Using Microsoft® Works for Windows

DOUG WOLF

Publisher: Lloyd J. Short

Acquisitions Manager: Rick Ranucci

Product Development Manager: Thomas H. Bennett

Managing Editor: Paul Boger

Book Designer: Scott Cook

Production Team: Jeff Baker, Claudia Bell, Mark Enochs, Bob LaRoche, Betty Kish, Laurie Lee, Anne Owen, John Sleeva, Kevin Spear, Mary Beth Wakefield, Lisa Wilson, Allan Wimmer, Christine Young

DEDICATION

To my grandmother, Pearl Wolf, who, despite all of her setbacks and personal losses, has never lost her basic faith in people and her God. She is surely one of the inheritors of the Earth and a guiding example to me.

CREDITS

Product Director
Brenda Carmichael

Production Editor
Mike La Bonne

Editors
Jo Anna Arnott
Kelly Currie
Don Eamon
Louise Lambert
Micci Swick-Volk

Technical Editor
Dana Schmeller

Acquisitions Editor
Tim Ryan

Composed in *Cheltenham* and *MCPdigital*
by Que Corporation

DOUG WOLF

Douglas J. Wolf has been involved in the microcomputer software business since 1982 when he and a partner started a software distribution company. The partners sold the company, and Mr. Wolf worked for several more software firms before starting his writing career in 1986.

Mr. Wolf holds business and journalism degrees, has authored more than 20 books on computer software, including Lotus 1-2-3, Agenda, First Choice, Sprint, Quattro Pro, Professional Write/File, and ACT!. He has also been active in the real estate business as a mortgage broker and authored the *Survivor's Guide to Financing Your Home*. His favorite author is H.L. Mencken.

He resides in San Diego with his wife, Gloria, and their children, Alexander and Ilsa.

TRADEMARK ACKNOWLEDGMENTS

The author thanks Brenda Carmichael and Mike La Bonne at Que Corporation for their excellent editing; Matt Wagner at Waterside Productions for his insouciance; the eugenic beta team at Microsoft; and Ed Wright at Amazing Bytes for his technical expertise.

CONTENTS AT A GLANCE

TABLE OF CONTENTS

II Word Processing

6   Using Advanced Word Processing Features and Printing 115

III   Spreadsheets

IV Databases

Introduction

Microsoft Works for Windows is the Windows version of the best-selling Microsoft Works for DOS. Works for Windows is really four programs, or components, in one: a word processor, a spreadsheet, a database, and a drawing program. The four programs are integrated so that information can be shared among them. Works also has another program—WorksWizards—designed especially for creating form letters and the mailing labels to match.

Microsoft Works, a virtual workhorse among software programs, can accomplish 95 percent of what most computer users need. For example, some of the tasks that Microsoft Works performs are as follows:

Feature	Capabilities
Word processor	Produces letters
	Produces memos
	Creates reports
Spreadsheet	Creates budgets
	Makes forecasts
	Accounts for profit and loss
Database	Keeps business records
	Stores names and addresses
	Creates mailing lists
Drawing	Creates freehand drawings

Feature	Capabilities
	Uses clip art to enhance drawings
	Uses images created in other programs such as Windows
	Uses Paintbrush
WorksWizards	Creates form letters
	Creates mailing labels
	Creates address books

Microsoft Works is designed to function with your computer hardware as a complete system so you don't have to spend time transferring files from one program to another. Your database can talk to your word processor, enabling you to create form letters and mailing labels to match. To make it even easier, *WorksWizards* helps you create an address book of people's names, addresses, and other information important to you. After creating the address book, you can then print form letters and matching mailing labels.

An important concept of Windows is the consistency of the user interface. For example, menus are always accessed from the top of the screen and the window control buttons are in the same place in every application. Such features make Windows and Works for Windows easy to learn and remember. Chapter 2 provides a quick run-down on the basics of operating in the windows environment.

Who Should Use This Book?

This book is written for small-business owners and department managers who want to use Microsoft Works to make their jobs easier. Most of the examples used in this book reflect actual business situations. Using Microsoft Works includes quick start lessons that enable you to learn the program quickly. In the chapters that follow the quick starts, you will find the details you need to do more intricate tasks with Microsoft Works.

How To Use This Book

Microsoft Works for Windows is divided into five parts that cover in detail each program of Microsoft Works. For example, you can turn to the part that examines the program you want to use and receive complete, detailed information about that program.

As mentioned earlier, this book includes quick start chapters that cover word processing, spreadsheets, and databases. If you want to use word processing, for example, and you want to start typing immediately, turn to the quick start chapter on word processing for helpful guidance on typing. Later, when you find that you need to move text or perform other more advanced procedures, refer to the remaining chapters in the word processing section of the book.

How This Book is Organized

If you browse quickly through this book, you can get a better sense of its organization and layout. The book is organized to follow the natural flow of learning and using Microsoft Works for Windows.

Part I—Getting Started

Chapter 1, "Learning about Microsoft Works for Windows," provides an overview of the tools available in and results produced by Works for Windows. Each program in Works is explained and an example of each program's products is displayed.

Chapter 2, "Understanding How Windows and Works Operate," explains how programs run in Windows, how windows can be manipulated to run programs simultaneously, and how you can use the keyboard and mouse mechanics to effectively work in the Windows environment.

Part II—Word Processing

Chapter 3, "Creating a Word Processing Document: Quick Start," gives you a quick start into the word processing tool of Works. Discussed in detail are the key procedures for opening, editing, printing, and saving a word processing document.

Chapter 4, "Entering, Editing, and Saving Documents," shows you how to enter text, make edits, and save your document. Also covered are the spell-checker and thesaurus.

Chapter 5, "Using Files, Styles, and Formatting," shows you how to open document files from other directories and drives, change text styles by altering fonts and typestyles, and format text by centering and aligning. You also learn how to set up the paper size, the margins, and tab stops.

Chapter 6, "Using Advanced Word Processing Features and Printing," allows you to search documents for misspelled words or style changes you want to make. Also covered are how to insert bookmarks, add headers and footers, insert tab stops, use advanced printing features, and examine additional Works features.

Chapter 7, "Creating Form Letters and Mailing Labels," introduces you to WorksWizards, the tool that Microsoft includes in Works to automate the process of creating your first database and creating a form letter. WorksWizards is a series of macros that stop at key points and get your input to create a name and address database and a form letter that has the inside address inserted.

Part III—Spreadsheets

Chapter 8, "Creating a Spreadsheet: Quick Start," gives you the key procedures for opening, editing, printing, and saving a spreadsheet.

Chapter 9, "Working with Spreadsheet Basics," provides the beginning steps in creating your first spreadsheet. Also covered are moving around the spreadsheet, entering labels, inserting columns and rows, and entering numbers and formulas.

Chapter 10, "Expanding Your Spreadsheet Knowledge," discusses more sophisticated techniques for entering data such as copying cell contents, combining relative and absolute formulas, setting column widths, freezing row and column labels, splitting the spreadsheet window into several panes, using the Go To function, formatting cells, creating and using range names, sorting and searching, and printing the spreadsheet.

Chapter 11, "Using Functions," identifies myriad built-in functions that can be used to create complex formulas. Each function discussed also shows an example of how it is used.

Chapter 12, "Creating Charts," offers a graphic representation of the numbers in the spreadsheet. With Works, you can create bar charts, line charts, pie charts, and an assortment of additional variations. Because of the windowing capability of Works, you can easily look at the spreadsheet and the chart at the same time.

Part IV—Databases

Chapter 13, "Creating a Database and Database Report: Quick Start," shows you how to enter, create, edit, and save information into a database.

Chapter 14, "Creating and Using Databases," explains how to build a sophisticated database file. Also covered are editing fields, moving fields, changing to List view, changing field sizes and alignment, sorting the database, searching the database, using formulas, formatting data, using different characters, hiding a field name, protecting data, and printing.

Chapter 15, "Creating and Using Database Reports," shows you how to design reports, sort a report, use formulas in reports, develop queries to find highly specific records, and customize reports.

Part V—Integrating Applications

Chapter 16, "Tying It All Together," shows you how to insert graphs into a spreadsheet and print them, insert drawings you create into word processing documents and print them, and link data so it is always accurate. Also covered are the calculator, the address book, and the clock.

Chapter 17, "Using Windows Accessories with Macros," shows you how to use the Recorder, a Windows tool that records keystrokes made in Works. This chapter also includes the steps you take to create several macros that you can use in Works immediately.

The appendix includes information on using files from other programs such as dBASE, Excel, Lotus 1-2-3, Word for Windows, and standard ASCII (text) file.

Using the Keyboard and Mouse

Works for Windows is designed to be used with a mouse. If you have worked with DOS applications that did not use a mouse, you will find quickly that using the mouse is much more natural and efficient than using keystrokes. Although Windows and Works for Windows are designed to be manipulated by using the mouse, Microsoft has included keystroke equivalents. Thus, if you are not comfortable using the mouse, you can use the keyboard. In this text, instructions are included for both the mouse and the keyboard.

Conventions

A number of conventions are used in *Using Microsoft Works for Windows* to help you learn the program.

Special typefaces used in this book include the following:

Type	Meaning
italics	New terms or phrases when they are initially defined
boldface	Information you are asked to type
`special type`	Information appearing on-screen

The following icons appear throughout this book:

Icon	Meaning
Note	Special notes on procedures that help you get the most from Microsoft Works for Windows
Tip	Special program features that the user might overlook; features that help the user gain proficiency with the program
Caution	Warns users about problem areas that may cause loss of data or damage to the program

Getting Started

PART

1

OUTLINE

Learning about Microsoft Works for Windows

Microsoft Works for Windows is the direct descendant of Microsoft Works for DOS. Like its predecessor, Works for Windows combines into one package its drawing capabilities and three of the most popular computer applications on the market: word processor, spreadsheet, and database. By combining the applications, Works for Windows enables users to share information from one application with another. This capability is the strongest feature of Microsoft Works.

Although the combined applications make for a powerful program, individually, each application is not the most advanced or powerful of its kind. For example, stand-alone word processing programs can create manuscripts that are printer ready, including a table of contents and an index. Not many computer users require applications that powerful. However, when less powerful applications are combined, as they are in this program, they can be just as powerful as the stand-alone programs. For example, Microsoft Works for Windows enables you to create documents that include multiple fonts, charts, and spreadsheet data. In other words, Works for Windows has everything you need to make a professional-looking document without having to become a desktop publishing expert. The same idea holds true for the spreadsheet and database applications. Each program can do what is necessary to accomplish the task.

In this chapter, you learn about the following:

- Works and Windows
- Works Word Processing
- Works Draw
- Works Spreadsheet
- Works Charts
- Works Database
- Works Integration

Works and Windows

Windows is like a huge desktop upon which you can run several different programs. For example, you can be creating a document in Works and move it to a "corner" of the desktop then access and run a totally different second application. When you finish your second application, you can return to Works at the same spot you were in when you left. Also, suppose that you are printing a long document in Works. You can start the printing process and then leave Works and work in another program. The printing continues in the background, while you accomplish other tasks.

Works Word Processing

Most businesses need to generate letters to clients or mail copies of the same letter to many clients. Works for Windows makes it easy to generate a single letter for one client or a form letter for all clients. Because Works includes a database, the names and addresses of your clients can be entered into the database and then retrieved into the form letter with mailing labels to match. In addition, because Windows is a graphics environment, you can add enhancements to text that highlight the key points in your letter. Figure 1.1 shows a sample letter created in the Works word processor with different typefaces and sizes plus a graphic object created in Works Draw and imported into the text.

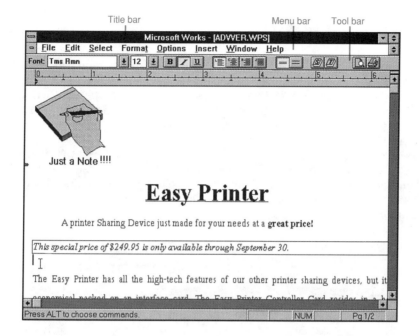

FIG. 1.1

A sample letter
using Works
features

In figure 1.1, the words Easy Printer are displayed in 30-point boldface and underlined type. The second line of text under Easy Printer is
in italic type and enclosed in a border. The look of your documents is
limited only by your creativity and good judgment.

The word processing screen in figure 1.1 shows the Title bar at the top
of the screen, followed by the Menu bar, then the Tool bar. The Title
bar displays a name to help you identify the contents of the window
and the current file name. The Menu bar contains the names of the pull-
down menus. The Tool bar enables you to select the font, type size,
boldface, italics, underlining, left justification, centering, right justification, full justification, and single- or double-spaced text, by using a
mouse. If you're using the keyboard, you can access the menus and
their programs by pressing the Alt key plus the first (or underlined or
boldfaced) letter. For example, to access the Edit menu with the keyboard, you would press Alt,E. You can also access the spell-checker
and thesaurus to edit your text. In addition, when you are ready to
print, you can first click the Print Preview icon to see if the final product matches your expectations, then you can click the Printer icon to
print the document.

Works Draw

From the word processor, you can access the Works Draw program to create your own drawings or to access ready-made clip art shipped with Works. In figure 1.2, the Draw program has been opened through the word processing Insert menu and a series of clip art pictures have been imported into the Draw work space. Any of these pictures can be imported into a document. For example, if you want to create a Fax cover sheet with a distinctive look, you can import a business-type picture into a word processing document, add the necessary phone numbers and addresses, and end up with a cover like the one shown in figure 1.3. Additional information on the Draw program is covered in Chapter 6.

FIG. 1.2

An example of the Draw Program

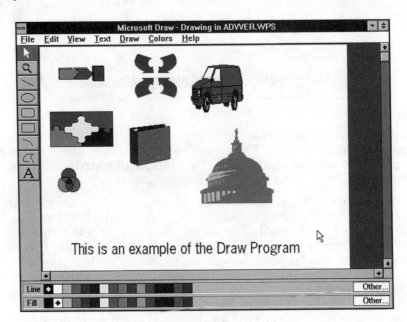

Works Spreadsheet

Operating a business or running any venture that involves numbers, is made easier by using the Works spreadsheet. Repetitive math problems that fatigue humans can be calculated by Works spreadsheets quickly, repeatedly, and accurately (providing you enter the problems correctly). Among many other uses, spreadsheets are used to create budgets, forecast sales, and develop multiple scenarios for planning purposes.

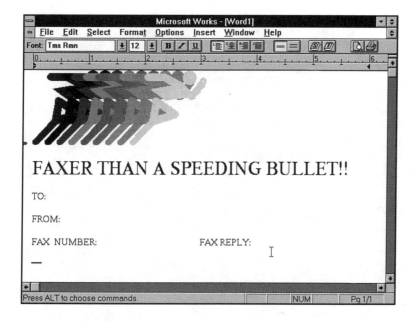

FIG. 1.3

A sample Fax
cover sheet

After spreadsheets are created they can be recalled at any time to enter
new information. Because you are using Works in the Windows environment, you can easily add enhancements (boldface, underline, italics,
and so forth) to the crucial numbers in the spreadsheet. In addition,
you can then link the numbers in the spreadsheet to Charts (discussed
in the following section), which display the spreadsheet data in graphic
form. Figure 1.4 is a typical spreadsheet that shows two quarters of
actual performance by a company and two quarters of planned sales.
The Total column calculates the total sales for each territory and
then the overall total. Spreadsheets are covered in greater detail in
Chapters 8 through 12.

Works Charts

Graphing the Total Sales by quarter from figure 1.4 results in the chart
you see in figure 1.5. The bar chart was created by highlighting the
numbers, including the overall total, and using the mouse pointer to
click on the Chart icon.

FIG. 1.4

A typical Works
spreadsheet

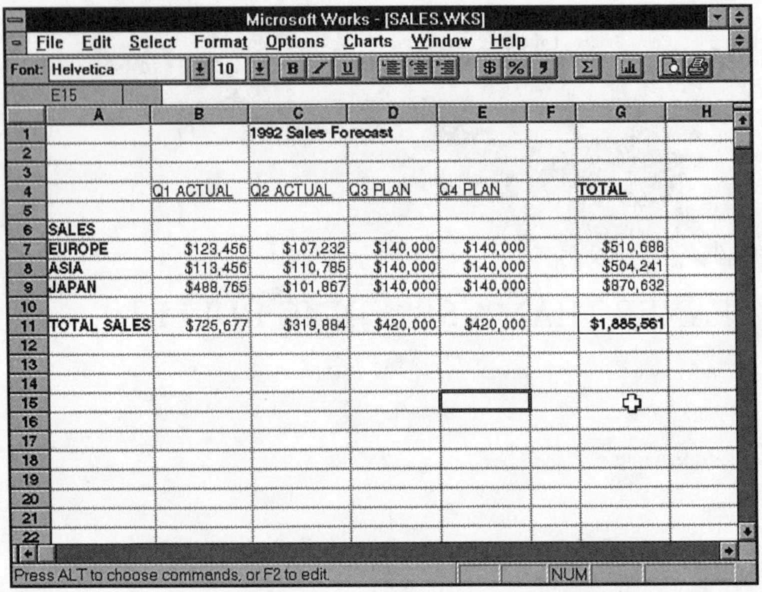

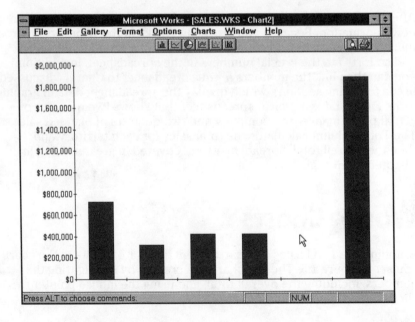

FIG. 1.5

The spreadsheet
totals in a chart

The chart in figure 1.5 has no legends, titles, or X-axis (horizontal axis)
labels. Also, the default chart created by Works when you use the Tool
bar icon is a bar chart. In figure 1.6, titles, the X-axis labels, and the bar
labels (the numbers over each bar) have been added.

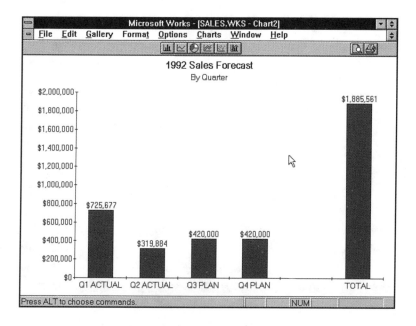

FIG. 1.6

Titles and labels
added to the
chart

Works Database

A database is a collection of information. Examples of databases include a phone book with names, addresses, and phone numbers, and a catalog of auto parts with part names and part numbers.

The Works database can be formatted two ways: in *form* view as shown in figure 1.7, and in *list* view as shown in figure 1.8. In the form view each record is displayed individually; in list view all the records are displayed at once.

A database can be rearranged or queried. For example, to rearrange records by the entries in the Last Name: field, you use the Sort command and tell Works in what order you want the records sorted. In a query, you ask Works to display only records that meet your needs such as all records in a specific ZIP code. Also, by inserting the name of the field, such as Last Name, into a word processing document, you can have Works insert the last name from each record into a separate letter.

FIG. 1.7

Database in form
view

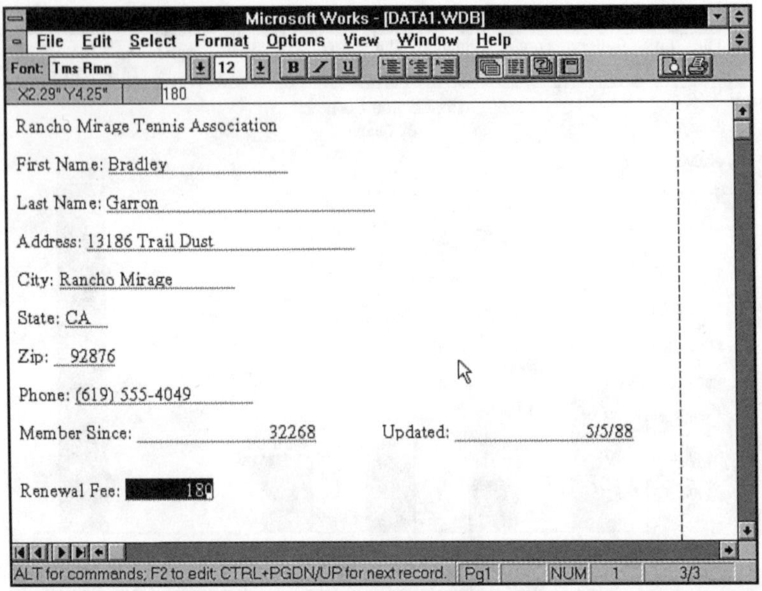

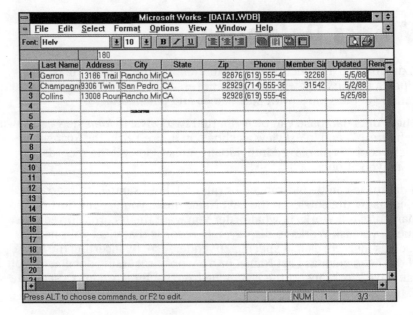

FIG. 1.8

Database in list
view

Works Integration

Because you are using Microsoft Works in a Windows environment, you can easily switch from a database window to a spreadsheet window to a chart window. In figure 1.9, the windows have been arranged by using the Tile icon from the Window menu. The database, spreadsheet, chart, and word processing windows are all visible.

To select the file you want to work with, move the mouse pointer to the appropriate window and click. That window then becomes the active window. You can then resize the window to make it full-screen.

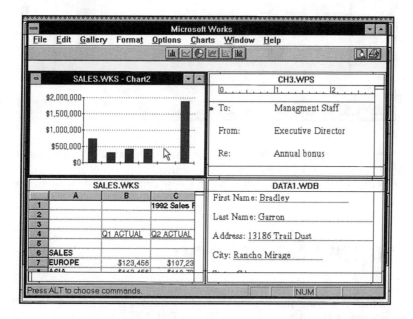

FIG. 1.9

Various windows displayed by using the Tile feature

Another way of looking at open windows is through the Cascade icon from the Window menu. When Cascade is selected the screen appears as shown in figure 1.10.

FIG. 1.10

Various windows
displayed by
using the
Cascade feature

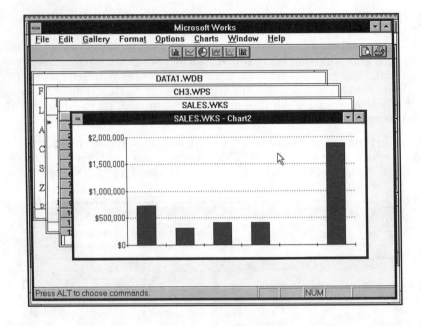

The active window is the foremost window in the stack. You can select a different window by pointing to the name at the top of the window border and clicking or by choosing the appropriate window from the Window menu.

Chapter Summary

In this chapter you were introduced to the four tools in Microsoft Works for Windows: the Works Word Processor, Works Draw, Works Spreadsheet with Charts, and the Works Database. Also, you were introduced to the special integration capabilities of Microsoft Works for Windows.

In the next chapter, you get a better understanding of how Microsoft Works for Windows operates.

Understanding How Windows and Works Operate

This chapter is written for those of you who have not had much experience with Windows. Because Works operates in the Windows environment, a working knowledge of Windows capabilities, Windows accessories, Windows sizing, and mouse techniques is essential to using Works.

 NOTE Although you can run Windows and Works with the keyboard, doing so is less efficient and usually slower than with the mouse. However, if you're still not comfortable with the mouse, or if you prefer to use the keyboard instead, keyboard equivalents are included throughout this book.

In this chapter, you learn how to do the following:

■ Use the Program Manager and the control menu.

■ Activate a Windows accessory.

■ Use the Main window, and move among active windows.

20

■ Install and start Works.

■ Navigate and manipulate windows, and use a Windows accessory while in Works.

■ Use the Help index, search for help topics, define bookmarks, and print help information.

■ Close applications and exit from Works.

Getting Started with Windows

The strongest feature of Windows is its capability of running several applications at the same time. For example, you can work in a spreadsheet while your modem is receiving a file over the phone. Or you can use Microsoft Works and access other tools to make calculations, record a macro, and so on. Windows includes several useful utility tools, such as a calendar, a calculator, and a macro recorder. You can load these tools before you run Works and then have them available as you need them. The following paragraphs explain how to use the basic Windows features and how to load these accessories so they are available in Works.

To use Microsoft Works for Windows effectively and understand directions in the rest of the book, you need to understand the terms described in table 2.1.

Table 2.1 Works for Windows Actions

General Actions Term	Procedure
Select	Highlight a menu command
	Turn on an option
	Highlight text
Unselect	Turn off an option
Choose	Execute a command from the menu
	Click the mouse pointer on a button or press Enter to complete a dialog box

Mouse Actions Term	Procedure
Click	Move the mouse pointer onto text or an object and then press and release the left mouse button once
Double-click	Move the mouse pointer onto text or an object and then press and release the left mouse button twice in quick succession
Drag	Move the mouse pointer onto text or an object, and hold down the left mouse button while you move the pointer

Keyboard Actions Term	Procedure
Type	Type but do not press the Enter key
Enter	Type and then press the Enter key
Alt+space bar	Opens the control menu for an application window
Alt+–	Opens the control menu for a document window
Alt+Tab	Switches to the next application window, restoring applications running as icons
Alt+Esc	Switches to the next application or minimized icon, including full-screen application
Press Alt,X	Press the first key, release it, and then press the second key
Press Ctrl+D	Press and hold down the first key while pressing the second key

Note that the term *mouse pointer* refers to the on-screen figure that represents the mouse location. As you work with Windows and Works, using the mouse becomes second nature and is the reason for the popularity of Windows.

Using the Program Manager

When you start Windows, the screen includes an icon labeled Program Manager. You use this icon to access the programs you want to run in Windows. If you have a mouse installed, a mouse pointer also appears on-screen. You can use the mouse to select an application, such as Works, that you want to run in the Windows environment.

To get to the Program Manager, you first need to start Windows by following these steps:

1. At the C:\> prompt, type the following command and then press Enter:

   CD\WINDOWS

2. At the C:\WINDOWS> prompt type the following command and then press Enter:

   WIN

To access the Program Manager, follow these steps:

1. Double-click the Program Manager icon. The Program Manager window appears.

2. To see the list of available windows, click **W**indow in the Menu bar, or press Alt,W. The **W**indow menu opens, as shown in figure 2.1.

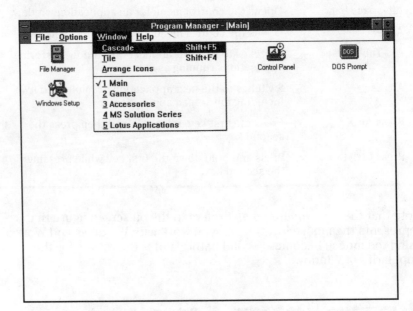

The **W**indow menu lists the available windows. If you have no other programs installed, three windows are available: Main, Games, and Accessories. In figure 2.1, two other programs are installed, MS (Microsoft) Solution Series, which includes Microsoft Works, and Lotus 1-2-3.

3. To open one of the windows or programs listed, use the mouse pointer to highlight the window or program name; then click the

left mouse button. (You use this point-and-click method to select options from all menus.)

Later on in this chapter, "Activating an Accessory" and "Examining the Main Window" sections show what happens when you choose Accessories or Main from the **W**indow menu.

Using the Control Menu

The minus sign in the upper-left corner of the screen (in the Title bar) is called the *Control-menu button*, which accesses the control menu. You use this menu to control the on-screen appearance of your windows. Figure 2.2 shows the control menu as it appears when the calculator is on-screen.

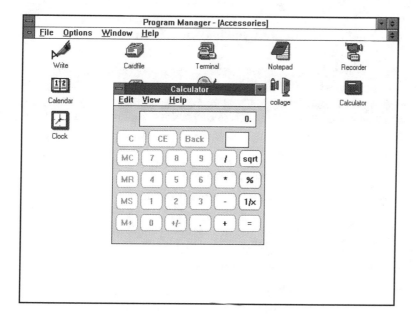

FIG. 2.2

The control menu with the calculator on-screen

Windows uses two types of Control menus. The first appears when you click the Control-menu button in the program manager, or any other application window. The second appears when you are in a document window and click its control-menu button. The key difference is that the document control menu includes the Next command, which allows you to switch among documents or icons.

If you don't have a mouse, you can run Windows by using the following keystrokes:

Table 2.2 Keystrokes for the Control Menu

Keystrokes	Results
Alt+spacebar	Opens the Control menu for an application window
Alt+hypen	Opens the Control menu for a document window
Alt+Esc	Switches to the next application or minimized icon, including full-screen application
Alt+Tab	Switches to the next application window, restoring applications running as icons
Ctrl+F6	Switches to the next document window
Arrow keys	Moves the highlight from one document to another within a window

Table 2.3 defines the options you find on the control menu.

Table 2.3 Using the Control Menu

Option	Effect
Restore	Restores the window to its previous size. For example, if you maximized the window with the Maximize option, then invoke **R**estore, the window shrinks back to its smaller size.
Move	Enables you to move the window to a different position on the desktop.
Size	Enables you to use the keyboard to change the size of the window.
Mi**n**imize	Shrinks the window to an icon.
Maximize	Enlarges the window to its maximum size.
Close	Closes the window and, if the window is an application such as the calculator, terminates the program.
Switch To	Opens the Task List dialog box. This box displays the active programs and accessories, such as Works and calculator, and enables you to choose among them. You also can rearrange the windows and icons on the desktop.
Ne**x**t	Switches among open document windows and icons.

Because you can have many applications open simultaneously in Windows, you often will minimize windows when you're not using them and then maximize them when you need to return to the full window. Maximizing is explained in the following section.

Activating an Accessory

After you use the Program Manager and choose Accessories from the Windows menu, the window shown in figure 2.3 appears.

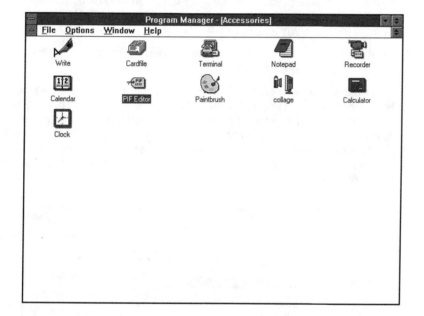

FIG. 2.3

The Accessories window

To make sure that you are seeing the entire Accessories window, you need to maximize it. To do so, follow these steps:

1. Move the mouse pointer to the maximize button, the upward-pointing arrow in the upper-right corner of the screen.

2. Click the mouse button.

Three of the Windows accessories are particularly useful: the Recorder for creating macros, the Calendar for setting alarms, and the Calculator for figuring calculations. If you want one or more of these accessories to be available while you're using Works, you must activate the accessories before running Works.

Windows is similar to a desk in that your Calendar, Calculator, and other business tools each occupy a place on the desktop. To have an accessory easily accessible, you must activate and then minimize it so that it resides in the background—that is, sits to one side on your desk while you complete tasks in other applications. You then, for example, can access the calculator and insert a value into a cell of a spreadsheet program. Or you can refer to your calendar at any time while you are working in a word processing document.

To activate and then minimize an accessory so that it waits in the background, follow these steps:

1. Move the mouse pointer to the icon in the Accessories window that represents the accessory you want to activate—the Calculator icon, for example.

2. Double-click the icon. The accessory opens. Figure 2.4, for example, shows the Calculator.

    The Calculator operates the same as any calculator. You may enter numbers into the display either from the keyboard (press Num Lock and use the numbered keys) or by pointing to the number and clicking. You can also activate the Calculater itself by clicking on the control-menu box (the negative sign) in the upper-left corner of the Calculator window, and the Control menu appears, as shown in figure 2.4.

FIG. 2.4

Activating the
Calculator

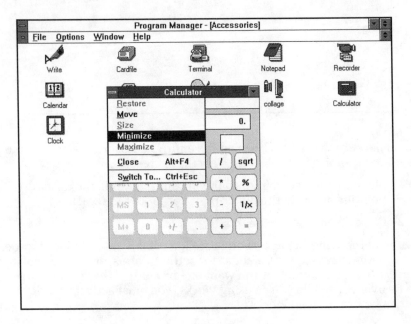

3. To minimize the accessory, choose Minimize.

The Calculator is now available and running in the background.

Examining the Main Window

When you use the Program Manager and choose Main from the Windows menu, the Main window appears. This window displays several other important components of Windows. Table 2.4 describes these elements briefly.

Table 2.4 Using the Main Window

Application	Function
File Manager	Used to set up directories for files and programs. When you install Works, this directory is set up for you.
Print Manager	Receives the files you want to print and sets up a print queue.
Control Panel	Controls the screen colors, fonts, communication and printer ports, the mouse click and tracking speed, the look of the desktop screen and the cursor blink rate, the 386 Enhanced mode, the installation of printers, the country conventions such as date and number format, the rate of the keyboard repeat, the current date and time, and the use of sound as a warning.
Clipboard	Enables you to cut and paste text from one application to another.
DOS Prompt	Closes windows and returns you to the DOS prompt.
Windows Setup	Displays the current hardware on your system.

For complete information on each of these Windows tools, see your Windows manual.

Moving among Active Windows

Windows gives you several ways to move among the active windows. Pressing the Ctrl and F6 keys at the same time (shown as Ctrl+F6 throughout this book) moves you from one window to another. If you start at the Accessories window, for example, pressing Ctrl+F6 cycles you to the Games window. If you press Ctrl+F6 again, the Main window appears. Pressing Ctrl+F6 again returns you to the Accessories window.

When you are running Works, you can use the Ctrl+F6 key combination to switch among the Works windows. When you are not in a specific application such as Works, the Ctrl+F6 combination rotates you through the active windows.

Getting Started with Works

As mentioned earlier, when you access the **W**indow menu it shows you which windows are available. If you have already installed Works, you can access the program by clicking the MS (Microsoft) Solution Series.

To start Works with a Mouse, follow these steps:

1. Click the document window containing the Microsoft Solution Series.

2. Click the icon labeled Microsoft Works.

To start Works with the keyboard, follow these steps:

1. Press Ctrl+F6 to make the Window containing Microsoft Solution Series window the active window.

2. Use the arrow keys to move the highlight to the label *Microsoft Works*.

3. Press Enter.

Press Alt plus the underlined letter to select a Works Tool, or to open an existing file.

Installing and Starting Works for Windows

If you have not already installed Works for Windows, you can accomplish this procedure from the Program Manager in Windows by following these steps:

1. Turn on your computer.

2. Start Windows. The Program Manager icon appears. (Depending on your system, the window may appear first.)

3. Open the Program Manager by double-clicking the icon.

4. Open the **F**ile menu (see fig. 2.5) by clicking the word *File*.

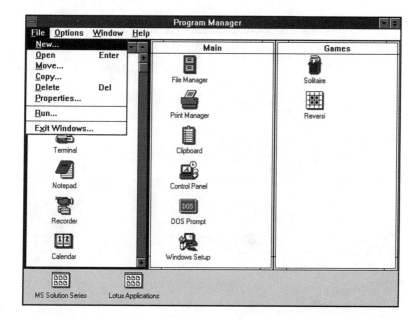

FIG. 2.5

The **F**ile menu

5. Select the **R**un... option (the three dots mean that additional choices are available when you select this option).

6. Insert disk 1 of Works for Windows in drive A or B.

7. In the Command Line box, type **A:Setup** if the disk is in drive A or type **B:Setup** if the disk is in drive B.

   The Works install program takes over and begins copying the files from the disks to the hard drive. A screen message (Insert disk x in drive x) appears when all the files have been copied to the hard drive.

8. Double-click the Works icon labeled Microsoft Works, or press Alt, F to open the **F**ile menu and then select **R**un.... In the Command Line box, type **C:\msworks\msworks** and press Enter. A screen appears showing the registered owner of Works. That screen is replaced quickly by a Welcome to Microsoft Works dialog box (see fig. 2.6).

FIG. 2.6

The Welcome to
Microsoft Works
dialog box

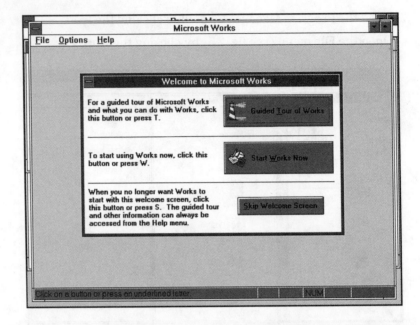

The Welcome to Microsoft Works dialog box has a Control-menu button in the upper-left corner of the box. But the only real choices are the three in the middle of the dialog box: Guided Tour of Works, Start Works Now, and Skip Welcome Screen. As is consistently true in Windows applications, these choices are written on what are called *buttons*. Pressing Alt and the underlined letter, or clicking the on-screen button—by moving the mouse pointer to the button and clicking the left mouse button—activates the choice, just as you might flip an on-off switch on an appliance.

T I P   Microsoft provides an excellent overview of the attributes and methods of using Works if you select the Guided Tour of Works option that appears when you start Works.

To begin the Works application, follow these steps:

1. Click the Start Works Now button, or press Alt,W. The Startup dialog box appears as shown in figure 2.7.

T I P   You can take every action in Works by combining the Alt key with a letter key or function key. Thus, if you prefer not to use the mouse, you can keep your fingers on the keyboard.

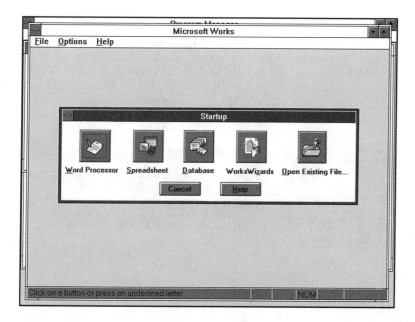

FIG. 2.7

The Startup
dialog box

Works gives you the opportunity to start working immediately
with the tool you want.

2. Select the word processing tool by pressing Alt,W or clicking the
   Word Processor button. The Microsoft Works screen with a blank
   document window appears (see fig. 2.8).

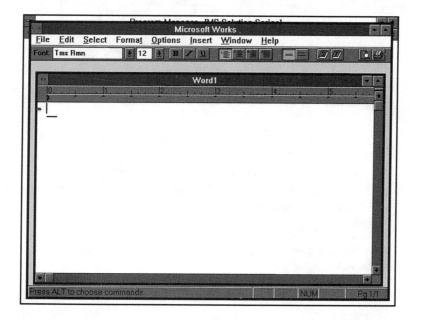

FIG. 2.8

The Microsoft
Works initial
screen

On your screen, you now have a large window labeled Microsoft Works and a smaller document window labeled Word1. When you start Works and access the word processing tool, the default file name is WORD1.WPS. In other words, Works has provided you with a blank electronic piece of paper. Notice that the Microsoft Works window contains a Control-menu button in the upper-left corner. You use this button to access the Microsoft Works control menu shown in figure 2.9.

FIG. 2.9

The Microsoft
Works control
menu

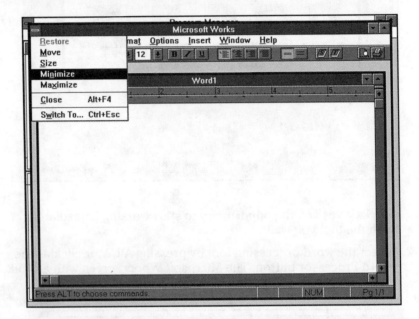

1. Click the Control-menu button or press Alt+space bar to display the control menu.

2. Click the Minimize option. (You have two keyboard alternatives: Use the down-arrow key to move the highlight to the Minimize option and press Enter; or press N.)

   Microsoft Works shrinks to icon size on the Windows screen. The Program Manager icon's caption is highlighted.

3. Click the Microsoft Works icon. (Or press Alt+Esc to move the caption highlight to Microsoft Works and then press Alt+space bar to open the control menu.)

4. Click **R**estore or press R.

Microsoft Works returns to full screen. You have just experienced one of the best features of Windows. You did not exit from Works to leave the program; you temporarily suspended its operation to go to Windows where you could have opened an entirely different program.

Maximizing the Works Word Processing Window

Make certain that you are viewing the entire word processing window by using the Control+menu button for the Word1 document window. To do so, follow these steps:

1. Click the Control+menu button in the upper-left corner of the Word1 window. Or press and hold the Alt key and press the hyphen (-) key.

NOTE   Remember to press Alt+-(hyphen) for the document control menu and Alt+space bar for the other control menus.

2. Click Maximize or press X.

The Word1 window fills the entire screen.

Minimizing the Works Word Processing Window

After you become comfortable working with multiple windows, you may want to minimize a particular window so you can view another one. Follow these steps to minimize a window:

1. Click the Control-menu button or press Alt+-(hyphen).

2. Click Minimize or press N.

The word processing document window shrinks to icon size. The caption under the icon is the same as the name of the file—Word1 in this example.

Using the Mouse To Navigate the Document Window

On the right and bottom borders of the document window are long bars with arrows at both ends. These bars are called *scroll bars*. Inside each of the scroll bars is a *scroll box* that moves within the bar. The position of the scroll box in the scroll bar shows you the insertion point, or where you are in your document.

When you open a word processing document, the scroll boxes are at the top of the right scroll bar and at the far left of the bottom scroll bar. The ruler line indicates that the insertion point is at the 0 position.

The mouse pointer assumes different shapes depending on where it is located on-screen. In the word processing work space, the pointer assumes the I shape, often called the *I-beam pointer*. In the scroll bar, the pointer changes to an arrow shape.

To see how the bottom scroll box works, follow these steps:

1. Move the mouse pointer to the bottom scroll box, above the word choose, and click.

   The document scrolls to the left as evidenced by the ruler line at the top of the work space. The ruler numbers 7 through 12 are visible.

2. Click the scroll box and hold the mouse button down, moving the pointer as far as possible to the left. The document scrolls to the right, and the insertion point is again at the 0 position.

When you click text, a scroll box, or anything else while holding the mouse button and moving the pointer across the screen, you are *clicking and dragging*. This procedure is a common one in Windows applications and greatly speeds up your work.

As you enter text in the work space, the scroll box in the right side scroll bar moves down with the insertion point.

Table 2.5 explains the mouse-scrolling options.

Table 2.5 Scrolling with the Mouse

To scroll	Use this method
One line	Click one of the scroll arrows.
One window	Click the scroll bar above or below the scroll box on the vertical scroll bar, and to the left or right of the scroll box on the horizontal scroll bar.
Continuously	Point to one of the scroll arrows and hold down the mouse button until the information you want comes into view.
To any position	Drag the scroll box up or down the scroll bar to the position you want.

Using a Windows Accessory While in Works

Previously in this chapter you learned how to open the Windows Accessories window and activate an accessory. The accessory—the Calculator in this chapter's example—is still there waiting for you to use it. Follow these steps to use a Windows accessory that you previously activated:

1. Click the Works Control-menu button in the upper-left corner of the screen. (Or press Alt+space bar.)

2. From the menu, select **S**witch To. The Task List dialog box appears, as shown in figure 2.10. All active programs are listed.

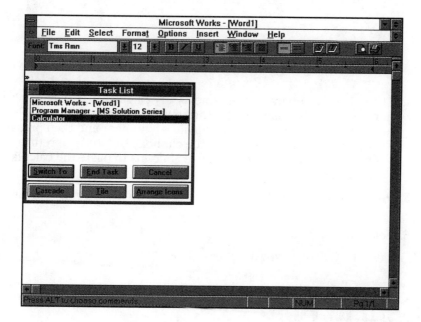

FIG. 2.10

The Task List dialog box

3. Double-click the name of the accessory you want to activate, or use the arrow keys to highlight the item and press Alt,S or Enter.

   The accessory then appears. Figure 2.11, for example, shows the Calculator.

FIG. 2.11

Displaying the
Calculator
accessory

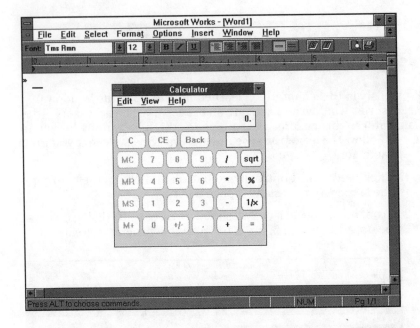

4. The Calculator operates the same as any calculator. You can enter
   numbers into the display from the keyboard or by pointing to the
   number and clicking. You can calculate a number and then press
   Ctrl+Ins to copy the result onto the clipboard. (After you return to
   your Works document, you can use Shift+Ins to paste the calculation into the document.)

5. When you're finished with the accessory, click the Control-menu
   button.

6. Select the Minimize option.

To access the Calculator again, press Alt+Esc.

Getting Help

Works has an extensive help system. When you access Help, the program assumes that you want information about the particular tool you
are using. When you access the Help window while in the word processor, for example, you get the word processing help screens.

To access a help screen at any point, press the F1 key, which is located
at the top or left of your keyboard. The appropriate help window then
appears, as shown in figure 2.12.

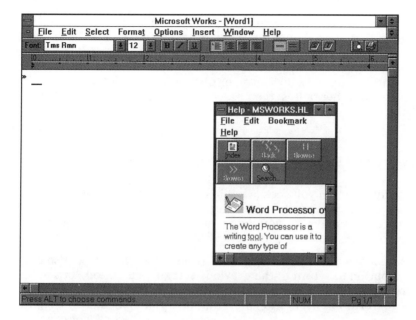

FIG. 2.12

A Microsoft
Works Help
window

You can enlarge the Help window in the same ways you maximize other
windows. You can open the control menu and select Maximize, or you
can click the up-arrow button (the maximize button) in the upper-right
corner of the window. Figure 2.13 shows the word processing Help
screen maximized.

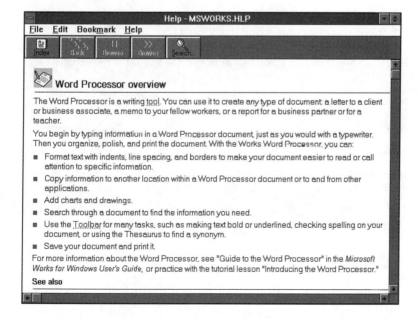

FIG. 2.13

The Help window
maximized

As you look at the Help screen, you can see that some of the words are enhanced by dotted underlines and others by solid underlines. If you move the mouse pointer to a word with the dotted underline and press and hold the left mouse button, a window appears with a definition of the word. If you click on a word or phrase with a solid underline, Works jumps to another help screen describing the word or phrase you clicked.

Maneuvering through Help

If the information you seek is not in the overview help window that first appears after you press F1, you can click the Index button to see a list of topics that may lead you to the information. In the index, click the word or phrase that you want to explore.

As you move through the Help screens in this way, you can use the Back button to return to the previous screen. In addition, look for underlined words in the text or words that appear in a different color. These words are *hyper-text jumps* that take you immediately from the overview screen to a specific help screen on that word. For example, in the word processor overview screen shown in figure 2.13, the word Toolbar is highlighted. Clicking it takes you directly to the screen of information on the Tool bar.

The Help screen also has the following buttons:

INDEX   Clicking this button returns you to the Help
                    index.

BACK   Clicking this button returns you to the previous
                    Help screen.

BROWSE   Clicking either browse button scrolls the Help
                    screens.

Using the Search Feature

If you know the help topic you want to find, but it is not on any of the Help screens you have accessed, click the Search button at the top of the screen. The dialog box shown in figure 2.14 appears.

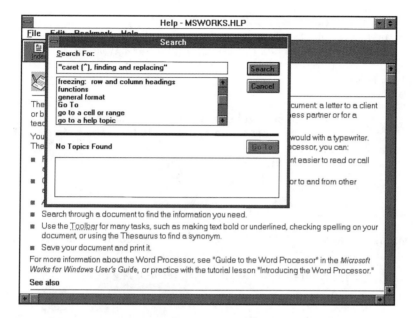

FIG. 2.14

The Search
dialog box

In the **S**earch For: box, type the subject you want to find, then click
Search or press Enter. After you select Search, Works displays the
Topics Found: box, which shows the information that most closely fits
your request. If you see the correct topic, highlight it and click the **G**o
To button to see the full screen of information about that topic.

When you have finished reading the help topic screen, click the minimize button, which is the down-arrow in the top right corner of the
window, or open the control menu and select Mi**n**imize.

Defining a Bookmark

If you find that a particular help screen contains information that you
want to access quickly, you can create a bookmark for that screen by
following these steps:

1. At the Help screen for which you want a bookmark, click Book-
   mark or press Alt,M.

2. Click **D**efine, or press Alt,D.

   The Bookmark Define window appears. Works inserts the name of
   the help screen as the default bookmark name. Click OK to accept
   the default name. Or, press the Backspace key to delete the default entry and type the name you want and press Enter.

The next time you select Bookmark while in the Help screens, Works lists the names of any bookmarks you have defined. To select the bookmark you want, either click the bookmark name or type the number preceding the bookmark name. Works takes you immediately to the Help screen.

 These Help screen bookmarks are not directly accessible from Works tools. You must already be in the Help system to get them.

Printing Help Information

If you find that you need to refer to the steps listed in the Help screen, you can print the information by following these steps:

1. At the Help screen you want to print, Click **File** or press Alt,F.

2. From the **File** menu, select **Print** Topic, or press P.

Works sends the file to the Windows print queue. If you have not set up a printer, you can select the Printer Setup command from the **File** menu to do so before printing the Help topic.

Closing Files and Exiting from Microsoft Works

When you are finished working in Works, you can close the applications, exit from the program, and return to Windows by performing the following procedure:

Click **File** and select **Exit**, or press Alt,F, then X.

If you've opened Works files and made changes, Works checks each file and asks you with a window prompt if you want to save the changes. You can select Yes or No, depending on your preference.

Chapter Summary

In this chapter, you learned about Windows and the ways to activate a Windows accessory. You learned how to get started in Works—how to install and start the program, control the appearance of windows, and scroll the document window. You also learned how to access a Windows accessory while running Works, and you explored the Works Help system. Finally, you learned how to close files and exit from Works.

In the next chapter, you begin creating a word processing document and learn how to save it to a file and print it.

Word Processing

Creating a Word Processing Document: Quick Start

This chapter briefly examines the Works word processing tool. Word processing programs such as Works provide the tools a writer needs to create, edit, save, and print text.

In this chapter, you learn how to do the following:

- Open a file.

- Enter, edit, insert, select, copy, and move text.

- Use the spell-checking program.

- Save, print, and close the file.

Opening a New File with Works

Remember that when you start Works, the Startup dialog box appears (see Chapter 2, "Understanding How Windows and Works Operate"). To open a new word processing file, click the **W**ord Processor button in the Startup dialog box or press Alt,W. A blank word processing screen appears.

Entering Text

You type text on the word processing screen the same way you type on a piece of paper when you're using a typewriter. When you type, characters are entered at the *insertion point*, which is the vertical flashing line that begins at the upper left corner of the screen. Works automatically starts a new line when the line you're typing is filled. This feature is called *word wrap*. You can also end a line by pressing the Enter key to move the cursor to the next line. The screen shows approximately 19 lines (with the window at full screen); after you fill the screen, Works scrolls the text up as you continue to type. The *default* start-up typeface is 12-point Times Roman.

 NOTE   A *default* setting is a command option the program uses automatically unless you specify something different. Thus, in this example, Works will always use 12-point Times Roman unless you select something else.

Before you begin typing in the work space of the word processing window, maximize both the application window and the document window. The application window is maximized by clicking on the Application control button in the top left of the computer screen and then clicking Maximize, or with your keyboard by pressing Alt+space bar to open the menu and pressing X. Next, maximize the document window by clicking the document control button in the upper left corner of the Word1 window and clicking Maximize, or with the keyboard by pressing Alt and the hyphen to open the window and then pressing X.

To help you quickly gain proficiency with Works word processing, follow these steps to enter a short memo (you can use the Backspace key to correct any errors you make):

1. Type **To:** and press the Tab key twice.

2. Type **Management Staff** and press Enter twice.

3. Type **From:** and press Tab twice.

4. Type **Executive Director** and press Enter twice.

5. Type **Re:** and press Tab twice.

6. Type **Annual Bonus** and press Enter twice.

Your screen should look like the one shown in figure 3.1.

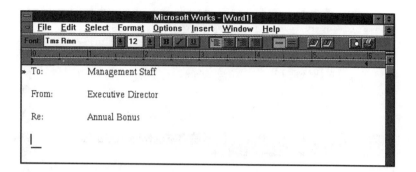

FIG. 3.1

The first part of
the memo

Notice that you ended each line by pressing Enter. Pressing Enter is similar to pressing Return on an electric typewriter or pushing the carriage return handle on a manual typewriter. The action brings you to the left margin of the next line.

Add a paragraph of text to the memo by typing the following (including the intentional misspelling of the word *Solstice*):

Look for the annual bonuses for each department in the interoffice mail during the week ending December 21. Happy Winter Solstoce!

(You learn how to correct the error in this chapter's section on "Connecting Text with the Backspace Key," and "Checking Your Spelling.")

Notice how Works moved the word *ending* (see fig. 3.2) to a new line when no more room was available on the current line. With the word-wrap feature, you do not have to press Enter to end every line. Notice also the short, horizontal line under the bottom line of text. This line is the *end-of-file marker*.

Correcting Text with the Backspace Key

In this sample memo, the word *Solstice* was misspelled as *Solstoce*. Take the following steps to correct the misspelling (if you made other typing errors, you can correct them with this same procedure):

1. Use the mouse or the left-arrow key to move the insertion point to the left until it is between the letters o and c in the word *Solstoce*.

2. Press the Backspace key one time to delete the letter o.

3. Press the letter *i*. The word Solstice now is spelled correctly (see fig. 3.2).

FIG. 3.2

The memo with
the paragraph
highlighted
and **Solstice**
corrected

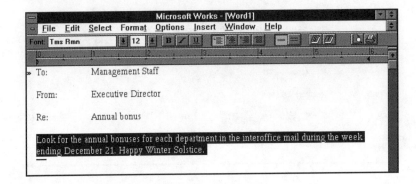

Inserting Text

Whether you want to insert text between other words, sentences, or
paragraphs, the steps are the same:

1. Move the insertion point to the position in the text where you
   want to insert more text. In the memo, for example, suppose that
   you learn the bonus is semiannual, not annual. You need to insert
   the prefix "semi" in front of the word "annual." Move the insertion
   point to the space between the words "the" and "annual."

2. Type the new text **semi**. The text that was already in the file
   moves to the right and down to accommodate the inserted text.

Selecting Text

Before you can move or copy text, you need to select it, as shown in
figure 3.2. Works doesn't know which text to move or copy unless you
have selected it previously. With Works, you can select text in several
ways. Use one of the following two methods when you want to select
small blocks of text:

With a mouse, follow these steps:

1. Move the pointer to the beginning of the text you want to select.

2. Press and hold down the mouse button and drag the pointer over
   the text until the text you want to select is highlighted.

With the keyboard, follow these steps:

1. Press and hold the Shift key.

2. Press the cursor-movement keys (the arrow keys) until the text
   you want to select is highlighted on-screen.

You can turn the selection off by pressing any cursor-movement key or by clicking the mouse button. Then the highlighting no longer appears over the text.

To select large blocks of text, use the F8 function key. Press F8 one time, and EXT appears on the status line to indicate that the selection mode is turned on. After EXT appears on the status line, you can highlight larger and larger blocks of text by continuing to press F8. Table 3.1 describes how F8 works.

Table 3.1 Selecting Text with F8

To select	Press F8
The current word	Two times
The current sentence	Three times
The current paragraph	Four times
The entire file	Five times

(The word *current* refers to the word, sentence, or paragraph in which the insertion point currently is positioned.)

When using the F8 key method of selecting text, turn off the selection by pressing the Esc key to leave the selection mode and then pressing a cursor-movement key or the mouse button to remove the highlighting.

You can also use some special steps to select text with the mouse. These techniques are described in table 3.2.

Table 3.2 Selecting Text with the Mouse

To select	Use this technique
The current word	Double-click the word
The current line	Click in the left margin
The current paragraph	Double-click in the left margin of the paragraph
The entire file	Hold down Ctrl and click in the left margin

Copying Selected Text

When you copy text, you leave the selected text in its original location and move a duplicate of that text to a new location. Here is the procedure for copying text:

1. Select the text you want to copy, by using one of the methods described in the preceding section.

2. Press Ctrl+C, or access the **Edit** menu and choose **Copy**.

3. Move the insertion point to the location where you want to insert a copy of the selected text.

4. Press Ctrl+V or choose **Paste** from the **Edit** menu. The selected text is inserted at the cursor position.

If you insert new text in the midst of existing text, Works moves the existing text to the right and down to accommodate the inserted text.

Moving Selected Text

Just as with copying text, to move text you must select it first. The text you select to move is removed from one location and then inserted in another location. You can use this feature, for example, when your boss tells you to delete a large section of text from a document. Be safe and move that large section to another file. Then if your boss has a change of mind, you still have the text on disk and can move the text back to the document electronically.

T I P   To avoid losing and having to re-create lost material when cutting and pasting text, copy the text to the insertion point first, then delete the duplicate copy.

Follow these steps to move text:

1. Select the text you want to move by using one of the procedures previously described in this chapter.

2. Press Alt,T or access the **Edit** menu and choose **Cut**. Works cuts the text from the document and copies the text to the clipboard.

3. Move the insertion point to the location where you want to insert the selected text.

4. Press Ctrl+V. Works moves the selected text from the original location to the cursor position.

When you insert text from the clipboard into the midst of existing text, Works moves the existing text to the right and down to make room for the new block of text.

NOTE The clipboard is an area of memory that Works uses to store the most recent edit of a document. For example, any text you cut is removed from the screen but saved on the clipboard. If you mistakenly cut text, you can use either the **Undo** or **Paste** option on the **Edit** menu to retrieve the text, provided you have not used the **Cut** or **Copy** options in the meantime. **Undo** reverses the most recent edit, and **Paste** inserts whatever is on the clipboard into the text at the cursor location. Similarly, when you copy text, it stays on the clipboard even after you have pasted it into the text. That way, you can paste the same text several times if necessary.

Checking Your Spelling

With Works, checking your spelling is easy, and you have many options from which to choose. You can use any of the following procedures with a misspelled word, depending on the situation:

- Replace the misspelled word with a correctly spelled word or a different word.

- Change all occurrences of the misspelled word.

- Ignore this instance of the word.

- Ignore the word each time it is found in the document.

- Add the word to the Works dictionary.

All these options are in the Spelling dialog box. Check the spelling in your sample Works memo by following these steps:

1. Click the **O**ptions menu or press Alt,O.

2. Choose the Check **S**pelling option.

   Assume that in your memo you had also misspelled the word *interoffice* as *interfoffice*. Works finds the word *interfoffice*, displays it in the Not in Dictionary: field of the Spelling dialog box (see fig. 3.3), and suggests alternative spellings.

3. From the Suggestions: box, choose the correctly spelled word.

FIG. 3.3

The Spelling
dialog box

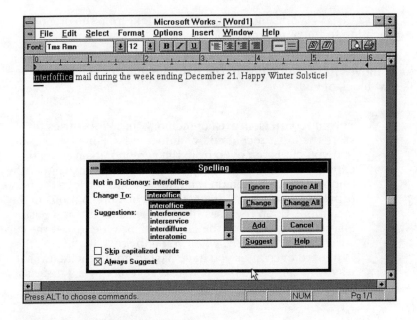

Working with Files

Works enables you to save, print, and close files. You have two options
when you save a file. After you have edited a file, you can save it under
the old file name, thereby replacing the old file with the edited version.
Or you can use the Save **As** option from the **F**ile menu to use a different
file name, thereby saving the new version of the file without modifying
the old version.

Saving a File

You should save text at 15-minute intervals and before you stop for an
interruption (such as a phone call or lunch break). After you have
saved a file, the information is at your disposal whenever you want to
see it again. The following steps show you how to save a Works file:

1. Click **F**ile and choose **S**ave, or press Alt,S.

   If you haven't previously saved the file, the Save As dialog box
   appears.

2. Enter a name for the file. Works writes the file's text to disk.

Printing a File

If you want to print only one copy of the entire file in which you are working, the following steps for printing are simple:

1. Click **File** and choose **Print**, or press Alt,F,P.

2. Check to see that the printer is on and that paper is ready to be fed through the printer.

3. Leave the Print dialog box's default settings as they are and press Enter.

Works sends a message to the printer to print one copy of the text in the on-screen file.

Closing a File

Closing a file takes that file off the screen. If you already have saved the file, it is on disk but is just not visible anymore. Close a file when you will not be working on it further or will not need to access it during the present work session. Use this procedure to close a file:

Click **File** and choose **Close**, or press Alt,F,C.

 NOTE A quick way to close any window or application is to double-click the control-menu button (the minus sign), or press Ctrl+F4.

The file is removed from the screen. If you haven't saved the file already, Works asks you whether you want to save it before closing. If you choose not to save the file and then proceed to close it, the text in that file is lost. Unless you want to abandon the file, save the document before closing it.

Chapter Summary

In this quick start, you learned the basic concepts for entering, editing, saving, printing, and closing a word processing document.

In the next chapter, you take a more detailed look at entering, editing, and saving your documents.

Entering, Editing, and Saving Documents

Word processing has become popular with business users, professional writers, and personal letter writers because it is such a convenient way to process text. You can type at your own speed and not be concerned about making mistakes. Editing the document is quick and easy. The document is recorded on magnetic media, not on paper. Instead of typing and then retyping an entire document so that it is perfect in the end, you can word process the document: type it on-screen, edit it, and then print a finished document. You have saved a great deal of paper and hours of frustration. As with most new technology, a little time invested in the beginning can save you hours in the future.

In this chapter, you learn how to do the following:

- Open a new word processing file.
- Create a document.
- Edit, select, copy, move, and delete text.
- Save a document.
- Close a document.

Opening a Word Processing File

As you learned in the previous chapter, you open a new word processing file by turning on your computer and starting Windows. In the Windows Program Manager, double-click the Works program icon. The Welcome to Microsoft Works screen appears. Click the **W**ord Processor button in the Startup dialog box or press Alt,W. A blank word processing screen appears as shown in figure 4.1, with a new, blank document named WORD1.

FIG. 4.1

Opening a new word processing file

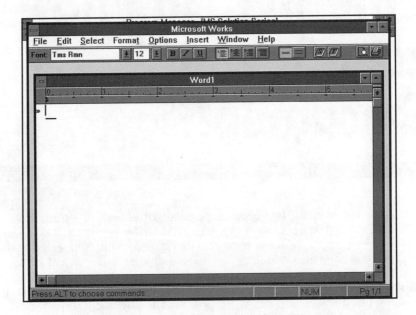

Examining the Word Processing Screen

On the word processor opening screen, the *insertion point*, a blinking vertical line, begins at the upper-left corner of the work space. The *work space* is where text is entered. Text you enter on this work space appears as it would if you were typing on paper. The insertion point indicates where the next character you type will be entered. As you type a character—any letter, number, symbol, or space—the insertion point moves to the next character position.

Across the top of the word processing screen (under the Title bar) is the *Menu bar*. The menu options available are **F**ile, **E**dit, **S**elect, Forma**t**, **O**ptions, **I**nsert, **W**indow, and **H**elp.

Beneath the Menu bar is the Works *Tool bar*, which houses shortcut buttons for the most commonly used document enhancements, plus information on the document. The Tool bar is covered more extensively in Chapter 5.

Below the Tool bar is the *ruler line*, which you use to set up your margins and tabs. The ruler line has default (automatic) margins established for standard 8 1/2-by-11-inch paper. The default margins are 1 inch for both the top and bottom margins, 1.3 inches for the left margin, and 1.2 inches for the right margin. You learn how to change margins and paper size in Chapter 5.

On your work space to the left of the insertion point are two right-pointing arrows. These arrows point to the beginning of page 1 of your document. Directly below the insertion point is a short horizontal line, the *end-of-file marker*, which indicates the end of your document. The end-of-file marker moves down the left margin as you type line after line of text.

Entering Text

Before you begin typing in the work space of the word processing window, maximize both the application window and the document window. Maximize the application window by clicking on the Application control button in the top left of the computer screen and then clicking Ma**x**imize, or with your keyboard by pressing Alt+space bar to open the menu and pressing X. Next, maximize the document window by clicking the document control button in the upper-left corner of the Word1 window and clicking Ma**x**imize, or with the keyboard pressing Alt+hyphen to open the window and then pressing X.

With your insertion point in the upper-left corner or the work space, begin by typing the following practice letter. Don't worry about making mistakes as you enter the text. Correcting mistakes and editing are covered later in this chapter.

As you type, you do not have to press Enter at the end of each line. As you learned earlier, works ends each line for you according to the default ruler line settings, a process called *word wrap*. Press Enter when you want to end a line without wrapping or when you want to end a paragraph. Pressing Enter twice leaves a blank line between paragraphs.

In the heading of the letter, for example, press Enter twice after the date line and after the heading and the salutation. In the body of the letter, let Works word-wrap for you. Press Enter twice to divide paragraphs. Type the following letter:

April 24, 1992

Rancho Mirage Town Council
c/o Louise Bezoldi
383847 Thundercloud Drive
Rancho Mirage, CA 92128

Dear Ms. Bezoldi:

As President of the Rancho Mirage Tennis Association, I feel it is my responsibility to voice a complaint regarding the hazardous right-hand turn that has to be made by motorists who wish to enter the Mirage Community Park.

The construction that has resulted in this hazardous turn has been proceeding for more than two years. We at the Rancho Mirage Tennis Association would like to see this hazardous situation come to a close.

To alleviate some of the danger, a warning light could be placed before the park entrance to encourage motorists to slow down before reaching the park entrance. While we are concerned about motorists, we are even more concerned about the thousands of children who frequent the park. It is for their safety that we express this concern.

Sincerely,

Arnold P. Schwarzkraut
President
Rancho Mirage Tennis Association

The beginning of your letter can be seen on the screen shown in figure 4.2.

Now that you have a draft of your letter, save it before you edit so that you have a copy on disk that you can use if you decide not to retain any edits. This is a good habit to get into as programs do occasionally crash (called an "Unrecoverable Application Error" in Windows parlance), and losing a large document is never pleasant. To save the new letter follow these steps:

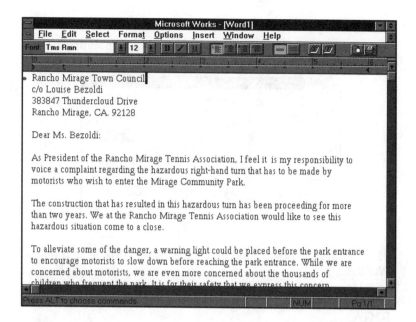

FIG. 4.2

The beginning of the sample letter

1. Click **File** or press Alt,F.

   The File menu appears as shown in figure 4.3

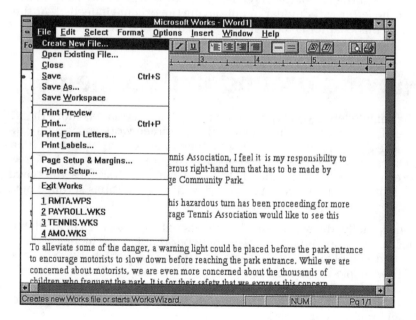

FIG. 4.3

The File menu

2. Click **S**ave or press Alt,S.

Works opens the Save As dialog box as shown in figure 4.4.

FIG. 4.4

The Save As
dialog box

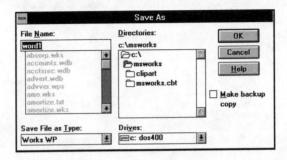

The highlight is positioned in the File **N**ame: box, which reads WORD1.

3. Type the new name as follows:

RMTA

4. Press Enter or click OK.

The file is saved to disk under the name RMTA.WPS, and the new name appears at the top of the screen in place of WORD1. Now you can freely edit the letter without fear of not having the original if needed. At the end of this chapter is more information on saving files.

Moving around in Documents

The sample letter you typed in the preceding section has more than 19 lines. Because only 19 lines can fit the on-screen work space, you cannot see the entire letter on-screen at one time. As you type more than 19 lines, Works scrolls the text up. The top lines move up and off the screen as new lines are added at the bottom. The first lines you typed are still there and stored. You can view the text that has scrolled out of view by pressing the PgUp key.

Conceptually, the screen display covers only a small area of available electronic paper. Imagine a piece of paper that is 8 1/2 inches wide but is hundreds of feet long. This imaginary long page is what you have to work with in a word processor. Microsoft Works takes care of deciding where to break pages when you print your work. Therefore, as you type more than 19 lines, the electronic paper simply is pushed up to make room for more characters.

Moving the Insertion Point with the Keyboard

Before you can perform editing functions, you have to know how to move the insertion point around within your Microsoft Works document. Table 4.1 describes how to move the insertion point to the error you want to change, the spot where text is to be inserted, or the beginning of text you want to delete.

Table 4.1 Using the Keyboard To Move the Insertion Point

To move	Press this key
Right one character	Right arrow
Left one character	Left arrow
Up one line	Up arrow
Down one line	Down arrow
Right one word	Ctrl+right arrow
Left one word	Ctrl+left arrow
Up one paragraph	Ctrl+up arrow
Down one paragraph	Ctrl+down arrow
To the beginning of the line	Home
To the end of the line	End
To the beginning of the file	Ctrl+Home
To the end of the file	Ctrl+End
Up one window	PgUp
Down one window	PgDn
To the beginning of the window	Ctrl+PgUp
To the end of the window	Ctrl+PgDn

As you can see, special keys enable you to move one character, line, word, paragraph, screen, or file at a time. With practice, you can move around in your documents quickly.

Using the Go To... Command

When you have created a long document, use the **G**o To... command (the three dots indicate that additional choices are available) to get to a certain page without having to move line by line or screen by screen. To use the **G**o To... command, follow these steps:

1. Click **S**elect or press Alt,S and the **S**elect pull-down menu appears (see fig. 4.5).

T I P   You can skip the **S**elect menu and go directly to the **G**o To dialog box by pressing shortcut key F5.

FIG. 4.5

The **S**elect menu

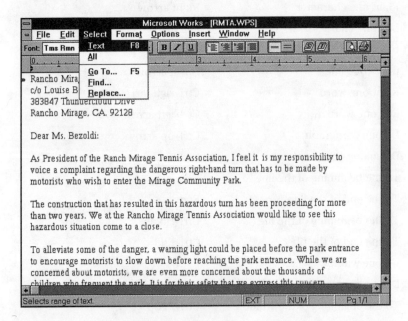

2. Choose the **G**o To... command. The **G**o To dialog box appears (see fig. 4.6).

3. In the **G**o To: field, type the page number to which you want to go.

4. Press Enter or click OK. Microsoft Works moves your insertion point to the first character on the indicated page.

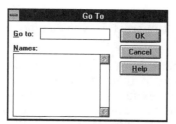

FIG. 4.6

The Go To dialog box

NOTE When using the **G**o To... command and you type a page number greater than the number of pages in your document, you get a warning saying that you have entered an invalid page number (see fig. 4.7). Press Enter to return to the Go To dialog box, and type in another page number. To exit from the dialog box without moving to another page, press the Esc key.

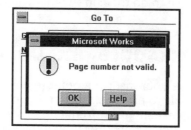

FIG. 4.7

The message that appears when you type an invalid page number

Moving the Insertion Point with the Mouse

The on-screen I marks the spot where the mouse pointer currently rests. With the mouse pointer on any character in your text, click the mouse. The insertion point appears where you clicked.

To move farther distances in a document, use the mouse and the scroll bars. On the far right side of the screen is a border area with a long gray bar. This *scroll bar* represents the entire length of the document. Inside the bar is a lighter-colored gray box called the *scroll box*. When the insertion point is at the top of the screen, the box is at the top of the scroll bar just below an upward-pointing arrow. By placing the mouse arrow on the box and then clicking and dragging, you can move the box up and down the bar. In a long document, you can move rapidly from top to bottom or vice-versa by dragging the box. To move a single line at a time, click the up or down arrow at the top or bottom of the scroll bar. With a little practice, you can move with precision through a document.

At the bottom of the screen is a horizontal scroll bar. Although you probably will not create documents with page widths greater than 80 characters, you can move the insertion point location from the farthest point on the left margin of the document to any point to the right. The procedure is identical to moving vertically. Position the arrow on the box and click and drag to where you want the insertion point to be.

Editing Documents

At this point, you may have found out how easy it is to use a word processor. But what if you discover errors in your document? What if you typed the same paragraph twice? What if you want to change the order of the paragraphs or insert or delete text? These tasks are all editing functions, and you learn to do them in the following sections.

Using the Backspace and Del Keys

You know how to move your insertion point to any location on-screen. Now you want to be able to erase misspelled words or delete certain information. The simplest and most frequently used method of editing text is to use the Backspace key. After typing the sample letter at the beginning of this chapter, for example, suppose that you check Ms. Bezoldi's name and find that it has two Zs rather than one. Move your insertion point to the end of her name in the inside address and press the Backspace key four times to erase i, d, l, and o.

Next type **zoldi** to correct her name.

Make sure that you find the incorrect word every time it occurs. Only one other occurrence of the incorrect *Bezoldi* is in this short letter, so you can move the insertion point there and correct that spelling, too. In a longer document, you need to do a search-and-replace to ensure that you catch all misspellings. (See Chapter 6 for instructions on how to search for a specific word and then replace it.)

No whiteout, correction tape, or fancy maneuvering are needed to edit text. Just backspace over the incorrect characters, and the information stored in the computer is gone. Type in new text, and new information replaces the old. The electronic typing page is that easy to use.

Inserting Text

Suppose that you decide to add a threatening paragraph to the sample letter you have typed. To insert the paragraph, move your insertion point to the line between the second and third paragraphs. Press Enter and then type the following:

Our attorney is being notified of our concern. We hope legal action will not be necessary. To protect our members, we will take any action necessary.

Press Enter again. Figure 4.8 shows how the inserted paragraph appears on-screen.

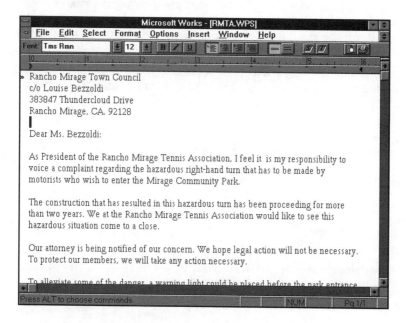

FIG. 4.8

The new paragraph inserted

Pressing Enter before and after you type the paragraph leaves a blank line before and after the inserted text, making it a separate paragraph. If you do not want this material to be a separate paragraph, start typing at the end of the preceding paragraph (after the word *close*).

Notice that when you insert new text, the text that already appears on-screen moves to accommodate the addition. The last paragraph and the closing scroll down automatically. All the information still exists even though it doesn't appear on your screen. The screen always shows you the insertion point location. Move your insertion point down, and the remaining text appears on-screen.

Selecting Text

Before you can do major editing jobs, such as moving paragraphs around or deleting large blocks of text, you must know how to select the text you want to delete, copy, or move. When you select text, that text is highlighted on-screen. The next command you choose affects only the text that is highlighted.

You can select just one character or an entire file. You may want to select one paragraph, one sentence, or one section. In a longer document, you may decide that Chapter 2 should be Chapter 5. In that case, you can select Chapter 2 and move it to the Chapter 5 location.

Remember, all these editing tasks are done with keystrokes or the mouse. You don't have to print out something, cut and paste, and then retype it. All the editing is done on an electronic screen. You arrange the text to your liking and then print it.

With Microsoft Works, you can select text in more than one way. In the following paragraphs, you learn how to use these various selection methods.

Selecting with the Shift and Cursor-Movement Keys

You can select text by using the Shift and cursor-movement keys. This method is most convenient when you are selecting small sections of text, such as a character, word, or small group of words. To select by using this method, follow these steps:

1. Use the arrow keys to move your insertion point to the beginning of the text you want to select.

2. Press and hold down the Shift key.

3. Use the cursor-movement keys (arrow keys) to highlight the text you want to select. Press the right-arrow key to highlight one character at a time, moving right across the screen. Press the down-arrow key to highlight one line at a time, moving down the screen.

Keep the Shift key pressed down the entire time you are selecting text.

To practice selecting text, go back to the example letter you typed. Move your insertion point to the beginning of the fourth paragraph, next to the word To (see fig. 4.9).

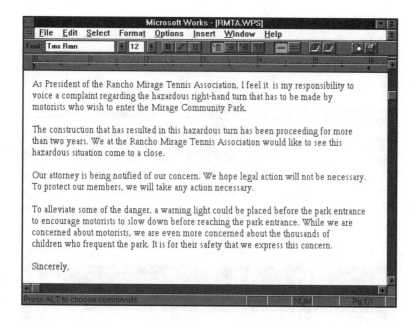

FIG. 4.9

Positioning the
insertion point to
select the fourth
paragraph

To select this paragraph for editing, press the Shift key and hold it
down. Press the down-arrow key four times until the entire paragraph
is highlighted (see fig. 4.10).

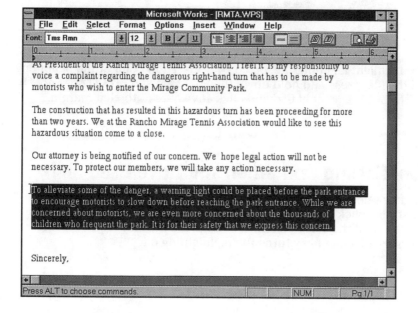

FIG. 4.10

Selecting a
paragraph

You also can use the other cursor-movement keys introduced previously in this chapter to highlight text. With the insertion point at the beginning of the fourth paragraph and the Shift key held down, for example, you can highlight the remainder of the page by pressing PgDn (see fig. 4.11).

FIG. 4.11

Selecting to the
end of the page

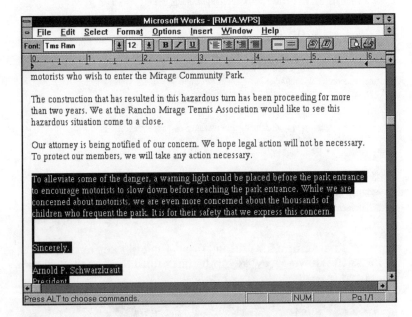

TIP   To highlight an entire file, place your insertion point at the beginning of the file, press and hold down the Shift key, and press Ctrl+End. Or with the mouse, hold Ctrl and click anywhere in the left margin.

Unselecting Text When You Have Used Shift

If after selecting a block of text you decide that you don't want to edit that text, click the mouse or press any cursor-movement key to unselect all the selected text. Do not press the Shift key. Pressing a cursor-movement key turns the highlighting off.

Selecting Text with the F8 Key

For the second method of selecting text, use the F8 function key. Just as you do when using the Shift key, move your insertion point to the beginning of the text you want to select. Then press F8. EXT, the abbreviation for the Extend command, appears on the status line at the bottom of the screen. You then can use the cursor-movement keys to select text. Press the right-arrow key to highlight one character at a time, moving right across your screen. Press the down-arrow key to highlight one line at a time.

As you can see, using F8 is similar to using the Shift key. An added advantage of using the F8 key is that it selects specific amounts of text in sequence. As you continue to press F8, more text is selected. Table 4.2 describes which text is selected, in sequence, when you press F8 repeatedly.

Table 4.2 Selecting Text with F8

To select	Press F8
The current word	Two times
The current sentence	Three times
The current paragraph	Four times
The entire file	Five times

(The word "current" refers to the current location of the insertion point.)

Figures 4.12 to 4.14 show how the sample letter looks when you begin pressing F8 with your insertion point at the beginning of the second paragraph in the example letter, the paragraph starting with The.

The F8 (Extend) command also works in conjunction with the **Go** To... command from the **S**elect menu. After you press F8 one time and EXT appears on the status line, press F5. The Go To dialog box appears (see fig. 4.15). Specify a page number, and all the text between the insertion point and the beginning of that page is selected.

FIG. 4.12

Selecting a word
with F8

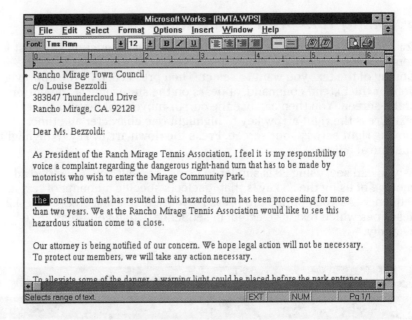

FIG. 4.13

Selecting a
paragraph
with F8

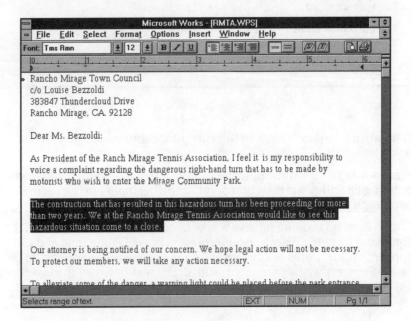

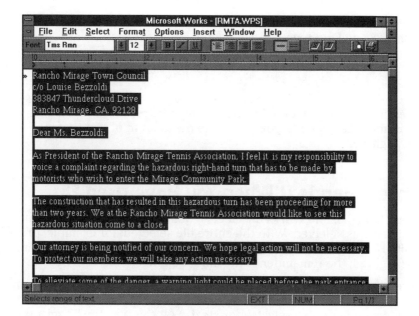

FIG. 4.14

Selecting the whole document with F8

FIG. 4.15

Using F8 and the Go To dialog box

In the same way, you can select text up to a specific word by following these steps:

1. Press F8.

2. Open the **S**elect menu.

3. Choose the **F**ind option.

4. When the Find dialog box appears, type a word. Works selects the text between your insertion point and the next occurrence of the specified word.

T I P   Using F8 and Find together works only if the insertion point is positioned in a portion of the file that precedes the occurrence of the word to find. Works does not search backward.

Pressing Esc turns off the Extend command. Pressing a cursor-movement key enables you to change the amount of text that is highlighted.

Unselecting Text When You Have Used F8

Press Shift+F8, and Works unselects text in the same increments in which it was selected. With the entire file selected, for example, press Shift+F8, and only the paragraph your insertion point was in remains highlighted; the remainder of the file is no longer selected.

After EXT appears, you cannot press a cursor-movement key to turn the highlighting off. Pressing a cursor-movement key only selects more text; pressing F8 also selects more text. You can turn the F8 selection process off only by pressing the Esc key. Then EXT no longer appears on the status line, and you can continue your editing functions.

Selecting Multiple Paragraphs

Use F8 with the Ctrl+down arrow combination to select a series of paragraphs. With your insertion point at the beginning of the second paragraph in the sample letter, for example, press F8. EXT appears on the status line. If you also want the third and fourth paragraphs selected, press Ctrl+down arrow to extend the highlighting to the third paragraph, and press Ctrl+down arrow another two times to select the next paragraph. (You have to press Ctrl+down arrow once for the blank line and once for the next paragraph.) Press Esc to turn off EXT.

Selecting Text with the Mouse

The last way to select text is to use the mouse. Place the mouse pointer on the first character in the section of text you want to select. Click and drag the mouse over the text to select it. If you want to select text as you move down the screen, for example, click the mouse and then drag down the screen until the necessary text is highlighted. Click the mouse again to unselect the text. Table 4.3 provides some additional mouse selection techniques.

Table 4.3 Selecting Text with the Mouse

To select	Use this method
A word	Double-click the word
A line	Click beside the line in the left window margin
A sentence	Drag through the sentence (or press and hold Ctrl and click the sentence)
Several lines	Drag the pointer up or down in the left margin
A paragraph	Double-click beside the paragraph in the left margin
A document	Hold down the Ctrl key and click in the left margin

Now that you know how to select text, you are ready to learn about the basic editing tasks that you can perform with selected text: moving, copying, and deleting blocks of text.

Moving Selected Text

Occasionally you may want to move a section of text from one position to another. In Works, to move text you must either *cut* or *copy* it from one position and *paste* it to another position. And before you can cut or copy text, you must select it. Suppose, for example, that in the sample letter to the Rancho Mirage Tennis Association you want to move the third paragraph to the end of the body of the letter. Follow these steps to move text:

1. Select the text you want to move. For example, move your insertion point to the beginning of the third paragraph—to the left of the letter O in the word Our. Press F8 four times to highlight the entire paragraph.

2. Access the Edit menu, as shown in figure 4.16. Note that the second option on the menu is Cut.

FIG. 4.16

The Edit menu

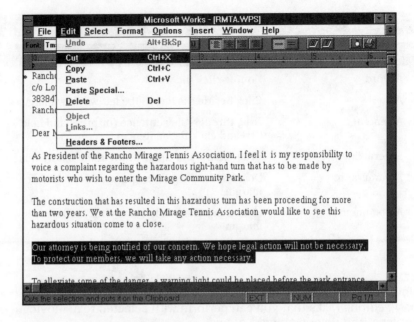

3. Choose the Cut option.

   The Edit menu disappears from the screen, as do the paragraph and the blank line following it.

4. Move the insertion point to the spot where you want to insert the cut text—to the left of the word Sincerely in the sample letter.

5. Press Ctrl+V. The highlighted paragraph is pasted to the new location (see fig. 4.17).

You can see from figure 4.17 that you have to make a few minor adjustments to clean up the letter. First, move your insertion point to the word concern, which ends the paragraph preceding the one you just moved. Press Enter to put a blank line between the two paragraphs. Now move the insertion point above the letter T in the word To—the beginning of what is now the third paragraph. Press the Backspace key one time to eliminate an extra blank line before that paragraph. Your letter is now neat and has consistent spacing.

If, while you are moving text, you decide that you don't want to complete the move, press Esc before you select Cut to cancel the Cut command.

Character styles and paragraph formats are moved with the text that is moved. Moving text from file to file is covered later in this chapter (see "Cutting and Copying Text between Documents").

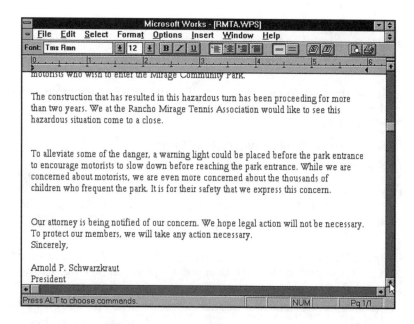

FIG. 4.17

Pasting the
paragraph to a
new location

Replacing Selected Text

You can use the **Edit Cut** command to replace text in another location
with selected text by following these steps:

1. Select the paragraph to be moved.

2. Click **Edit** and choose **Cut** or press Alt,T.

3. Move your insertion point to the new location and highlight a
   second paragraph (the paragraph you want replaced).

4. Press Ctrl+V, or choose **Paste** from the **Edit** menu. The first highlighted paragraph replaces the second highlighted paragraph.

This feature saves you the steps of deleting one paragraph before you
move another paragraph to that location.

Copying Selected Text

Suppose that you are preparing four documents for various staff
members. Each of these documents, though different, has the same
introduction. Save yourself time and potential errors by copying the
introduction to each document. When you copy text, you duplicate the
selected text without removing it from the original location. You then
insert, or paste, that text into a new location.

Practice copying text in the sample letter you have on-screen. With your insertion point to the left of the letter O in Our—in what is now the last paragraph of the body of the letter—follow these steps to copy text:

1. Select the text you want to copy. For the practice example, select the last paragraph by pressing F8 four times or click four times in left margin.

2. Access the **E**dit menu and choose **C**opy.

3. Press Enter.

4. Move the insertion point to the spot where you want to insert the copied text. In the example, move the insertion point up to the line between the second and third paragraphs of the letter (after the word close and before the word To).

5. Press Ctrl+V or choose **P**aste from the **E**dit menu, and the selected text is inserted at the insertion point's position (see fig. 4.18).

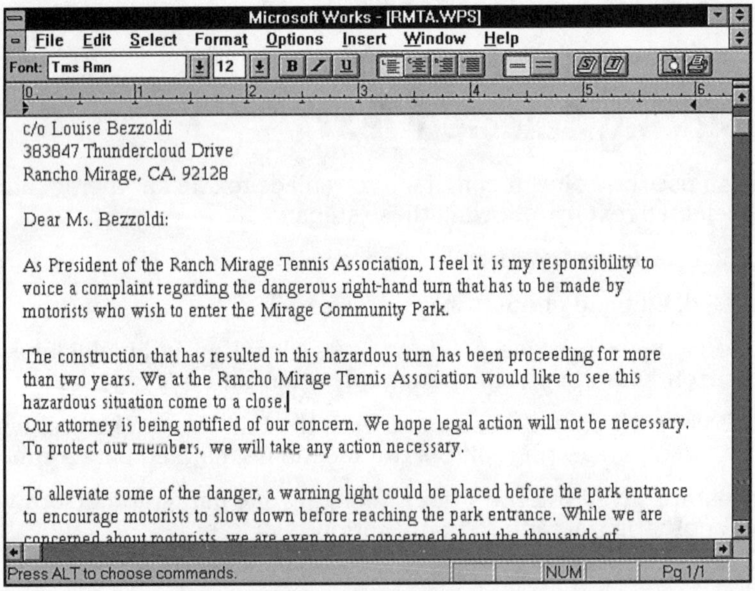

FIG. 4.18

Copying a paragraph

```
═                    Microsoft Works - [RMTA.WPS]                    ▼ ▲
─  File   Edit   Select   Format   Options   Insert   Window   Help        ▲
Font: Tms Rmn          ± 12 ±  B / U  ▩▩▩▩  ─═  ▨▨  ▧▨
  0. . . . . . |1. . . . . |2. . . . |3. . . . |4. . . . |5. . . . |6. . . ▲
c/o Louise Bezzoldi
383847 Thundercloud Drive
Rancho Mirage, CA. 92128

Dear Ms. Bezzoldi:

As President of the Ranch Mirage Tennis Association, I feel it is my responsibility to
voice a complaint regarding the dangerous right-hand turn that has to be made by
motorists who wish to enter the Mirage Community Park.

The construction that has resulted in this hazardous turn has been proceeding for more
than two years. We at the Rancho Mirage Tennis Association would like to see this
hazardous situation come to a close.|
Our attorney is being notified of our concern. We hope legal action will not be necessary.
To protect our members, we will take any action necessary.

To alleviate some of the danger, a warning light could be placed before the park entrance
to encourage motorists to slow down before reaching the park entrance. While we are
concerned about motorists, we are even more concerned about the thousands of
Press ALT to choose commands.                          NUM      Pg 1/1
```

You also can use the **E**dit **C**opy command to replace text. Select text at the new insertion point location and, with the Typing Replaces Selection command selected, press Enter. Works replaces the selected text with the copied text. Access this toggle option by pressing Alt,O, and then Y.

Deleting Selected Text

You often may find yourself with unwanted text on your hands. After completing the practice copy operations on the sample letter, for example, you have two identical paragraphs—the third and the fifth paragraphs. The next step is to decide which to keep and which to delete, and then to delete the unwanted paragraph. As with the copy and cut functions, you can delete any amount of text you can select, from one character to an entire file. Take the following steps to delete unwanted text:

1. Move the insertion point to the beginning of the text you want to delete. For the sample letter, move the insertion point to the first letter in one of the identical paragraphs.

2. Select the text you want to delete. For the example, press F8 four times or click twice in the left margin beside the paragraph to select the entire paragraph.

3. Access the **E**dit menu and Choose **D**elete.

You can bypass the **E**dit menu by pressing the Del key after you select the text you want to delete.

T   I   P

Cutting and Copying Text between Documents

Now that you have worked with cutting and copying, you can distinguish the difference between the function of each. When you cut text, it is removed from its original location and inserted in a new location. When you copy text, it remains in the original location and is inserted in the new location.

Before you can cut and copy from one file to another, you must have both files open. With the original open on-screen, start by opening a new file to hold your copy. Open the **F**ile menu and select Create **N**ew File. Four options appear on-screen, one for each component of Works. Click the **W**ord Processor icon or press W to open a new word processing file.

The default name of this new file (assigned by Works) is WORD2. You probably want to rename the new file. Open the **F**ile menu and choose

Save. The Save dialog box appears with the name WORD2. at the top. In the File **N**ame: field, type a new name for the file, such as *copy*, and press Enter or click OK.

To copy from the original file to the new file, follow these steps:

1. First make sure that the insertion point is back in the file from which you want to copy. To return to that file, open the **W**indow menu, move the highlight to the source file name, and press Enter.

2. Move the insertion point to the beginning of the text you want to copy. Suppose, for example, that you want to copy the name and address at the beginning of the sample letter. The insertion point thus should be to the left of the letter R in Rancho.

3. Select the text you want to copy. For the example, hold down the Shift key and press the down-arrow key until the inside address is highlighted.

4. Access the **E**dit menu and choose **C**opy or just press Alt,C.

5. Open the new file to which you want to copy the selected text.

6. Open the **W**indow menu.

7. Select the appropriate window—COPY.WPS, for example. The new file is superimposed on the second file, which still is open (see fig. 4.19).

FIG. 4.19

Two open windows

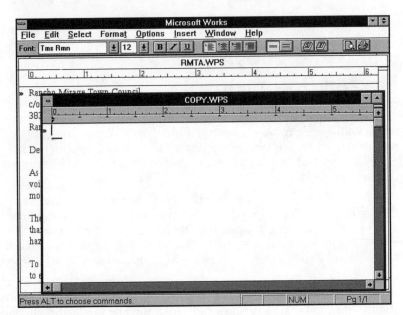

8. Press Ctrl+V or choose **P**aste from the **E**dit menu, and the highlighted text from the source file is inserted into the destination file
   (see fig. 4.20).

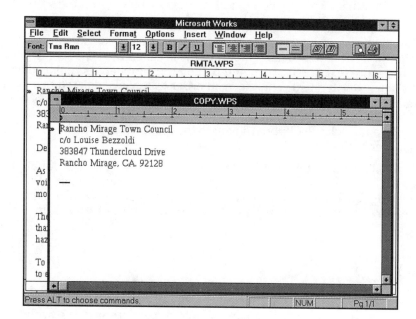

FIG. 4.20

Copying text to
the new file

Undoing Mistakes

The first option on the **E**dit menu is Undo. This option is a valuable
feature that helps you correct mistakes. Imagine how you would feel if
you selected an entire chapter from a book you had written and then
accidentally pressed Del. Reproducing the lost prose might take consid-
erable effort. With the Microsoft Works word processor, however, all is
not lost. Immediately after you press the Del key, press Alt,E and then
U, or press Alt,Backspace. You undo the deletion, and the text you have
deleted accidentally is restored.

CAUTION   To restore deleted material, you must use the Undo
command immediately after deleting. If any new deletions occur between the mistaken deletion and the use
of the Undo command, the deleted text is lost.

Undo reverses not only deletions but also many of your other most
recent editing and formatting actions. Following are other examples of
commands you may want to undo:

■ All commands on the Format menu

■ All commands on the Edit menu (except Undo)

■ The Check Spelling command (undoing all the corrected words)

When you delete text, Microsoft Works stores the deleted text in RAM (random-access memory) in a temporary file that holds only one occurrence of deleted text. This temporary file is called the *clipboard*. If you delete more text, the first deleted text on the clipboard is replaced with the newly deleted text. Therefore, in order to retrieve deleted text, you must retrieve it immediately, or the clipboard may no longer be holding the text you want. (To view the contents of the clipboard, minimize Works and click the Clipboard icon in the Main window of the Program Manager.)

Your skills at selecting, cutting, copying, and deleting text undoubtedly are improving. As your documents take form, get ready to put a few finishing touches on them for the sake of clarity and accuracy. Your tools are the spell-checking and thesaurus functions of Microsoft Works.

Checking Your Spelling

The Microsoft Works spell-checking program electronically searches the text you have entered and finds misspelled words. Works also finds incorrectly capitalized words such as *WOrks*, incorrectly hyphenated words such as *hyp-henated*, and repeated words such as *and and*.

For practice, look through the sample letter you created in this chapter. If no spelling errors exist, you may want to create some to see how well the spell-checking program works. Follow these steps to check your spelling in a document:

1. Press Ctrl Home to move the insertion point to the upper-left corner of the word processing document. In a longer document, you may choose to move the insertion point to where you want to begin checking the spelling. Works moves forward when checking spelling, starting with the insertion point location to the end of the file.

2. Click **O**ptions and choose Check **S**pelling, or press Alt,O,S.

   Works starts searching through the text for words it does not recognize. When such a word is found, the Spelling dialog box appears. Figure 4.21 shows the first word that Works does not recognize in the sample letter: Bezzoldi.

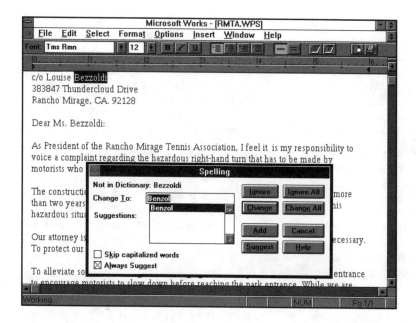

FIG. 4.21

Finding an
unrecognized
word

3. Notice that in the Spelling dialog box Works offers alternative
   spellings for the found word and also provides several other options. When a word is not recognized, you can take one of these
   approaches:

   ▪ Replace the word with a correctly spelled word.

   ▪ Change all occurrences of the misspelled word (press Alt,E).

   ▪ Ignore this instance of the word (press Alt,I).

   ▪ Ignore the word each time it is found in the file (press Alt,G).

   ▪ Ask Works to suggest some other spellings of the word
     (press Alt,S).

   ▪ Select a word from the list of suggestions and then press
     Alt,C to change the word.

   ▪ Add the word to the Works dictionary (press Alt,A).

When you have made a decision about the word Works does not recognize and have chosen the appropriate option to implement your decision, Works follows your instructions and then begins searching for the
next questionable word. Notice that with each word Works finds, a
brief description of the problem appears in the upper-left corner of the
Spelling dialog box. Bezzoldi, for example, is considered to be a misspelled word.

T I P

If Works flags a proper name you know is correct and that may appear more than once in the document, the best response is to press Alt,G to tell Works to ignore all occurrences of the found word in the file. If Works displays in the Spelling dialog box your name or another person's name that will appear often in your documents, you may want to press Alt,A to add the name to the dictionary so that Works will not stop at that name again.

Works does not recognize most proper names—except ones such as Cook or Fish. And even these common types of words may appear in the Spelling dialog box under the `Irregular Capitalization` prompt. If the text you want to check contains many proper names, you can prevent continuous interruptions by pressing Alt,K to select the S**k**ip Capitalized Words option in the Spelling dialog box. Keep in mind, however, that if you select this option, Works does not catch some errors. A misspelled but capitalized word such as *Presibent*, for example, will go unnoticed.

If you have selected Al**w**ays Suggest or if you press Alt,S, Works lists suggested replacements for misspelled words. Figure 4.22 shows the list you might see for the word *Presibent*. To correct the misspelling, highlight the correct word in the Suggestions: field—*President*—and press Enter or click OK. The word *President* replaces the incorrect *Presibent*.

FIG. 4.22

Finding a new spelling for an incorrect word

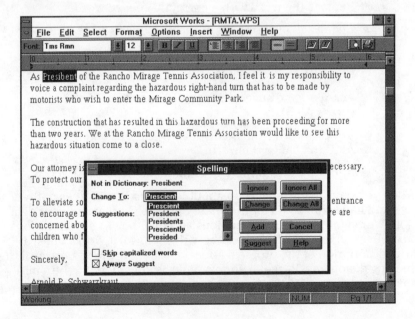

If you didn't start checking the spelling at the beginning of the file, a prompt appears when Works reaches the end of the file asking whether you want to continue to check spelling from the start of the file. Choose OK (press Enter), and Works continues to check the spelling. Or press the right-arrow key to move the highlight to the right to select Cancel (or press Esc). This action stops the spell-checking process. To get help, press Alt,H.

Press Esc anytime during the spell-checking process to stop it.

Using the Thesaurus

Use the Microsoft Works thesaurus to improve your clarity and style when writing. The thesaurus helps you find exactly the right word or interject a little variety in your choice of words.

When you want to use the thesaurus to find a synonym for a word in your text, follow these steps:

1. Move the insertion point to the first letter of the word.

2. Press Shift and the right-arrow key until the word is selected, or double-click the word.

   In the second paragraph of the sample letter, for example, the writer has used the word *hazardous* two times. You thus might want to select the second occurrence of *hazardous* and find a synonym for it.

3. Access the **O**ptions menu.

4. Select the **T**hesaurus option.

   The Thesaurus dialog box appears. At the top is information concerning what is contained in the dialog box. The word you selected appears next to the Synonyms For: field, and the **M**eanings: field displays other meanings for the selected word. After each word in the Meanings list a small letter in parentheses tells you what kind of word it is. The small a next to the word *risky* in figure 4.23, for example, indicates that this word is an adjective. On the right side of the dialog box are the synonyms.

5. Use the Tab key to move the highlight to the Synonyms: field.

6. Highlight the word you want to use instead of the word you selected in the text.

7. Press Alt,C or Enter or click **C**hange. The new word replaces the selected word in your document.

You also can search for the synonym of a synonym. With one synonym highlighted, press Alt,S. Works lists any synonyms for the highlighted word. You can choose a replacement from this list.

FIG. 4.23

The Thesaurus
dialog box

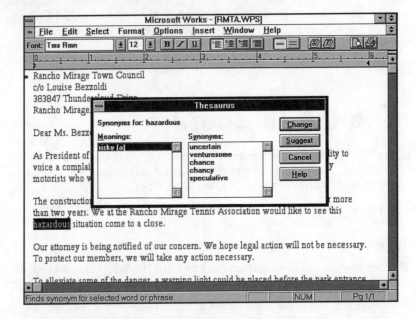

Saving Your Documents

If you exit Works without saving or if a power loss occurs, you lose all of your work. Many computer users make a habit of saving their files every few minutes. Saving a document creates a copy of your text on either your hard drive or a floppy disk. If you don't need to use a document again and have no need to keep a record of it, you do not have to save it. Usually, however, you want to keep a copy that you can call up anytime.

Earlier in the chapter you saved the letter, naming it RMTA. Now that you have finished your edits, you will want to save it again in its corrected form. To save your letter, perform the following procedure:

Open the File menu and select Save

Works automatically saves the letter, replacing the file on disk with the changes you have made on-screen.

NOTE Works names your files for you in the following sequence: WORD1, WORD2, and so on. Because these names aren't descriptive, you probably want to rename the documents you create. Names of files can be eight characters in length with a one- to three-character extension. Works automatically adds the WPS extension to your word processing files if you don't add one yourself. Add your own extensions if you want to identify your files even further. If the name of your company is Hot Cross Buns, for example, you may want to use HCB as a file extension for everything that has to do with your business.

CAUTION If you use extensions other than the default WPS, Works doesn't automatically list these files in the Open Existing File dialog box. You have to type *.* in the File Name: field to see all the files, regardless of name or extension.

Changing the File Name

The two options you can use to save text are **S**ave and Save **A**s. Most of the time, you will use the **S**ave command to save the file to your hard disk. At other times, however, you may want to use other saving options or change the file name. You can save files in other file formats, for example, making them compatible with other word processors. And you can give a file a new name. For these tasks, you use the **F**ile menu's Save **A**s command.

Some of the Save **A**s options are covered here. First, look at the Save As dialog box that appears when you choose Save **A**s from the **F**ile menu (see fig. 4.24).

In the File **N**ame: field, the Save As dialog box shows the name you have given the file. The directory is listed (C:\MSWORKS), telling you where the file is to be saved. You can change the name of the file by typing a new name in the File **N**ame: box. To change the file format, click on **T**ype or press Alt,T to select a different format.

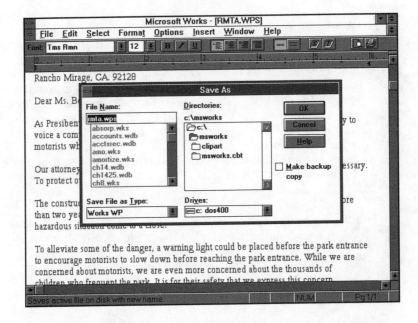

FIG. 4.24

The Save As
dialog box

Saving to Another Drive or Directory

If the correct drive and directory are not selected, follow these steps to
change to another drive or directory:

1. Press Alt,V to move to the Drives: field in the Save As dialog box.

2. Press the down-arrow key to choose a different drive. (Most computers have at least A, B, and C available.)

3. Press Alt,D to move to the **D**irectories: field.

4. Use the down-arrow key to select the correct directory. (The directory currently selected is shown above the box.)

5. Press Enter or click OK to save the file.

When you use this method, the new drive and directory you select becomes the new current drive and directory. To save the file to another
drive or directory without changing the current directory, choose Save
As from the **F**ile menu and type the complete path name and file name
in the File **N**ame: field. To save a file to the WORKS directory on drive A,
for example, type the following and then press Enter:

A:\WORKS\RMTA.WPS

Saving Files in ASCII Format

When you save files in Works, the files are saved in Works format. Use ASCII format to save files that you may want to use with other word processing programs. (ASCII files also are called text files.) An ASCII file contains only the text and numbers from the file without the Works formatting.

While in the Save As dialog box, press Alt,T to move to the Save File As Type field and press the down-arrow key to select the Text option. Then press Enter or click OK. The specified file is saved to the current directory—or to any other directory you have specified—in ASCII format.

Closing Files

After you have saved a file, you can close it to clear the screen. Usually you close a file when you are finished working with it.

With the mouse pointer in the file you want to close, open the File menu and select the Close option. The file is removed from the screen (and from RAM). If other files are open, the insertion point moves to the next open file. Use the Close option to close each subsequent file. After all files are closed, the Works screen becomes empty, with only three menus remaining: File, Options, and Help. Even though your files are closed and not visible, if you have saved them you can retrieve them by using the Open Existing File option from the File menu.

If you have not saved your files before you attempt to close them, Works prompts you with a dialog box, asking whether you want to Save changes to <filename>. If you select Yes and press Enter, Works saves the files before closing them. If you choose No in this dialog box, Works closes your file without saving it, which means that you do not have a permanent copy of the file. If you select Cancel, the procedure to close the file is terminated, and the file remains on-screen.

Exiting from Microsoft Works

To exit from Microsoft Works, follow this procedure:

Click File and choose Exit, or press Alt,F,X.

Microsoft Windows takes over, and you are returned to the Windows screen.

Chapter Summary

In this chapter, your word processing skills have been improved—including opening a new file; entering text; moving around in your documents; correcting, inserting, selecting, cutting, and copying text; and saving your document. If the electronic page is new to you, you are learning about the convenience and ease with which you can create documents. If you are an experienced word processor, you have learned how the particular features of the Works word processor can help you create professional documents.

If you are looking for different ways to format your text, look at Chapter 5. You find in that chapter information on formatting, creating tables with columns, using boldface and italics, and changing fonts. Chapter 5 takes you through the advanced word processing features of Works. You learn how to search, search and replace, add headers and footers, create form letters by merging documents, and print all or part of a document.

Using Files, Styles, and Formatting

I n the previous chapter, you learned how to enter and edit documents for accuracy and style, and then save the documents. Now you're ready to learn more about opening and closing documents, enhancing the contents of documents, and adding the finishing touches to a document's appearance.

In this chapter, you learn how to do the following:

- Open Works files in different drives and directories.
- Change type styles and fonts.
- Center and justify text.
- Change spacing and margins, indent paragraphs, and use tabs.

 NOTE Remember to save your documents so you don't lose formatting changes.

Opening Works Files

In Chapter 4, when you created the letter named RMTA.WPS, (Rancho Mirage Tennis Association), you opened a file. You then created another new file, which you named COPY.WPS. At the end of the chapter, you closed the two files. In this section, you practice opening files that you previously closed. To open a closed file, follow these steps:

1. From the Program Manager, double-click the Works icon. The Works Startup dialog box appears.

2. Click the Open Existing File icon. The Open file dialog box appears, as shown in figure 5.1.

FIG. 5.1

The Open
Existing File
dialog box

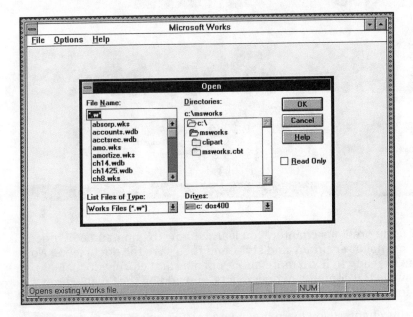

3. In the File Name: field, press the down-arrow to select the RMTA.WPS file, or click on the file name RMTA.WPS, or press Alt,N.

4. Click OK or press Enter.

You now have a file, easily opened, with which to work.

Understanding the Open Dialog Box

You also can use the File Name: box to type the name of the file you want to open. For example, typing ***.*** displays a list of all files from which you can choose.

Existing files are listed in alphabetical order, and the different extension determines the kind of file, as described at the end of chapter 4.

In the center of the Open dialog box is the **D**irectories: field that tells you the drive and directory in which you are working. Here, you see C:\MSWORKS. Two subdirectories, CLIPART and MSWORKS.CBT, also are visible.

In the bottom-left corner of the screen is the List Files of Type: box, which you use to change the default extension of files to list. The entry *.W*, for example, lists all the Works files. To see only word processing files, click the down-arrow in that box and Works shows a list of files and possible extensions. Then click on the Works WP (*.wps) option, and the files listed in the File Name: box change. Figure 5.2 shows the Open dialog box, listing only word processing files.

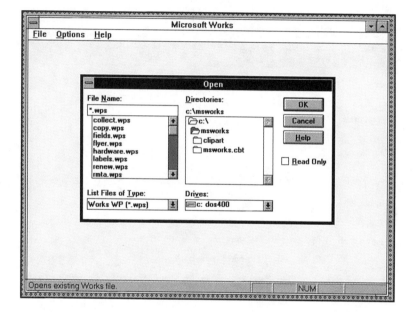

FIG. 5.2

A listing of word processing files

The Read Only option, for use on a network, keeps files from being overwritten when more than one person is allowed to use the same file at the same time.

Opening a File from Another Drive

Suppose that you just purchased a template designed for use with Microsoft Works. (A template is a file created to do repetitive jobs so you don't have to reinvent formats or documents.) You have a hard disk drive and want to load this template file into Works. To do so, place the template disk in drive A and close the drive, click on File or press Alt,F to access the File menu, then press O (for Open Existing File), and the Open dialog box appears.

1. Press Alt,V to move to the drives.

2. Click the down-arrow or press the down-arrow key. Works lists the available disk drives. Click on drive A.

In the **Directories:** box, you see A:\, indicating the drive from which Works is reading the files. The File **Name:** box lists the files found on the disk in drive A (see fig. 5.3).

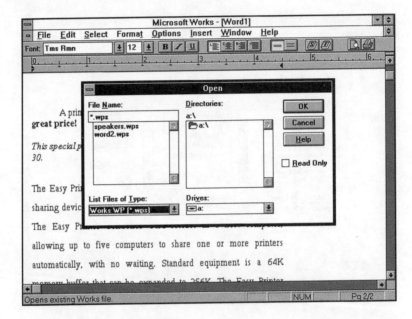

Highlight the file you want to open (here, SPEAKERS.WPS). Click OK. This file is read from drive A and appears on-screen (see fig. 5.4).

Repeat the preceding steps to continue opening files from drive A. If you are done opening files from drive A, follow the remaining steps to open files from drive C.

Click **File** or press Alt,F and then O to access the Open dialog box.

Click the down-arrow in the Drives: list box. From the list of drives, click drive C. You can now open files from drive C rather than drive A. To close the dialog box, click OK or press Enter.

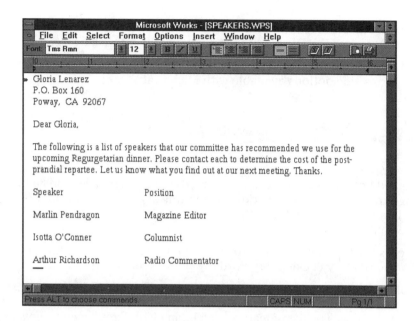

FIG. 5.4

The file from
drive A,
on-screen

Opening a File from Another Directory

In the preceding sequence, you opened a file from another drive. In this
section, you open a file from another directory by typing the complete
path and file name in the File **N**ame: box. For example, to open the file
LETTERS.MAY from Microsoft Word in the WORD directory, type the
following line and press Enter:

C:\WORD\LETTERS.MAY

The file LETTERS.MAY appears on-screen.

You can open a file from another drive without moving out of the
current drive (in this case, C). For example, suppose that you are
looking for BOS_AUTO.WP. Type the following line in the File **N**ame:
box then press Enter:

A:\BOS_AUTO.WP

This file is read from drive A while you continue to work in drive C.
This method saves the step of returning to the Open dialog box
and changing the drive to A. The method described in the preceding
section is useful if you don't remember or don't know the files on the
disk in drive A. By changing to drive A, you see a list of all the files.

T I P

With the insertion point in the file you copied from the template in drive A, access the File menu then close the file by clicking C.

RMTA.WPS is on-screen. The next step is to prepare a document to test the formatting options available with Microsoft Works.

Creating a New File

Now, practice some formatting options in a new file. Open a file to create and hold the text for a catalog advertisement. This file holds a one-page advertisement with various formatting styles, including boldfaced and italicized text, to draw attention to specific sections of the advertisement.

Access the File menu, click N to start a new file, then select the kind of file you want by clicking the Word Processor icon.

A blank work space appears, ready for input. Type the advertisement printed here, and then you can experiment with some of Works' formatting functions. The list of features beginning with *Simultaneous inputting* is indented by pressing the Tab key once.

Double Data Announces the Easy Printer.

A Printer Sharing Device just made for your needs at a great price!

This special price of $249.95 is available only through September 30th.

The Easy Printer has all the high-tech features of our other printer sharing devices, but it is economically packed on an interface card. The Easy Printer Controller Card resides in a host computer, allowing up to five computers to share one or more printers automatically, with no waiting. Standard equipment is a 64K memory buffer that can be expanded to 256K. The Easy Printer has room for high-speed, simultaneous storage of each print job from each computer. Fantastic features are

Simultaneous inputting

Built-in, high-speed memory buffer

Automatic action

Parallel output port

Eighteen-month limited warranty

Examining the Options in the Font & Style Dialog Box

Look at the Font & Style dialog box by accessing the Format menu then clicking F. The Font & Style dialog box appears, as shown in figure 5.5.

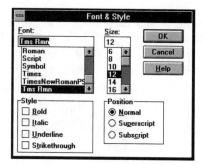

FIG. 5.5

The Font & Style
dialog box

Font refers to one complete set of characters in a given point size, type-face, and weight (or attribute) such as 12-point Times Roman bold. However, font often is used to refer to typefaces. By using different fonts, you can change the look or length of documents. Some fonts available in Works are shown in the following list:

Tms Rmn

Roman

Script

Symbol

Times

The number of fonts available to you depends on the capability of the printer you use. Some printers can print only one basic font in pica, elite, large type, double-wide, and other variations. Other printers offer as many as 50 different fonts. Find out what fonts are available by click-ing the Format menu or pressing Alt,T and then accessing the Font & Style dialog box. The fonts available are listed in the box under Fonts.

NOTE If the printer's available fonts aren't listed, you probably set up Works with the wrong printer. Return to the Printer Setup dialog box and select another model or printer until the correct fonts appear in the list. To find out which printer selection works with, or *emulates*, your printer, read the printer's manual.

The style, or attributes, of text refers to the way the characters look compared with the surrounding text. A variety of styles are available with Microsoft Works, as shown in the following list:

Plain
Bold
Underline
Italic
Strikethrough

Some text styles are commonly used for specific reasons. For example, words sometimes are emphasized with bold text, foreign words and phrases usually are italicized, and book titles are underlined. Often, the Strikethrough style is used in legal documents.

Another characteristic of type is position. At the bottom of the Font & Style dialog box, you see the Position options. The Superscript option places the text above the normal line level, as you often see in a footnote reference number. Choosing Subscript places the text below the normal line level; subscript is used for technical or scientific references, such as H_2O.

The last choice available on the Font & Style dialog box is the type Size. Type size is measured in points: 1 point equals 1/72-inch. Most text (such as what you're reading here) appears in 12-point. You find that 6-point text is small, sometimes known as *the fine print*. Point sizes of 14 or 18 usually are used for headings or titles.

Changing the Style of Text

Now that you are familiar with the options featured in the Font & Style dialog box, you're ready to edit the advertising text. You've already typed the text, so now you need to determine what style you want to use.

Many options are available for style, font, size, and position. You can combine any of these options to form almost endless permutations of typefaces. For example, you can have a portion of the text italicized, underlined, and in an 8-point Times font. You can make other text bold, in a 12-point Courier font. You even can have italicized superscript.

Style changes are most often used to emphasize a particular item. When sending out letters with the names of products, for example, you may want to have the names appear in italics or boldface. In business reports, you can emphasize headings and titles with different styles or fonts so that the readers easily recognize them.

Be careful, however, not to overdo font and style changes. You do not want to have so many different fonts and styles that the reader has difficulty reading the text. If you put too much variety in your letters or publications they will look like circus posters.

To begin experimenting with fonts and styles, start with the advertisement you just typed. First, make the words *Double Data* appear in boldface text. With the insertion point at the beginning of the file (press Ctrl+Home), follow these instructions to change the style of text:

1. Click and drag on the words *Double Data*, or select the text you want to change by holding down the Shift key and using the right-arrow key to move the cursor to the right until Double Data is highlighted.

2. Click Format or press Alt,T to activate the Format menu, then access the Font & Style option.

3. Click on **B**old then click OK. With the keyboard, press Alt,B and when an X appears in the box next to the option, press Enter.

When you return to the text on-screen, Double Data is still highlighted. Press the down-arrow key, and the highlighting disappears. The text you selected is now in boldface.

Changing Styles by Using the Tool Bar

For a quicker way to change a style, use the Tool bar. (The Tool bar can be accessed only with the mouse. Later on in this section are instructions to help keyboard users get to the Tool bar.) In the advertising material you typed earlier, perform the following steps to italicize the sentence that talks about the great price of Easy Printer:

1. Move the insertion point to the beginning of the text you want to italicize. The insertion point should be to the left of the T in the text, This special price.

2. Highlight the entire sentence by clicking in the left margin next to the paragraph.

3. Click on the letter I in the Tool bar.

4. You are now back in the text with the sentence still highlighted. Press a cursor-movement key or click the mouse to turn off the highlighting.

NOTE If your printer cannot italicize, you can indicate which words you want italicized by underlining them. The words are underlined when printed.

Some screens show styles differently. Like the variability in printers, you also may see differences in screens. Some screens may show underlined text; others may just boldface all type styles not in plain text. Some color monitors show different styles in different colors. You quickly become familiar with how the screen and printer handle these options.

Changing Styles by Using Command Keys

Using a command key, or hot key, is an even quicker method of selecting styles with Microsoft Works. When you become familiar with the different styles available with Works, you may find that you often use one option more than others. By using the hot key each time you use the option, you will save time and energy.

To experiment with the hot key, start by selecting the text you want to change. In this example, place boldface text in part of a sentence. Move the insertion point to the words great price in the second sentence. Click and drag great price or hold down the Shift key and press the End key to highlight great price. Then press Ctrl+B.

After you move the cursor out of the highlighted area, you see that the text appears bold-faced on-screen.

The following list shows the hot keys for the style options:

Bold	Ctrl+B
Italic	Ctrl+I
Underline	Ctrl+U

Inserting Text after Choosing the Style

At times you may want to enhance your text by making specific letters or words stand out after you choose the style you want. For example, assume that you want to insert and underline a phone number at the end of the advertisement you are formatting. To do so, follow these steps:

1. Press Ctrl+End to move the cursor to the end of the document.

2. Click U in the Tool bar and type the following text:

Call now to order Easy Printer at 1-800-EZPRINT.

3. When you finish typing, click U or press Alt,U in the Tool bar. The sentence is underlined and the underline style is turned off.

When you use this method, remember to turn off the type style by reclicking the button, or your text will continue to be inserted in the style you selected.

Choosing Two Styles for Text

You can choose more than one style for text. For example, to apply the boldface and underline styles to the words *Easy Printer*, follow these steps:

1. With the insertion point to the left of the E in Easy, click and drag `Easy Printer` or hold down the Shift key and press the right-arrow key until `Easy Printer` is selected on-screen.

2. In the Tool bar, click B then U or press Ctrl+B+U.

Use a cursor-movement key or click the mouse, and the highlighting disappears. The words `Easy Printer` appear in boldface and underline on-screen.

Removing Styles

You can remove a style whenever you want. For example, assume that you're not happy with *Double Data* in boldface. To remove the bold-face, click and drag or use the Shift and arrow key to highlight the words.

Notice that when you highlight the words the Tool bar reflects the attributes of the selected text—in this case, the B is turned on. Click B or press Ctrl+B to turn off the boldface.

Once more, you are back in the text with Double Data highlighted. Press a cursor-movement key or click the mouse, and the highlighting disappears. Double Data no longer appears in boldface (see fig. 5.6).

To tell which style you are using for lines of text, move the insertion point to Double Data at the top of the screen. Use an arrow key or the mouse to move down one line at a time. When you reach the words `Easy Printer`, the B and U buttons turn on. Continue moving the insertion point down and you see the buttons change to B when the insertion point is in `price` and to I when insertion point is in `This`. The B tells you the text is in boldface, and the I tells you the text is italicized.

FIG. 5.6

Double Data in
plain text

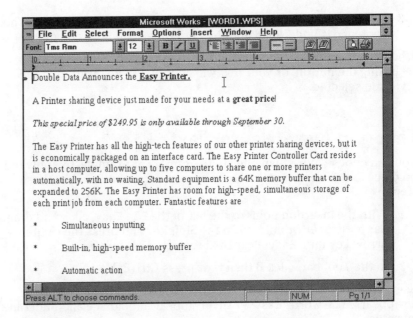

Changing the Font

Applying and changing the font is a little different from applying and
changing styles. Although you can have more than one style applied to
text at the same time, you can have only one font or size per character
at a time.

T I P Font names and sizes direct a laser printer to print in different
modes. You can add more fonts with laser cartridges or special software that works with Windows.

You can change the font for the entire file by following these steps:

1. Move the insertion point to the beginning of the file (here, to the
   left of the D in Double Data).

2. Highlight the entire file by pressing F8 five times or by pressing
   Ctrl and clicking in the left margin.

3. Click Format or press Alt,T to access the Format menu then open
   the Font & Style option.

4. Click the font you want and then click OK. With the keyboard, press Alt,F and then use the up- or down-arrow keys to highlight the font and press Enter.

The entire file is now converted to the font you selected. Use this same method to change fonts in smaller blocks of text by highlighting them. In the same way, you can change the point size for the document or for individual blocks of text. Press an arrow key or click the mouse to remove the highlighting.

After you accent the appropriate words and text in the file, you can move on to other formatting options available with Microsoft Works.

Changing the Font by Using the Tool Bar

Changing the Font by using the Tool bar is a faster way to modify the font. Select the text you want to modify and click the down arrow next to the Font box in the Tool bar. The list of fonts appears, as shown in figure 5.7:

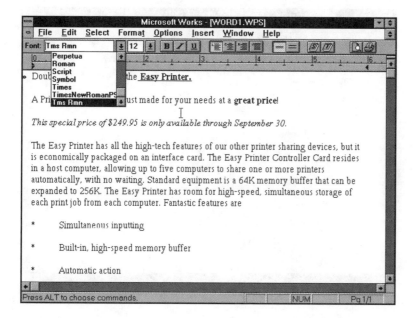

FIG. 5.7

The Tool bar font list

After you click the font you want, it changes immediately. To see how a different font would look, click the down arrow next to the Font box again and the list reappears. Click the font you want and it changes immediately.

The text remains highlighted until you press an arrow key or click the mouse.

Formatting Text

As with the selection of text styles, more than one way is available for you to change the formatting of sentences, paragraphs, or files. You can use either the Tool bar or the Format menu to make the following changes:

Normal paragraph (left justified)
Centered
Right justified
Full justified (aligned both right and left)
Single-space
Double-space

The Tool bar and related options are shown in figure 5.8.

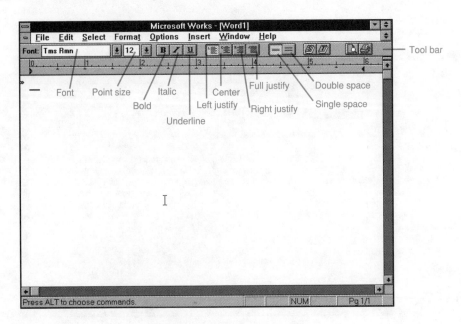

FIG. 5.8

The Tool bar

Using the Tool Bar To Center Text

Suppose that you want to center the first sentence in the text you're working on. Because centering (as are left, right, and full justification) is a paragraph format, you don't have to select all the text you want to center. Make sure that your insertion point is in the first sentence or that some portion of the first paragraph is selected.

Point to the Tool bar Center icon and click. The text is immediately centered.

Using the Command Keys To Center Text

After you've placed the insertion point in the paragraph you want to center, use the centering command key. Press Ctrl+E and highlighted text is centered without the need for accessing the Format menu.

> To center more than one paragraph at a time, make sure that a portion of each paragraph you want to center is selected.
>
> **T I P**

The formatting command keys are shown in the following list:

Left justified	Ctrl+L
Centered	Ctrl+E
Right justified	Ctrl+R
Full justified	Ctrl+J

Justifying Text

Left-justified text is commonly used in all kinds of word processors (the left margin is aligned, and the right margin is not). Use the left-justify command to undo justification or right-justified text.

Right-justified text is used only in special situations (the right margin is aligned, and the left margin is not). Right justification occasionally is used for headers or for aligning columns in tables.

Use the same procedures for justifying text as you use for centering text. For example, to full justify the paragraph in the sample advertisement, move the cursor to the left of the T in The at the beginning of the paragraph. Press Ctrl+J or click the Justify item in the Tool bar. The text shifts, especially on the right margin, so that the right margin is straight and aligned, as is the left margin.

Changing the Spacing

To determine whether the document is going to be single- or double-spaced, choose the one you prefer from the Tool bar or from the Format menu.

For example, to double-space the justified paragraph of text follow these steps:

1. Move the insertion point to the left of the T in The at the beginning of the paragraph.

2. Click the double-space item on the Tool bar.

The selected text appears full justified and double-spaced on-screen (see fig. 5.9).

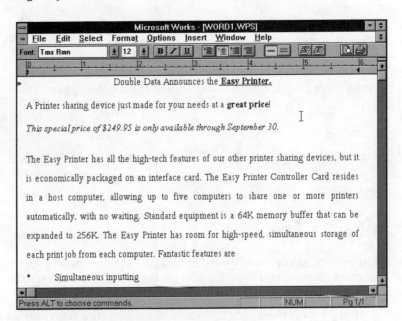

Examining the Spacing Options

Beyond single-and double-spacing, you can specify any number of spaces between lines. For example, to triple-space your material click Format or press Alt,T to activate the Format menu. Then select A and the Indents & Spacing dialog box appears (see fig. 5.10).

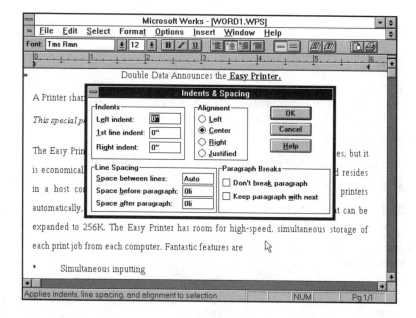

FIG. 5.10

The Indents &
Spacing dialog
box

Place the insertion point in the paragraph, or if you are formatting more than one paragraph, drag and click to select the text you want to print triple-spaced.

Press Alt to activate the menu bar and T for the Format menu. Select A and the Indents & Spacing dialog box appears.

Auto is the same as the default value, which is single-spaced. Press Alt,S. Type **3**. The text you selected is triple-spaced on-screen and prints the same way.

Choose other spacing options the same way. You can specify 1.2, 1.8, and 2.33 as the spacing values. The default dimension is lines. Press 3 and Works assumes that you mean three lines. You can specify other dimensions, including inches, centimeters, points, or picas, in the Options menu by selecting Works Settings and clicking the Units you want to use.

When you choose an alternative line-spacing amount, Works searches for the largest font size in the selected text and makes all lines in the selected text proportional to this font size. If you choose double-spacing, 1/6-inch is added between lines.

If you choose a fractional amount of line spacing, such as 2.33 lines, you see only double-spacing on-screen. However, when you print the document, the line spacing prints as you specified.

Adding Space before or after a Paragraph

To set off a paragraph or heading, select the paragraph, access the Indents & Spacing dialog box, and perform the following steps:

1. Place the insertion point in the paragraph, or if you are formatting more than one paragraph, click and drag the mouse pointer to highlight the number of paragraphs you want included.

2. Press Alt,B.

3. Type the number of lines you want before the selected text.

4. Press Alt,A.

5. Type the number of lines you want after the selected text and then press Enter or click OK.

Works adds the designated amount of space before and after the selected text.

Indenting Paragraphs

Several options are available for indenting paragraphs. You can indent the first line of a paragraph, indent levels in an outline, create numbered and bulleted lists, or create a hanging indent (first line of the paragraph flush left and all subsequent lines indented).

Normally, paragraphs appear on-screen and are printed in left-justified format with a ragged-right edge. The paragraph also is set off by one blank line above and below the text. You can change this default format within the Format menu.

For example, in your advertising material, begin by indenting the line that starts with the words, A Printer Sharing Device. Using the following method indents only the first line in a paragraph:

1. With the cursor to the left of the A for A Printer Sharing Device, press F8 three times to highlight the sentence or click once in the left margin beside the sentence.

T I P   If you have a long document and want the first line of each paragraph indented, press F8 two more times to highlight, or select, the entire file. Every paragraph now will have an indented first line, providing you follow the remaining steps for indenting the first line of a paragraph.

2. Click **Format** or press Alt,T to access the Format menu, then access the Indents & Spacing dialog box.

3. Press Alt,1.

4. Type **.5** and press Enter or click OK. This dimension is in inches, so you chose to indent 1/2-inch. (You can enter any number of inches to indent.)

In the text, the line remains highlighted and is indented five spaces (see fig. 5.11).

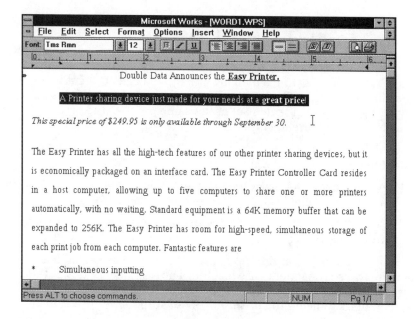

FIG. 5.11

The text, indented 1/2-inch

You may want to indent all the lines in a paragraph to set a block of text apart from the rest of the text. Often, you use this format for quotations, which distinguishes the quotes from the remaining text. To try this format, take the following steps:

1. Select the paragraph(s) to indent.

2. Click **Format** or press Alt,T and then press A for the Indents & Spacing dialog box.

3. Press Alt,E and type **1** in the Left indent box.

4. Press Enter or click OK.

If you correctly followed these steps, all lines of the selected text are now indented 1 inch.

Removing Indents

To remove indents, use the same procedure you used with each of the indent steps. However, rather than typing in the number of inches to indent text, type **0** (zero) inches in each box as follows:

Left indent: [**0**"......]

1st line indent: [**0**"......]

When the value in either box is 0 inches, the indenting is removed.

Creating a Hanging Indent

The text at the end of the advertisement you typed lists the features of Easy Printer. By creating a hanging indent, you can add text to the feature list and Works will wrap the text at the new indent. In this example, the hanging indent is set at the same point as the first tab stop to match the text already typed.

Move the insertion point to the text for which you plan to use a hanging indent by taking the following steps:

1. For this example, place the insertion point at the beginning of the word Simultaneous.

2. Press Ctrl+H. This step creates the hanging indent, for the single line of text as Works adds hanging indents a paragraph at a time.

Look at the ruler line at the top of the screen. The two small diamonds indicate where the indents are located. The first diamond is at the .5" position and the second, at the 1" position. The smaller triangles at each .5" mark indicate the positions of tab stops.

3. Add enough text at the end of Simultaneous inputting to see the effect of the hanging indent. As your typing reaches the right edge of the line, it will word wrap to the new hanging indent. Figure 5.12 shows the effect of the hanging indent.

If you wanted to add a hanging indent to each of the listed features in the advertisement, you would place the insertion point at the beginning of each line and press Ctrl+H.

Making Tab Stops with Works

You can select custom tab stops, or you can use the Works default tab stops. The tab stops appear on-screen when the Show All Characters option is on from the **O**ptions menu.

Figure 5.12 shows the effect of the hanging indent, the tab stops and the paragraph marks.

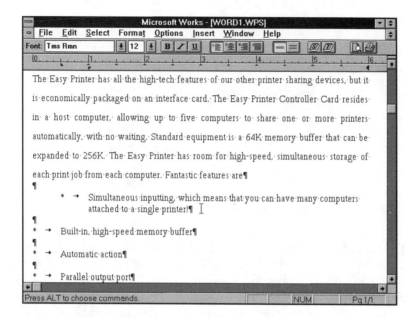

FIG. 5.12

Tab Marks visible, and the effects of the hanging indent

T I P

You can show all characters by pressing Alt,O to see the **O**ptions menu and **L** to toggle on the Show All Characters option. Repeat this procedure to turn this option off. With Show All Characters on, the screen shows paragraph marks, tab marks, spaces between typed characters, and so on.

The default Works tabs are 1/2-inch apart. Usually, you can use these default tab stops to line up columns or indent text. For custom tables and indentations, you can customize the tab stops. Set custom tab stops in this example at the end of the file in which you are working.

Add more products at the end of the file with stock numbers and prices. You now see how well Works can create tables.

To create a table, follow these steps:

1. Type the following three lines at the end of the draft advertisement (use the Tab and Enter keys):

    Disk Notcher (tab)DN8845 (tab)$5.95 (Enter)

    Ribbons (tab)R7633 (tab)3.99 (Enter)

    Keyboards (tab)K89900 (tab)100.25 (Enter)

The table you are setting up is not yet aligned properly. Do not add extra tabs to line up the table because you are going to align the table in a following step.

2. Select the three lines by click and dragging.

3. Click Format or press Alt,T to open the Format menu and then T to display the Tabs dialog box (see fig. 5.13).

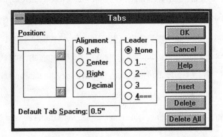

FIG. 5.13

The Tabs dialog box

4. In the Position: box (Alt,P), type **2.5**. Click the Center alignment option or press Alt,C, and click Leader or press Alt,L for the dotted Leader. Click Insert (Alt,I).

5. In the Position box type **4.5**. Click right for alignment (Alt,R) and Alt,L) which is the dotted Leader. This step inserts leading dots to the third column. Click Insert (Alt,I). The Tabs dialog box appears with settings as shown in figure 5.14.

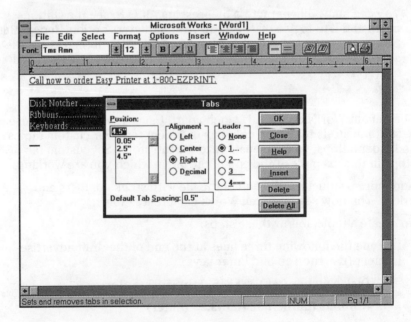

FIG. 5.14

The Tabs dialog box with settings

6. Click OK. The custom tabs should appear similar to the tabs in figure 5.15

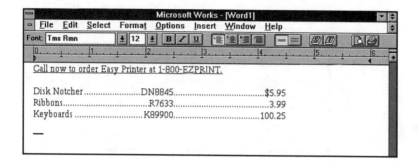

FIG. 5.15

Custom Tabs

Notice that the first column is left justified, the second column is centered, and leading dots bring you to the third column, which is right justified. Figure 5.15 gives you an idea of the many options available with tab stops. With tab stops, you can create well-crafted and professional-looking tables.

Changing Custom Tab Stops

Suppose that you are not happy with the way this table turned out. Access the Format menu and then press T for the Tabs dialog box. Move the cursor to the same locations and reset the values you chose previously. If you don't like a tab stop altogether, highlight the stop and click delete (Alt,T). The tab stop is removed.

Removing Custom Tab Stops

Go back to the Tabs dialog box. Click the Delete **All** button (or press Alt,A). All custom tab stops are removed.

Changing Margins

You can see the default values for the Works page in figure 5.16. Works has page and margins already established for 8 1/2-by-11-inch paper. The top and bottom margins are 1 inch, the left margin is 1.25 inches, and the right margin is 1.25 inches. If you create a header or footer, this information is placed 1/2-inch and .75 inch inside the top and bottom margins, respectively. For more information about creating headers and footers, see Chapter 6.

FIG. 5.16

The default
margins

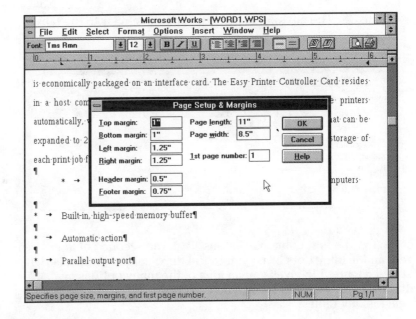

When you are ready to change margins for the printed page, you will
use the Page Setup & Margins dialog box. To reset the advertisement's
margins for a smaller piece of paper, take the following steps:

1. Click **File** or press Alt,F for the File menu, then M for the Page
   Setup & Margins dialog box (see fig. 5.17).

2. With the highlight in **T**op margin, type **2**.

3. Use the arrow pointer to move the highlight or press Alt and the
   letter underlined. For example, to move the highlight to the **R**ight
   Margin setting, type Alt,R.

   Bottom margin: 2

   Left margin: 2

   Right margin: 2

Keep the header margin settings because these settings don't affect
this text. The dialog box should look like figure 5.17.

4. Click OK or press Enter.

You see some changes to the screen. When you print this text, it fits
within the margins specified. Return to the Page Setup & Margins dialog
box to reset the margins to the default values.

If you plan to bind the text you are printing, consider increasing the left
margin. A left margin of 2 inches ensures that the binding doesn't inter-
fere with the left margin of the text.

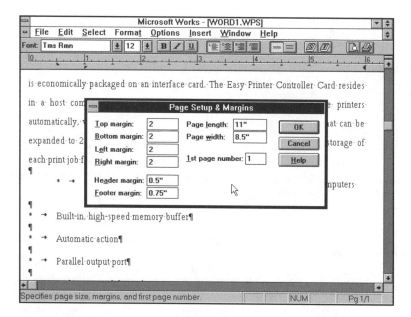

FIG. 5.17

New Settings for
Margins

Changing Paper Size

Using the Page Setup & Margins dialog box, change the paper size.
Imagine sending out an invitation on specially ordered paper. You are
going to use the office printer to invite business customers to an open
house. You prepared the text on-screen and need to change the page
size. Click File or press Alt,F to activate the File menu then press M.
The Page Setup & Margins dialog box appears. Click the Page length
option (or press Alt,L) and type **6**. Click Page width (or press Alt,L) and
type **4.5**. Now, click OK or press Enter.

The text on-screen changes to fit the page size you established. The
text is printed with the Works' default margins. Although the paper is
smaller, you still have 1-inch top and bottom margins just as you do on
8 1/2-by-11-inch paper. When you change the paper size, also consider
changing the margins. A 1-inch margin may be unreasonable for this
small piece of paper because little room is left for text. With paper only
4 1/2-inches wide, for example, a 1.2-inch and 1.3-inch margin takes up
2 1/2-inches of room. You are left with only 2 inches of space to print
text. Right and left margins of 0.6-inch or 0.75-inch may be a more rea-
sonable setting. In contrast, you may want to increase the margins for
larger paper.

Return to the Page Setup & Margins dialog box to set the page size back
to the default values. You need to type **8 1/2** and **11** in the associated
text areas.

Saving Changes to the File

You completed a great deal of formatting in the text on-screen. Save this file with all the formatting changes.

To save the file, click File or press Alt,F to open the File menu then A to select the Save As option. Choose this option because you haven't yet saved this file and you want to name the file something other than WORD3.WPS (the default title Works gave this file). In the File Name: box, type **adver.wps** so you remember that this advertisement is a word processing file. Press Enter and, along with the text, all formatting changes are saved to disk.

Chapter Summary

In this chapter you practiced opening and creating word processing files. You learned how to take advantage of the formatting options available with Works, including justification, single- and double-spacing, and indentation. You created tables with Works' tab stops, adjusted the margins to print text on various sizes of paper. You now have the skills to prepare advertisements, mailers, and announcements with the variety of styles and fonts available on the equipment and Works.

In Chapter 6, you learn more advanced formatting and editing techniques, such as searching a document by using the search and replace features, creating headers and footers, and learning to create objects with the Draw program.

Using Advanced Word Processing Features and Printing

C hapters 4 and 5 introduced the most commonly used editing and formatting functions in Works. Many more options are available, however, including search functions, headers and footers, page breaks, and printing. As you create longer and more complicated documents, you will find that these advanced functions help to streamline your work.

In this chapter, you learn how to do the following:

- Find characters and words in your text by using the search functions.

- Globally or selectively replace characters or words by using Find and Replace.

- Use bookmarks to find material in documents.

- Use Works Draw to create objects to insert into word processing documents.

- Review the printing options available with Works.

Using the Find Feature

With the Find feature, you can search for specific words and phrases in your document. For example, assume that you want to search a document to see if you overused the word *business*. You activate Find, and Works searches from the insertion point to the end of the document. If you don't want to use the word *business* too often in a report, you can use the thesaurus to find suitable synonyms, such as *trade, corporation, industry,* or *firm*. You can use a variety of these substitute terms to make the report more colorful.

You can also use the Find feature to refer to a specific location in your text. For example, suppose that on page 10 of your document, you refer to taxes. You know that you've already covered taxes earlier in the document but are not sure where. By using Find, you can find the section in a few keystrokes.

To find the section, press Ctrl+Home to move the insertion point to the beginning of the file and then search the document for the word *taxes*. Works finds the word on page 3. Now you can move your insertion point back to the page 10 reference to taxes and type: **(See page 3 for more information on taxes)**.

You can search an entire document by moving the insertion point to the beginning of the document before activating Find. When text is selected, Works searches from the selected text to the end of the document. When Works finds the text you are looking for, the program highlights the text.

Searching for Text

To start searching for text, open the RMTA.WPS file by clicking **F**ile or pressing Alt,F, then choosing the **O**pen Existing File. . . option. In the File Name: box, type **RMTA.WPS** and press Enter.

After the file is open, search for the word *President* in the text by following these steps:

1. Press Ctrl+Home to move the insertion point to the beginning of the file.

2. Access the **S**elect menu and choose **F**ind. The Find dialog box appears (see fig. 6.1).

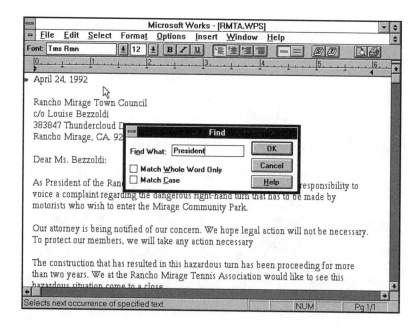

FIG. 6.1

The Find dialog
box

3. Type **President** in the Find What: text box, as already shown in
   figure 6.1.

4. Click OK or press Enter.

   Works highlights the first occurrence of *President* in the
   document.

After you designate a word or phrase for Works to find, you don't have
to reenter that material for the next search. To continue searching for
President, press F7. Works finds the next occurrence of *President* in the
text.

If you press F7 again after your search reaches the end of the document, Works tells you that it no longer can find a match (see fig. 6.2).
Click OK or press Enter to cancel the search.

FIG. 6.2

The No Match
Found dialog
box

If you decide to cancel the search before you reach the end of the
document, press Esc.

T I P

You also can make your search more specific with the Match **W**hole Word Only and Match **C**ase options in the Find dialog box, or broaden your search by using wild-card characters. The following sections focus on each feature.

Finding Whole Words

If you have Works look for the word *and* in a document, the program finds *and* in *hand* (see fig. 6.3). In another example, if you search for the word *the*, Works stops at *together*, *their*, *there*, *Thesaurus*, *theory*, and so on.

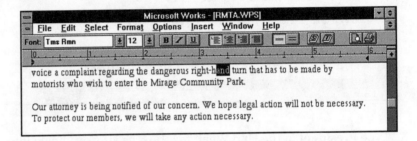

You can see that in a lengthy document, such a search can become bothersome. With the Match **W**hole Word Only option in the Find dialog box, however, you can have Works search only for the word you specify. In RMTA.WPS, have Works search for the word *and*. Before clicking OK or pressing Enter this time, however, choose Match **W**hole Word Only so that an X appears in its check box (see fig. 6.4).

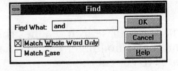

In this case, Works tells you that no match has been found. The word *and* does not appear alone in this letter.

NOTE   The Match **W**hole Word Only option is a toggle. Pressing Alt,W again or reclicking the Match **W**hole Word Only check box turns off the option.

Finding Uppercase and Lowercase Words

When searching through documents, sometimes you want to find only a capitalized version of a word, not the lowercased version. You may want to find the occurrence of the word *Works*, for example, when referring to the product name but not *works* when referring to whether a task works. To conduct such a search, use the Match **Case** option in the Find dialog box.

With the insertion point at the beginning of the file RMTA.WPS, search for the word *We* (but not *we*) by following these steps:

1. Access the **Select** menu and choose **Find**. The Find dialog box appears.

2. In the Find What: text box, type **We**.

3. Choose the Match **Case** option so that an X appears next to it.

4. Click OK or press Enter.

    Works finds and highlights *We* in the text.

Continue the search by pressing F7. The No match found dialog box appears. (The word *we* occurs later in the letter, but the *w* is lowercased.)

Using Wild-Card Characters in Searches

If you are not sure how a word is spelled or how it appears in the text, use wild-card characters to find the word.

Works uses a question mark (?) as a wildcard that represents any single character. Substitute the question mark for any variable character when you type the word in the Find dialog box. If you search for *f?x*, for example, Works finds *fix*, *fax*, and *fox*.

Using Find and Replace

The Find and Replace feature goes a step beyond the Find feature. Find and Replace finds the character sequence you enter and then replaces it with another character sequence of your choice. You also can match whole words in the search, use wild cards, and match uppercase and lowercase letters.

Suppose that you are a developer writing a bid on a project. In the bid, you specify that you need 3/4-inch pipe. Just before submitting the bid you find that you really need 1/2-inch pipe. Use Find and Replace to find and replace each occurrence of 3/4 with 1/2.

You also can use Find and Replace when you are not sure of some information as you write a report. If you are not sure whether you are going to need 3/4- or 1/2-inch pipe, for example, place a symbol in the position where the value should be. Type **##-inch pipe**. After you find that you need 3/4-inch pipe, search for and replace the # symbols with 3/4.

In another example, suppose that the president of the Rancho Mirage Tennis Association shares a letter with the president of the Rancho Mirage Golf Association. The golf association president decides to send the same letter to the Rancho Mirage Town Council. Use Find and Replace to change the letter appropriately by following these steps:

1. Make sure the insertion point is at the beginning of the document.

2. Access the **S**elect menu and choose **R**eplace. The Replace dialog box appears (see fig. 6.5).

3. In the Fi**n**d What: text box, type **Tennis**.

4. Move to the Re**p**lace With: text box and type **Golf**.

5. Because you want to find *Tennis*, not *tennis*, choose the Match **C**ase option.

6. Choose **R**eplace. By selecting this option, you can view and decide on each replacement.

7. Click OK or press Enter. A dialog box with the message Replace this occurrence? appears (see fig. 6.6).

8. Click Yes or press Enter.

   Works moves to the next occurrence of *Tennis* and prompts you again.

9. Click Yes or press Enter.

10. Choose Yes or press Enter again to replace the last occurrence. A No more occurrences message appears (see fig. 6.7).

11. Click OK or press Enter.

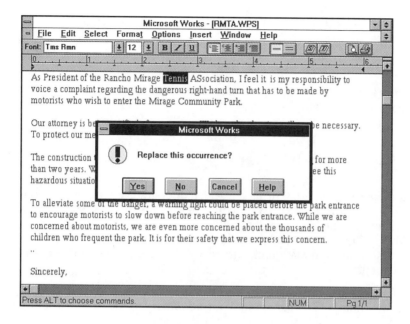

FIG. 6.6

A dialog box asking whether you want to replace the found word

FIG. 6.7

No more occurrences

You successfully have replaced every occurrence of *Tennis* with *Golf*. To finish the letter, you would replace the name *Arnold P. Schwarzkraut* with the name of the president of the golf association.

Replacing three occurrences of a text string may not seem like such an overwhelming task, but imagine how easy replacing the text is if you have many more occurrences than that. If you want to replace all the occurrences at one time, choose Replace **A**ll in the Replace dialog box.

Another way to use the Find and Replace feature is to search for and replace special characters. Suppose that you want to replace all occurrences of two spaces in a document with a tab stop. A space is considered a character, but tab stops are special characters. In Works, the Find and Replace feature recognizes tabs when they are typed as **^t**.

To replace the spaces, follow these steps:

1. Press Ctrl+Home to move to the beginning of the document.

2. Access the **S**elect menu and choose **R**eplace.

3. In the Find What: text box, press the space bar twice.

4. In the Replace With: text box, type ^t.

5. Click Replace or Replace All.

Works locates all occurrences of two spaces together and replaces them with a Tab stop.

Using Bookmarks

Suppose that you are writing a 50-page document with several sections on the High Middle Ages. With your cursor-movement keys, you quickly can move to the beginning and end of your document (press Ctrl+Home and Ctrl+End, respectively). In this longer document, however, you will also want to move quickly to specific places in the middle of the document.

Bookmarks are your answer. A *bookmark* places a hidden marker in your document. You can name your bookmark in the Bookmark Name dialog box and then use the Go To dialog box to find the bookmark. Works moves the insertion point to the beginning of a document when the document is opened. By placing a bookmark in the document, you can easily find any stop you want.

For example, assume that you are working in a file named COPY.WPS, which has part of the text of the 50-page document. You would insert a bookmark in the middle of this sample document by following these steps:

1. Move the insertion point to where you want the first bookmark— in this example, move the mouse pointer to the left of the M in Many in the second paragraph (see fig. 6.8).

2. Access the Insert menu and choose Bookmark Name. The Bookmark Name dialog box appears (see fig. 6.9).

3. In the Name: text box, type the name of the first bookmark. Choose a name that reflects the subject matter so that you can easily recognize the marker later. In this example, type **Viking**.

4. Click OK or press Enter.

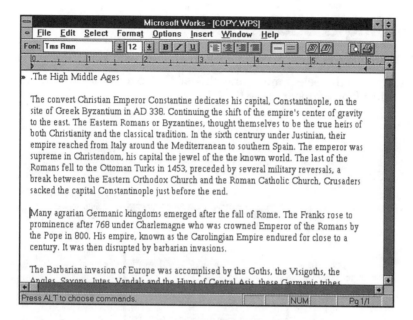

FIG. 6.8

Finding a place
for the bookmark

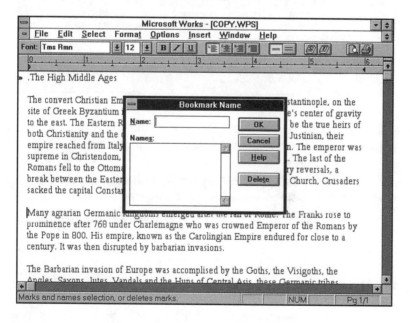

FIG. 6.9

The Bookmark
Name dialog
box

You have created a bookmark in your text. Now, move the insertion
point to the beginning of the document, because in the next section you
see whether you can find the bookmark again.

Finding a Bookmark

You can find the bookmark you just created by following these steps:

1. Access the **S**elect menu and choose **G**o To or press F5. The Go To dialog box appears (see fig. 6.10).

FIG. 6.10

The Go To dialog box

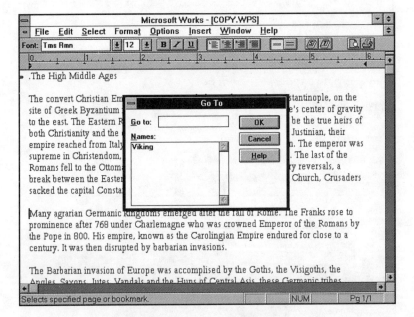

Below the **G**o To: text box is the **N**ames: list box, which contains the names of the bookmarks you created in the active file. In this example, you see Viking.

2. You can enter the bookmark by typing **Viking** in the **G**o To: text box or by choosing the bookmark name from the Names list: box.

3. Click OK or press Enter. Works moves the insertion point to the hidden bookmark in your text.

Deleting a Bookmark

If you end up with several bookmarks that have become useless, you can delete them by following these steps:

1. Access the **I**nsert menu and choose Bookmark Name. The Bookmark Name dialog box appears.

2. In the **Name:** text box, type the name of the bookmark you want to delete. In this case, type **Viking**.

   You can also select the bookmark name from the Names: list box.

3. Choose Delete. Works deletes the bookmark from the list.

4. Click Close or press Escape.

Using Headers and Footers

A *header*, sometimes called a running header, is text that appears at the top of every page in a document. A header may include the name of the document's author, the date the document was prepared, page number, the title of the document, or the subject covered.

A *footer* appears at the bottom of every page of a document and can contain information similar to a header.

Works offers two types of headers and footers: paragraph and standard. A paragraph header or footer is formatted like regular text, including tab marks and multiple lines. You can center or align this text at the right margin. A standard header or footer, on the other hand, most often is used in the spreadsheet and database components of Works. Standard headers and footers are centered, and dates and times are printed in a predetermined format.

Because this chapter focuses on word processing, this section concentrates on the paragraph header and footer.

The standard header or footer can be seen only when you use Print Preview or actually print to a printer. The length is restricted to a single line of text.

To add a single-line header or footer, take these steps:

1. Open the **Edit** menu.

2. Select **Headers & Footers**. The Headers & Footers dialog box appears (see fig. 6.11).

	Headers & Footers	
H_eader:		OK
_Footer:		Cancel
☐ **N**o header on 1st page	☐ **U**se header and	Help
☐ N_o footer on 1st page	footer paragraphs	

FIG. 6.11

The Headers & Footers dialog box

3. Click the **U**se header and footer paragraphs option or press Alt,U to turn the option on. An X appears in the box next to the option. Enter a header or footer or both. If you want, you can designate that the header or footer not print on the first page of the document. After making the entries, click OK or press Enter. Your screen should look like the one shown in figure 6.12.

The paragraph header or footer allows for a variety of formats, several of which are explained in the following sections.

The example file, COPY.WPS, is a three-page document that you have not created. You can create the example headers without having first entered a long document. The limitation is that you cannot see the printed effect of the header on a second page.

FIG. 6.12

The header and footer format on-screen

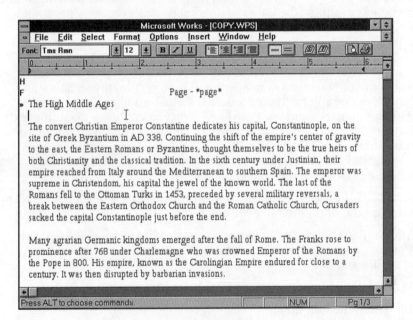

NOTE   Footers appear at the bottom of the page when printed or when viewed by using Print Preview.

4. Move the insertion point up to the H to type text for the header. Type **The Middle Ages** and then press Tab.

5. To insert the date, access the **I**nsert menu and choose **S**pecial Character (see fig. 6.13).

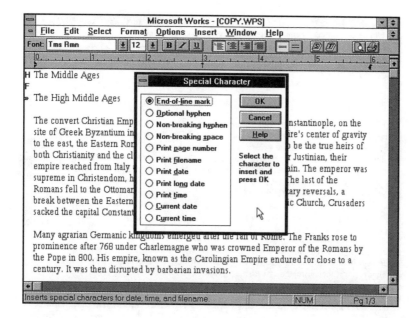

FIG. 6.13

The Special
Character dialog
box

T I P

The date is especially useful if you have a document that you are revising frequently. If you are printing several revisions a day, you may want to add to the header the time the document is printed. That way, you always know which copy is the most recent revision.

6. Choose Print **d**ate. A solid mark is inserted into the leading circle. Click OK or press Enter. The *date* symbol appears in the center of the header line. Works inserts the date in the MM/DD/YY format.

NOTE

In this step, you may select any special character from the Special Character option on the Insert menu. You may want to include the page number or time in any header. Do so by following steps 5 and 6, and selecting the option you want.

7. Press Tab to put the insertion point on the right margin. Type **By Charlie Main**.

Your screen should look like the one in figure 6.14. The header spaces evenly across the top of the screen and prints that way on every page.

FIG. 6.14

A finished
header

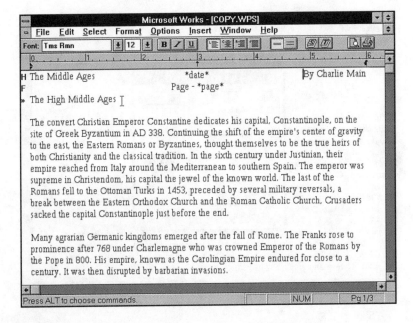

The footer line also is still on-screen with Page - *page* in the center.
You can add to the footer by typing more text on the footer line, the
same way you add text to a header. In this example, however, leave the
footer as is. A page number is printed in the document at the bottom
center of every page. Figure 6.15 shows the printed document with
header and footer.

FIG. 6.15

Printed document
with header and
footer

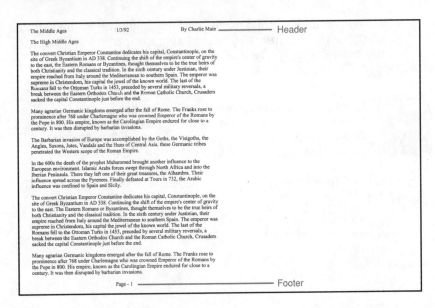

Creating Complex Headers or Footers

Instead of having the header spread across the page, you can have all the header information at the right or left margin. The following steps show you how to make a multiple-line, right-justified header in your Works document:

1. Access the **E**dit menu and choose **H**eaders & Footers.

2. In the Headers & Footers dialog box, choose **U**se header and footer paragraphs. An X appears next to the option.

3. Click OK or press Enter.

4. Move the insertion point to the header (H) or footer (F) mark at the top of the file and type the text you want.

   For this example, move the insertion point to the header line, press Tab twice, and then type **The Middle Ages**.

5. Access the **I**nsert menu and choose **S**pecial Character. The end-of-line mark is the default selection. Click OK or press Enter.

   Your screen should look like the one shown in figure 6.16. Another H appears at the top of the screen.

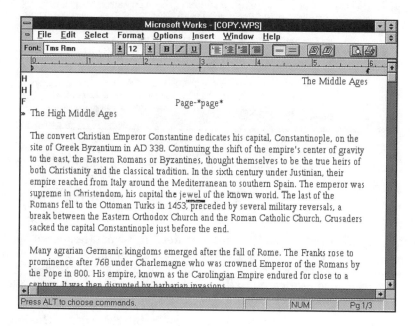

FIG. 6.16

A two-line header

6. Now add the next line to the header by pressing Tab twice and then choosing **S**pecial Character from the **I**nsert menu.

7. Move to the Print **d**ate option and press Enter or click OK. A `*date*` symbol appears under `The Middle Ages`.

8. Access the **E**dit **I**nsert menu and choose **S**pecial Character.

9. Move to the end-of-line mark and then click OK or press Enter. Another header line appears at the top of the file.

10. Press the Tab key twice. Type **By Charlie Main**.

The screen should look like the one shown in figure 6.17, with a three-line, right-justified header.

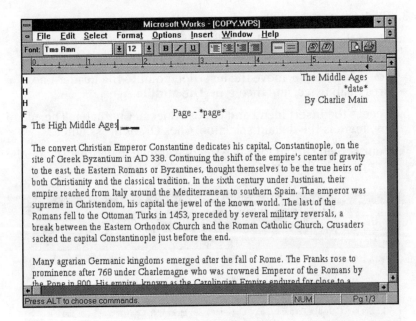

11. Move the insertion point out of the header area and continue typing or editing text.

You can see the effect of a header or footer by printing it out or by selecting the Print Preview button on the Tool bar.

If only two lines of the header print, you need to adjust the margin allowed for a header. The standard margin setting for headers is 1/2 inch. To print a header or footer with three or more lines you may have to increase the space allocated to the header by reducing the margin setting. To do so, take these steps:

1. Access the **F**ile menu and choose Page Setup & **M**argins. The Page Setup & Margins dialog box appears (see fig. 6.18).

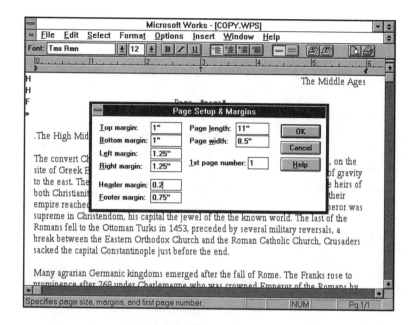

FIG. 6.18

The Page Setup
& Margins
dialog box

2. In the Header margin: text box, type **0.2**.

> You may think that you should make the header margin larger by using .8 or 1.0. Instead, you want to make the header margin smaller to make room for the extra line of text. If you type .8, only one line of the three-line header is printed. If you type 1.0, the three-line header is not printed. By typing .2, you are having the printing start higher on the page, making room for the three lines of the header.

T I P

3. Click OK or press Enter.

Now when you print the document, you have a three-line, right-justified header. Figure 6.19 shows how the printed header looks, now that you have made room for the extra line.

After you create a header and choose an end-of-line mark for the right-justified header, Works inserts a hidden symbol at that location.

In this example, Works inserts a down left-arrow at the end of the line. You can see this symbol by choosing Show All Characters from the Options menu. On-screen, you see the down-arrows at the end of the header lines. You also see arrows facing right, which show tabs.

FIG. 6.19

A three-line, right-justified header

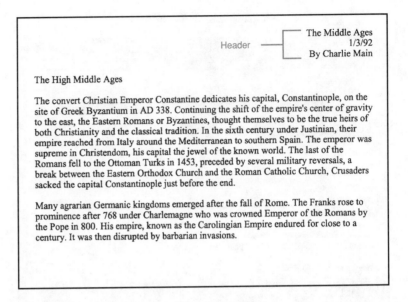

Use the Show **All** Characters option when you want to see exactly what you've done to format your text (see fig. 6.20). Repeat the preceding procedure to turn off the option and to hide the characters.

FIG. 6.20

The Show All Characters option to show the effects of text formatting

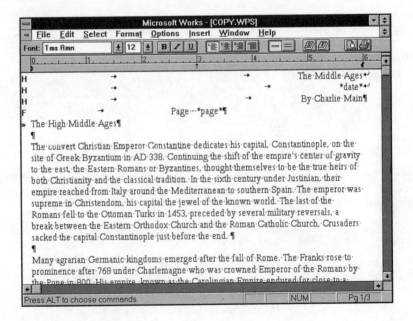

Using Only Page Numbers

If you want to put page numbers on the pages but don't want any other text in the header or footer, follow these steps:

1. Access the **E**dit menu and choose **Headers & Footers**.

2. In the Headers & Footers dialog box, choose **U**se header and footer paragraphs to put an X in its check box.

3. Click OK or press Enter.

4. The header and footer lines appear at the top of the file. Do not enter any text in either line.

   Page - *page* appears by default on the footer line. This formatting command places a page number at the bottom center of every page.

 NOTE If you want to right-align page numbers in the footer, move the insertion point to the footer line and click the centering button in the Tool bar. With the keyboard, move the insertion point to the footer line and press Ctrl+E.

Removing Headers or Footers

Removing headers and footers from a document is easily accomplished by following these steps:

1. Access the **E**dit menu and choose **Headers & Footers**. Works displays the Headers & Footers dialog box.

2. Choose **U**se header and footer paragraphs to remove the X.

3. Click OK or press Enter. The header and footer lines are removed from the top of the file.

Using the Draw Program

The Works Draw program is similar to the Paintbrush program in Windows. With Works Draw, you can use clip art and create logos or other drawings that you can incorporate into a document. If you are going to send out party invitations to guests who do not know how to reach the party location, for example, you can create and insert a map into the text of the invitation.

The Draw program can be accessed only through the word processor, and any object you create can only be inserted into a document. If you insert an object into the middle of text, Works adjusts the text to fit.

NOTE The Draw program is virtually worthless if you do not have a mouse connected to your system.

Before inserting clip art or a drawing you create in Draw into a blank document, place the insertion point where you want the drawing to appear. Works assumes that the position of the insertion point in the text is where you want the drawing inserted. You can move the drawing after you insert it into the text.

After selecting the insertion point, access the **I**nsert menu and choose **D**rawing to call up the Draw program screen (see fig. 6.21). Click the up-arrow button in the upper-right corner of the Draw window to maximize the window.

FIG. 6.21

The Draw program screen

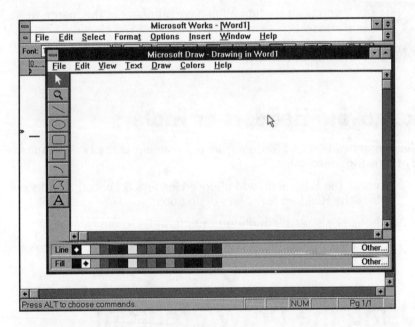

At the top of the screen, Works tells you that you are in the Draw program and displays the name of the document from which you accessed the drawing program.

From here, you can import clip art into the document or create your own drawing to be inserted. For your first example, you import and edit a piece of clip art. Later, you create your own drawing.

To import clip art, follow these steps:

1. Access the **File** menu and choose **Import Picture**. The Import Picture dialog box appears (see fig. 6.22).

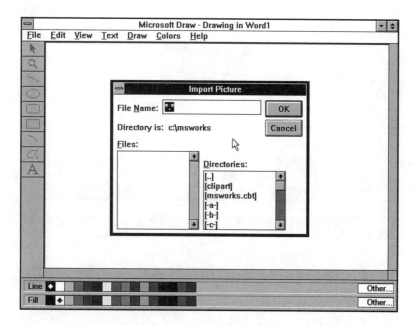

FIG. 6.22

The Import Picture dialog box

2. Double-click CLIPART in the **Directories:** list box or press Alt,D and press Enter. A list of clip-art files appears in the **Files:** list box.

3. In the **Files:** list box, press Alt,F or click the scroll arrow until a file named HNDWRTNG.WMF appears.

4. Double-click HNDWRTNG.WMF. The piece of clip art appears on the drawing screen (see fig. 6.23).

5. Edit the clip art, as discussed in the following sections.

6. Access the **File** menu and choose **Exit** to return to the blank word processing document.

   Works closes the Draw program and then asks you whether it should update the document.

7. Answer Yes. The drawing is inserted at the insertion point (see fig. 6.24).

FIG. 6.23

Clip art on the
drawing screen

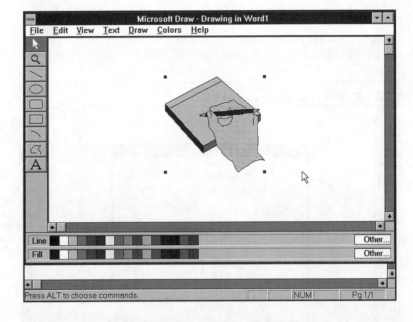

FIG. 6.24

Clip art inserted
into the blank
document

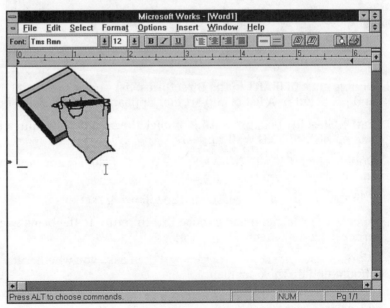

After you insert a drawing into a document, you can save the word
processing file as a memo template by saving the document as
MEMO.WPS, with the appropriate graphic a part of each memo.

Editing Clip Art

On the left of the screen is the Tool bar of nine design tools. At the bottom of the screen are two color spectrums, which are discussed in the section on "Changing Colors."

The Draw Tool bar tools are described as follows. To use a tool, click on the tool desired with the mouse pointer.

Tool	Function
Arrow	The arrow-shaped tool is the mouse pointer, which is used when you want to click an object and manipulate it.
Magnifying Glass	The magnifying glass tool is used when you want to look at an object in 200, 400 or 800% size. When an object is magnified, you can edit it at the pixel level, which is the smallest point in an object.
Line	The line tool is used to draw straight lines. When you select the line tool, the arrow pointer appears as a crosshair symbol. When you click and hold the right mouse button, that point becomes the beginning point of the line. Then you drag the crosshair to the end point of the line. When created, a line becomes an object.
Oval	The oval tool is used to create ovals. When Oval is selected, the mouse pointer appears as a crosshair symbol. Clicking and holding the mouse button defines one point on the oval. Dragging the mouse defines the shape and size of the oval.
Rounded-Corner Rectangle	The rounded-corner rectangle tool is used to create rectangles with rounded corners. When this tool is selected, the mouse pointer appears as a crosshair symbol. Clicking and holding the mouse button defines the upper-left corner of the rectangle. Dragging the mouse determines the shape and size of the rectangle.
Square-Corner Rectangle	The square-corner rectangle tool creates square-cornered rectangles in the same manner as the rounded-corner rectangle tool.

continues

Tool	Function
Arc	The arc tool creates objects that have a right angle connected by an arc line. When Arc is selected, the mouse pointer appears as a crosshair symbol. Clicking and holding the mouse button defines the right-angle portion of the object. Dragging the mouse determines the shape and size of the arc object.
Wavy Line	The wavy line tool is a freehand drawing tool that operates like a pen. With this tool, you can draw anything possible with a pen and paper. The pen begins drawing when you click the mouse button and continues until you click on the start point.
A-Letter	The letter tool is for adding text to a drawing. Clicking the tool changes the mouse pointer to a modified insertion point symbol, until after you click in the drawing area. At that point, the symbol becomes identical to the insertion point symbol seen in the word processor.

After you create an object, it can be changed in size, rotated, or deleted. If the object has enclosed areas, it can be filled in with a color or a pattern.

Figure 6.25 shows objects created with the drawing tools.

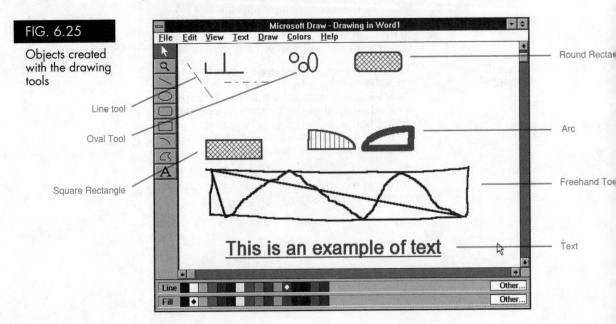

FIG. 6.25

Objects created with the drawing tools

Each component of a drawing is called an *object*. A drawing may have one object or several.

Moving an Object

You can move each object in a drawing. Click the middle of the object until you can see the small dots. Then, with the pointer still in the middle of the object, drag to where you want the object positioned. (On a line object, a dot appears at each end of the line.) Release the mouse button to reposition the object.

Resizing an Object

The four black dots that form a square around the clip art are *handles* for changing the size of the drawing. As an example, click the dot in the lower-right corner and drag the dot toward the upper-left corner dot. As you drag, the size of the clip art reduces proportionally. Figure 6.26 shows the clip art in a reduced form.

The handles work to enlarge an object, too. Or, if you want to move the object without adjusting its size, click the middle of the object and drag it to the new location.

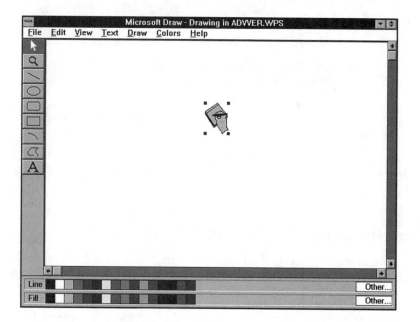

FIG. 6.26

Reduced clip art

Changing the View of an Object

The View menu offers options that determine the scale of an object. You can magnify an object up to 800 percent, for example, or down to 25 percent of the way it appears on-screen. For a complex drawing, scaling means that you can see the individual objects in fine detail.

To scale an object, access the View menu and choose the **8**00% Size. The drawing is magnified on-screen (see fig. 6.27).

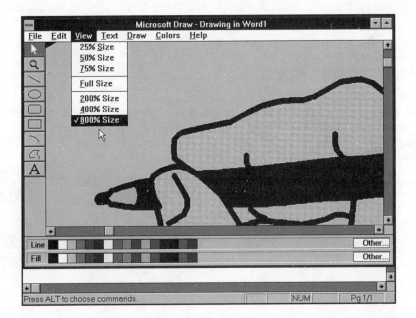

FIG. 6.27

Clip art scaled to **8**00% Size

To return the drawing back to its original size, choose **F**ull Size from the View menu.

To view a single object in greater detail, click the magnifying glass tool in the Tool bar and then click the object until the desired magnification is achieved.

Rotating and Flipping an Object

Because of the flexibility of an electronic art pad, you not only can resize objects to your liking, but also you can rotate and flip them. Rotating an object means to turn it clockwise or counterclockwise on its center. Flipping means to turn over the object, either horizontally, which means that the right side and left side exchange places and the reverse is displayed, or vertically, which means the top goes to the bottom and the object is displayed in reverse.

Follow these steps to rotate an object:

1. Click the object you want to rotate.
2. From the **Draw** menu choose Rotate/Flip. A cascading menu appears (see fig. 6.28).
3. Choose Rotate **L**eft. The clip art rotates in a counterclockwise fashion (see fig. 6.29).

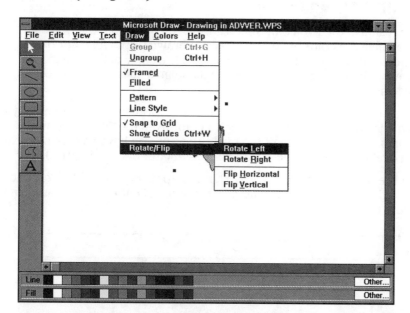

FIG. 6.28

The Rotate/Flip cascading menu

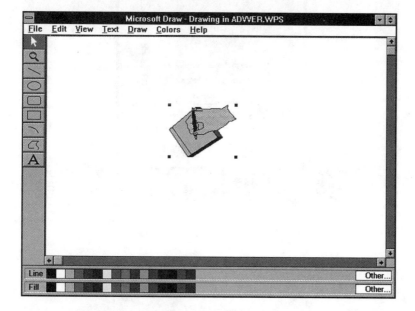

FIG. 6.29

Clip art rotated counterclockwise

Rotate the clip art back to normal by choosing R**o**tate/Flip from the **D**raw menu and Rotate **R**ight from the submenu.

You also can use these steps to flip objects by using the Flip **H**orizontal or Flip **V**ertical option on the submenu in step 3.

Changing Colors

You can use the two-color spectrums at the bottom of the Draw screen to change the color of lines as they are drawn or the fill color of an object. The top spectrum, Line, changes the color of the line that is drawn. The bottom spectrum, Fill, fills objects such as circles with a specific color.

If you create an ellipse by using the Oval drawing tool, for example, you can click the object and then click a color from the Fill spectrum. Works paints the inside of the oval the color you have selected. (Creating ovals and other objects are discussed later in this chapter.)

On the bottom right, the word Other... appears twice. When clicked, the Other options access a far greater range of color choices, as seen in figure 6.30.

FIG. 6.30

The Other Color dialog box

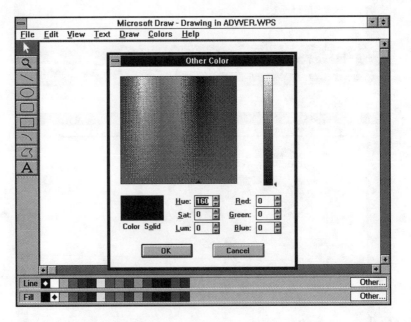

Adding Text to a Drawing

One tool in the Tool bar is identified by the letter A. By using this tool, you can enter text into the drawing and change the text as you want.

To insert text, click the letter A. Place the pointer in the draw area where you want the text to begin and type the letters. After you have typed the text, click the arrow tool. Click the text, and the small dots appear as a box around the text. Choose the attribute you want from the Text menu. In figure 6.31, boldfaced text has been added to the clip art.

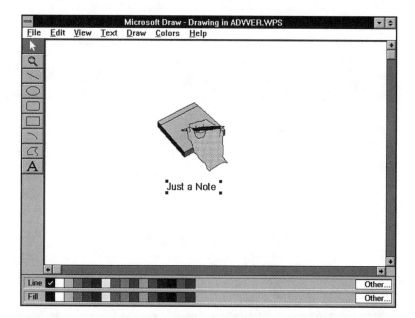

FIG. 6.31

Boldfaced text added to the clip art

Printing Your Document

Now that you have edited and added to your document, you can print it.

You already have printed several documents by choosing **P**rint from the **F**ile menu and pressing Enter or clicking OK in the Print dialog box. This section discusses the printing options available with Works, such as previewing a document before printing it and forcing page breaks.

The Print dialog box (see fig. 6.32) offers the following options to give you greater control over your document:

■ *Number of Copies* enables you to choose the number of copies you want to print of your document. The default value is 1; enter a new number when you want to print multiple copies of any document.

■ *Print Range* allows you to choose which pages of a document to print. The default, **A**ll, prints from the beginning of the file to the end. With the **P**ages option, instead of printing an entire 50-page document, you can specify printing to begin with page 20, for example, and end with page 35.

■ *Draft Quality Printing* enables you to choose the quality of your printed document. The option prints more quickly but does not print charts, drawings, graphics, or different fonts.

FIG. 6.32

The Print dialog box

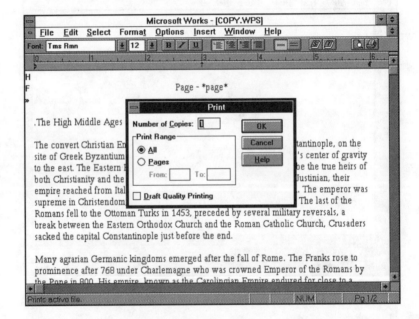

Now that you are familiar with the Print dialog box's options, you can print a document. For example, to print two copies of the second page of a document several pages in length, follow these steps:

1. Access the **F**ile menu and choose **P**rint. The Print dialog box appears.

2. In the Number of **C**opies: text box, type **2**.

3. Choose **P**ages so that the circle next to the option is filled with a black dot.

4. In the From: text box, type **2**; in the To: text box, type **2**.

5. Click OK or press Enter.

Previewing a Document

In Chapter 5, you worked primarily in ADVER.WPS, a one-page adver-tisement with boldfaced, underlined, justified, and italicized text. In this file or a comparable file with many formatting options used, you may want to look at the file before you print it, or *preview* the document.

The Preview feature shows you how a whole page looks with the for-matting adjustments you have made, before you print the document. You may find through previewing that you want to make some last-minute changes before you actually print the document.

As with many word processing features, this feature may not seem like too much of a timesaver with a one-page document. With a lengthy document and a slow printer, however, you can get an electronic pic-ture of how the finished product looks before taking the time necessary to print the document.

Open ADVER.WPS. Access the File menu and choose Print Preview to call up the Preview screen (see fig. 6.33). You can preview specific pages, several copies, or an entire document.

The print preview screen includes the following six buttons:

Print Preview Options

Option	Function
Previous	Click this button or press Alt,P to see a page previous to the one on-screen. Or press Page Up.
Next	Click this button or press Alt,N to see a page after the one on-screen. Or press Page Down.
Zoom In	Click this button or press Alt,I to magnify the document. The zoom feature goes up in scale twice then reverts to the full-page view.
Zoom Out	Click this button or press Alt,O to reduce the magnification of the document.
Print	Click this button or press Alt,P to send the document to the printer.
Cancel	Click this button or press Escape to return to the word processing screen.

FIG. 6.33

The Preview screen

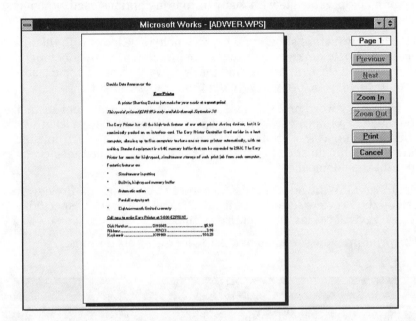

The buttons on the right control how you view the document. To zoom in on part of the text, move the pointer (which looks like a magnifying glass when moved onto the previewed page) to the text you want to examine and press the mouse button. The text is magnified more with each click until it returns to print preview. With a keyboard, press Alt,I to increase the magnification and Alt,O to decrease it.

To exit Print Preview, click Cancel or press Esc.

Previewing Two Parts of a Document Simultaneously

After you create a document longer than a single page, you may want to see pages 1 and 10 at the same time. At any point in the document, you can split the window and then scroll text in either window to see different parts of the document.

Follow these steps to use the split-screen feature:

1. Access the **Window** menu and choose **S**plit.

   Works inserts a gray horizontal line across the screen, with a double arrow in the middle.

2. Use the mouse to click and drag or the up- and down-arrow keys to move the gray line on-screen to where you want the split to occur. Because you can scroll either window after making the split, you do not have to position the split exactly.

3. To create the split, click or press Enter (see fig. 6.34). Press Esc if you want to cancel the split.

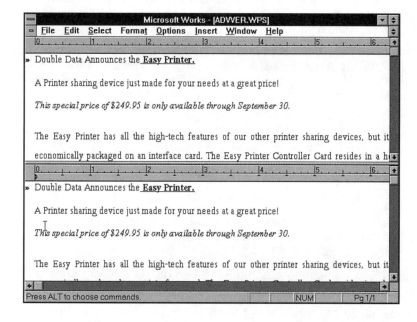

You also can create a split by clicking and dragging the split icon, located directly above the up-scroll arrow on the right side of the window, into the document.

To move between the window panes, press F6 or click the pane desired.

To revert to one window, place the pointer in between the split windows and grab the gray bar. With the keyboard, choose **S**plit from the **W**indow menu. Use the up- or down-arrow key to move the gray bar to the top or bottom of the window and then press Enter.

Forcing Page Breaks in Printed Documents

The default margins established in Works tell the printer when to stop one page and start another. This method of establishing page breaks is done with the values you see on the Page Setup & Margins dialog box. If you insert paragraphs or pages of text or delete pages of text, the page breaks are adjusted according to the amount of text on-screen.

You can force a page break in places where you want to control what text is on a page. You may want to force a page break just before a section heading, for example. You then can be sure that the heading is on the top of the page, not on the bottom of one page with the text that follows it on the next page.

On the two-page document now in COPY.WPS, move toward the end of the document. A double right-facing arrow » to the left of the text shows you where the page break occurs. Instead of having the page break divide the paragraph, force a page break between the paragraphs. To do so, follow these steps:

1. Move the insertion point to where you want a page break to occur. For this example, move the insertion point to a spot between the paragraph in which the page break now occurs and the preceding paragraph.

2. Choose Page **B**reak from the **I**nsert menu.

   A dotted line appears on-screen above the insertion point with a double right-facing arrow to the left. Notice these changes on-screen (see fig. 6.35).

Print this document now, and the last two paragraphs are printed on the second page. No paragraphs are divided.

If you change your mind about the location of a forced page break, you can delete it. To do so, move the insertion point to the forced page break and press Del. The dotted line symbolizing the page break disappears, as do the page break arrows.

 Before editing page breaks, make sure that they are current by choosing Paginate **N**ow from the **O**ptions menu to update the page break locations.

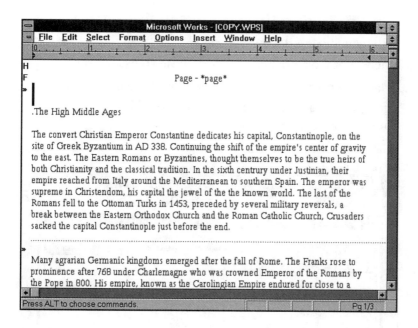

FIG. 6.35

The inserted
page break

Examining Additional Works Features

Besides offering you word processing, spreadsheets, databases, graphics, and communications—the five essential tools common to most computer users—Works provides several additional features: using note-it notes, counting words in documents, showing and hiding the Tool bar and Ruler, and dialing a phone.

Using Note-It Notes

3M Corporation made a fortune with Post-it Notes because the notes enable people to attach information to many things, including documents, without disturbing the original text. One Works item on the Insert menu is called Note-It. With this option, you can attach notes as you would Post-it Notes for reference at any place in the text.

A good example of using a Note-It is a research paper. In the text, you may assert some information. By attaching a note at that point in the text, you can quickly ascertain the source for your information. Or, you can insert a note into the text to remind yourself that you have not completed the work needed for a particular passage or paragraph.

The note is located by a graphic. After you click the graphic in the text, the underlying text of the note appears.

To attach a note to a document, follow these steps:

1. Place the insertion point where you want the note to be located.

2. Choose Note-It from the Insert menu. The Note-It dialog box appears (see fig. 6.36).

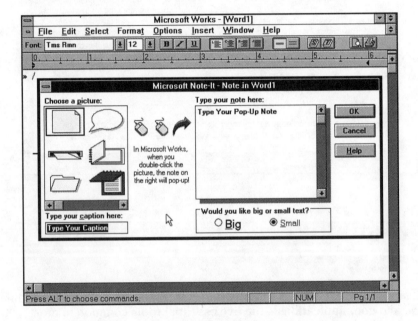

3. Click the graphic symbol you want from the Choose a picture: list box or press Alt,P and the arrow keys to select a graphic.

4. Type a caption for the note in the Type Your Caption text box. On the keyboard, press Alt,C. The caption will appear under the graphic in the text. Captions may be up to 30 characters long.

5. Type the note itself in the Type your note here: list box.

6. Select the size of the text you want. For Big, press Alt,B. For Small, press Alt,S.

7. Choose OK or press Enter. Works inserts the graphic in the document at the insertion point (see fig. 6.37).

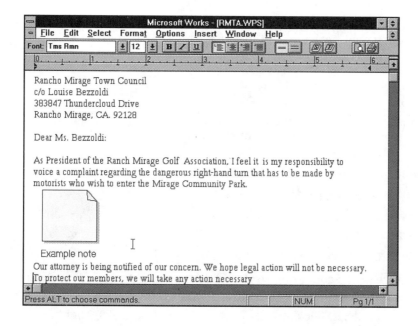

FIG. 6.37

A Note-It inserted
in a document

To read the note in the document, double-click the graphic symbol. The text of the note appears (see fig. 6.38).

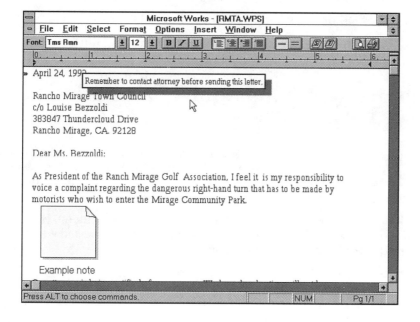

FIG. 6.38

The underlying
note exposed

You cannot resize a note, but you can move it to a different location in the document by using the **Cut** and **Paste** options from the **Edit** menu.

Counting Words in a Document

Works can count the number of words for you in a document. Thus, if you are writing a paper or a column that has a required word length, you can monitor your progress.

To have Works count the words in your document, follow these steps:

1. Access the **O**ptions menu and select Word Count.

Works displays a dialog box with the total number of words in the document.

2. Click OK or press Enter to dismiss the dialog box.

To have works count the words in a portion of a document, such as a paragraph, page, or several pages, take these steps:

1. Press F8 or click and drag the mouse pointer to highlight the text from which you want to extract the word count.

2. Access the **O**ptions menu and select Word Count. Works displays the number of words in the selected text in a dialog box.

3. Click OK or press Enter to dismiss the dialog box.

4. Press an arrow key or click to remove the highlighting.

Showing and Hiding the Tool Bar and Ruler

You can hide or display the Tool bar and the Ruler. By hiding the Tool bar and the Ruler, you increase the space on-screen for text. You also may want to hide the Tool bar if your system does not include a mouse. Figure 6.39 shows the screen minus the Tool bar and Ruler.

To hide the Tool bar, choose Tool **b**ar from the **O**ptions menu. Hide the Ruler by choosing **R**uler on the **O**ptions menu. Follow the same steps to show the Tool bar or Ruler again.

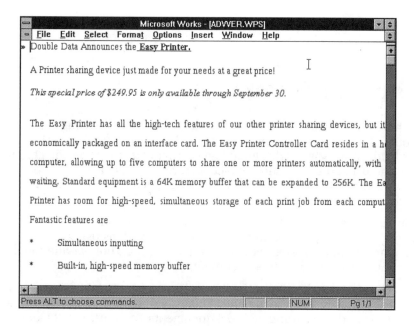

FIG. 6.39

The screen with
the Tool bar and
Ruler hidden

Dialing a Phone Number

If you have a modem installed, highlighting a phone number in a document and choosing the **D**ial this Number command causes Works to access the modem and dial the number, connecting you to a person.

A sample use of this feature would be to set up a word processor file that has a list of names and phone numbers of your business associates. You can open this file every time you run Works, and then switch to it when you want to call someone. You can use the Find command from the **S**elect menu to locate the name of the person and then highlight the number for your modem to dial.

NOTE   You cannot use this option to dial into a different computer.

To use the modem, follow these steps:

1. In a document, click and drag to highlight a telephone number or move the insertion point to the number and press F8. If the number has a hyphen in it, press F8, then the arrow key to select the number.

2. Choose **D**ial This Number from the **O**ptions menu.

3. After you hear the ring, pick up the phone handset or press the button on your speaker phone, and select OK or press Enter.

Before you can use this option, you must have installed your modem from the **O**ptions menu and the **W**orks Settings option.

Chapter Summary

In this chapter, you learned some advanced word processing techniques and then printed your document. You started with practicing the Find features in Works, including searching text for specific characters and using the Find and Replace feature. You also learned about using bookmarks, which help you to find a specific section within a document.

You learned about headers and footers and the various ways to use them. You also learned about special features such as using notes in a document, dialing a telephone number, hiding the Tool bar and Ruler, and counting the words in a document.

This chapter also discussed the Works Draw feature and how you can use it to enhance your documents. Finally, you reviewed more printing details, including printing multiple documents and portions of a document. You learned that you can insert page breaks and preview a document on-screen to get a look at the overall layout of the pages.

In the next chapter, you examine the built-in WorksWizards tool. Microsoft has designed WorksWizards to help you create form letters and mailing labels. Although you can do this yourself without using WorksWizards, it makes it much easier.

Creating Form Letters and Mailing Labels

Microsoft Works includes the *WorksWizards* program, which provides you the step-by-step process for creating an address book, a form letter, and mailing labels.

An address book is a type of database that contains the names and addresses of friends or business associates. After the address book is complete, you make a form letter. A form letter is a standard letter sent to one person or a group of people; however, this letter looks as if it were created individually because the inside name, address, and salutation are personalized. That is, each letter is unique to the person. For example, instead of saying "Dear Occupant," the letter reads "Dear Joe" or "Dear Sally" or whatever is appropriate. Finally, when the letters are personalized, you can easily print mailing labels to match.

In this chapter, you learn how to do the following:

- Use WorksWizards.
- Create an address book of names and addresses.
- Use the merge feature.
- Create a form letter.
- Preview the form letter.
- Print the form letter.
- Print mailing labels to match the letter.

Using WorksWizards

To create a form letter, choose WorksWizards from the opening screen of Works (see fig. 7.1) to call up the WorksWizards dialog box (see fig. 7.2). Alternatively, access the File menu, choose Create New File, and select WorksWizards.

FIG. 7.1

The opening screen of Works

FIG. 7.2

The WorksWizards dialog box

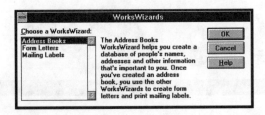

Because WorksWizards cannot create a form letter unless it has data to insert, you must first enter several names and addresses into an address book. Enter data by following these steps:

1. In the WorksWizards dialog box, select Address Books from the Choose a WorksWizards: list box.

2. Click OK or press Enter.

   Works presents an information screen.

3. Click the Next button.

4. From the next screen, click Personal as the kind of address book and then click Next.

   At any point in WorksWizards you can click the Exit, Hint, or Back buttons. The Exit button terminates the process. The Hint button provides more information about the particular step you are on, and the Back button returns you to the previous screen.

5. From the next screen, accept the structure of the database as suggested by Works. Click Next.

6. Click **No** or type **2** in response to the next screen question and then click **Next**.

7. Click the Create **Address** Book button. Works creates the form for the address book. When finished, Works then gives you an opportunity to learn more about the address book. Click **No** and the **Next** button.

8. Save the address book form by clicking **Yes** or typing **1** and then **Next**. Click **Save** in the dialog box. Click **Next** when you want to exit the WorksWizards box.

   The Save **As** dialog box appears.

9. You can enter a file name of up to eight letters. For this example, type **persnl** as the name in the File **Name** and click **Next**.

10. Follow the on-screen instructions to begin entering data (see fig. 7.3). Click **Next** to exit from the WorksWizards box.

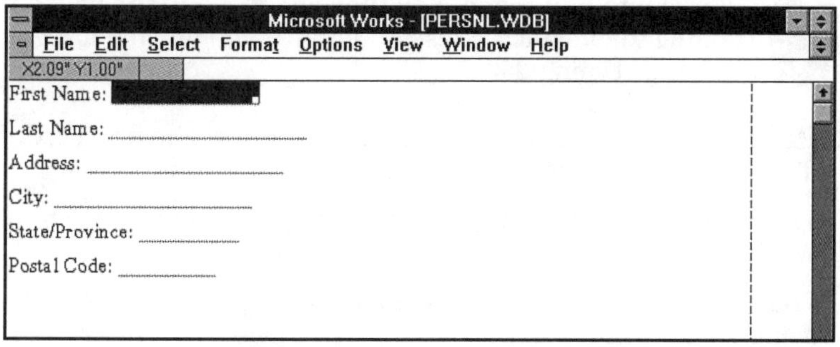

FIG. 7.3

The PERSNL database form

11. If the highlight is not in the First **Name**: field, click that field or use the up-arrow key to highlight it.

12. You now can begin entering data. Type as you normally do. After typing in a field, press Tab to move the highlight to the next field.

   Enter the following data:

Field	Data
First Name	Arthur
Last Name	Kanum
Address	12234 Double Fault Ct.
City	San Diego
State/Province	CA
Postal Code	92129

After you finish the Postal Code entry, press Enter instead of Tab to complete your first address book record. Your screen now should look like figure 7.4.

FIG. 7.4

First address
book record

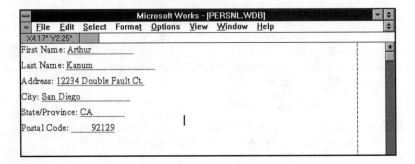

> **NOTE** If you make an error while typing the text, press F2 to put Works into Edit mode. You then can move to the field containing the mistake. Press Enter after you finish editing to continue typing data.

13. Move to the Postal Code entry, then press Tab. The first record disappears and a blank record form takes its place.

    The record has not been lost. When you pressed Enter in step 12, Works saved the data in the PERSNL database file.

14. Create one more record before going on to the form letter by using the following data:

Field	Data
First Name	William
Last Name	Gladrock
Address	444 Doubles Drive
City	San Diego
State/Province	CA
Postal Code	92004

> **NOTE** Remember to press Tab to move among the fields and Enter to save the record.

You have created two records. To see the first record, press and hold the Ctrl and PgUp keys. Now, press Ctrl+PgDn. If you press Ctrl+PgDn again, a blank entry form appears.

Using the Merge Feature

Use the Microsoft Works Merge feature to print form letters when you must send the same letter to many different people.

The WorksWizards program guided you through the creation of your first database, the address book. The program also can take you step-by-step through the process of creating the form letter. At this point, however, it is not necessary because the same result is achieved by performing the procedures provided in the following sections.

Using a form letter enables you to personalize the letter for each name on your list. You can use a form letter, for example, when you are sending letters to people who owe your company money. In each letter, you can specify the amount owed. You also can send form letters when you want to remind several people of their next appointment with you. In the example for this chapter, you are sending party invitations.

To print form letters, you need the following items:

- A database file that contains records from which you retrieve information that you insert into the form letter. The address book you just created will work fine.

- A word processing document into which you insert information from the database file.

Creating a Form Letter

In the example letter, you insert fields that Works later fills with information from the database. Each field in the typed form letter holds a place for one piece of information, and each field in the database holds one piece of information. Although you can follow the WorksWizards format to create a form letter, for this example create the form letter without its help.

When you want the first name of the person listed in the database to be printed in the form letter, insert a field as a place holder in the letter. A short database of two members has been created for this example in the file PERSNL.WDB. (For more information on fields and creating databases, see chapters 13-15.)

To create a form letter, take these steps:

1. Create a new file by accessing the **File** menu and choosing Create New File.

A new document window opens on top of the window containing the PERSNL database. Maximize the new window.

2. Type **May 1992** and press Enter twice.

Next, you start adding field names for the inside address.

3. Access the Insert menu and Choose Database Field. You see the Insert Field dialog box.

4. The database file you want to use as the source for field names must be open. Click the database file you want to use (PERSNL.WDB). The fields in the database are listed in the Fields: list box (see fig. 7.5).

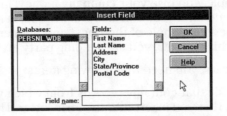

With many databases, remembering the exact names of all the fields can be difficult. Works, however, displays the field names unique to each database file.

5. In the Fields: list box, select the field you want to insert in the form letter. In this case, select First Name.

Because the highlight is on First Name, double-click the field. First Name appears on-screen at the insertion point (see fig. 7.6).

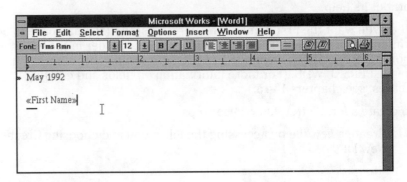

All punctuation and spacing must be added to the word processing document, just as if you were typing the letter itself.

6. Press the space bar once and then choose Database Field from the Insert menu.

7. Double-click Last Name in the Fields: list box.

   The Last Name field appears next to the First Name field in the document.

8. Press Enter to move to a new line in the letter. Then, choose Database Field from the Insert menu.

9. Double-click Address and then press Enter.

10. From the Insert menu, choose Database Field.

11. Double-click City in the Fields: list box.

12. Type a comma (,) and then press the space bar to insert a blank. Again choose Database Field from the Insert menu. Double-click State/Province in the Fields: list box.

13. Press the space bar twice. Choose Database Field from the Insert menu. Double-click Postal Code in the Fields: list box.

   The letter's address now is complete (see fig. 7.7).

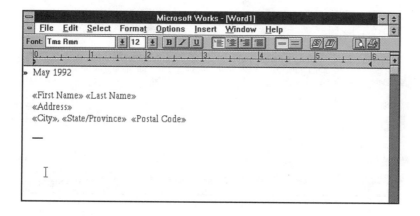

FIG. 7.7

The completed address

14. Press Enter twice. Type **Dear** and press the space bar.

15. Choose Database Field from the Insert menu. Because this letter has a friendly tone, double-click First Name.

16. Type a colon (:) and press Enter twice.

17. Type the following text:

With the coming of spring we want to invite you to the big party at our Golf Club. This is the 33rd year of our spring gala and this year's theme is "Drive for Show, Putt for Dough," on Friday the 13th.

Press Enter twice.

18. Close the letter with the salutation, and then press Enter twice to make room for the signature.

Sincerely,

Molly Gross
Social Chairman

The letter on-screen should look like the one shown in figure 7.8. Chevrons (< >) set off each field inserted in the letter.

FIG. 7.8

The finished form letter

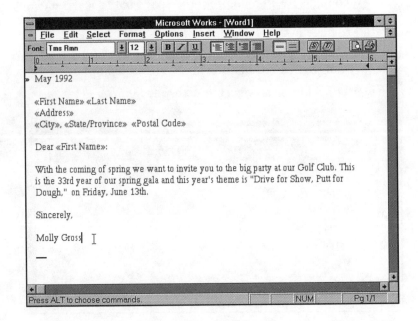

When Works prints the letter, it reads the field name and inserts the value you have for that field in the database. Although you are using only two records for this example, you can see how much time this procedure can save if you must type many letters.

Save this file by choosing **S**ave from the **F**ile menu. Rename the file as PARTY.WPS and then click OK or press Enter. The new name is inserted at the top center of the work space.

Printing the Form Letter

One letter is printed for each record you have entered in the database.

Follow these steps to print the example form letters:

1. Open the database file that holds the records you want to use, if you already have not done so. Choose **O**pen Existing File from the **F**ile menu. Point to the file name you want and double-click the mouse.

2. From the **W**indow menu, highlight PARTY.WPS and press Enter. The form letter appears.

3. Make sure that your printer has enough paper for the number of letters you are printing and is ready to print.

4. Choose Print **F**orm Letters from the **F**ile menu. The Print Form Letters dialog box appears (see fig 7.9).

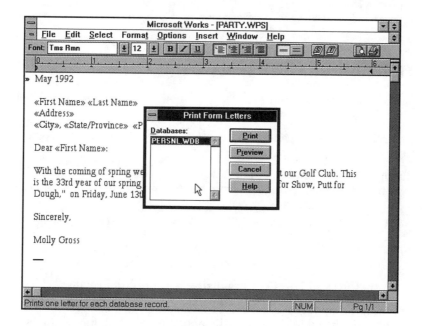

FIG. 7.9

The Print Form Letters dialog box

5. Double-click the database you want to use for the form letter. In this example, double-click PERSNL.WDB in the **D**atabases: list box.

6. The Print dialog box appears. Click OK.

The form letter is printed. Figure 7.10 shows an example of a letter, in which the information from the fields in the database is inserted. The name, address, and salutation are inserted.

FIG. 7.10

The printed letter

May 1992

Arthur Kanum
12234 Double Fault Ct.
San Diego, CA 92129

Dear Arthur:

With the coming of spring we want to invite you to the big party at our Golf Club. This
is the 33rd year of our spring gala and this year's theme is "Drive for Show, Putt for
Dough," on Friday, June 13th.

Sincerely,

Molly Gross

Previewing the Form Letter

If you are planning to print many letters, you can test your form letter
for accuracy before printing it.

This process gives you an example letter for proofreading and review.
To preview your letter, take these steps:

1. Open the database file that holds the records you want to use.
   Choose **O**pen Existing File from the File menu. Select a database
   file and then click OK or press Enter.

2. On the **W**indow menu, highlight PARTY.WPS and press Enter. The
   form letter appears.

3. Choose Print **F**orm Letters from the File menu.

4. From the Print Form Letters dialog box, choose **P**review.

The first letter appears (see fig. 7.11). Click Zoom **I**n. Instead of the field
names being placed in the letter, the actual database information is
inserted. From this previewed form letter, you can make any necessary
changes or additions to the letter without having to spend time printing
incorrect letters.

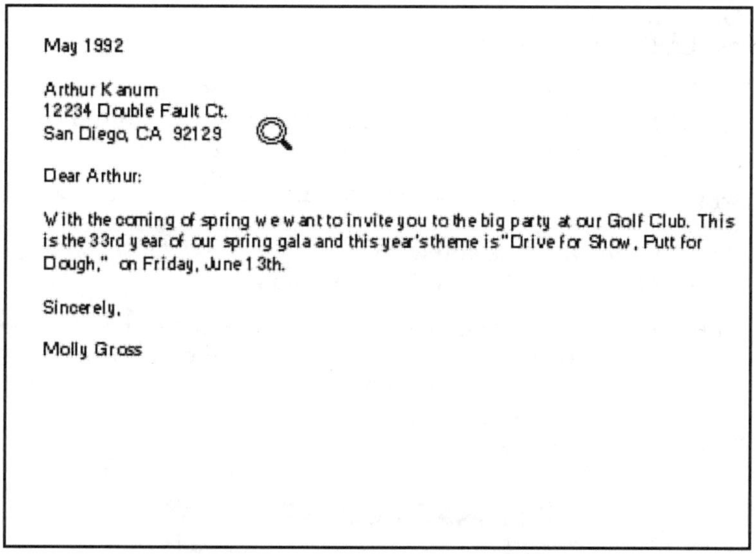

May 1992

Arthur Kanum
12234 Double Fault Ct.
San Diego, CA 92129

Dear Arthur:

With the coming of spring we want to invite you to the big party at our Golf Club. This is the 33rd year of our spring gala and this year's theme is "Drive for Show, Putt for Dough," on Friday, June 13th.

Sincerely,

Molly Gross

FIG. 7.11

The previewed form letter

Printing Mailing Labels

Now that you've printed the form letters, you can print the mailing labels to match. However, you must first insert the labels into your printer so they're ready when you start printing. Before you can start printing mailing labels, you must create a mailing label document. This document is similar to the form letter, in that you designate which fields from the database are going to print on the label. To create the labels, take these steps:

1. Open the database for which you want to create the labels. In this example, the PERSNL database is already open, assuming you have followed the correct steps for creating the form letter.

2. Open the File menu and select Create New file.

3. Choose Word Processor as the new file type.

4. Open the Insert menu and select Database Field. From the dialog box, select the database you want to use (in this example, PERSNL). The list of field names appears.

5. Double-click the field name that you want to appear on the label. For example, click First Name. Works inserts the placeholder <<First Name>> into the document. Repeat the steps to insert the remaining fields needed to complete the label.

6. Open the File menu and save the document. A simple name such as "LABEL" should work fine.

   You now have two files open, the LABEL document file and the PERSNL database file. To create mailing labels, both the database file and the word processor file must be open.

7. Open the File menu and select Print Labels. The Print Labels dialog box appears and lists the databases currently open. Click the name of the database you want to use, or press Alt,D and use the arrow keys to highlight the database name.

   The dialog box also contains the settings for label size. The vertical size is the distance from the top of one label to the next. The horizontal size is the distance from the left edge of a label to the left edge of the label to the right, assuming you are printing more than one label across.

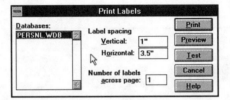

If you're printing with a single label across, (left to right) these settings should work fine with standard labels. If the labels you are printing are larger, or you are printing two across, adjust the settings. For example, if the labels are the correct size, but you are printing two across, change the setting in the Number of labels across page: box.

8. If you are printing more than one label across, select Test, which opens the Page Setup and Margins dialog box.

   The default settings should work, unless you are using a wide carriage printer. If so, change the number for the page width setting. Click OK or press Enter. If you are not printing more than one label across, Click Print, or press Enter and from the Page Setup and Margins box, click OK or press Enter.

9. The Print dialog box appears. Click OK or press Enter.

If you are printing a Test, Works prints two rows of labels that enable you to see if the size settings are correct. If they are not, enter new values in the Vertical or Horizontal settings and Test print again.

At any time while you are printing, you can press Escape to stop. However, because Windows has a print manager, the printer probably will not stop immediately, but continue to print until the data already sent to the print manager is printed.

Chapter Summary

In this chapter, you learned how to use WorksWizards to help set up a database. From there, you learned how to use the merge feature, set up a form letter, preview the form letter, and print the mailing labels from a database.

The next chapter introduces you to the Microsoft Works spreadsheet.

Spreadsheets

PART

III

OUTLINE

Creating a Spreadsheet: Quick Start

A spreadsheet is an electronic ledger sheet in which you can enter labels, values, and formulas. Spreadsheets exploded onto the computer scene with the 1978 introduction of VisiCalc for the Apple computer, followed by Lotus 1-2-3 in 1982 for the new IBM PC. The popularity of spreadsheets is directly linked to the ability of anyone with a computer and a spreadsheet program to quickly develop budgets, cost estimates, pricing schemes, and all matters of financial calculations. Previously, these tasks had to be tackled with paper, pencil, eraser, and lots of sweat. With an electronic spreadsheet, the task became much easier because the computer does the calculations while you can manipulate the numbers. Properly entered, a spreadsheet virtually guarantees accuracy as opposed to paper and pencil methods. This chapter covers the basics of building a spreadsheet.

In this chapter, you learn how to do the following:

- ■ Create, open, format, edit, print, and save spreadsheets.
- ■ Enter labels, numbers, and formulas.
- ■ Perform calculations.
- ■ Copy and erase cells, and cut and paste cells.
- ■ Insert rows and columns.

Creating a Spreadsheet File

To create a spreadsheet file, access the File menu, click Create New File..., and choose Spreadsheet. Or press Alt,F,N,S. You see the spreadsheet with the file label SHEET1 shown at the top.

A spreadsheet can contain three types of data: labels, numbers, and formulas. *Labels* are text entries you use to describe and explain the information entered into the spreadsheet. *Numbers* are the values used in spreadsheet calculations. *Formulas* tell Microsoft Works what to do with the values that have been entered. Formulas contain operators that act on the values—for example, formulas divide, multiply, or add the values. Works also has sophisticated built-in formulas called *functions* that relieve you of the task of creating complex formulas.

In the following sections, you learn how to enter labels, numbers, and formulas into the spreadsheet.

Entering Labels

An entry beginning with an alphabetic character is a label. In addition, an entry containing a mixture of numbers and alphabetic characters (such as 123 Elm Street) is also a label. The only exception is scientific notation—12.34E, for example—which is a number. To enter a number as a label, you must precede the entry with a double quotation mark (").

Before you enter labels into the spreadsheet, you need to maximize Works and the spreadsheet document. To maximize Works, press Alt+space bar to open the Control menu. Then, select Maximize (Alt,X) or click the upward pointing arrow in the upper-right corner of the Works window. To maximize the spreadsheet, press Alt+hyphen. Select Maximize or click the upward pointing arrow in the upper-right corner of the spreadsheet window.

Note the border around cell A1. This border is the highlight that indicates this is the active (selected) cell.

To enter labels into your spreadsheet, take the following steps:

1. In cell A3, type **SALES**.

2. Press the down-arrow key. The label is entered into cell A3 and cell A4 is now the active cell.

3. Type **EUROPE** in cell A4 and press the down-arrow key.

4. Type **ASIA** in cell A5 and press the down-arrow key.

5. Type **JAPAN** in cell A6 and press the down-arrow key twice.

6. Now type **TOTAL SALES** in cell A8, and press the down-arrow key once.

Your spreadsheet should look like the one shown in figure 8.1.

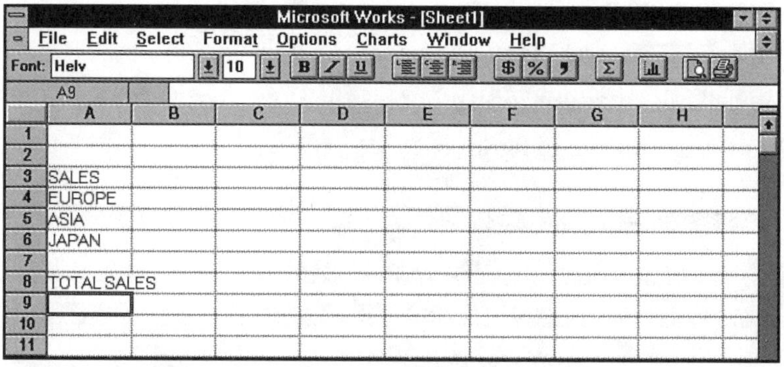

FIG. 8.1

Labels entered into cells

To finish entering the labels in cells B2 through F2, respectively, type **Q1 ACTUAL, Q2 ACTUAL, Q3 PLAN, Q4 PLAN**, and **TOTAL** (see fig. 8.2). Use the right-arrow key to move the cell pointer after each entry.

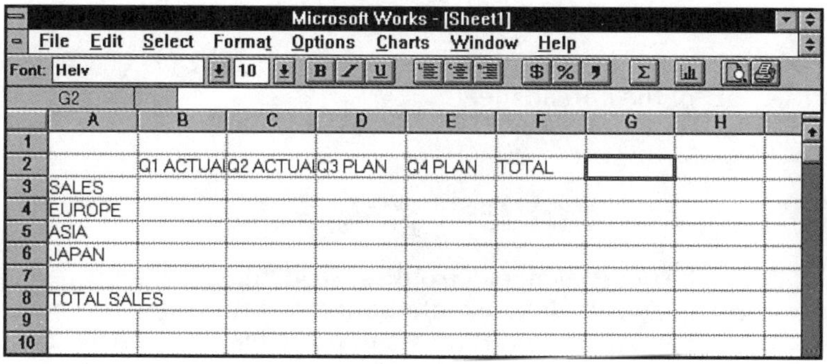

FIG. 8.2

The spreadsheet with column headings entered

Entering Numbers

Numeric entries can contain the numbers 0 through 9, the minus sign, and the decimal point. Your entries must be in the appropriate form to be interpreted as numbers.

You can enter other characters, but Works either ignores them or performs appropriate conversions. (Remember that the exception is the letter E for exponentiation.) Dollar signs are ignored, and commas are deleted if not correct. An entry with a percent sign (%) is converted to a percent. When you enter 4567% into a cell, for example, the formula bar displays 45.67, without the percent sign.

To enter numbers into the example spreadsheet, follow these steps:

1. In cell B4, type **123456** and press the down-arrow key. The number appears in cell B4, and cell B5 is now active.

2. In cell B5, enter **113456** and press the down-arrow key.

3. In cell B6, enter **488765** and press the down-arrow key.

The results are shown in figure 8.3.

FIG. 8.3

The spreadsheet shows numeric entries

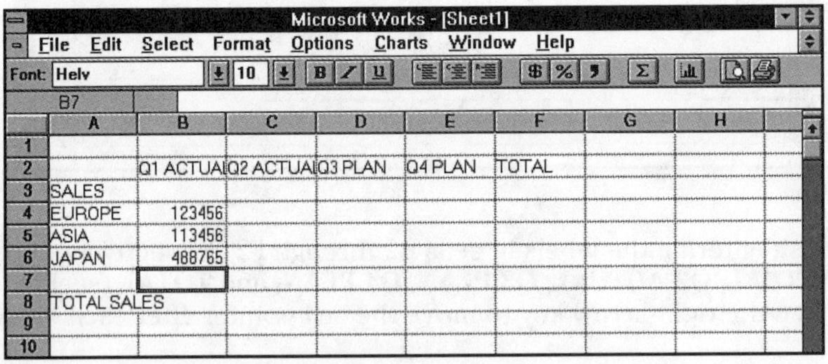

Enter **107232** in cell C4, **110785** in cell C5, and **101867** in cell C6 to complete this part of the spreadsheet.

Entering Formulas

Formulas are the heart of an electronic spreadsheet. Without the capability of performing calculations automatically, spreadsheets would be little more than expensive alternatives to using pencils, paper, and erasers.

Every Works formula begins with an equal sign (=). The equal sign is followed by either a function name or cell address. To enter a formula into the example spreadsheet, move the cell pointer to cell B8. Type the following formula and then press Enter:

=B4$plB5$plB6

The result is displayed immediately in cell B8. If you make a change in any of the cells in the equation, a new value is calculated by the formula.

Entering formulas in this way is fine, but the task is tedious and can lead to typing errors. With Works, you can point to the cells you want to add, which is a faster and more accurate method.

To add cells by pointing, follow these steps:

1. In cell C8 enter an equal sign (=).

2. Type **SUM(** after the equal sign.

3. Move the cell pointer to cell C4. Works inserts the cell name C4 into the formula.

4. Press and hold the Shift key. Use the down-arrow key to highlight cells C4, C5, and C6 (see fig. 8.4), or hold down the mouse button and drag down to select cells C5 and C6.

5. Type **)** and press Enter.

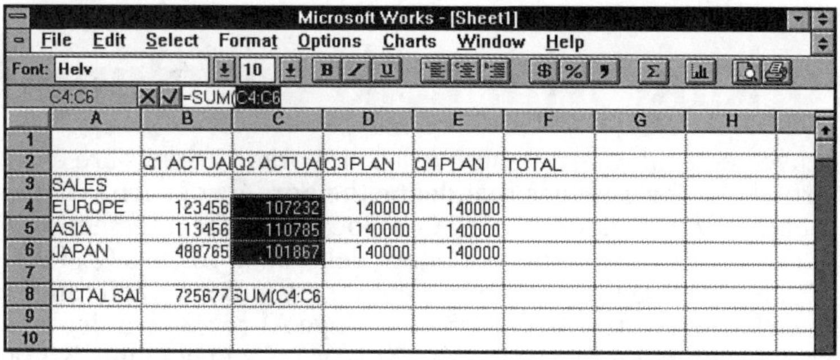

FIG. 8.4

Highlighting the cells to be added

NOTE   If you use the mouse, the first cell is outlined, not highlighted. If you use the keyboard, the cell is highlighted.

The total is entered into cell C8. Now you can use the **Edit** menu and the Fill **Right** option to copy the formula to cells D8 and E8. When you copy a formula, Works assumes that the formula should be relative to its position in the spreadsheet. Thus, when you copy this formula, it adjusts so that it sums the values in column D and column E, respectively.

To subtotal the sales areas in column F, type formulas in cells F4, F5, and F6. The formula to enter in cell F4 is =SUM(B4+C4+D4+E4). After you enter the formula, highlight the cells F4, F5, F6, F7 and F8, open the **Edit** menu and select Fill **Down** to copy the formula down the column. You will get a 0 entry in cell F7, which can be erased by moving the cursor to the cell and pressing Delete and Enter. The total should reflect the numbers in cells B, C, D, and E in each respective row. Cell F4 sums the values in cells B4, C4, and D4. The last formula, in cell F8, is of the total sales row and reflects the sales for every area (see fig. 8.5).

FIG. 8.5

The spreadsheet displays the total sales for every area

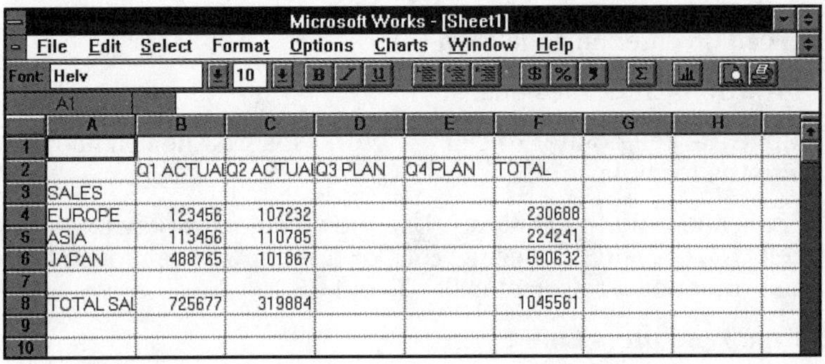

	A	B	C	D	E	F	G	H
1								
2		Q1 ACTUAL	Q2 ACTUAL	Q3 PLAN	Q4 PLAN	TOTAL		
3	SALES							
4	EUROPE	123456	107232			230688		
5	ASIA	113456	110785			224241		
6	JAPAN	488765	101867			590632		
7								
8	TOTAL SAL	725677	319884			1045561		
9								
10								

Microsoft Works - [Sheet1]
File Edit Select Format Options Charts Window Help
Font: Helv   10   B I U $ % , Σ
A1

Working with Cells and Ranges

You have been entering data into cells. In Works, the cells are easily discernible by the gridlines that define the borders of each cell. Cells are located by their address. Cell C4 is located at the intersection of row 4 column C. A group of contiguous cells, such as cells C1, C2, C3, C4, C5, constitute a range of cells. Another example of a cell range is all of the cells from cell A1 to cell D8. The range A1 to D8 includes all of the cells in column A to row 8, and all of the cells in columns B, C and D down to row 8, forming a rectangular range of cells.

Data is entered into cells either by using the arrow keys to move the cursor to the cell and typing, or by using the mouse pointer to point to a cell and clicking, then typing.

Copying Cells

Many spreadsheets contain entries that are repetitive. Rather than re-keying every entry, Works provides the Copy option, which makes it easy to copy entries and ensure accuracy.

Copying cell information is an easy way of making entries into a range of cells. Follow these steps to copy cell information:

1. In cell D4, type **140000** and press Enter.

2. To highlight the area you want to copy the number into, press and hold the Shift key and press the right- and down-arrow keys until the cell pointer is in cell E6. Alternatively, with a mouse, click cell C4, hold the mouse button, and drag the pointer to cell E6.

3. Release the Shift and arrow key (or release the mouse button). As you can see, the entire area is now displayed in a different color from the rest of the spreadsheet (called reverse video.)

4. Click **Edit** or press Alt,E.

5. From the **Edit** menu, select Fill Down and press Enter. The number 140000 is copied to cells D5 and D6.

6. Click **Edit** or press Alt,E and select Fill **Right**. The number 140000 is entered into cells E4, E5, and E6 (see fig. 8.6).

	Microsoft Works - [Sheet1]						
File Edit Select Format Options Charts Window Help							
Font: Helv		10	B / U		$ % ,	Σ	
D4:E6	140000						
	A	B	C	D	E	F	G	H
1								
2		Q1 ACTUAL	Q2 ACTUAL	Q3 PLAN	Q4 PLAN	TOTAL		
3	SALES							
4	EUROPE	123456	107232	140000	140000	510688		
5	ASIA	113456	110785	140000	140000	504241		
6	JAPAN	488765	101867	140000	140000	870632		
7								
8	TOTAL SAL	725677	319884			1045561		
9								
10								

FIG. 8.6

The number is copied to a range of cells

Erasing Cell Contents and a Range of Cells

Suppose that your analysis of the first quarter reveals an increase in the sales for ASIA. The best way to enter the new number is to move the cell selector to cell B5 and delete the current entry in its entirety by taking these steps:

1. Move the cell pointer to cell B5 and press Del. If you have made a mistake and don't want the contents deleted, press Esc and the contents are returned. In this example, you want to delete the contents, so press Del and then Enter.

2. Now enter the new number, **120000**.

Alternatively, you can type over the old entry. If you use the type-over method, be certain that the entire entry is overwritten.

You cannot erase a range of cells without using the menu system. To erase a range, select the cells with the Shift and arrow keys and then open the Edit menu and choose Clear. With this method of deletion, you have no second chance. After you choose Clear, the cell information is erased for good.

Cutting and Pasting Cells

Because you are working in an electronic medium, it is easy to copy information from one spreadsheet to another or to move information. Moving information is called "cutting and pasting," as you are imitating what is often done with scissors and glue on paper. It is better to cut and paste information if you need to move it than to erase the information and then re-create it elsewhere.

Suppose that you want to move the quarterly totals in cells F2 to F8 and move them to below your table, in column C. To move the totals, follow these steps:

1. Select the range of cells F2 to F8.

2. Press Alt,E.

3. From the **E**dit menu, select Cut. Works cuts the cells to the clipboard.

4. Move the cell selector to cell C10, then press Ctrl+V or choose Paste from the Edit menu. The cells are relocated (see fig. 8.7).

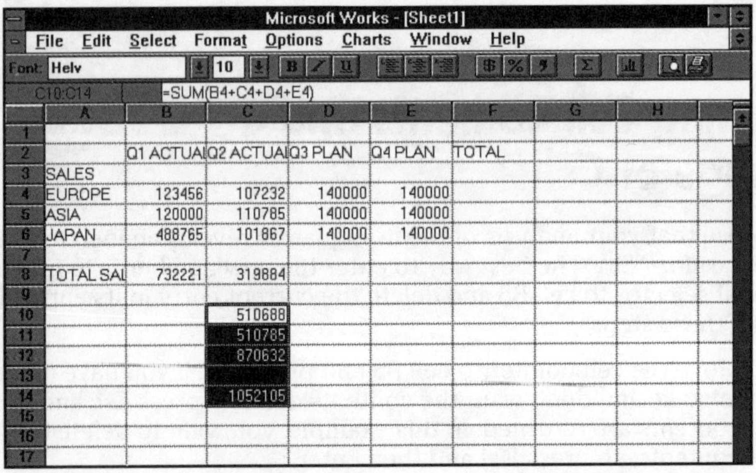

FIG. 8.7

The cell information has been moved

The formulas all calculate correctly. Because you used the Cut and Paste command, Works did not adjust them relative to their new location.

Working with Spreadsheets

Now that you have a grasp of how a spreadsheet works, you will explore some of the editing and enhancing techniques that make a spreadsheet more readable and accurate.

Editing the Spreadsheet

Suppose that after you print your spreadsheet, you decide to make changes. Editing the spreadsheet is relatively easy if you follow some simple safeguards before making any changes.

The best thing you can do is make a backup copy of the spreadsheet before editing. Select the Save **As** option from the **F**ile menu to save the file under a different name. When you use the Save **As** option, the spreadsheet file is saved with a new name and your changes are made on the file with the new name.

Another way to make a backup copy is to select Save **As** and select the **M**ake backup copy option from the dialog box that appears (press Alt,M). Works makes a second file with the extension BKS. Then, if you make an error while editing, you can refer to the backup copy.

The procedure for making changes to text, numbers, and formulas is the same. For practice in editing techniques, follow these steps:

1. Make cell B4 the active cell.

2. Press the F2 function key. A flashing vertical line (the insertion point) appears in the formula bar at the end of the entry.

3. Press the Home key to move the editing line to the beginning of the entry.

4. Press the Del key to delete the number 1.

5. Press 2 and that number takes the place of the deleted number 1.

6. Press Enter. The entries in cells B4 and B8 both change because cell B8 is a calculated cell.

Enhancing the Spreadsheet

In this section, you change the appearance of the spreadsheet by adding boldface, underlining, and other enhancements. Microsoft Works enables you to change a single cell, an entire column or row, or the entire spreadsheet.

To make changes in the example spreadsheet, follow these steps:

1. Move the cursor to cell A1.

2. Press Shift-down arrow to highlight all the label entries in column A (A3 through A8). (With a mouse, you can click the column letter to highlight the entire column—in this case, A.)

3. Press Alt,T to display the Format menu. Select Style to display the Style dialog box.

   You can choose items from this dialog box in three ways. You can press and hold down the Alt key while you type the letter that is underlined in the format you desire. Or you can use the Tab key to move from style to style and press the space bar to select the desired style. Or you can use the mouse to click the desired item. When you choose a Style or an Alignment, an X appears in the box or a dot appears in the circle by that selection.

   For this example, choose Bold, and then choose OK.

4. Next, select cells B2 through F2.

5. From the Format menu, select Style. From the Style dialog box, choose Underline, and press Enter or click OK.

6. Now select the range of cells B4 to F8 (all the numeric entries) and open the Format menu. Choose Currency and leave the setting at two decimals. Click OK.

The entire screen is filled with number signs (see fig. 8.8), which indicates that the entries in the cells are longer than 10 characters, the default width of the cells. You have two options: change the format or change the width of the columns. The cells remain highlighted until you move the cell pointer, so open the Format menu and choose Currency and then set the number of decimal places to 0.

 NOTE To reset the width of a column, select the column or columns, open the Format menu and select Column Width. In the Column Width dialog box enter a number that is greater than the number of characters entered into the column. For example, if a label has 15 characters, enter 16 and click OK or press Enter.

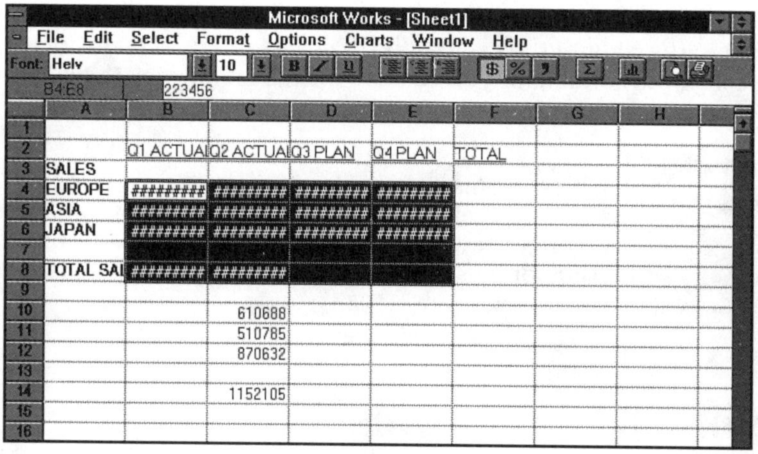

FIG. 8.8

The screen filled with number signs

Inserting Rows and Columns

Because the spreadsheet is electronic, it is adaptable. Rows or columns can be inserted as needed. In the example spreadsheet, a good place to insert a row would be above the SALES label entry so that the entries can be read more easily. To insert a row, follow these steps:

1. Move the cell selector to cell A3.

2. Click **E**dit or press Alt,E.

3. Select the **I**nsert Row/Column option. A dialog box opens and asks for the type of insertion you want (a row or column).

4. Select the **R**ow option and click OK. A row is inserted above SALES (see fig. 8.9).

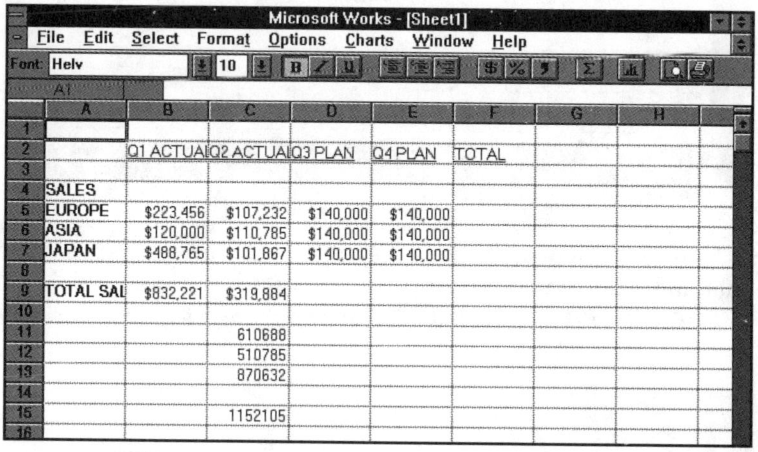

FIG. 8.9

You can insert a new row to make your spreadsheet easier to read

When inserting a column, remember that the new column will be inserted to the right of the cell pointer. The cell pointer can be located in any cell of the column, or you can use the mouse to click the column letter and then insert the column.

CAUTION When you insert a row or column, the old formulas adjust to their new location but will not extend to cells that may have been moved out of a range. Always test your spreadsheet for accuracy after making such an adjustment.

Saving the Spreadsheet

To save the spreadsheet, click **F**ile and choose **S**ave, or press Alt,F,S. The first time you save a spreadsheet file, the Save **As** dialog box appears (see fig. 8.10).

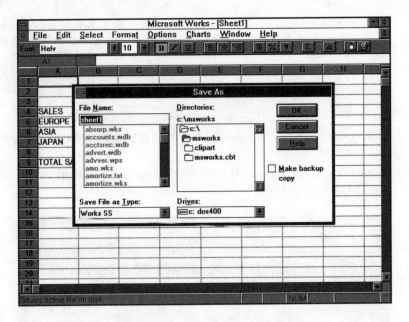

Works supplies the default file name SHEET1 for any new spreadsheet, but that name is not very descriptive. Try typing a more specific name, up to eight characters long, with no spaces. Works automatically adds the WKS extension to the name you type. If you want, you can save the file to a disk drive other than the default. For example, type **TEST** and click OK or press Enter. The spreadsheet file is saved to disk and the new name appears at the top of the spreadsheet screen.

Printing the Spreadsheet

Creating a paper copy of the spreadsheet is straightforward. A paper copy of the spreadsheet allows you to share your findings with colleagues or to present a proposal. Works does not automatically print the gridlines you see. To print gridlines open the **File** menu and select the Page Setup & **Margins** option. Click on Print **Gridlines** or press Alt,G. In the chapters that follow on spreadsheets, more information on the myriad printing options is considered.

The next logical step is to print your work by following these steps:

1. Click **File** or press Alt,F.

2. Click Se**t** Print Area or press Alt,T.

3. Use the Shift and arrow keys to highlight cells A1 to F8 (or click and drag by using the mouse).

4. Click **File** or press Alt,F and select **Print**.

5. The Print dialog box appears. Click OK or press Enter.

Microsoft Works prints only the cells that have entries. You must specify for anything else to be printed.

Closing the Spreadsheet

To close the spreadsheet, click **File** and choose **Close**, or press Alt,F, C. If you have made any changes since the last save or close, Works asks whether you want to save those changes or discard them.

Because Works allows for more than one open file, you also can use the mouse to squeeze down the display of the spreadsheet and then switch to another file by using the Window menu. For more on this procedure, see Chapter 16, "Tying it all Together."

Chapter Summary

In this chapter, you learned how to create, open, format, edit, print, and save your spreadsheets. You also learned how to enter labels, numbers, and formulas, and perform calculations. You also learned how to copy and erase cells, and cut and paste cells. Finally, you learned how to insert rows and columns.

In the next chapter, you learn more about working with spreadsheet basics.

Working with Spreadsheet Basics

If you've ever worked with budgets, invoices, tax statements, or payrolls, you're familiar with ledger paper. Ledger paper has rows and columns in which labels and numbers are entered. Also, with ledger paper you manually enter the labels and numbers you need and when you want to make a change to a number or label you must erase what is already there. And if the number you change alters other numbers in the ledger, all of those numbers must also be erased and changed. A spreadsheet program is an electronic ledger. With a spreadsheet program, all entries are made by using a keyboard or a mouse. Also, when a number is changed in a spreadsheet, all other numbers affected are automatically and accurately changed for you.

Spreadsheets are the tools that helped create the market for personal computers. Up until the advent of Lotus 1-2-3, businesses bought main frame computers primarily for large scale operations or specialized computers for word processing. The spreadsheet made it possible for any manager to create a quick budget in a short time and examine a variety of variables.

The Works spreadsheet is comprehensive. Most of the features found in the more expensive spreadsheet programs, such as Lotus 1-2-3, Excel, or Quattro Pro are available. On the other hand, because Works is integrated, you can move or copy information from the spreadsheet to the word processor, from the database to the spreadsheet, or from the spreadsheet to the database. Because Works operates under Windows, you have the other Windows tools at your command, such as the calculator, address book, and file manager. For example, with the calculator, you can easily make a simple calculation that can be inserted into a spreadsheet formula.

In this chapter, you learn how to do the following:

■ Create, open, and close a spreadsheet file.

■ Format a spreadsheet.

■ Enter labels, numbers, and formulas.

■ Use the Windows calculator.

■ Insert rows and columns.

■ Copy cells.

■ Edit, save, and print your spreadsheet.

Creating a Spreadsheet File

Getting started with a spreadsheet file requires that you access the same menu you use to begin a word processing file. After starting Works, the opening screen appears (see fig. 9.1).

Choose Spreadsheet so that a blank spreadsheet appears (see fig. 9.2).

T I P When you begin using Works, you open a window that may not fill the entire screen. To maximize the program window, click the Control button in the top left corner of the screen or press Alt+space bar, and then click the Maximize option. Repeat this process with the spreadsheet window by clicking the Control button next to the File menu name, or pressing Alt+hyphen, and then clicking the Maximize option.

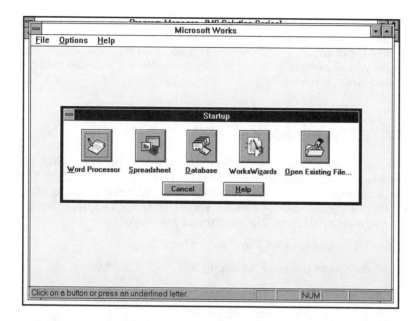

FIG. 9.1

The opening
screen

FIG. 9.2

A blank spread-
sheet screen

The application window (in this case, Works) is controlled by the Control button menu in the top-left corner of every application. Within the program, the current window, known as the document window, is controlled by the Control button in the upper-left corner of the document window. The application Control button menu has an option that the document Control button menu does not. That extra option is the "Switch to" option, which allows you to access a different application. Thus, as you are working in the Works spreadsheet, you can switch to the Windows calculator.

Saving the Worksheet

Works automatically names the first spreadsheet you open when you begin a work session by selecting Create New File. . . as SHEET1. This name is a temporary file name. By taking the following steps, create a permanent file name now, so that if you are interrupted while working you can quickly exit from Works without losing your work:

1. Click **F**ile or press Alt,F and select **S**ave.

   Works opens the Save As dialog box.

2. Type **SHEET1.**

3. Click OK or press Enter.

Works creates the permanent file name and displays it at the top center of the screen. At the end of this chapter are more extensive details on saving spreadsheet files.

Understanding the Spreadsheet Window

At the top of the screen is the document Title bar. If your spreadsheet is not maximized, the document Title bar of the active file appears below the formula bar. When you first open a new spreadsheet file, Microsoft Works assigns a name to the new spreadsheet, such as SHEET1, SHEET2, and so on. All spreadsheet files in Microsoft Works end with the extension WKS after they are saved.

Below the Title bar is the Menu bar, which is discussed in the next section, "Using the Menu Bar."

Below the Menu bar is the Tool bar, which is similar to the word processor's Tool bar, except for five different buttons. The buttons with the $, %, and comma symbols are used to format the appearance of numbers. The $ button formats the cells as currency, the % button as a percent, and the comma button as a comma. The button to the right of the format buttons, with the (SUM) symbol, is used to enter a summing formula quickly for a range of cells. The button with the bar chart on it is used for creating charts.

The next line on-screen is the *formula bar*. The block of information on the left—the cell reference box—shows the location of the cursor. Figure 9.2 shows the spreadsheet with the active cell being A1 (column A, row 1), as indicated in the cell reference box. When you move the cursor, or cell pointer by using a direction key or the mouse, the cell address in the cell reference box changes to reflect the new location.

When you type information into a spreadsheet cell, Works displays the information simultaneously in the cell and in the formula bar, so that you can edit the entry before entering it into the cell. As you move the cursor around the spreadsheet, entries of the cells you move to also appear in the formula bar.

Using the Menu Bar

You can access the menus on the Menu bar by clicking the menu name or by pressing the Alt key and the letter underlined in the menu name. To close a menu without choosing any commands, press Esc.

Pull down the File menu (see fig. 9.3) to see its similarity to the File menu found in the Works word processor. If you choose Create New File. . . from this menu, you get the same file options that you have in the word processor. Microsoft Works is consistent in that you can move easily between Works applications because all have similar menus. Switching from the spreadsheet to the word processor and back again is easy.

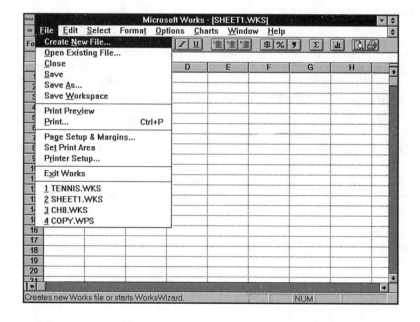

FIG. 9.3

The **File** menu

Other menus are specific to using spreadsheets. The Format menu, for example, contains options that control how Works displays data entered into cells (see fig. 9.4).

FIG. 9.4

The Format menu

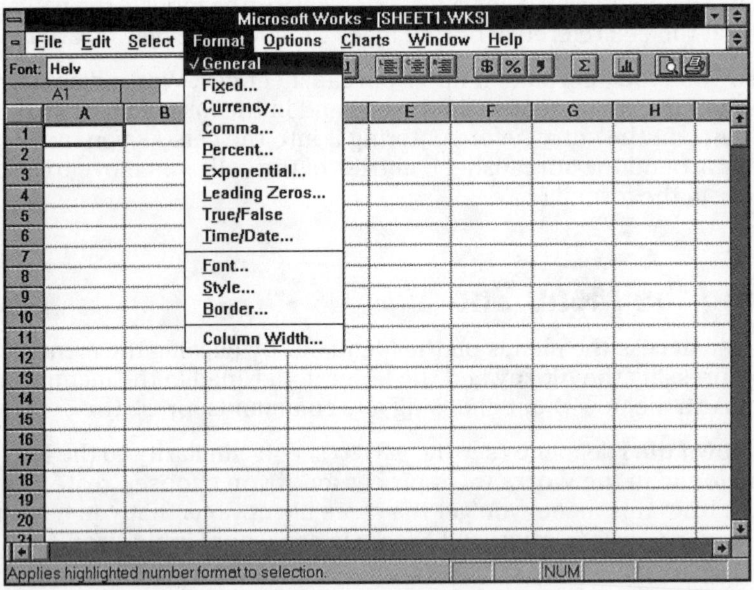

Using the Mouse Pointer and Cursor

The mouse pointer changes shapes according to its location. In the spreadsheet itself, the pointer takes the shape of a fat cross. In the Menu bar and Tool bar, the pointer has an arrow shape. In the formula bar, it becomes an I-beam for editing cell entries. Use the visual shape as a guide to where the mouse pointer is located.

The cursor is designated by a heavy border around a spreadsheet cell. When you open a new spreadsheet, the cursor is located in cell A1 (column A, row 1). After you press the down-arrow key once to move the cursor to A2, two things occur. The heavy border appears on cell A2 and the cell reference box now displays the new location (see fig. 9.5). When you begin typing, the characters are inserted into the cell at the insertion point.

The best way to move the cursor is to use the mouse. Just click the cell where you want the cursor to move.

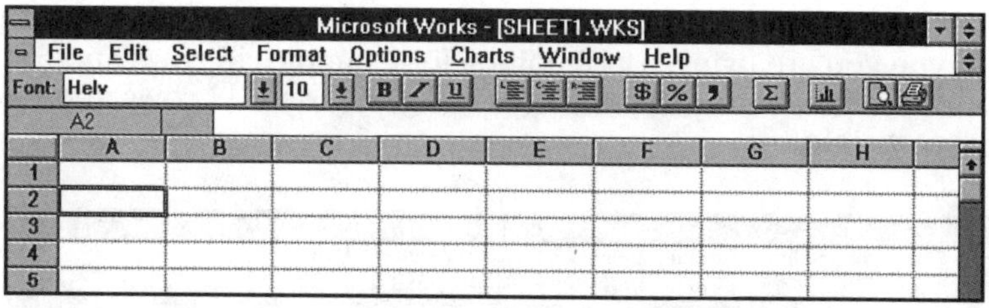

FIG. 9.5

The cursor on cell A2

Manipulating the Spreadsheet Screen

Below the formula bar, the next line across the top of the working area is lettered, beginning with A, B, C, and so on. The *column letters* run from A to Z and then begin repeating—AA, AB, AC, and so on—until the letters reach IV, totaling 256 columns.

Along with those 256 columns are 16,384 rows, which means that a Microsoft Works spreadsheet has 4,194,304 cells. Take a quick tour of the spreadsheet to see for yourself how large it is.

Move the cursor to the end of the columns by pressing Ctrl+right arrow. Almost instantly, the cursor appears under the IV column heading, as shown in figure 9.6.

Down the left side of the screen are the row numbers (1, 2, 3, and so on). To move the cursor to the bottom of the spreadsheet while still in column IV, press Ctrl+down arrow. The cursor jumps to cell IV16384.

Press Ctrl+left arrow to move the cursor to A16384 (column A, row 16384). To move the cursor back to cell A1, press Ctrl+Home.

As you move the cursor to the four corners of the spreadsheet, only a small portion of the available cells are visible at a time. In fact, only 20 rows and 8 columns are normally visible. Therefore, the screen you see is only a small opening on a large electronic grid of rows and columns.

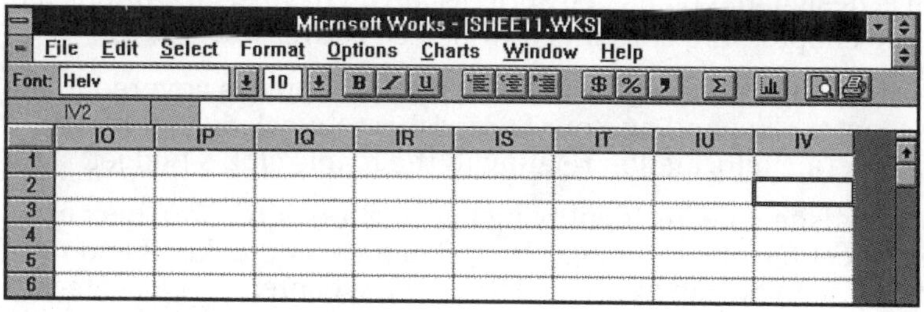

FIG. 9.6

The cursor in cell IV2

The number of rows and columns that you can see depends on the size of the type you are using. At 12 points, for example, 15 rows and 6 columns are visible, but at 18 points (as in fig. 9.7) only 11 rows and 4 columns are visible.

FIG. 9.7

The spreadsheet at 18 points

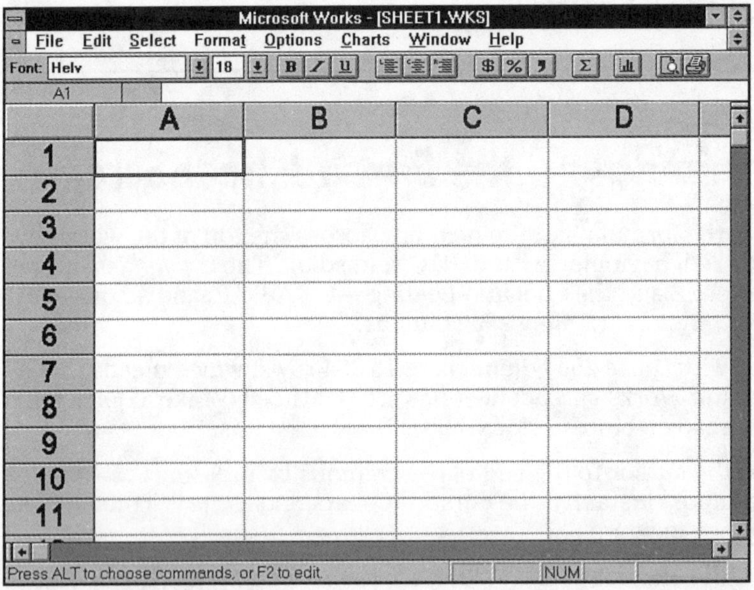

Entering Information into Cells

In preparing a spreadsheet, you enter all information into the cells. A *cell* is an area at the intersection of a row and a column. With the cursor in cell A1, you can see the size of an individual cell by looking at the length and height of the cursor.

A cell is designated by its cell address. If you have been working along with the chapter, the cursor is now on cell address A1.

You can change cell sizes as needed, but that topic is covered in the next chapter, "Expanding Your Spreadsheet Knowledge." For now, begin entering information relating to the tennis club's budget.

The spreadsheet needs identifying information at the top. Because a spreadsheet has the form of a chart, you must add column and row labels so that you can easily understand the contents. A *label* is any cell entry that begins with a letter or any entry that has as its first character an apostrophe (') or quotation mark (").

Begin by typing the spreadsheet title for a proposed budget, as follows:

1. Move the cursor to cell C1. (Verify that you are positioned correctly by looking at the cell reference box on the far left of the formula bar.)

2. Type **Budget June 1992**.

   Notice as you type that Works displays this information in two places: in cell C1 and on the formula bar. Because this entry is longer than the width of the cell, the text scrolls through the cell, enabling you to see only a portion of the entry at any time. In the formula bar, the entire entry is visible (see fig. 9.8).

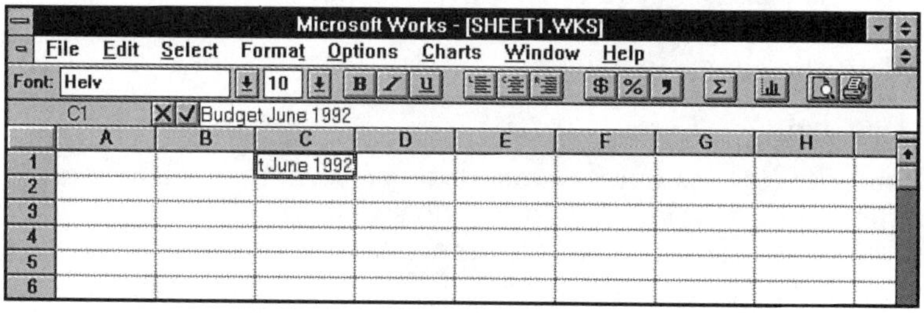

FIG. 9.8

The entire entry is visible in the formula bar

3. Press Enter to insert the information into the cell. As you can see in figure 9.9, the entire entry now appears in the spreadsheet.

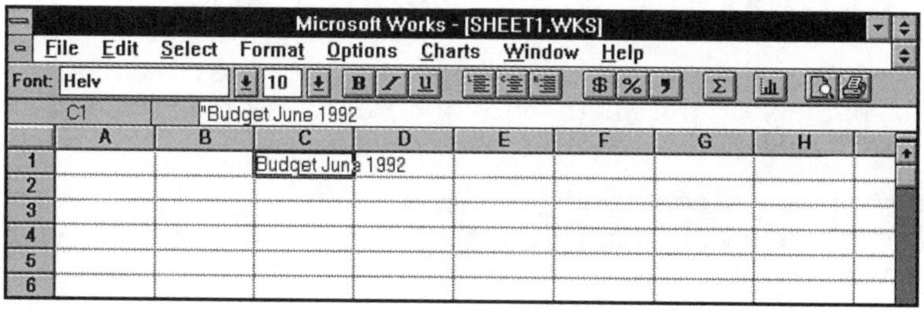

FIG. 9.9

The entire entry becomes visible across cells

Although you can see the entire entry, if you make an entry in cell D1, that entry will overwrite the C1 entry. The entry in cell C1 is not changed if overwriting occurs; the entry in C1 is only in cell C1, even though Microsoft Works displays a long entry across cell boundaries when the spreadsheet has the room to do so.

With the spreadsheet title entered, move the cursor to cell A4. Because a budget is a statement of income and expenses over a specific period of time, you must add the months of the year as column heads. To do so, take these steps:

1. With the cursor in cell A4, type **Jan** and press Enter.

   Works assumes that you want to enter the month name *January* and fills in the remaining letters for you. Notice, too, that no character precedes the letter *J*. Move the cursor back to the entry in cell C1.

> **NOTE** With the cursor in C1, take a close look at the formula bar: a quotation mark precedes the word Budget. Works adds the quotation mark when the program detects a label entry. This method is Microsoft Works' way of designating the entry in the cell as a label. Works' manner of handling January enables you to enter month names quickly.

2. Move the cursor to cell B4.

3. Type **Feb**.

This time, don't press Enter to insert the name in the cell. Instead, press the right-arrow key. When you do so, the month name *February* is entered into the cell, and the cursor moves to the next logical cell (C4) for an entry. Much faster than pressing Enter, this technique simultaneously enters information into a cell and moves the cursor to the next cell.

Using the Fill Series Command

You easily can move across the columns and type the remaining months of the year. But Microsoft Works has a feature for entering the months of the year that requires fewer keystrokes.

With the Fill Series command, you can enter subsequent numbers or labels into a series of cells. This method involves less work and eliminates typing errors.

Using the Fill Series command requires that you know how many entries you must enter. In this case, you have 10 more entries, because you already have January and February in place.

To make the entries, follow these steps:

1. Move the cursor to cell B4, the one containing the February entry.

2. Hold the Shift key and press the right-arrow key until the cursor is on cell L4. You now have selected the cells into which you want to insert the month names.

NOTE You haven't made a mistake by including cell B4 in this selection because B4 tells Works what kind of data you want in the rest of the cells. To determine that data, the first cell selected must contain the first entry in the series. February works well as the first entry because Microsoft Works is smart enough to know that the rest of the entries should be the months after February, even though February is not the first month of the year.

3. Click **Edit** or press Alt,E and choose Fill Series. The Fill Series dialog box appears (see fig. 9.10).

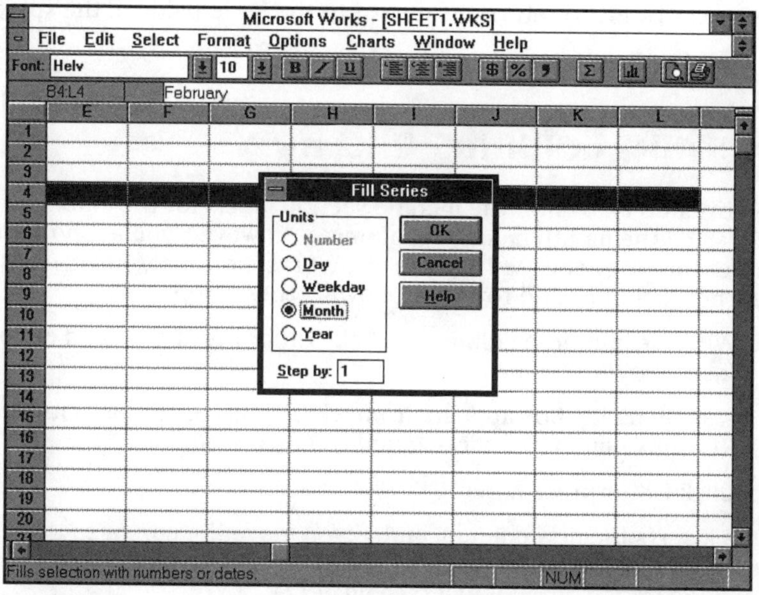

FIG. 9.10

The Fill Series dialog box

Works now needs two pieces of information: the type of data you want to insert and the size of the increment.

In the Units section of the Fill Series dialog box, you can choose from five types of data: Number, **Day**, **Weekday**, **Month**, and **Year**.

The **Step** By: option tells Works the size of the increment. The default option is 1. You also can use an increment such as 3, which enters the months of the year by quarter.

4. For this example, choose **Month** for the type of data and leave the **Step** By: text box at the default of 1.

5. Press Enter or click OK.

Works inserts the rest of the months (see fig. 9.11).

Now, press Home to return the cursor to the far left side of the spread-sheet.

Inserting Columns and Rows

The next step is to enter the income section labels for the club. When you started the month names in column A, however, you left no room to enter the row items. With Microsoft Works, however, you can easily insert new columns and rows by following these steps:

1. With the cursor in column A, click **Edit** or press Alt,E and choose **Insert Row/Column**.

2. A small dialog box appears from which you can choose either **Row** or **Column**. For this example, choose **Column**.

3. Click OK or press Enter.

Works inserts the new column, and, if you move the cursor to the right, you see that all the month names have been shifted over one column to accommodate the new column (see fig. 9.12).

To move the cursor to the right edge of the spreadsheet, press End. Microsoft Works moves the cursor to the farthest right entry in the current row.

You now have room for labels. Move the cursor to cell A5 and type **Dues**. Press the down-arrow key to enter the *Dues* label.

The next source of income is a fee charged to a local professional tennis player who gives lessons on the club courts. In cell A6 type **Fees**, and then press the down-arrow key.

Move the cursor to cell A8. For the next label (which begins a new section), type **Expenses** and press Enter to enter the label but leave the cursor on cell A8.

Now, underline Expenses to set off the labels for this section of the spreadsheet. To underline, follow these steps:

1. Click Format or press Alt,T and choose **S**tyle... (see fig. 9.13).

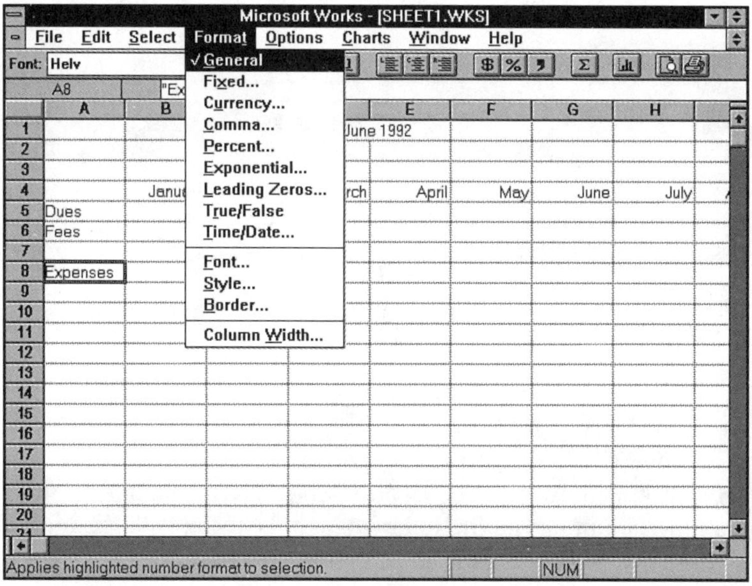

FIG. 9.13

The Format menu

The Style dialog box appears (see figure 9.14), from which you can change the appearance of the label in this cell.

2. Choose Underline and then click OK or press Enter.

The label Expenses is underlined, and you can begin to enter expense subheadings. (See the next section, "Adding Labels.")

To use the underline attribute without using the Style dialog box, click the U button on the Tool bar.

T I P

FIG. 9.14

The Style dialog box

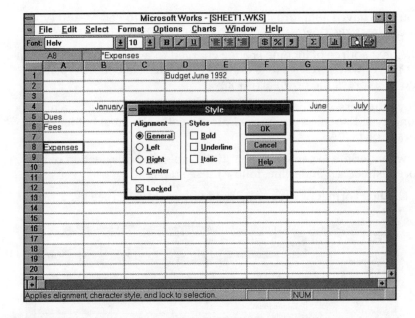

The options in the Style dialog box fall into three categories: Alignment of cell entries, Styles of entries, and the Locked check box.

If Locked is selected, you cannot edit the information in the cell(s) unless you return to the Styles dialog box and unlock the cell(s).

Adding Labels

Now that you have the Expenses label entered, you can add to the list. To finish the column, type the following labels in the cells, as indicated in the following table:

Cell	Label
A10	Salaries
A11	Trailer Rental
A12	Electric
A13	Telephone
A14	Supplies
A15	Postage
A16	Printing

Cell	Label
A17	Tournaments
A18	Accounting
A19	Miscellaneous

Your spreadsheet now should resemble figure 9.15.

FIG. 9.15

Expense labels added

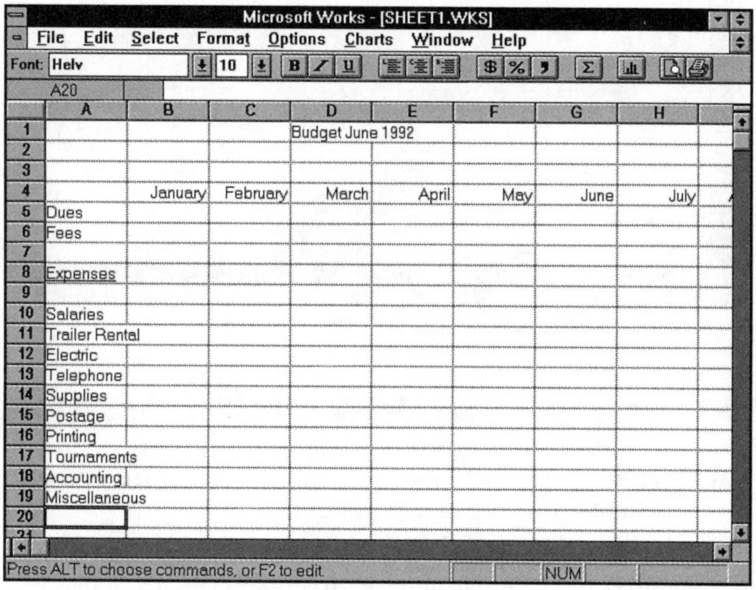

No section head has been entered for the two items set out as income items in cells A5 and A6. To be consistent, add such a heading.

First, insert a row by putting the cursor on cell A5. Then, follow the steps in the preceding section, "Inserting Rows and Columns," except choose **Row** in the Insert Row/Column dialog box. Works inserts the new row above the cursor.

Now type **Income** in the new cell A5. Finish the entry by adding underlining to the word (see fig. 9.16).

FIG. 9.16

Income header
added

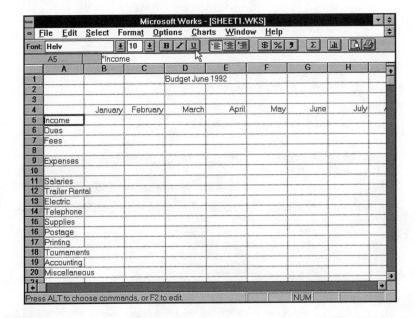

	A	B	C	D	E	F	G	H	
1				Budget June 1992					
2									
3									
4		January	February	March	April	May	June	July	
5	Income								
6	Dues								
7	Fees								
8									
9	Expenses								
10									
11	Salaries								
12	Trailer Rental								
13	Electric								
14	Telephone								
15	Supplies								
16	Postage								
17	Printing								
18	Tournaments								
19	Accounting								
20	Miscellaneous								

Entering Numbers and Formulas

You have built the skeleton of the spreadsheet. To use the spreadsheet, you now must enter numbers and formulas.

If you are new to spreadsheets, you must grasp the concept of the way labels, numbers, and formulas interact to create a financial model. A *financial model* puts labels, numbers, and formulas in ledger form for such items as a budget, a profit-and-loss statement, or a cost estimate.

Numbers come in many forms, but as long as the first character Works encounters is a numeral or an arithmetic operator such as a plus sign (+) or minus sign (-), the character is considered a number.

A *formula* always begins with an equal sign (=) or a plus sign (+). The formula itself follows the leading equal sign or plus sign. A cell formula calculates values in the spreadsheet the same way a formula calculates values on paper. That is, to calculate totals, percentages, or amortization schedules.

Using the Windows Calculator

According to the club's accountant, member dues total $30,000 annually. This total is helpful, but you need monthly figures for your budget.

You find that 30,000 divided by 12 months is easy to calculate with the Windows popup Calculator. The Windows Calculator must be active in memory before you can access the feature.

Follow these steps to activate the Calculator:

1. Move to cell B6, which will have the first entry for dues.

2. Click the Control button in the upper-left corner of the screen, or press Alt+space bar. The Control menu appears (see fig. 9.17).

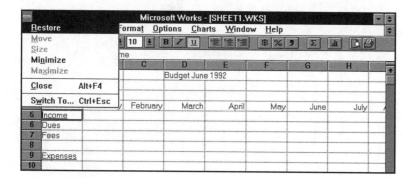

FIG. 9.17

The Control menu

3. Choose Minimize.

   You can also quickly minimize by clicking the down-arrow button in the upper-right corner of the window.

4. From the Program Manager screen, click the Accessories icon. If you can't see the icon, choose Accessories from the **Window** menu. The Windows Accessories appear (see fig. 9.18).

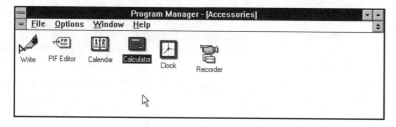

FIG. 9.18

The Windows Accessories screen with the Calculator icon highlighted

5. Double-click the Calculator icon. The Calculator appears (see fig. 9.19).

FIG. 9.19

The Calculator

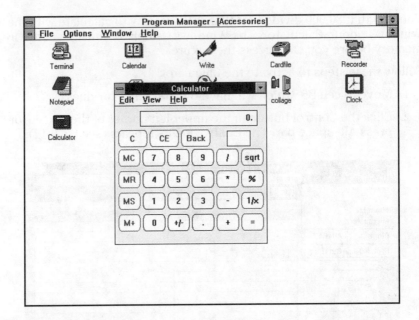

6. Type **30000** and press the / (slash) key.

7. Type **12** and press Enter. The value 2500 appears in the Calculator display.

8. From the Calculator's **E**dit menu, choose **C**opy to copy the value in the display onto the Windows Clipboard.

9. Press Alt+space bar or click the Control menu button at the upper-left corner of the Calculator window.

10. Choose **S**witch To.

   The Task List dialog box appears, listing the active programs, one of which is Microsoft Works. You can also quickly open the Task List by pressing Ctrl+Esc.

11. Click Microsoft Works, and then click the **S**witch To button from the Task List dialog box.

   The Microsoft Works spreadsheet reappears.

12. Press Shift+Ins. The value, 2500, is copied from the Clipboard and inserted into cell B6.

Next, you must enter the fees from the tennis pro. Move to cell B7. Because the Windows Calculator is loaded into memory, you can easily retrieve it for the next calculation by following these steps:

1. Press Ctrl+Esc to open the Task List.

2. Click Calculator and then click Switch To.

   The Windows Calculator appears on top of the spreadsheet.

3. Type **5880** (the total annual fees from the tennis pro) and then press /. You can enter the numbers and operator from the keyboard or by clicking the numbers and operator with the mouse.

4. Enter **12** and press Enter or click the equal sign.

   The Calculator window displays 490 as the value.

5. Press Ctrl+Ins to copy the value onto the Clipboard.

6. Click the down-arrow button at the top right of the Calculator window to minimize the Calculator, or press Alt+space bar and select Minimize. To quickly jump back to the spreadsheet, click the spreadsheet window.

7. Press Shift+Ins.

Works inserts the value of 490 in cell B7.

Table 9.1 describes the Calculator's features.

Table 9.1 Calculator Features

Button	Keystroke	Result
C	Escape	Clears calculation
CE	Delete	Clears number in display
Back	Backspace	Deletes rightmost number in display
MC	Ctrl+C	Clears value stored in memory
MR	Ctrl+R	Recalls value in memory
MS	Ctrl+M	Stores displayed value in memory
M+	Ctrl+P	Adds displayed value to value in memory
+	+	Addition
-	-	Subtraction
/	/	Division
*	*	Multiplication
sqrt	@	Calculates square root of displayed number
%	%	Calculates percentages

continues

Table 9.1 Continued

Button	Keystroke	Result
1/x	r	Calculates reciprocal of displayed number
+/-	F9	Changes the sign of displayed number
.	.	Inserts decimal point in displayed number
=	=	Performs calculation

T I P   Repeatedly pressing the = key repeats the calculation.

In the next section, you find the total income for the month. Because you have no room for another cell entry beneath the Fees entry, however, you must insert an additional row at cell A9 by following the steps in "Inserting Columns and Rows," earlier in the chapter. Then, in cell A9, type the label **Total Income**.

The spreadsheet still looks a little crowded, so repeat the steps to insert a second blank row under row 9 to give a neater appearance.

Entering a Formula

Before entering formulas into a Microsoft Works spreadsheet, you must understand this simple concept: Formulas are calculated based on the information in the cells by using the cell addresses.

In the example, 2500 is entered in cell B6 and 490 is entered in cell B7. You want the total of 2500 and 490 to appear in cell B9. Therefore, the formula you type in cell B9 is **=B6+B7**. The formula is based on the cell addresses (B6 and B7), not the values in those cells. If you read aloud the formula, it reads as "Cell B9 equals (=) the sum of the values entered in cells B6 and B7."

Enter the formula by taking these steps and see what happens:

1. In cell B9, type the equal sign (=) to begin the formula. All formulas begin with an equal sign (=).

2. Type **B6** as the cell address containing the first value you want to include in the formula.

3. Type the mathematical operator—in this example, the addition sign (+).

4. Then, type **B7** as the cell address containing the second value you want in the formula.

5. Press Enter. Your spreadsheet should resemble figure 9.20.

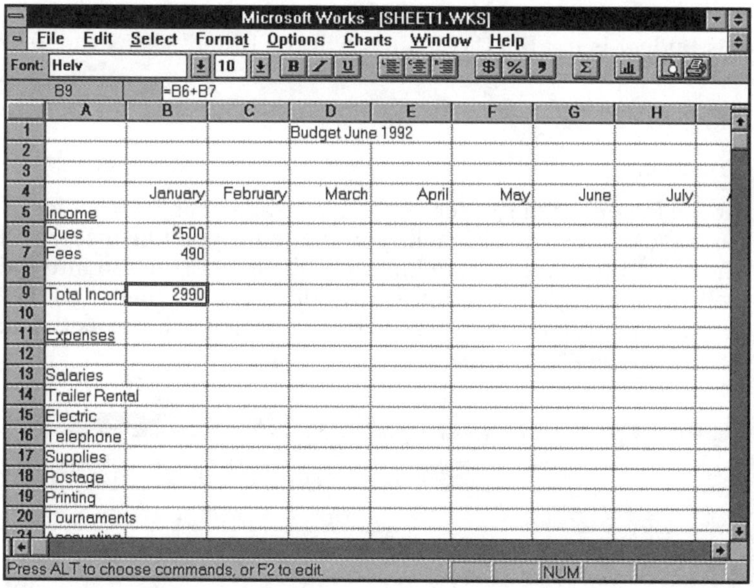

FIG. 9.20

The first formula

Notice that the text from cell A9 has been overwritten by the entry in cell B9.

All formulas in Microsoft Works follow the same principle. The cell addresses in the formula determine what values Works acts on, and the mathematical operator determines the result of that action.

To illustrate the power this concept provides, move the cursor to cell B6 and change the value there. Type **1000** and press Enter. Microsoft Works recalculates the total of the values in cells B6 and B7 and displays the result, 1490, in cell B9.

Editing Cell Entries

In the preceding section, you edited a cell by replacing one entry with another. With the cursor in the cell you want to change, you can edit cell entries in one of two ways: type the new entry, or press F2 and use the arrow keys to move through the cell entry to make changes. Using F2 to edit is helpful if you have a long or complex cell entry, such as a long title or a formula.

As an example, look at the title for this spreadsheet, Budget June 1992. You have left out an important word: *Proposed*. To make it clear that this budget is not final, you must edit the title by using the following steps:

1. Move to cell D1.

2. Press F2.

   At the lower-left of the screen, the message Press ENTER or ESC to cancel (see fig. 9.21) tells you that after you finish correcting the cell contents, pressing Enter inserts the correction into the cell. If you decide not to make any edits or make them and then decide the original entry was better, pressing Esc leaves the cell as it was before the edit.

FIG. 9.21

The edited line

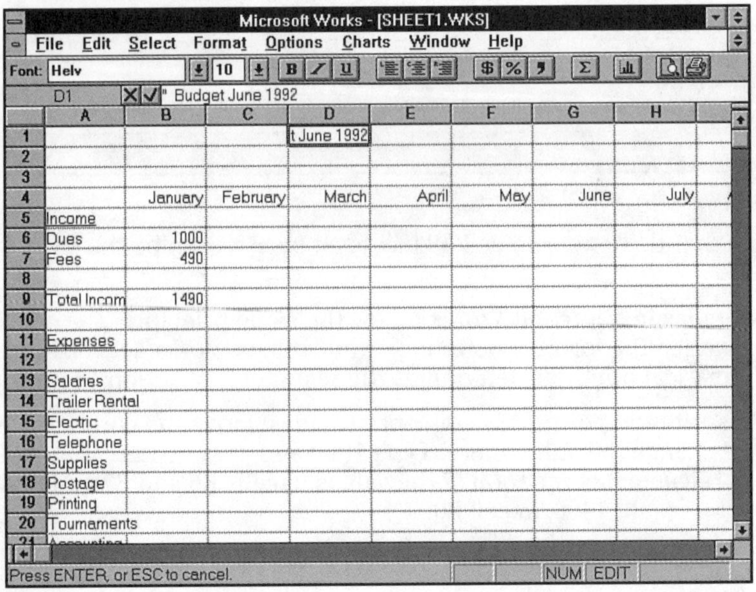

	A	B	C	D	E	F	G	H	
1				t June 1992					
2									
3									
4		January	February	March	April	May	June	July	
5	Income								
6	Dues	1000							
7	Fees	490							
8									
9	Total Incom	1490							
10									
11	Expenses								
12									
13	Salaries								
14	Trailer Rental								
15	Electric								
16	Telephone								
17	Supplies								
18	Postage								
19	Printing								
20	Tournaments								
21	Accounting								

Microsoft Works - [SHEET1.WKS]

File Edit Select Format Options Charts Window Help

Font: Helv   10   B I U $ % , Σ

D1   Budget June 1992

Press ENTER, or ESC to cancel.   NUM EDIT

3. You must insert *Proposed* at the beginning of the title, but the insertion point—a small vertical line—is at the end of the title. Use the left-arrow key to move the insertion point in front of B in the word Budget.

4. Type **Proposed**.

5. Press the space bar to insert a space and then press Enter. Your spreadsheet now should look like figure 9.22.

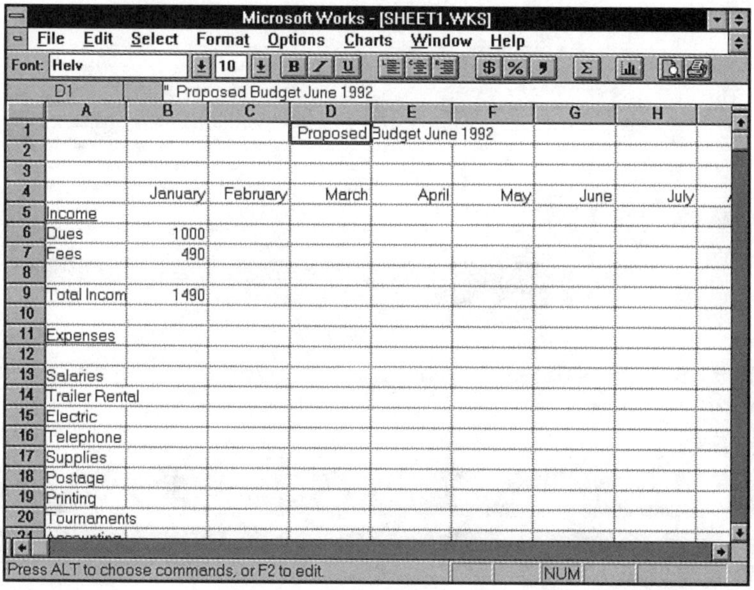

FIG. 9.22

The new title

Something else is amiss. The title says that this proposed budget is for June 1992, not January, as the spreadsheet reads. As long as you are making changes, go back and change the month by following these steps:

1. With the cursor in D1, press F2 to enter Edit mode.

2. Move the insertion point to the left of the letter u in June.

3. Press Del three times to delete the letters une in June.

4. Type **anuary** and press Enter. The spreadsheet title should resemble the one in figure 9.23.

FIG. 9.23

January replaces
June

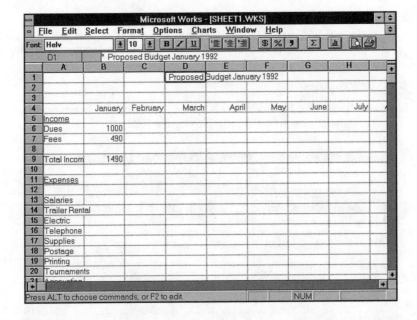

Table 9.2 identifies the keys to press for the Works editing functions in the formula bar.

Table 9.2 Formula Bar Editing Keys

Key	Action
Home	Moves edit line to beginning of entry
End	Moves insertion point to end of entry
Left arrow	Moves insertion point left one character
Right arrow	Moves insertion point right one character
Backspace	Deletes character to left of insertion point
Delete	Deletes character to right of insertion point
Shift+left arrow	Selects character(s) left
Shift+right arrow	Selects character(s) righ
Enter	Accepts edits
Up/down arrow	Accepts edits
Esc	No change

Deleting Cell Contents

Suppose that instead of changing the contents of a cell, you want to delete the contents. Earlier, you changed the number in cell B6 from 2500 to 1000. To delete the new value so that you can restore the correct number, follow these steps:

1. Move the cursor to cell B6.

2. Press Del to delete the current entry, 1000, and press Enter.

3. The cell is now blank, and the formula in cell B9 has correctly recalculated to show the total of cells B6 and B7, which is 490 (0+490).

4. Type **2500** and press Enter.

The formula is recalculated. The correct value of 2990 is now in cell B9.

Aligning Cell Entries

Microsoft Works aligns labels and numbers when they are entered into a cell. The default is that labels are left-justified in the cell and numbers are right-justified.

You can change the alignment for labels in one of two ways: by using the Format Style. . . command or by clicking the Alignment button in the Tool bar. In the Proposed Budget spreadsheet, you already have set off the section heads, *Income* and *Expenses*, by underlining them. Now move the *Income* head to the right side of cell A5. Follow these steps:

1. Move the cursor to cell A5. Because you already have underlined this cell, the U button in the Tool bar is activated.

2. Click the right-align button on the Tool bar.

Income now is right-justified (see fig. 9.24).

Entering Values into Cells

To determine the budget for the month of January, you must insert the numbers related to the expense section items.

FIG. 9.24

A right-justified
Income label

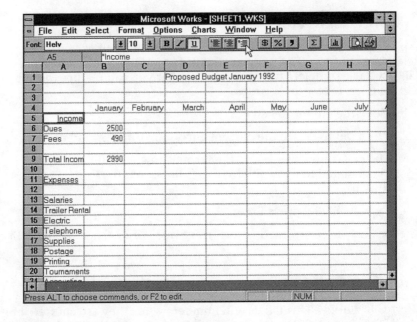

Type the numbers from the following table in their corresponding cell address:

Cell	Number to Type
B13	1290
B14	190
B15	120
B16	39
B17	179
B18	79
B19	79
B20	100
B21	100
B22	29

With these expenses entered, you can calculate whether the club made money. Earlier, when you calculated the income section of the spreadsheet, the formula (=B6+B7) involved only two cells.

In the Income section, having only two cells to total makes entering the formula easy. You also can add every cell individually in a long formula, like +B13+B14+B19+B16 (and so forth). That method works, but the complexity of the process and the possibility of typing errors render such a method impractical. Of course, Microsoft Works provides a better way.

Summing a Range of Cells

You want to add the values in a range of cells. (A *range* is any contiguous group of cells.) In this example, the range is B13 to B22, the cells that contain the values relating to expenses.

Earlier, you used the Fill Series command to insert the names of the months of the year into a selected range of cells. This time, select the cells to include in the range to be totaled. Follow these steps:

1. Move the cursor to cell B24, where Works will show the total expenses.

2. Start the formula by typing the equal sign (=).

3. Add a function name. For this example, type **SUM** after the equal sign so that the formula bar displays =SUM.

> Microsoft Works has many functions with which you can construct formulas. The SUM function totals a range of values. See Chapter 11, "Using Functions," for details on other functions.

T I P

4. Because you are going to add a range of cells, parentheses must surround this range in the formula. Type the opening parenthesis (.

   The formula now looks like =SUM(.

5. You can use menu commands to add the range of cells, but Microsoft Works provides an easier way. First, move the cursor to cell B13.

   Cell B13 displays in the formula. Near the lower-right corner of the spreadsheet, a screen message also appears, indicating that you are in POINT mode. This mode means that you are going to point to the range of cells desired.

6. Hold down Shift and then press the down-arrow key. The cursor goes into the Extend mode and stretches as you continue pressing the down-arrow key. You can also drag the mouse pointer to select the cells you want.

7. When the cursor reaches cell B22, stop pressing the Shift and down-arrow keys. The range B13 through B22 is highlighted (see fig. 9.25).

FIG. 9.25

Range B13..B22
highlighted

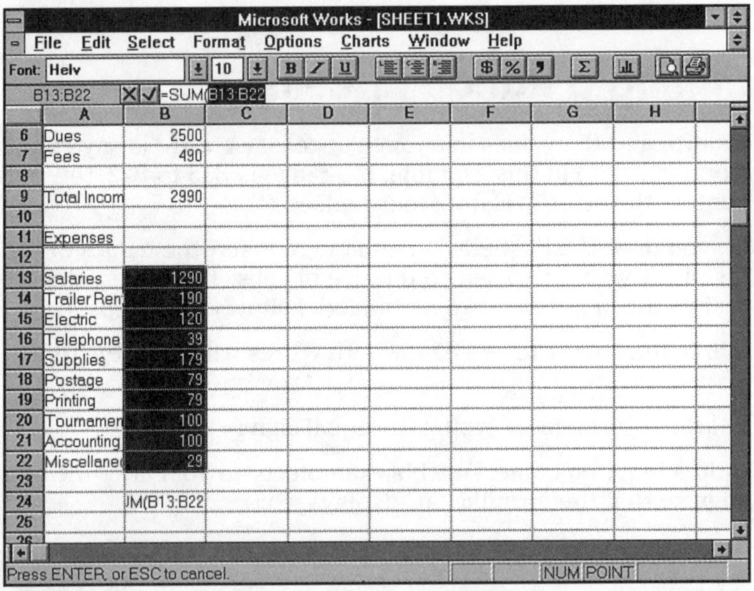

8. Type the closing parentheses, **)**, and then press Enter to finish the formula.

If you have followed the steps closely, your screen should resemble figure 9.26.

You have taken a big step toward mastering one of the key concepts of working with the Microsoft Works spreadsheet. You can use a function and then select a range of cells on which the function operates. This technique opens a wide range of formulas to you. Chapter 11, "Using Functions," demonstrates all the built-in functions with working examples.

Computing the Final Tally

To determine the final tally for the month of January, you must subtract the total expenses from the total income. You already know those figures, but you must include a cell for that result. Follow these steps:

1. Move the cursor to cell B26.

2. Type **=B9-B24** and press Enter.

The result—785 (from 2990-2205)—is entered in this cell.

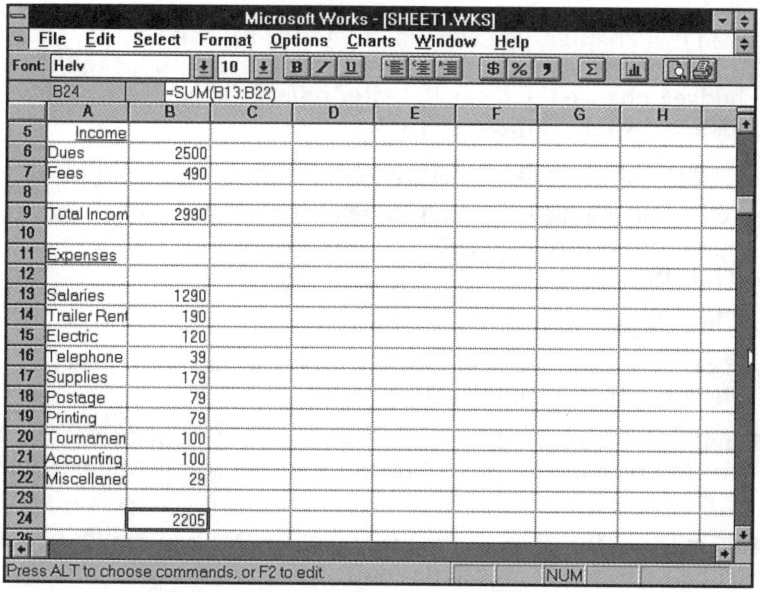

FIG. 9.26

The finished
formula

Add the labels **Total Expenses** in cell A24 and **Net Income** in cell A26 to
finish this spreadsheet (see fig. 9.27).

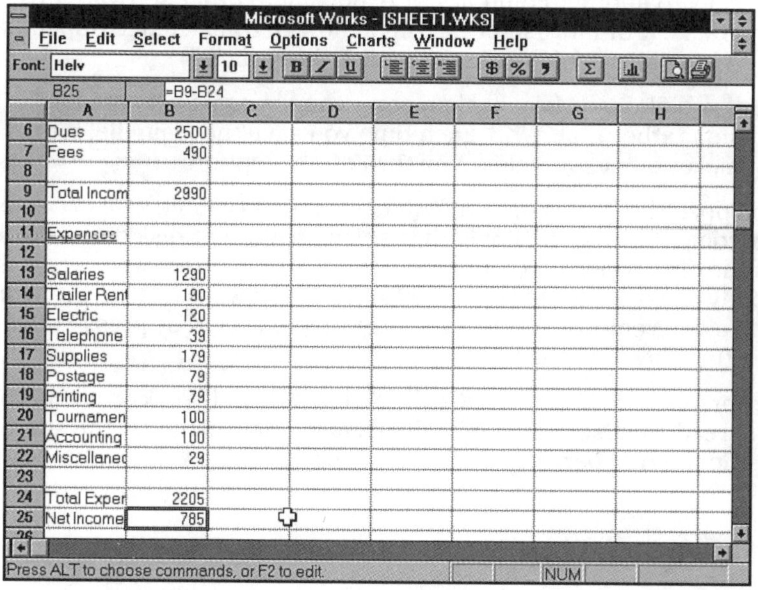

FIG. 9.27

Total expenses
and net income

Resaving the Worksheet

Earlier in this chapter, you were instructed to save the spreadsheet as SHEET1.WKS. However, because this spreadsheet pertains to the tennis club budget, change the name to better reflect the contents of the spreadsheet by taking these steps:

1. Open the **File** menu and choose the Save **As**. . . command.

2. Works opens the Save As dialog box, with the current name of the spreadsheet, SHEET1.WKS in the File **Name**: text box. Type **TENNIS**.

3. Click OK or press Enter.

Works saves the spreadsheet file under its new name, as reflected in the title bar at the top of the screen.

- In the File **Name**: text box is the spreadsheet file name Works thinks you want to use. If you prefer to use another name, type one here.

- Next is the **Directories**: list box, in which you can see files in other subdirectories or switch directories to save the file where you choose.

- With the Save File as **Type**: list box, you can save the spreadsheet as a Works file or as a text file. If you save the spreadsheet as a text file, you can send the spreadsheet by transferring electronically to another computer or exporting to other software programs. (For more information on how to transfer, see Appendix A, "Using Microsoft Works with Other Programs.")

- If you choose **Make** backup copy, the file name gets the BKS extension rather than WKS. Each time you save the main file, Works makes a backup unless you turn off this option.

If you open the Drives option, Works lists the available disk drives on your computer system. If you then select a different disk drive, Works lists the directories on that drive. If there are no directories, such as on a floppy drive, a list of files is presented. If you want to save the Works file to a different drive, select the drive and click OK or press Enter. The file is then saved to that drive.

The spreadsheet file is saved as TENNIS.WKS, and Works returns you to the spreadsheet screen. Works displays the new name for the spreadsheet in the title bar.

Chapter Summary

In this chapter, you learned how to enter labels, numbers, and formulas into the cells of the spreadsheet. You also used the Fill Series command to insert the names of the months of the year, edited text, formatted and aligned label entries, and used a function in a formula to sum a range of numbers.

In the next chapter, you do more work with the TENNIS.WKS spreadsheet: copying formulas and data, using fonts, manipulating columns, naming ranges, freezing column and row titles, and searching the spreadsheet.

Expanding Your Spreadsheet Knowledge

In the preceding chapter, you began entering in spreadsheet cells the basic elements that make up a spreadsheet: the labels describing the information contained in the spreadsheet, the numbers associated with the labels, and the formulas that make the numbers useful.

In this chapter, you finish the TENNIS.WKS sample spreadsheet and work with a couple of other spreadsheet examples. In doing so, you learn more about the basics of using the Microsoft Works spreadsheet. Also in this chapter, you learn how to do the following:

- Open a saved spreadsheet file.
- Copy cell contents.
- Set column widths.
- Freeze row and column titles.
- Split the spreadsheet window.
- Use the **G**o To... command.
- Format cells.

■ Create range names.

■ Hide columns.

■ Protect cell contents.

■ Display formulas.

■ Recalculate and sort spreadsheets.

■ Search and print spreadsheets.

Opening a Saved Spreadsheet File

At the end of Chapter 9, you saved the proposed budget for the tennis club in a file called TENNIS.WKS. To open that spreadsheet file, take these steps:

1. From the Microsoft Works Startup dialog box (see fig. 10.1), select the Open Existing File... command. The Open dialog box shown in figure 10.2 appears.

FIG. 10.1

The Startup dialog box

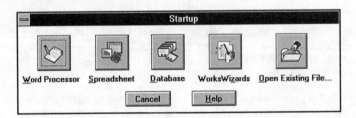

Click Drives or press Alt,V and the Drives: field drop-down menu appears. Works determines which disk drives your computer has and displays them in the Drives: field. Notice that in figure 10.2 Works detects four drives: A, B, C, and D. The files already saved in the current drive and subdirectory (C:\MSWORKS by default and in fig. 10.2) are listed in the File Name: field.

2. If the file you want to open is not in the MSWORKS subdirectory of drive C, you need to change to the drive and directory where the file is stored. If you saved the TENNIS.WKS spreadsheet on a floppy disk, for example, use the Drives: field to select the drive in which you have inserted your files disk (usually drive A). After you switch drives, Works displays in the File Name: field the files contained on the disk in that drive. (If you need more information on files, see Chapters 3 and 5.)

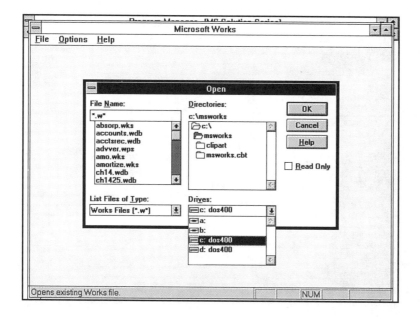

FIG. 10.2

The Open dialog box

Notice also that in the File Name: field, Works displays *.w* as the suggested file name parameters for the file to open. This notation is a shorthand method used by DOS to select all files with a W as the first letter of the extension. The files listed in the File Name: field are sorted alphabetically.

3. Select the file you want to open—TENNIS.WKS in this example— by clicking the down arrow until the file is highlighted in the File Name: field. The highlighted file name is inserted at the top of the field, replacing the *.w* entry.

4. Double-click the mouse button, and the file appears on-screen. Figure 10.3 shows the TENNIS.WKS spreadsheet.

NOTE Remember to maximize the program and spreadsheet windows as you begin your work, as described in Chapter 9.

The values and formulas that make up the month of January are already in place in the sample worksheet. Your first step is to copy those values and formulas to the remaining 11 months of the year.

FIG. 10.3

Opening the
TENNIS.WKS
spreadsheet

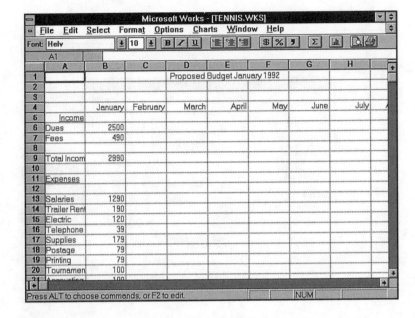

FIG. 10.3

Opening the
TENNIS.WKS
spreadsheet

Copying Cell Contents

When you have created a spreadsheet with values that you want to repeat over time, for example the cost for rent per month, you can copy the first value across the row with the copy command. By copying rather than typing each entry individually, you increase the accuracy of the spreadsheet.

To copy cell contents, follow these steps:

1. Move the cell pointer to the beginning of the group of cells you want to copy. In this example, move the cell pointer to cell B6, the beginning of the Income section of the TENNIS.WKS spreadsheet.

2. Select the cells you want to copy. For the TENNIS.WKS example, press and hold the Shift key while pressing the down-arrow key until cells B6 and B7 are selected. You want to copy the values in these cells to the right through column M.

3. Use the cell pointer to highlight the cells to which you want to copy. In the TENNIS.WKS spreadsheet, highlight the cells across rows 6 and 7. With the Shift and right-arrow keys pressed, stretch the cell pointer across to column M, which is the December column.

4. Access the Edit menu.

5. Highlight the Fill **R**ight option. Notice the prompt at the bottom of the screen that shows the effect of choosing this command. You see the prompt `Copies leftmost cell(s) to rest of selec-tion`. Press left arrow to turn off the highlighting.

Instantly, Microsoft Works copies the information (see fig. 10.4).

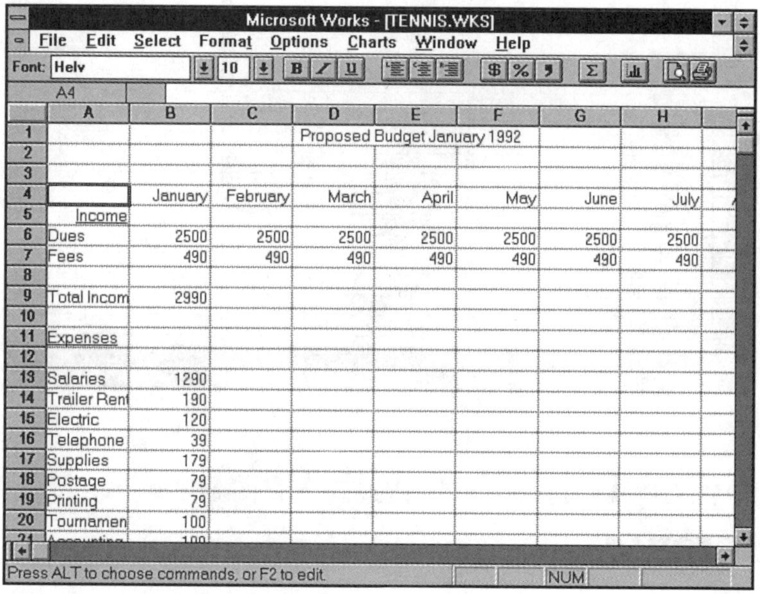

FIG. 10.4

Copying cells B6 and B7 across rows 6 and 7

You can use the same method to copy column B in the Expense section across the spreadsheet. Move the cell pointer to cell B13, press Shift-down arrow until the highlight stretches to cell B26, press Shift-End to select the entire range C13..M26, and select Fill **R**ight from the **E**dit menu. As shown in figure 10.5, Microsoft Works quickly fills in the cell contents over many cells.

You now have a complete TENNIS budget, which is flexible because you can change assorted numbers and immediately find the effect on net income.

Filling numbers is certainly much faster than typing the same numbers in every cell. But this method has a potential problem. Suppose you discover that the pro's fees are going to be higher than you originally thought. You can go back and type the new number in the January column and then refill the cell contents across the row for the entire year. But Microsoft Works offers a faster method, as you discover in the following section.

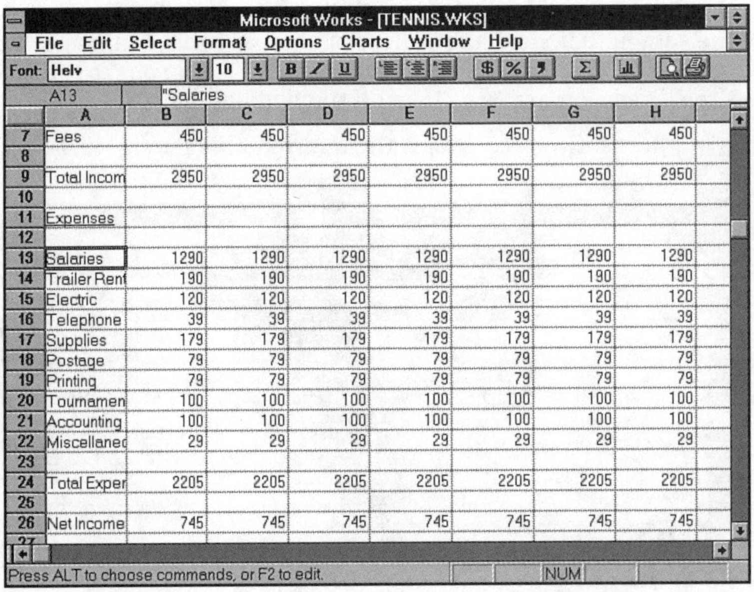
Microsoft Works - [TENNIS.WKS]
File Edit Select Format Options Charts Window Help
Font: Helv 10
A13 "Salaries
A B C D E F G H
7 Fees 450 450 450 450 450 450 450
8
9 Total Incom 2950 2950 2950 2950 2950 2950 2950
10
11 Expenses
12
13 Salaries 1290 1290 1290 1290 1290 1290 1290
14 Trailer Rent 190 190 190 190 190 190 190
15 Electric 120 120 120 120 120 120 120
16 Telephone 39 39 39 39 39 39 39
17 Supplies 179 179 179 179 179 179 179
18 Postage 79 79 79 79 79 79 79
19 Printing 79 79 79 79 79 79 79
20 Tournamen 100 100 100 100 100 100 100
21 Accounting 100 100 100 100 100 100 100
22 Miscellaned 29 29 29 29 29 29 29
23
24 Total Exper 2205 2205 2205 2205 2205 2205 2205
25
26 Net Income 745 745 745 745 745 745 745
Press ALT to choose commands, or F2 to edit.
NUM

FIG. 10.5

Copying a larger range of cells

Copying Formulas with Relative References

By using formulas in your spreadsheet, you can make certain cell entries dependent on other cells. In the TENNIS spreadsheet, for example, you can make each cell in row 7 dependent on the adjacent cell to the left. By using this method, you can change one entry in the row and automatically change all cells to the right in that row. This type of cell reference in a formula is called a *relative reference*.

Move the cell pointer to cell B7, the cell containing the initial entry for fees, and type **500** in the cell. The number is inserted, but the rest of the months in that row remain the same at 490. Instead of refilling row 7 with the new value, enter a short formula in cell C7 and then copy the formula across the row. Follow these steps:

1. With the cell pointer in cell C7, type =**B7** and press Enter. Works interprets the formula as "This cell (C7) equals the contents in cell B7," and so the value 500 is entered in cell C7.

2. Move the cell pointer to cell C7 and then press the Shift and End keys together. This command stretches the cell pointer across the spreadsheet.

3. Access the **E**dit menu.

4. Select the Fill **R**ight option.

The new value 500 is entered in every cell in row 7. These entries, however, are different from those cells in which you simply entered numeric values. Move the cell pointer back to cell B7, enter 450 as another new value for fees, and press Enter. All the cells in row 7 change to contain the value 450.

Look at the contents of cell E7 by moving the cell pointer there. The cell displays 450, but the formula bar displays the formula =D7. Although you copied the formula =B7 into cell C7, the formula bar shows =D7 as the contents of cell E7 because Microsoft Works has adjusted the copied formula so that it is *relative* to its column position. The formula in each cell thus refers to the cell to its immediate left. When you are creating a spreadsheet, the best policy usually is to make the cells to the right dependent on the cells preceding them. By using this method as a habit, you can avoid errors when playing what-if scenarios.

Copying Formulas with Absolute References

Microsoft Works assumes, as the default, that a copied formula is to be adjusted to its new location in the spreadsheet. If you scroll the cell pointer across row 7 in TENNIS.WKS, for example, you see that every formula has been adjusted to copy the cell just to its left, not to copy the original cell copied, C7. In most instances, this adjustment is welcome. You can, however, make a cell reference within a formula an absolute reference.

An *absolute reference* is an address for a specific cell; an absolute address does not adjust to the relative cell location. The dollar signs in an absolute reference (as in B4) indicate that no matter where the formula is copied in the spreadsheet, only the contents of that specific referenced cell are used.

Microsoft Works has a special key for creating an absolute reference: the F4 function key. To use this key, you must activate it *at the same time* the formula is entered not *after* the formula is entered. To use the relative/absolute key for the TENNIS.WKS example, you first must erase the formulas in the cells in row 7. Take these steps to replace the formulas in row 7 with formulas containing absolute references:

1. With the cursor in cell C7, press the Shift and End keys to stretch the highlight across the entire row, or click and drag the row.

2. Click **E**dit or press Alt,E.

3. Select the Clear command. All the contents of the cells in row 7 are cleared.

4. Move the cursor to C7 and type an equal sign (=) to begin the formula.

5. Move the cursor to cell B7. Works inserts the B7 cell address in the formula bar.

6. Press the F4 key once. Dollar signs are inserted in front of the B and the 7 to make the cell reference absolute (see fig. 10.6).

FIG. 10.6

Inserting an
absolute
reference

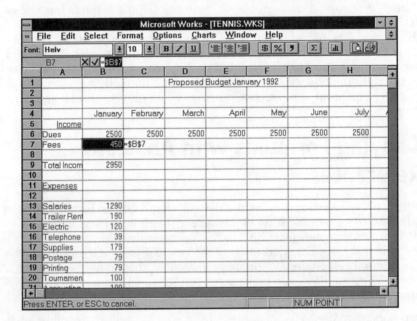

NOTE You can make just one component of the cell reference—the column or the row reference—absolute. If you press F4 again after making a cell reference absolute, the dollar sign in front of the column reference disappears, but the one in front of the row number remains (B$7). This reference is called a *mixed reference*. If you copy the cell contents at this point, only the row reference remains constant, not the column reference. Pressing the F4 key again reverses the situation. The dollar sign moves to the column reference, so the column reference is constant while the row reference is relative ($B7). The F4 function key cycles through the choices of absolute and relative references.

7. Press Enter to insert the new formula into C7.

8. Use the Fill **R**ight command from the **E**dit menu to insert the formula into cells D7 through M7.

If you scroll across the cells in row 7, you see that the formulas are now absolute. The absolute formula gives you new flexibility. For example, suppose that in the month of July the teaching pro takes a month off. In that month, the fees revenue is 0. By having the formulas absolute, you can adjust one month without disturbing the formulas for all the months following July.

Finish the Income section of the TENNIS spreadsheet by copying the formula in cell B9 to cells C9 through M9 by using relative references.

Combining Relative and Absolute Addresses

To try different economic assumptions easily, make the Expenses section depend on the entries in cells B13 to B26. Follow these steps:

1. Move the cell pointer to C13 and press Shift-down arrow to highlight the cells in the range C13..C26., or click and drag C13..C26. The cursor is still on cell C13.

2. Press F2 to edit.

3. Press the Backspace key to delete the characters 1290.

4. Type =$B13 and press Enter.

   When you copy this formula with its mixed reference, the column reference remains absolute, but the row reference changes to reflect its new position. By making the column entries absolute, you can make changes in midyear numbers without disturbing the entire spreadsheet.

   The next step is to copy the contents of cell C13 to the other cells in column C, C14 through C26.

5. Access the Edit menu.

6. Highlight (don't click) the Fill Down option (see fig. 10.7).

   Microsoft Works displays the message Copies topmost cell(s) to rest of selection.

7. Because you want to have all the cells dependent on the entries in column B, this choice is correct. Press Enter to confirm.

   Check to see whether the cells have the correct entries by moving the cell pointer down the C column. The entries in the Formula bar reflect the cell addresses from column B. Cells C23 and C25 display zero values. The zeros are logical because no entries in the B column have been copied to those cells. For cosmetic reasons, you can clear the entries in those two cells, either by using the Del key.

8. The final step in preparing the spreadsheet is to copy the formulas in column C to the rows for the rest of the year. Use the Shift and arrow keys to highlight cells C13 through M26. Open the **Edit** menu and choose the Fill **R**ight option. The entire Expenses section is now dependent on the entries in column B.

FIG. 10.7

Highlighting the
Fill Down option

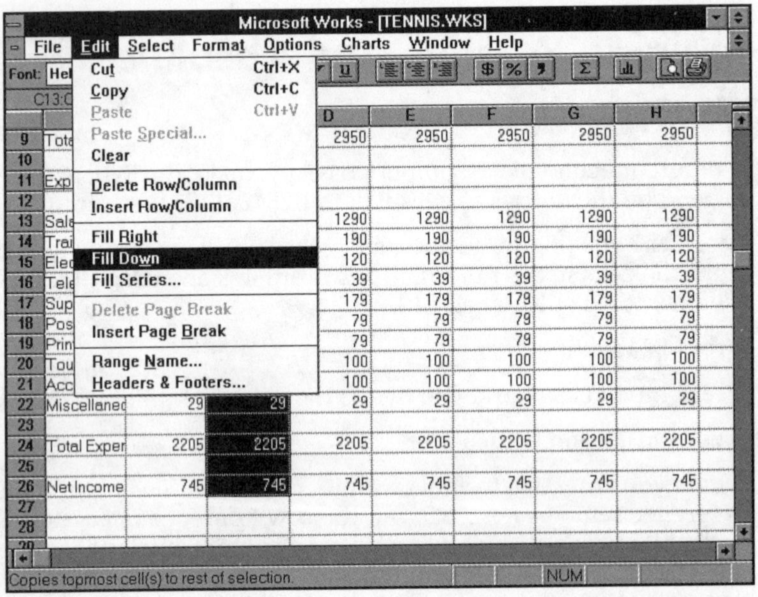

Before making any more changes to the spreadsheet, save it so you can retrieve a copy of the work you have done, just in case you make a mistake. To save the file, access the **File** menu and choose **S**ave.

The TENNIS sample spreadsheet can be used to illustrate more aspects of using absolute and relative entries. Suppose that you want to find out the percentage each expense represents of the total expenses. Figure 10.8 shows the spreadsheet with only columns A and B of the Expenses section. Column B has been formatted to display as currency, and column C has been formatted to display as percentages with no decimals. (For more information on these cell formats, see "Formatting Cells" in this chapter.)

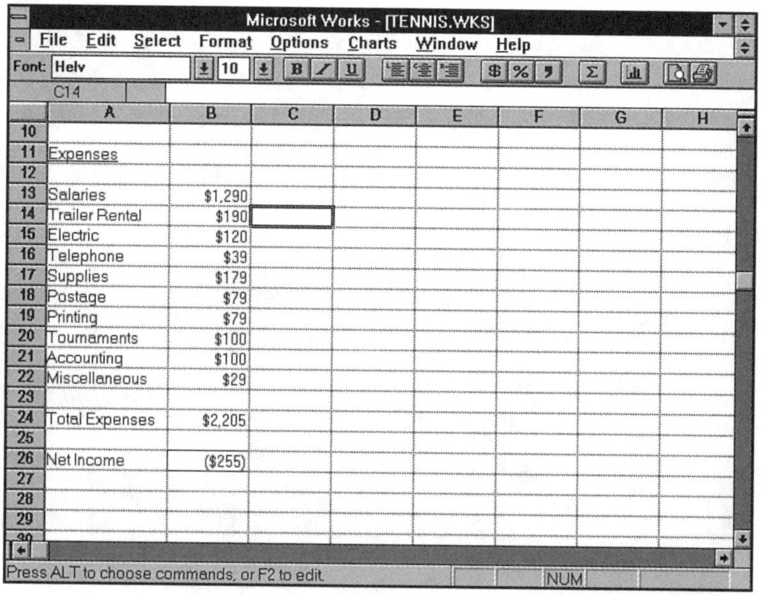

FIG. 10.8

The Expenses section of the TENNIS spread-sheet

To begin your computation, make the following entry in cell C13:

=B13/B24

Next, copy the formula into the range C14..C22 with the **Edit** menu's Fill Down command.

Because the cell references in the formula adjust relative to the formula's position, and because Works cannot divide by blank cells, the ERR message appears in all the copied cells except C15. Cell C15 displays an erroneous value that is the result of Works dividing by the Net Income number in cell B26.

To fix this problem, adjust the formula so that the divisor is absolute. Move the cursor back to cell C13 and press the F2 (Edit) key. Move the insertion point after the slash (/) and type a dollar sign ($). Move the insertion point between the B and the 2 and again type a dollar sign. The formula should read as follows:

=B13/B24

Press Enter and recopy the formula with the Fill Down command. The correct results are shown in figure 10.9.

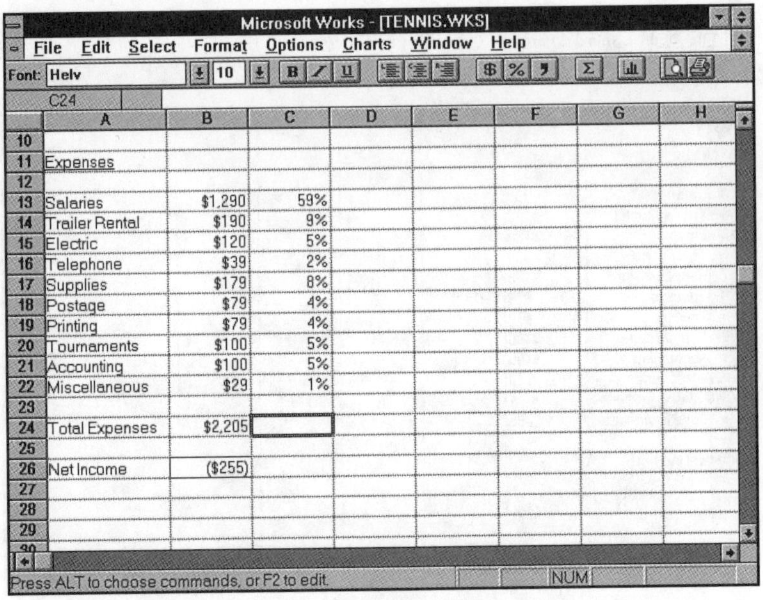

FIG. 10.9

Computing
percentages
with a mixed-
reference
formula

FIG. 10.9

Computing percentages with a mixed-reference formula

Setting Column Width

An entry longer than the width of a cell spills over into the cells to the right if no entries are in the adjoining cells. You cannot read all the labels in column A of the TENNIS spreadsheet, for example, because some of them are longer than the width of the column. You can change a column's width, however, so that all the cell entries fit within the column boundaries.

To change a column's width, follow these steps:

1. Move the cell pointer to any cell in the column whose width you want to change—column A in the TENNIS spreadsheet, for example.

2. Click **Format** or press Alt,T.

3. Select the Column **W**idth option. The Column Width dialog box appears, as shown in figure 10.10.

   The default column width is 10 characters. Try another width and see whether it is enough to hold all the cell contents.

4. In the **W**idth: field, type a number and press Enter.

Figure 10.11 shows the TENNIS spreadsheet with column A widened to 15 characters. All the labels are now entirely visible.

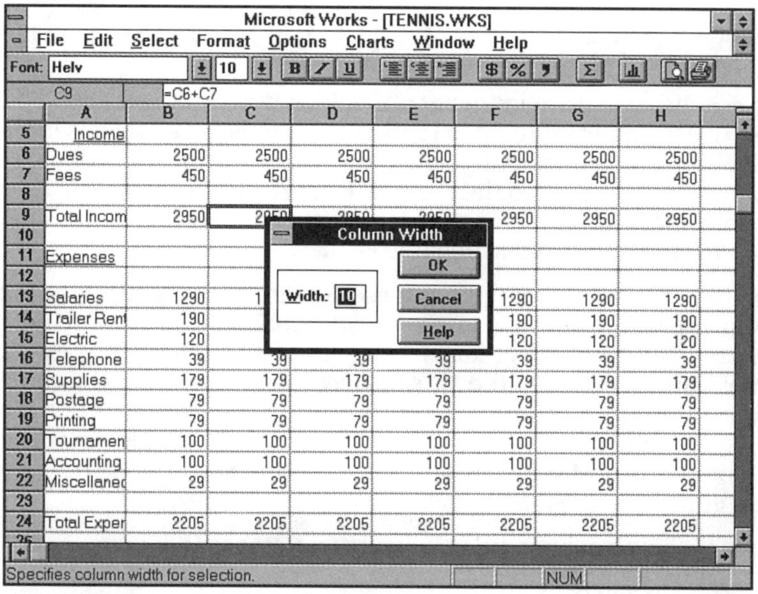

FIG. 10.10

The Column Width dialog box

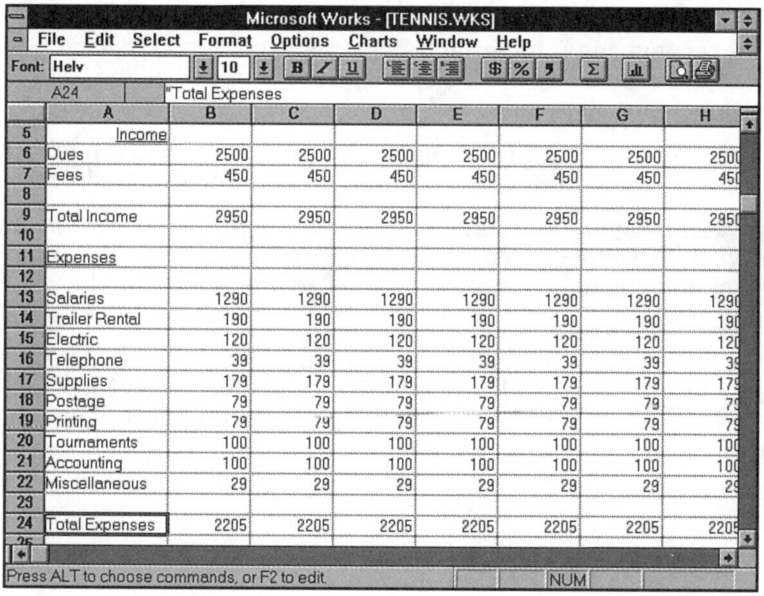

FIG. 10.11

Widening column A

You can make any column wider or narrower on the spreadsheet. Narrowing columns allows more columns to be visible on the display; the action does not affect the contents of the cells.

Freezing Row and Column Titles

Suppose that you learn in the month of October an extraordinary expense will be incurred relating to the item titled Miscellaneous in the TENNIS spreadsheet. Identifying the exact cell you need to edit is not easy because scrolling to the right in the spreadsheet removes the entries in column A—and thus the identification labels—from the screen. The month names also disappear from view.

Microsoft Works enables you to freeze column or row entries, or both, to help you identify cells in large spreadsheets. You can freeze the titles so that they always remain visible no matter where the cell pointer happens to be in the spreadsheet. After you freeze the row and column titles for the month names and the label entries for the Income and Expense lines in the TENNIS spreadsheet, for example, you easily can modify a cell with the visual assurance that indeed it is the correct cell to edit.

To freeze row or column titles, follow these steps:

1. Move to cell B5.

2. Access the **O**ptions menu. Notice that the menu contains a Freeze Titles option. The location of the cell pointer when you choose this command is important. When selected, this command freezes all the columns to the left of the cell pointer and all the rows above the cell pointer.

3. Choose the Freeze Titles option. With the cell pointer in B6 of the sample worksheet, column A and rows 1 through 5 are frozen.

Figure 10.12 displays the screen as it looks when you move to the intersection of the October column and the Miscellaneous row when the title row and column are frozen. As you can see, cell K22 is the cell you need to edit.

To eliminate frozen titles and return the spreadsheet display to its original form, access the **O**ptions menu again. The Freeze **T**itles option on the menu has a checkmark preceding it. Selecting the option again removes the checkmark and unfreezes the rows and columns.

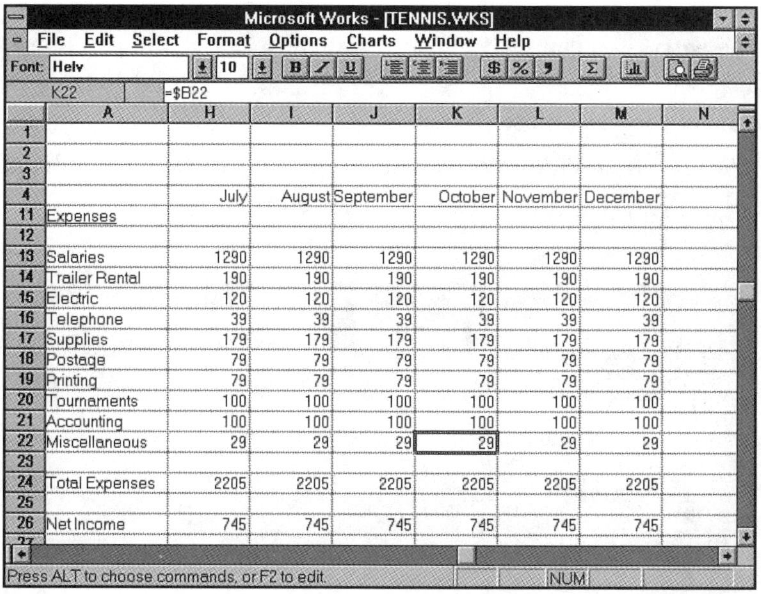

FIG. 10.12

Freezing a row
and a column of
the spreadsheet

Splitting the Spreadsheet Window

When you have finished setting up a spreadsheet in terms of the numbers, labels, and formulas, you can begin entering numbers or modifying formulas throughout the spreadsheet to see the effects of changes.

One of the problems with spreadsheets is that they are larger than the computer's screen display. Consequently, when you make changes in the numbers that affect important calculations, you may not be able to see the results without moving the cell pointer to the cell that contains the modified result.

If you change the entry in cell G6, the dues income for June, for example, the effect on the total income is displayed in cell G9, but the effect on the net income is not visible unless you move to cell G26. Seeing both cells at the same time would be better.

Remember that the display is electronic and therefore can be manipulated according to your needs. Microsoft Works enables you to split the screen display into windows; each window can display the same or different areas of a spreadsheet. Think of these displays as window panes overlaid on a single large window, the spreadsheet as a whole.

To see both the Income section of the TENNIS spreadsheet and the Net Income entry, you can split the spreadsheet window into two panes. Follow these steps to split the spreadsheet window:

1. Move the cell pointer to cell B9.

2. Access the **W**indow menu (see fig. 10.13). The bottom of the menu displays the name of the current window next to the number **1** (TENNIS.WKS in this example).

The **W**indow menu

3. Highlight the **S**plit command. At the bottom of the screen, Microsoft Works describes this command, which creates individual window panes to display the different parts of the spreadsheet file.

   When you select the **S**plit command, Works responds with two additional double lines on-screen: one for a vertical split and one for a horizontal split.

4. If you want to create four windows on the spreadsheet, press Enter to execute the command. Use the arrow keys to move the split lines to the desired location, and press Enter.

5. If you want to create only two windows, eliminate one of the split lines by positioning the mouse pointer on the line and dragging it off the screen. Remove the vertical split line if you want to create two horizontal windows, or remove the horizontal split line if you want to create two vertical windows.

For the TENNIS example, eliminate the vertical split line and then click the horizontal line and drag it to row 10 (see fig. 10.14). Press enter.

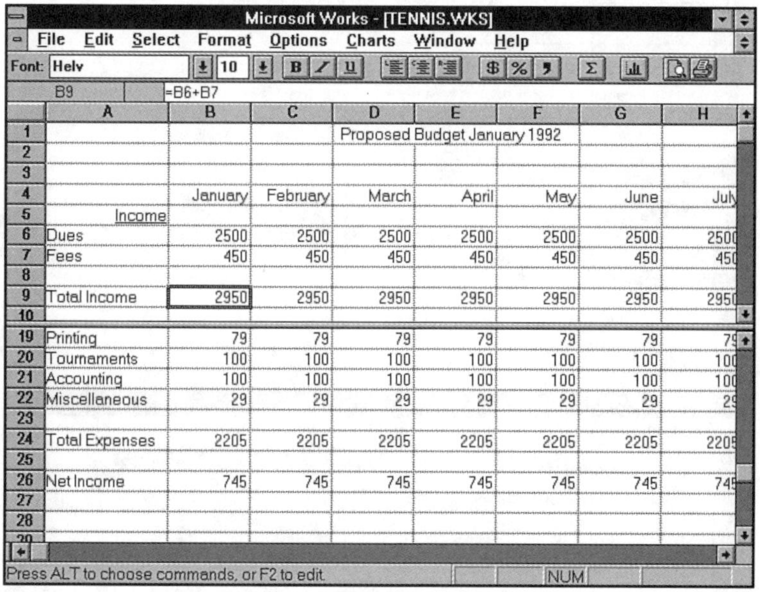

FIG. 10.14

Splitting the spreadsheet window horizontally

Moving between Split Windows

You move from one split window to another by moving the mouse pointer and clicking or by pressing the F6 key. In your TENNIS spreadsheet, press F6 to move to the bottom window. Then scroll the screen up by pressing the down-arrow key so that the Total Expenses and Net Income lines are the only rows displayed (see fig. 10.15).

Press F6 again to move the cell pointer to the top window. With the screen split, you easily can see the results of any change made in the income figures. For example, what effect will a change in the dues income entered in the month of January have on net income? The current January dues income is $2,500, producing a net income of $745 dollars per month. Enter **1500** in cell B6 to see what happens when dues drop off to a total of $1,500 per month. As you might expect, the picture changes dramatically for the club. Net income becomes a negative number, –255 (see fig. 10.16).

FIG. 10.15

Scrolling
the bottom
window up

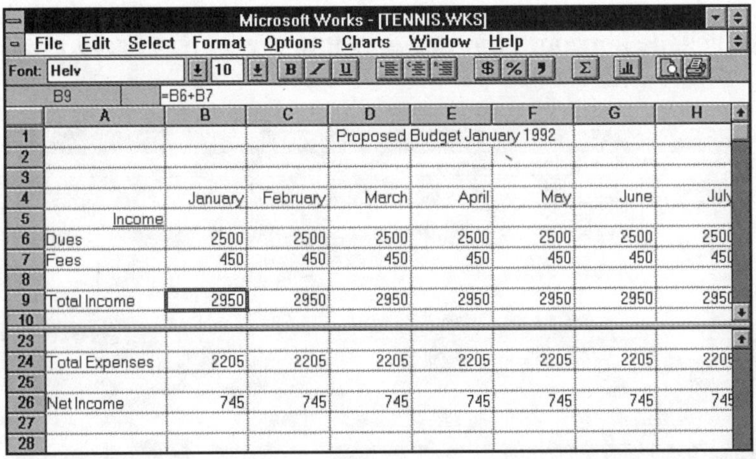

FIG. 10.16

Changing a
number in the top
window and
viewing the
resulting change
in the bottom
window

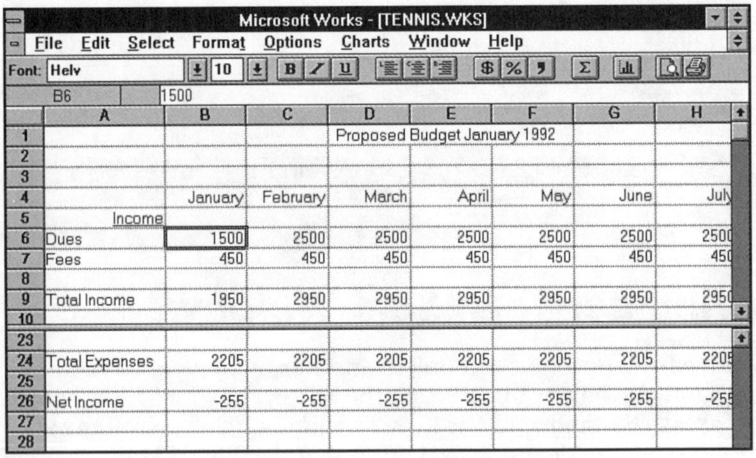

This example uses the split window technique to show how you can see the net effect of a change on the income side of the club. In a more complex business situation, the window pane allows for simultaneous viewing of information on changes in pricing, allocation of profits, increases in expenditures, and other variations. By viewing the different parts of the spreadsheet through a window pane, you can evaluate a proposed change immediately.

Consider a vertical split of the screen. In figure 10.17, the screen has been split vertically so that you can look at the label entries for each row while creating a Totals column for the TENNIS budget.

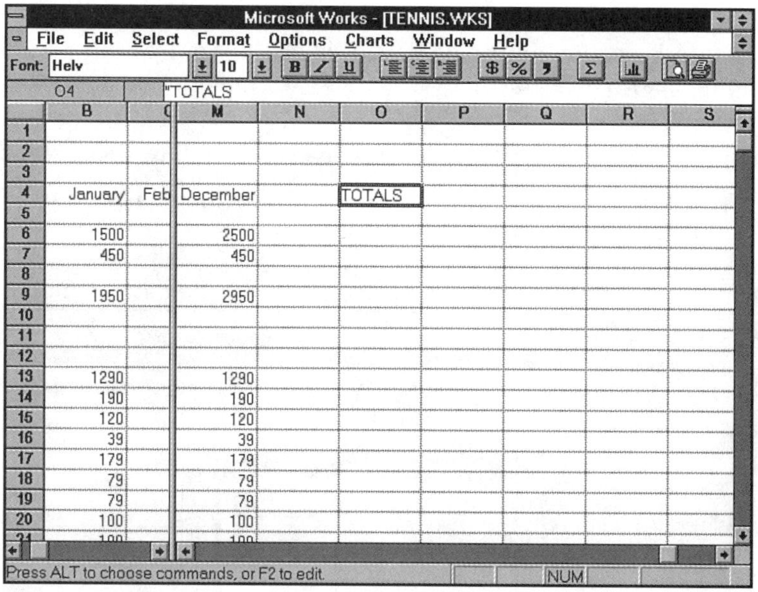

FIG. 10.17

Splitting the window vertically

Removing a Screen Split

To remove a screen split and restore the display to a single window, follow these steps:

1. Access the **Window** menu.

2. Select the **S**plit command.

3. Use the arrow keys or the mouse to move the gray split line off the edges of the screen.

4. Press Enter, and the screen is restored to normal display.

Using the F5 (GoTo) Function Key

Many times as you are working in a spreadsheet you need to go back and forth between different cells. If you make a note of which cells you need to travel to, you can speed the journey by using F5, the GoTo key.

With F5, you can move the cell pointer to named ranges of cells (see this chapter's section on "Using Range Names" for more information on named ranges). You also can access the GoTo function by using the **S**elect menu's **G**o To... command.

To move to another location in your spreadsheet, follow these steps:

1. Press F5 or choose **G**o To... from the **S**elect menu. Figure 10.18 shows the Go To dialog box that appears.

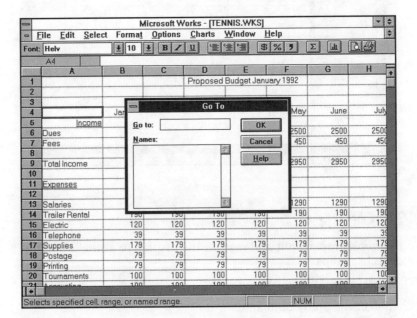

FIG. 10.18

The Go To dialog box

2. In the **G**o To: field, type the cell address or range name of your destination. Enter the cell address as you enter cell addresses in a formula: A1, B2, and so on. The **N**ames: field lists names of ranges already created. You also can use the mouse to click and drag the scroll box on the right side of the list of range names to select the range.

3. Press Enter or click OK.

Immediately, Works closes the dialog box and moves the cell pointer to the designated cell address.

Formatting Spreadsheets

After you finish the hard work of entering all your labels, numbers, and formulas into a spreadsheet, you can add formats to the values and labels to add variety, highlight critical values, and add a real-world look to the numbers and labels.

Formatting Cells

To this point in building the TENNIS spreadsheet, you have not formatted any numbers to reflect the kinds of values they represent. If you don't specify a format, Microsoft Works displays numbers in a default format called General, which is plain with no symbols of any kind. Other formats are available on the Format menu (see fig. 10.19).

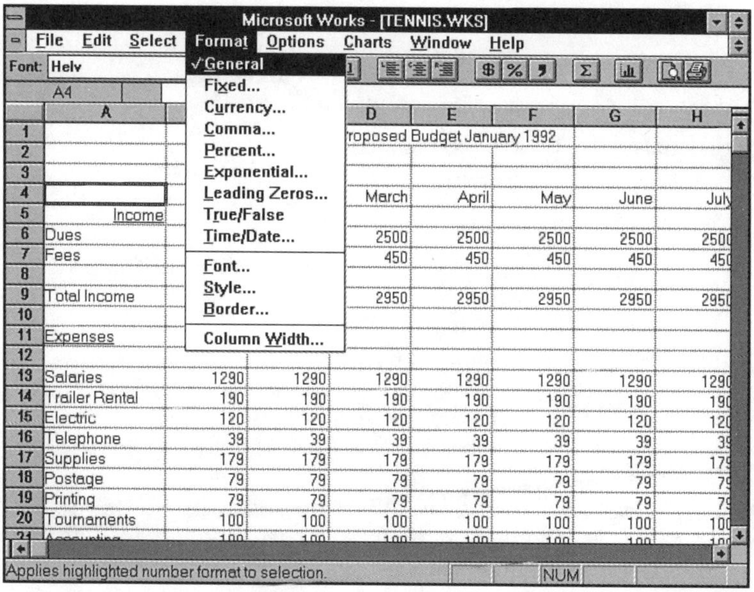

FIG. 10.19

The Format menu

Table 10.1 lists the formats and describes their effects. Figure 10.20 demonstrates how the different formats appear in the spreadsheet.

Table 10.1 Using the Format Menu To Format Cells

Option	Effect
General	Formats numbers as precisely as possible: 466, 4.66 or 4.66E+6.
Fixed	Formats numbers to the number of decimal places you specify. If you specify three places, a number like 456.7896 becomes 456.790. Any negative numbers are displayed with a leading minus (–) sign.
Currency	Formats numbers to include a leading dollar sign and a comma every three places to the left of the decimal point.
Comma	Formats numbers by inserting a comma every three places. Negative numbers are displayed in parentheses.
Percent	Formats numbers so that they are displayed with a trailing percent sign and the decimal place moved two positions to the right. A number such as .0567 becomes 5.67%.
Exponential	Displays numbers in scientific notation. 9999999 displays as 9.99E+06. An exponent has a range of ±300. Negative numbers are displayed with a leading minus (–) sign.
True/False	Formats cells to display either TRUE or FALSE. All numbers are displayed as TRUE. Cells with zero entries are displayed as FALSE.
Time/Date	Formats cells to display entries as a time or date in the format you specify (see "Entering Dates and Time" for more information).

In the TENNIS spreadsheet, all numbers currently are in the **General** format. A better way to display them is in the **Currency** format. To change a cell format, follow these steps:

1. Select the cells to be reformatted. Microsoft Works has a command that selects every cell in the spreadsheet. To select all the cells, open the **Select** menu (see fig. 10.21) and choose the **All** option. Selecting **All** changes the screen display, indicating that the entire screen has been selected. On a color monitor, the selected range becomes a different color.

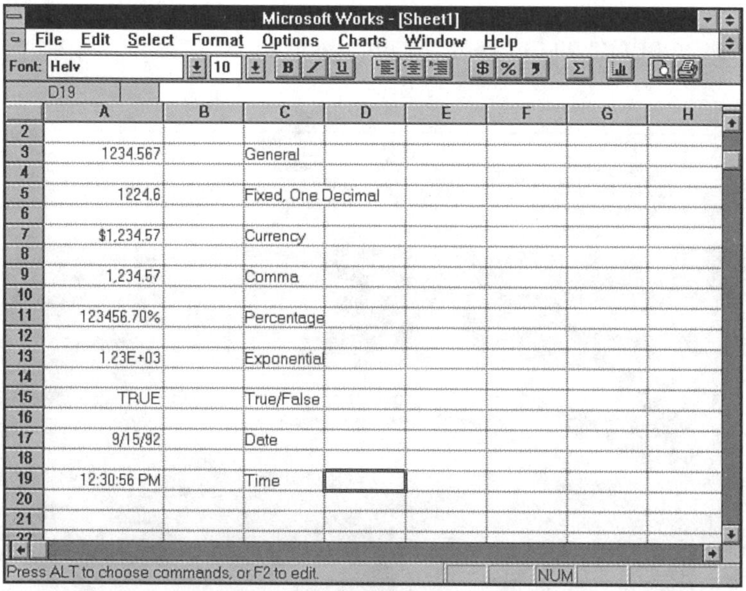

FIG. 10.20

The results of
formatting cells

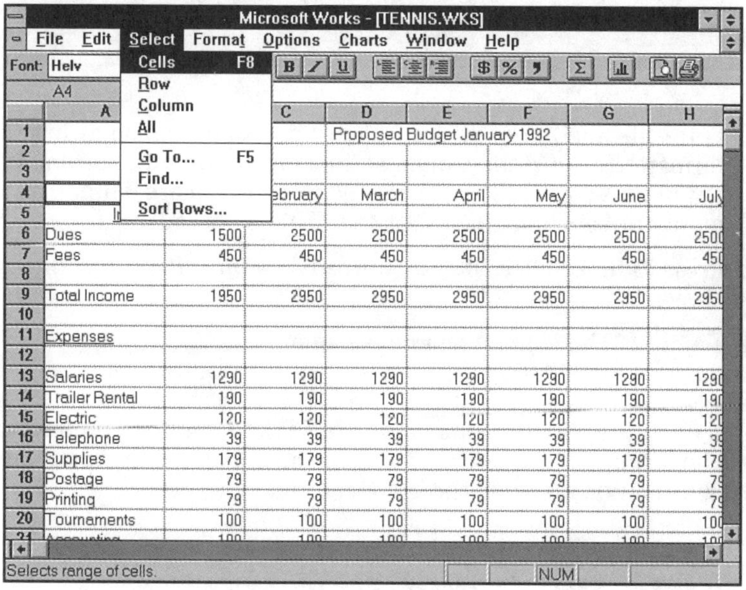

FIG. 10.21

The **S**elect menu

To select the entire spreadsheet with a mouse, click the box in the upper-left corner of the spreadsheet border.

2. Access the Forma**t** menu.

3. Select the **Currency** option. The Currency dialog box appears, prompting you for a specific number of decimal places to display (see fig. 10.22).

FIG. 10.22

The Currency
dialog box

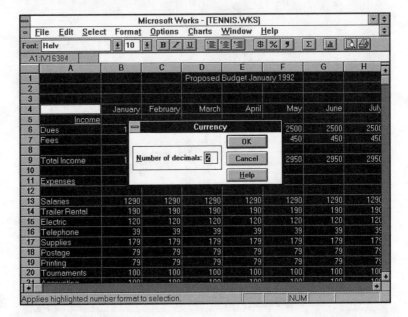

4. Enter the number of decimal places you want to display in cells formatted as currency. In most financial reports, the decimals are not necessary for the sake of precision. Therefore, enter 0 as the number of decimal places for the TENNIS spreadsheet.

5. Press Enter or click OK. The spreadsheet now looks like the one shown in figure 10.23.

Wait a minute! The column headings naming the months have changed to numbers with dollar signs. The reason is that dates are considered numbers by Works. To rectify this problem, select the range of cells B4:M4, open the Format menu, and choose the Time/Date option to reset the format of those cells to Month Only. (See the next section for more information on using the Time and Date formats.)

Entering Dates and Time

You have several ways to use date and time entries. They are helpful for creating labels, making calculations, time-stamping a spreadsheet, or separating into time segments the data you enter into the spreadsheet. Works accepts time and date in the specific formats described in table 10.2.

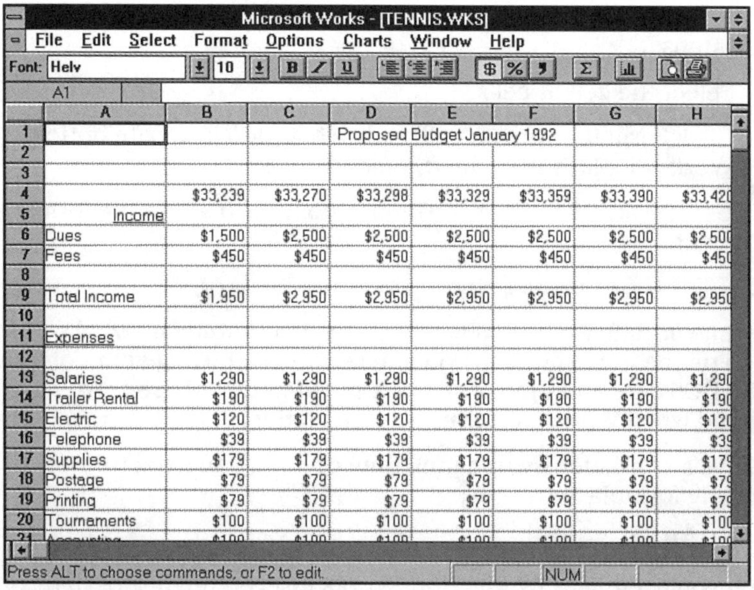

FIG. 10.23

Viewing the TENNIS spreadsheet cells in the Currency format

Table 10.2 Using Works Date and Time Formats

Long Date Format	Example
Month, Day, Year	July 17, 1992
Month, Year	July, 1992
Month, Day	July 17
Month Only	July

Short Date Format	Example
Month, Day, Year	07/17/92
Month, Year	07/92
Month, Day	07/17

24-Hour Time Format	Example
Hour, Minute, Second	10:15:00
Hour, Minute	10:15

12-Hour Time Format	Example
Hour, Minute, Second	3:30:00PM
Hour, Minute	3:30PM

To format a cell or range of cells for specific times and dates, follow these steps:

1. Select the cell or cells.

2. Click Format or press Alt,T and select the Time/Date option. Works displays the Time/Date dialog box.

3. Use the arrow keys or the mouse pointer to select the format you want.

4. Click OK or press Enter.

The time or date is entered based on the computer's internal clock or based on the date and time you entered when starting your computer at the DOS date and time prompts. Unfortunately, these entries are not updated when Works performs a recalculation.

To have a continuously updating time or date, you need to enter the following formula in the cell:

=NOW()

When you use the NOW function, Works inserts the time or date, depending on how you have formatted the cell with the Format Time/Date option. The cell entry is updated to the current time or date as you recalculate the spreadsheet.

Adding Cell Borders

A formatting feature that financial spreadsheets often include is a line to separate the Income section from the Expense section. Works goes a step further in that you can add a special border to cells to which you want to draw attention. If you want to emphasize the Net Income row of the TENNIS spreadsheet, for example, you can add a heavier border around cells B26 to D26. Follow these steps to add a border around certain cells:

1. Select the cells you want to border—B26 through M26 in the example.

2. Open the Format menu.

3. Choose the Border option.

4. In the Border dialog box, choose Outline.

5. Press Enter or click OK.

6. Click a different part of the spreadsheet to remove the highlighting and see the effect of the new border (see fig. 10.24).

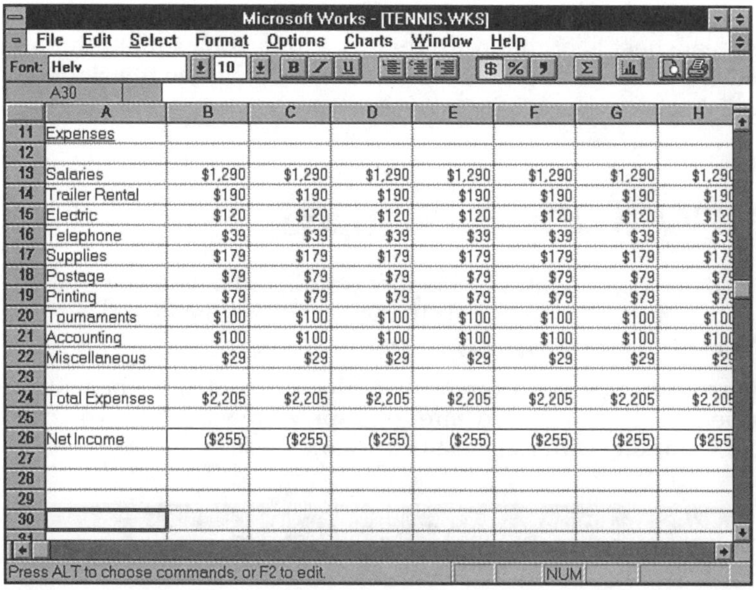

FIG. 10.24

Adding a border
around a group
of cells

The default setting in Works is to display gridlines around each of the
cells. Figure 10.24 shows the screen without gridlines to better demon-
strate the outline option. To turn gridlines off, click **O**ptions and select
the Show Gridlines option.

> When you print the spreadsheet, the borders are most effective if
> you turn off the gridlines. To turn off the gridlines, open the File
> menu, choose Page Setup & Margins, and make sure that Print
> Gridlines is set to off (unchecked).

T I P

Before going to the next section and the next example, save and close
your TENNIS spreadsheet.

Changing Fonts

Another option on the Format menu is Font. *Fonts* are type styles that
Microsoft Works can send to your printer. Whether your printer can
print a certain font is a separate issue. Microsoft Works checks with the
type of printer you have installed and displays the types of fonts your
printer is capable of printing.

A selected font applies to the entire spreadsheet file. Every character in the spreadsheet is printed with the same font; you cannot print a selected cell or range of cells in a font different from the remainder of the spreadsheet.

Using Range Names

You can use range names to simplify your spreadsheet work. A *range name* identifies a group of cells that normally is considered a single unit for use in formulas, copying, or searching.

In figure 10.25, you see a spreadsheet that calculates the payment for a specified mortgage rate. To enter this spreadsheet so that you can practice working with range names, follow these steps:

FIG. 10.25

A new sample spreadsheet

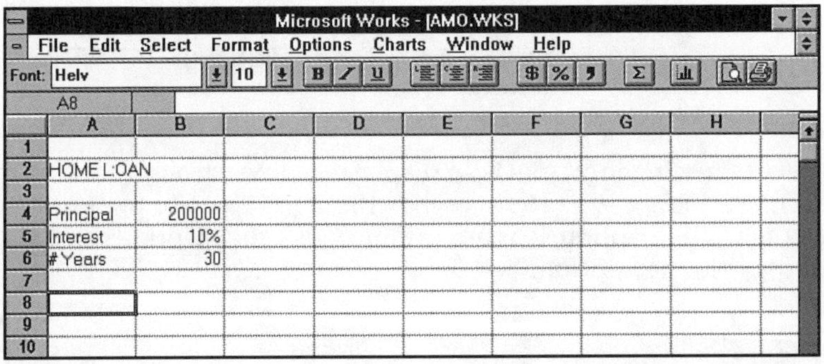

1. Access the **File** menu.

2. Select Create New File.

3. In cell A2, enter the following title:

   HOME LOAN

4. In cell A4, enter the following label:

   Principal

5. In cell A5, enter the following label:

   Interest

6. In cell A6, enter the following label:

   # Years

7. Across from the labels, enter the values **200000** for Principal, **10%** for Interest, and **30** for # Years. Because Works understands the percent sign following the number 10, the program formats the cell as a percentage.

Naming Ranges

The next step is to connect the labels with the corresponding values— name the ranges. Follow this procedure:

1. Move the cell pointer to B4.

2. Access the **Edit** menu.

3. Choose the Range **Name**... command. The Range Name dialog box appears (see fig. 10.26).

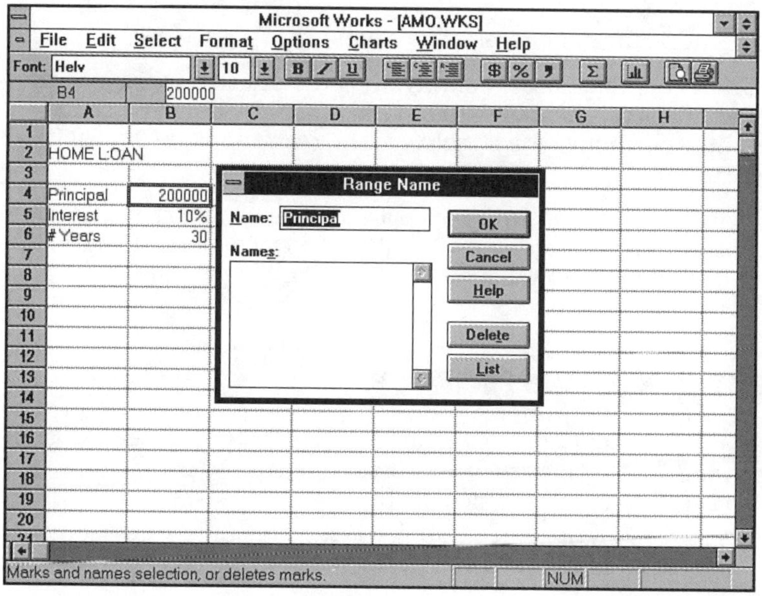

FIG. 10.26

The Range Name dialog box

Because the cell pointer is in cell B4, Microsoft Works assumes that range B4 is the range to use. The label Principal is the default range name because when you use the Range **Name**... command, Microsoft Works assumes that you want to name the selected range with the text in the cell in which the cell pointer is positioned, the text in the cell directly to the left of the cell pointer's location (as in this case), or the text directly above the cell pointer's location. The assumed range name is displayed in the **Name:** field of the Range Name dialog box. (Keep in mind that the length of any range name cannot exceed 15 characters.)

4. Press Enter or click OK. Cell B4 is now a range named Principal.

For this example spreadsheet, you can repeat the Range Name procedure with the Interest and # Years labels so that cell B5 is named Interest and cell B6 is named # Years.

You can use named ranges in a formula. Move the cell pointer to cell A8 in the new sample worksheet, for example, and enter a formula for computing the monthly loan payment. Instead of entering cell addresses, use the range names in the formula. Do not leave any spaces between the arguments of the formula unless the spaces are part of the range names; use only commas as separators. The following formula computes the monthly payment based on the data entered in the three named ranges:

=PMT(Principal,Interest/12,# Years*12)

The interest is calculated monthly, thus the division by 12, and the number of years is also figured monthly (30*12=360). If you enter everything correctly, you should see the result 1755.1431 displayed in cell A8.

Any cell or contiguous group of cells can be a named range. Later in this chapter, in the section on "Printing a Spreadsheet," you treat the entire spreadsheet as a named range to simplify printing.

Listing Range Names

After you have created many range names in a spreadsheet, a list of those range names may be useful for reference and for creating formulas. To list all the range names, follow these steps:

1. Move the cell pointer to any area of the spreadsheet where you want the upper-left corner of the list to begin.

2. Access the Edit menu.

3. Choose the Range Name... command.

4. In the Range Name dialog box, choose the List button or press Alt,L.

The range names are displayed beginning in the cell pointer's position and extending down in the spreadsheet. To erase, press Alt,E,C or click **Edit** and select **Clear**.

Changing and Reassigning Range Names

If you want to change the cell reference for a named range, follow these steps:

1. Click **Edit** and select the Range Name... command.

2. Click the range name you want to rename or press Alt,S to move the highlight to the Name**s** box. Use the arrow keys to highlight the name and enter it into the **Name** box.

3. Click on the name in the **Name** box or press Alt,N.

4. Type in the new name and press Enter, or click OK.

The new range name is in effect. However, Works retains the old name, so you must reopen the **Edit, Range Name** dialog box and delete the old range name. Use the mouse pointer to select the name or press Alt,S to move the highlight to the Name**s** box and then select the old range name. Press Alt,T or click Delete to erase the old name.

If you want to change the cell reference for a named range, follow these steps:

1. Select the new range.

2. Access the **Edit** menu and select Range Name.

3. In the **Names:** field, press Alt,S and press the down-arrow key until the named range you want to modify is displayed in the **Name:** field.

4. Press Enter or click OK to create the new cell reference.

5. Press Enter or click OK.

Hiding and Unhiding Columns

In some situations in which spreadsheets are to be distributed to a number of people, you may want to hide some information from certain individuals. You can hide information by setting to 0 the width of the column or columns that contain the information. Follow these steps:

1. Place the cell pointer in the single column you want to hide or, with the Shift key and the arrow keys, select the multiple columns you want to hide.

248

2. Access the Format menu.

3. Choose the Column **W**idth option.

4. In the Column Width dialog box, press 0 and Enter.

The column is now hidden. To redisplay a hidden column, first use the GoTo key, F5, to access a cell in the column. When the column address is displayed in the upper-left corner of the screen, access the Format menu, choose the Column **W**idth option, and change the width to a nonzero setting.

Protecting Cell Contents

After working diligently on a spreadsheet, you do not want to alter a critical formula inadvertently and destroy all your work. You can take two steps to prevent this kind of mistake. First, make a copy of the spreadsheet and save it on a separate disk. Second, lock the critical cells so that neither you nor anyone else can ruin the labor mistakenly.

In the loan amortization example, you can lock the cells containing the labels to avoid erasing the range names accidentally. Or you can lock the entire spreadsheet.

Locking an Entire Spreadsheet

To lock all the cells in a spreadsheet, follow these steps:

1. Access the **O**ptions menu.

2. Select the **P**rotect Data command. This command is a toggle; selecting it again turns off the protection. A check mark precedes the command when it is activated.

All cells in the spreadsheet are now protected. Move the cursor to a cell and press F2 to attempt to make an edit. Erase a few characters and press Enter. Microsoft Works displays a dialog box, letting you know that you cannot change locked cells.

Unlocking Cells

Unlocking cells requires that you reverse the process of locking. You may, for example, want someone else to enter data into a spreadsheet but not be able to alter the formulas or labels. The loan spreadsheet is a good example. Anyone can be allowed access to the cells that determine the mortgage payment: B4 for the principal amount, B5 for the interest rate, and B6 for the term.

To unlock an entire spreadsheet, take the following steps:

1. Open the **O**ptions menu. If your spreadsheet is locked, a check mark appears next to the **P**rotect Data option.

2. Select **P**rotect Data to turn off the locking. The check mark disappears, and the spreadsheet is unlocked.

At this point, if you want only specific cells unlocked, continue the procedure (after unlocking the entire spreadsheet) by following these steps:

1. In the spreadsheet, select the cell or cells that you want to remain unlocked after you turn the **P**rotect Data command back on.

2. With the cell or cells selected, open the Forma**t** menu.

3. Select the **S**tyle command. The Style dialog box appears (see fig. 10.27).

4. Press Alt,K to erase the X in front of the Loc**k**ed option.

5. Press Enter or click OK.

6. Reopen the **O**ptions menu.

7. Select the **P**rotect Data command.

The cells you have selected are unlocked, but the remaining cells in the spreadsheet are again locked.

FIG. 10.27

The Style dialog box

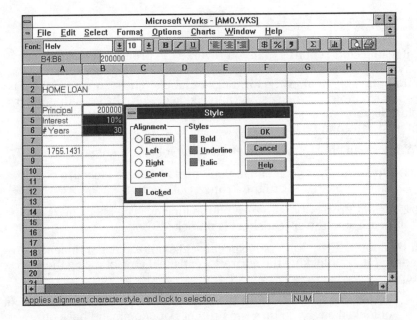

Use the Locked option to protect the contents of cells vital to correct spreadsheet results.

Showing the Spreadsheet Formulas

Unfortunately, many spreadsheet users have the tendency to believe whatever the spreadsheet produces. As you build more complex spreadsheets, however, auditing your formula trails is a good idea. A small error when inserting a formula can lead to gross errors later, because one formula result builds on another.

One method of auditing is to change the spreadsheet display to show only the formulas rather than the results of the calculations. You then can analyze your formulas to make sure that your spreadsheet is doing what you want it to do. To reveal the formulas, access the **O**ptions menu and select the Show **F**ormulas option. Figure 10.28 shows the TENNIS spreadsheet with the formulas displayed.

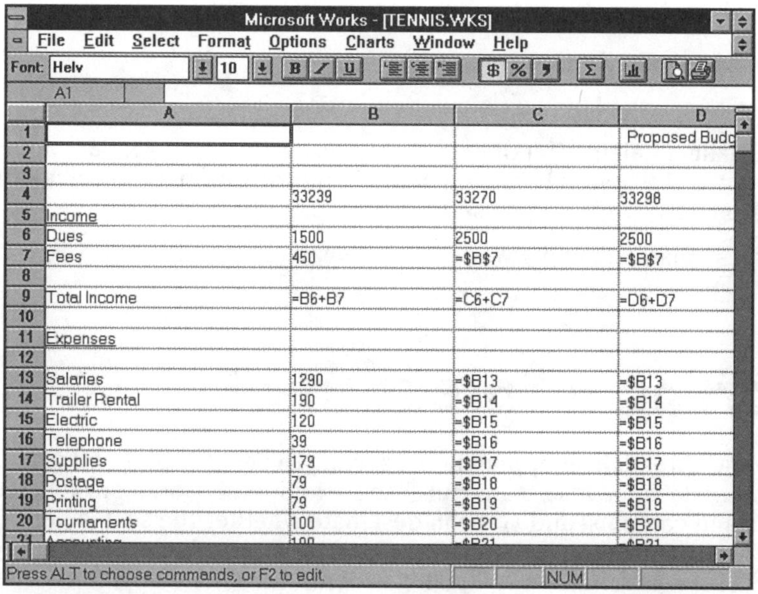

FIG. 10.28

Showing the
formulas

Of particular interest in this example are the entries in row 4. Those cells contain the names of the months, but Works displays values rather than the text entries because the month names are serial dates. Remember, when you inserted the names of the months, you used the Fill Series command to complete the row. If you had entered the name of the month with a specific year included, such as January 1980, the entry would have remained a text entry.

Manual versus Automatic Recalculation

Works has the capability of recalculating your formulas whenever a change is made in the spreadsheet. You can turn off this automatic recalculation, however, so that the recalculation is performed only when you specify. Turning off recalculation can be helpful if your spreadsheet gets so large that a recalculation takes a long time or if you want to make several changes before the recalculation takes place. When you're in this mode, the CALC message appears on the status line.

To turn off the automatic recalculation, follow these steps:

1. Access the **O**ptions menu.

2. Choose the **M**anual Calculation option.

The **M**anual Calculation option is a toggle switch. A checkmark appears in front of the option in manual mode. To turn automatic recalculation back on, repeat the steps used to turn it off.

To recalculate manually when the automatic recalculation is off, press F9.

Sorting a Spreadsheet

In some spreadsheet applications, sorting the entries alphabetically or by numeric value may be useful. The sort function works on selected rows and columns, and you can designate whether the sort is performed in ascending order (1, 2, 3... or A, B, C...) or in descending order (9, 8, 7... or Z, Y, X...). In ascending order, if the column contains numbers and text, the text comes before the numbers. In descending order, text follows the numbers.

When sorting, Works adjusts the relative references but not the absolute ones. Use caution whenever formulas are included in the sorted material.

T I P   Before performing a sort on any spreadsheet, make a copy of the spreadsheet under a unique name. If you complete a sort and are not happy with the results, you still have a copy that reflects the spreadsheet's condition before the sort.

Figure 10.29 shows a spreadsheet used for performing payroll calculations. Notice that the first column of the spreadsheet gives a unique number to each record. If you forget to make a copy of a spreadsheet before you sort the contents, a column such as this one provides a measure of protection and enables you to re-sort a list to its original order based on the numbers in the column.

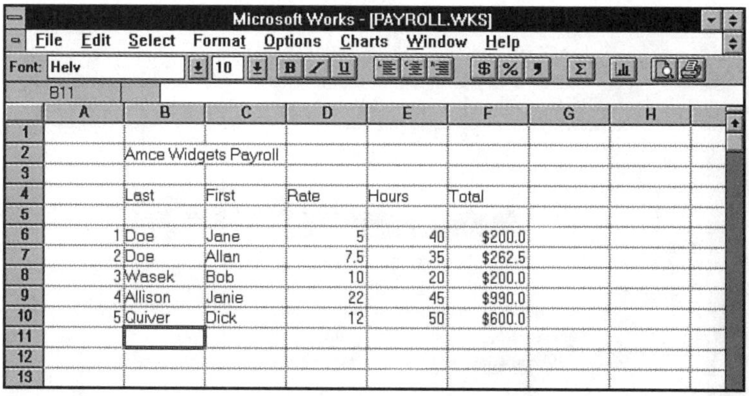

FIG. 10.29

A sample payroll spreadsheet

Make a copy of this spreadsheet if you want to follow the sorting examples in this section. The only formula is in column F. A formula computing the Rate times the Hours (=D6*E6) is copied down the column.

Because the rates of pay and the number of hours worked vary, even a small payroll can be difficult to sort. First you might want to do a simple alphabetical sort based on the employees' last names.

To perform a sort, do the following:

1. With the Shift and down-arrow keys, highlight the range you want to sort. You always must select a minimum of two cells to begin a sort. To sort the employees' last names in the payroll spreadsheet, for example, highlight the range B6..B10.

2. Access the Select menu.

3. Choose the Sort Rows option. The Sort Rows dialog box appears (see fig. 10.30).

   With the Works sort function, you can sort on three columns. In the example, you have highlighted only a single column of cells: column B is listed in the 1st Column field of the Sort Rows dialog box. By default, Works selects Ascend A, ascending sort order.

4. Press Enter or click OK or choose Descend B to accept ascending order. Figure 10.31 shows the names sorted in ascending order.

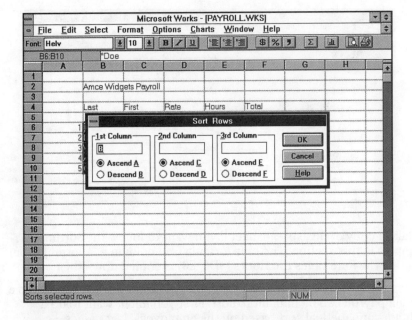

FIG. 10.30

The Sort Rows
dialog box

FIG. 10.31

The spreadsheet
after you have
sorted on the first
column

You can add another sort column that requires Works to break a tie.
Because records for Jane and Allan Doe have the same last name, you
can sort the column of first names, too, to arrange the first names in
alphabetical order within the first sort's order. To sort a second column, do the following:

1. Select the second column to be sorted—cells B6..C10 in this
   example.

2. Open the **S**elect menu.

3. Select **S**ort Rows.

4. Press Alt,2 to move the cursor to the **2nd** Column field.

5. Press the letter of the column you want to sort. To sort column C, which contains the first names in the example spreadsheet, press C.

6. The default sort order is Ascend **C**. Press Enter or click OK or choose Descend D to accept that setting.

Figure 10.32 shows the results of the second sort on the sample spreadsheet. As you can see, Jane Doe and Allan Doe have switched spots in the sort because the A in Allan comes before the J in Jane.

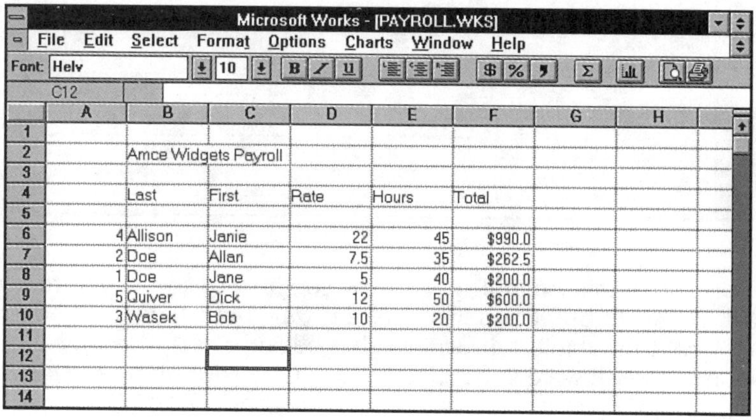

FIG. 10.32

The results of sorting the second and first columns in ascending order

Suppose that you want to sort on a descending scale the total dollars earned (as reflected in column F) and the rate of pay (as listed in column D). Because the two columns are not juxtaposed, you must use the sort function a little differently. Follow these steps:

1. Select the first range of cells to be sorted—column F, F6..F10, in this example.

2. Access the **Select** menu.

3. Select **Sort Rows**.

4. In the Sort Rows dialog box, press Alt,B to change the order of the sort in the **1st** Column field to Descend **B**.

5. Press Alt,2 to access the **2nd** Column field.

6. Press the letter of the second column on which you want Works to sort. For this example, you want to sort column D because it contains the rate of pay, so press D.

7. Change the setting to **Descend** by pressing Alt,D.

8. Press Enter or click OK.

The sorted spreadsheet is shown in figure 10.33.

	A	B	C	D	E	F	G	H
1								
2		Amce Widgets Payroll						
3								
4		Last	First	Rate	Hours	Total		
5								
6	4	Allison	Janie	22	45	$990.0		
7	5	Quiver	Dick	12	50	$600.0		
8	2	Doe	Allan	7.5	35	$262.5		
9	3	Wasek	Bob	10	20	$200.0		
10	1	Doe	Jane	5	40	$200.0		
11								
12								
13								
14								

The purpose of this example is to show you how to sort separated columns and how to break ties in a different way. Both Jane Doe and Bob Wasek have the same total earnings, but because of the second sort on rate of pay, they have distinct positions in the order of the sorted file.

Summing a Series of Numbers with the Tool Bar

One of the buttons on the Tool bar is the mathematical SUM symbol. When you have entered a series of numbers that you want summed, either in a row or a column, you can position the cell pointer in any blank cell beneath or to the right (or left) of the series and then click this SUM button. The button invokes a *macro*, a programmed series of keystrokes, that inserts the equal sign, the SUM function, and an open parenthesis; moves the highlight to the top or the end of the series; and finally enters a close parenthesis. If you press Enter, the SUM formula is inserted into the blank cell.

Using the payroll spreadsheet as an example, follow these steps to enter a sum at the bottom of the Total column:

1. Move the cursor to cell F12.

2. Click the SUM button. In an instant the formula is created (fig. 10.34).

3. Press Enter to finish the entry.

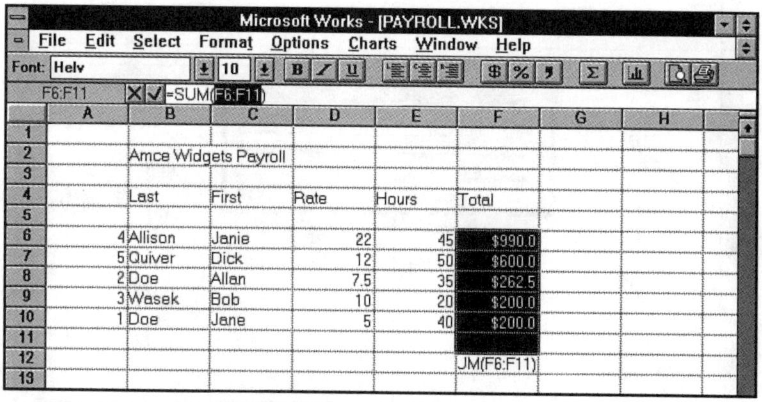

FIG. 10.34

Using the Tool bar to enter a SUM formula

Searching Cells

Previously in this chapter, you learned how a sort can rearrange your lists of entries into more usable forms. In some cases, however, even a sort cannot be much help. Suppose, for example, that you have several hundred employees or formulas included in a large spreadsheet. To find a certain employee or a specific formula, you need to use the Find option. Even if you need to find a certain employee but aren't sure of the exact spelling of the employee's name, you can use the Find option with wild cards to assist your search.

Follow these steps to search for a particular entry in your spreadsheet:

1. Access the **Select** menu.

2. Choose the **Find** option. The Find dialog box appears (see fig. 10.35).

3. In the Find What: field, type the entry you want to find. If you want to find an employee named Jane or Janie in the sample payroll database, for example, type **Jan?** in the Find What: field. The question mark acts as the wild card and asks Works to find any entry that begins with the specific letters *Jan* and ends with any other letter.

FIG. 10.35

The Find dialog
box

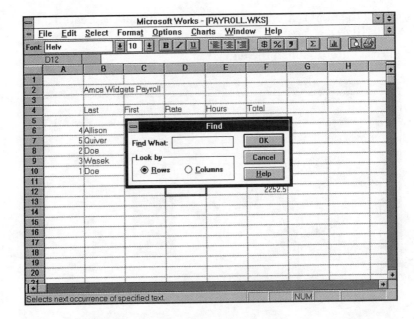

4. Direct Works to search row by row or column by column. If you choose **C**olumns in the Look By box, the search commences in column A and goes across. If you choose **R**ows, the search starts in row 1 and goes down.

5. Press Enter or click OK to begin the search. Works stops on the first entry that makes a match—Janie Allison in the example.

6. Press F7 to move to each subsequent match. In the example, pressing F7 once moves the cell pointer to Janie Allison, and pressing F7 again jumps the cell pointer back to the Jane Doe entry because those are the only two matching entries.

As a wild card, the question mark stands for a single character. You can use an asterisk (*) to perform a broader search. If you want to find all entries that start with the letter Q, regardless of the number of characters, for example, type **Q*** in the Find What: field.

The search function works just as well for finding formulas. You cannot use operators, such as / or <, but you can use wild cards, as in 5?5 or 6*.

In the TENNIS spreadsheet, many numbers are calculated with the SUM function. If you want to find all the cells containing this function (or any other one contained in your spreadsheet), first format the spreadsheet to show formulas. Then follow the steps described previously for using the **F**ind option, typing the word **sum** in the Find What: field of the Find dialog box.

Printing a Spreadsheet

Printing a spreadsheet enables you to share your completed spreadsheet with your colleagues. Five printing-related options are found on the File menu: Print Preview, Print, Page Setup & Margins..., Set Print Area, and Printer Setup... (see fig. 10.36). In the following paragraphs, you learn how to use these options in your printing tasks.

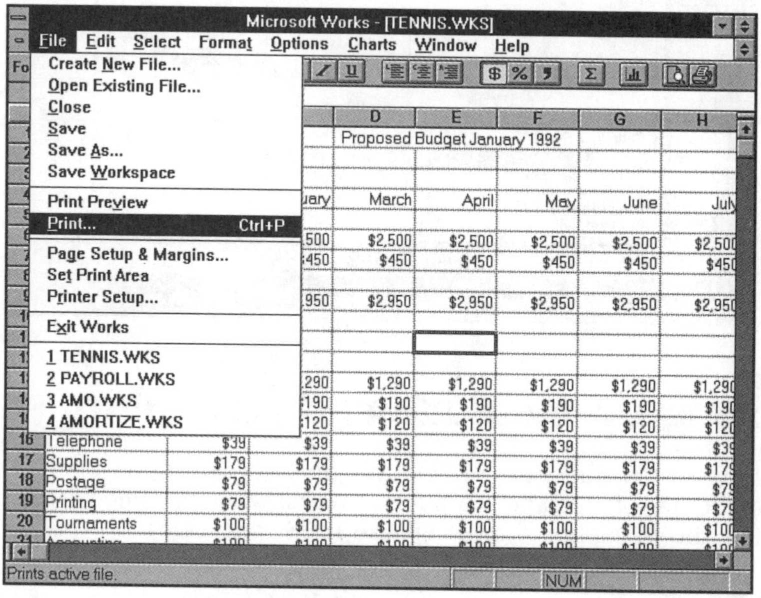

FIG. 10.36

The **File** menu

Setting Up the Printer

Printer Setup... is an option on the File menu. Choose this option and check the Printer Setup dialog box before you begin printing. The information shown in the dialog box depends on what you told Windows about your printer when you installed the program. Figure 10.37, for example, shows the Printer Setup dialog box for a system using an HP LaserJet Series II printer.

If you described your printer correctly when installing Windows, you should have no trouble printing. If you have more than one printer attached to your computer, you can select the second printer from this dialog box.

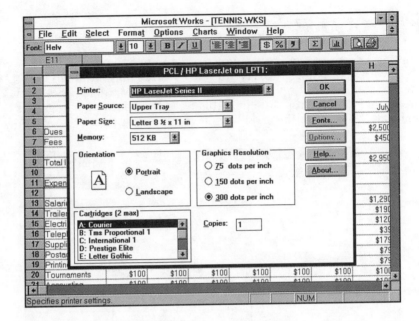

Setting Up the Page and Page Margins

With the File menu's Page Setup & Margins... option, you can determine the size of the paper output for Works. When you choose this
option, the dialog box shown in figure 10.38 appears.

FIG. 10.38

The Page Setup
& Margins
dialog box

The default print settings are for standard 8 1/2-by-11-inch paper. As you add headers or footers, you may want to adjust these settings. For most applications, the defaults work well. You also can print gridlines or row and column headers.

To change any of the settings in this dialog box, click on the setting or press Alt plus the underlined letter. For example, to change the top margin press Alt,T.

To print **Gridlines**, click the box preceding the option or press Alt,G. A further option is to print the row and column headers. The row headers are the numbers on the left side of the workspace, and the column headers the letters that run across the top of the workspace. To print the row and column headers, click the preceding box or press Alt,O. By printing both the gridlines and row and column headers your printed copy closely resembles what you see on screen.

The option **1**st page number option allows you to specify which number should be printed on the first page. Works suggests 1 but you can enter any number you want.

The **Edit** menu also contains some options for controlling the setup of your page. After printing a spreadsheet, you may find that it looks better on paper with a page break or with breaks different from the ones Works has selected. Selecting Insert Page **B**reak from the **Edit** menu displays a dialog box that enables you to pick a new page break at a specific row number. If you change your mind, you can use the Delete Page Break option from the **Edit** menu to delete any manual page break you have inserted.

Another option on the **Edit** menu—Headers & Footers—takes you to the dialog box shown in figure 10.39.

A header or footer is information that prints at the top for headers, or bottom for footers, of every spreadsheet page. Keeping track of multipage worksheets is much easier with headers and footers. Works does not automatically add page numbers to multipage spreadsheets. You can include the page number in either a header or footer by adding the correct symbol.

With the **Headers & Footers** dialog box, you can enter any header or footer you need and also choose whether you want Works to print headers or footers on the first page. You can use special formatting commands within your headers and footers by combining the ampersand character (&) with a letter, as described in table 10.3.

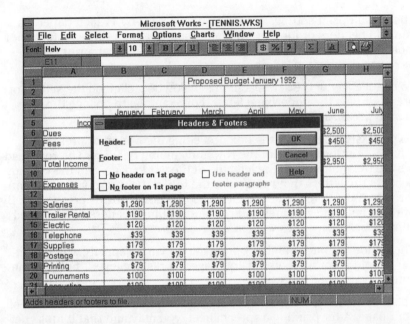

FIG. 10.39

The Headers &
Footers dialog
box

Table 10.3 Formatting Your Headers and Footers

Special Formatting Function	Command
Left or right align	&l or &r
Center	&c
Print page number	&p
Print file name	&f
Print the date	&d
Print the time	&t
Print an ampersand	&&

Previewing the Printout

Because judging where everything will come out on a printed spreadsheet is difficult, Works offers you an on-screen preview of the printed
pages. This preview gives you the opportunity to add or delete formatting as appropriate.

To see the print preview, open the **File** menu and select the Print Preview option or click the Preview button on the Tool bar. Microsoft Works displays the pages, one at a time, as they will print. If you are using a color monitor, note that the preview pages are displayed in black and white. You can print directly from the preview screen by selecting the **Print** button or by pressing Alt,P.

Using the Print Option

After you have checked your printer setup, set up the page, and previewed it if you prefer, you're ready to print your spreadsheet. Selecting the **Print** option from the File menu opens the Print dialog box, which is shown in figure 10.40.

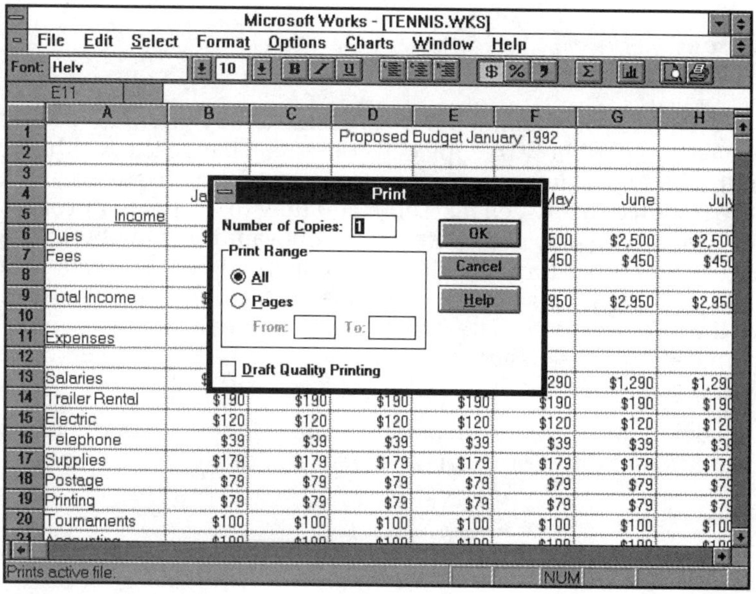

FIG. 10.40

The Print dialog box

Works is flexible in its printing capabilities. It allows for multiple copies, prints entire spreadsheets or only specific pages, or prints to a disk file so that you can use the file with other applications.

To print only specific pages, enter the page numbers in the **P**ages field of the Print dialog box. If your spreadsheet is 10 pages long and you need to print only pages 3 through 6, for example, enter 3 in the From: field and 6 in the To: field.

T I P Use the File Save As command and select the Text&Tabs [DOS] option as the File Type to create a DOS print file that can be printed with the DOS Print command. Other applications, such as some word processors, can read this file. In the Type box, select the option that fits your needs. If you want to share the spreadsheet with a colleague who uses Lotus 1-2-3, for example, select the Lotus 1-2-3 Only option. Or select the Text & Tabs (DOS) item to create a DOS file.

When you choose the Set Print Area option from the File menu, Works prints only the cells you select. Use this option when you need to have a hard copy of a small area of the spreadsheet.

Chapter Summary

In this chapter, you examined how to create a fully interactive spreadsheet. You learned how to copy cell contents, change the width of columns, and split the screen. You also learned how to use the Go To feature to move to any cell instantly; and how to format features, which enables you to display cell contents as you want them in percentage, currency, and other formats. Finally, you learned how you can name cell ranges so that you can use the names in formulas, and you learned other techniques, such as how to hide and unhide columns, protect cell contents, show spreadsheet formulas, sort a spreadsheet, search cells, and print a spreadsheet.

In the next chapter, you learn about the built-in functions you can use with your Microsoft Works spreadsheets and databases.

Using Functions

Microsoft Works contains many built-in functions that you can use with your Microsoft Works spreadsheets and databases. These functions are abbreviations of longer formulas that would be difficult to use in a spreadsheet or database if they were not already a part of Microsoft Works.

An example of a complex formula that is encapsulated into a function is the PMT function, which calculates the payment on a loan. The whole formula is complex and involved; however, Microsoft has devised this shorthand function method to make it easy to use the loan formula and many others. Every function must have arguments, and the arguments must be enclosed in parentheses. For example, the loan function has three arguments: the loan amount, the loan length, and the loan interest rate.

Using Microsoft Works functions in spreadsheet formulas requires that you use the correct format. Doing so is not difficult, but the format is exacting. If you always take care to enter your functions and their arguments correctly, you can save yourself much frustration.

The format of a function is called the *syntax*. The general syntax for each function is the same. An equal sign (=) and the name of the function come first, followed by a left parenthesis, then one or more arguments separated by commas, and finally a right parenthesis. An example of a spreadsheet formula using a function is as follows:

=DATE(*Year,Month,Day*)

The equal sign indicates to Works that a formula is to follow. Next, the name of the function, DATE, appears. Following the name of the function is the left parenthesis and then three arguments: *Year*, *Month*, and

Day. The function is closed with the right parenthesis. Notice that no spaces are included between the function name, the parentheses, and the arguments.

This chapter defines and explains each Microsoft Works function. The functions are covered in alphabetical order by function name. An example usage of each function follows the syntax and the usage description.

Microsoft Works functions can be divided into several categories:

- Date and time
- Financial
- Information
- Logical
- Lookup
- Mathematical
- Statistical
- Text
- Trigonometric

As mentioned earlier, the following Works functions are listed in alphabetical order. The best way to learn how these various functions operate is to read the examples and then try one on your own data. Some of the functions are specialized as indicated in the preceding list, but many can be used to extend the power of your spreadsheet calculations. For databases, the best way to use these functions is in **List View** where the data is arranged like the spreadsheet format.

ABS

Syntax: ABS(*x*)

Usage: Returns the absolute value of *x*.

Example: =**ABS(-8)** returns 8.

ACOS

Syntax: ACOS(*x*)

Usage: Returns the arccosine of *x*, which is the angle whose cosine is *x*. The value of ACOS is returned in radians. *x* must be in the range from −1 through 1. The angle may be between 0 radians (0 degrees) and pi radians (180 degrees).

Example: **=ACOS(-.05)** returns 1.6208172 (2pi/3 radians).

ASIN

Syntax: ASIN(*x*)

Usage: Returns the arcsine of *x*, which is the angle whose sine is *x*. The value of ASIN is returned in radians. *x* must range from −1 through 1. The angle ranges from −pi/2 radians (−90 degrees) through pi/2 radians (90 degrees).

Example: **=ASIN(-0.5)*180/3.146** returns -30 (degrees).

ATAN

Syntax: ATAN(*x*)

Usage: Returns the arctangent of *x*, which is the angle whose tangent is *x*. The value of ATAN is returned in radians. The angle ranges from -pi/2 radians (-90 degrees) to pi/2 radians (90 degrees).

Example: **=ATAN(1)** returns 0.785 (pi/4 radians).

ATAN2

Syntax: ATAN2(*X coordinate,Y coordinate*)

Usage: Returns the arctangent of an angle defined by the X and Y coordinates. The arctangent is the angle, in radians, determined by the point described by the coordinates. The angle ranges from -pi radians (180 degrees) to but excluding pi radians (180 degrees). Table 7.1 shows the ATAN2 results with different combinations of X and Y coordinates.

Table 11.1 ATAN2 Results with X and Y Coordinates

Sign of X Coordinate	Sign of Y Coordinate	Angle Result
positive	positive	between 0 and pi/2
negative	positive	between pi/2 and pi
negative	negative	between -pi and -pi/2
positive	negative	between -pi/2 and 0

When both X and Y coordinates are 0, ATAN2 returns the error value ERR.

Example: **=ATAN2(-1,-1)** returns -2.356 (-3pi/4 radians).

AVG

Syntax: AVG(*RangeReference0,RangeReference1,...*)

Usage: Returns the average of the values specified in *RangeReference*. The values in *RangeReference* may be numbers, cell references, or formulas. When you use cell references, blank cells are considered 0. When you use range references, blank cells are ignored. Text is treated as 0 in all references.

Example: If the range B2..F2 includes the values 97, 83, 78, 85, and 97, **=AVG(B2:F2)** returns 88.

CHOOSE

Syntax: CHOOSE(*Choice,Option0,Option1,...*)

Usage: Uses *Choice* to select an option from a list. If *Choice* is 0, CHOOSE selects *Option0*; if *Choice* is 1, CHOOSE selects *Option1*, and so on. If *Choice* is 0 or is greater than the number of options available in the list, CHOOSE returns the error value ERR.

Example: When cell A1 holds the number 2, **=CHOOSE(A1-1,10,20,30)** returns 20.

COLS

Syntax: COLS(*RangeReference*)

Usage: Returns the number of columns in *RangeReference*.

Example: If the range B2..D5 is named Sales, **=COLS(Sales)** returns 3.

COS

Syntax: COS(*x*)

Usage: Returns the cosine of *x*, which is an angle measured in radians.

Example: **=COS(1.047)** returns 0.5.

COUNT

Syntax: COUNT(*RangeReference0,RangeReference1,...*)

Usage: Returns the number of cells contained in *RangeReference*. COUNT adds 1 for every cell that holds a number, a formula, text, ERR, and N/A. *RangeReference* may be numbers, cell references, range references, or formulas. When you use range references, blank cells are ignored. When you use cell references, blank cells add 1 to the count.

Example: **=COUNT(B2:F2)** returns 5.

CTERM

Syntax: CTERM(*Rate,FutureValue,PresentValue*)

Usage: Returns the number of compounding periods needed for an investment earning a fixed rate per compounding period to grow from a present value to a future value. *Rate* is the interest rate for a single compounding period.

Example: You have $1,000 in a savings account with an annual rate of 8 3/4 percent. Interest is compounded monthly. This formula tells you how long it will take you to double your investment:

   =CTERM(8.75%/12,2000,1000)

The formula returns 95.41 months (nearly 8 years).

DATE

Syntax: DATE(*Year,Month,Day*)

Usage: Returns a date number for the date specified by *Year, Month,* and *Day.* The date number is an integer ranging from 1 to 65534, representing the dates from January 1, 1990, to June 3, 2079.

The value for *Year* must be a number ranging from 0 (1900) to 179 (2079). *Month* must range from 1 to 12. *Day* must range from 1 to 31. If you enter a value outside these ranges, DATE adjusts the value to the correct date. Works adjusts the entry this way. If you enter 63 for the minutes value, Works adds one to the hours value and leaves 3 as the minutes value. Or, if you enter 70 as the number of seconds, Works adds one to the minutes value and leaves 10 as the seconds value. If *Year, Month,* and *Day* do not comprise a valid date in the Works range of dates, ERR is returned.

With DATE, you can enter a constant date in a cell by using a formula.

Example: Although you can use a formula such as =**DATE(60,11,30)**, typing the date directly (as 11/30/60 in this case) generally is easier. A better use for DATE is within a longer formula to calculate the number of days between two other dates. If cell B5 holds the number of the current quarter (1, 2, 3, or 4) of 1989, for example, the following formula returns the date number of the first day of the next quarter:

=**DATE(89,B5*3+1,1)**

DAY, MONTH, YEAR

Syntax: DAY(*DateNumber*)

MONTH(*DateNumber*)

YEAR(*DateNumber*)

Usage: Returns the day, month, or year of the date specified by *DateNumber.* DAY returns a number from 1 through 31. MONTH returns a number from 1 through 12. YEAR returns a number from 0 through 179.

Date numbers use the integers 1 through 65534 to represent the dates January 1, 1900, through June 3, 2079. January 1, 1900, is date number 1, and June 3, 2079, is date number 65534.

Example: =**YEAR('4/15/89')** returns YEAR(31882), which returns 89.

DDB

Syntax: DDB(*Cost,Salvage,Life,Period*)

Usage: Uses a double-declining balance method to find the amount of depreciation in the period specified. *Cost* refers to the amount paid for the asset. *Salvage* is the value of the asset at the end of its working life. *Life* refers to the number of time periods you expect to use the asset, usually entered in years. *Period* is the period of time for which you want to find the depreciation.

The formula for computing depreciation for a given period is Double Declining Method.

> *Value**2
>
> *Life*

Example: You buy machinery for $50,000. The life expectancy of the machinery is 10 years. The salvage value is $8,000. The depreciation expense for the seventh year, using the double-declining balance method, is computed as follows:

> **=DDB(50000,8000,10,7)**

This formula returns $2,621.44.

ERR

Syntax: ERR( )

Usage: Returns the error value ERR. Use this function to force a cell to display ERR whenever a specified condition exists and to find cells whose formulas depend on the erroneous cell.

Example: If B2 contains the number 0, the following formula returns ERR:

> **=(IF(B2=0,ERR( ),B2))**

EXP

Syntax: EXP(*x*)

Usage: Returns *e* to the power of *x*, where *e* equals 2.71828...., the base number of natural logarithms. Use the exponentiation operator (^) to compute the powers of other bases. EXP is the inverse of LN.

Example: **=EXP(1)** returns 2.718... (the value of *e*).

FALSE

Syntax: FALSE( )

Usage: Returns the logical value 0 (FALSE). Use FALSE rather than 0 to create more readable logical formulas.

Example: If B2 contains the number 5, the following formula returns =IF(B2>10,1,0), which returns 0:

=IF(B2>10,TRUE( ),FALSE( ))

FV

Syntax: FV(*Payment,Rate,Term*)

Usage: Returns the future value of an ordinary annuity of equal payments earning a fixed interest rate per term compounded over several terms. Microsoft Works assumes that the first payment occurs at the end of the first period. The program uses the following formula to calculate the future value of an ordinary annuity:

$$\frac{Payment*((1+Rate)\ Term-1)}{Rate}$$

Example: You deposit $1,500 into your savings every year for 8 years. The interest rate is 8.75 percent, compounded annually. The following formula tells you how much money will be in the account at the end of 8 years:

=FV(1500,8.75%,8)

This formula returns $16,393.61.

HLOOKUP, VLOOKUP

Syntax: HLOOKUP(*LookupValue,RangeReference,RowNumber*)

VLOOKUP(*LookupValue,RangeReference,ColumnNumber*)

Usage: These two functions find an entry in a table. HLOOKUP searches the top row of the specified *RangeReference* until finding the number that matches *LookupValue*. The function then goes down the column the number of rows specified in *RowNumber* to find the entry. Arrange the numbers in the top row in ascending order. Works searches the top row for the largest number that is less than or equal to *LookupValue*.

VLOOKUP searches the leftmost column in *RangeReference* until finding the number that matches *LookupValue*. VLOOKUP then goes to the right the number of columns specified in *ColumnNumber* to find the entry. Arrange the numbers in the left column in ascending order. Works searches the left column for the largest number that is less than or equal to *LookupValue*.

You get an error value (ERR) if *ColumnNumber* or *RowNumber* is negative or is greater than or equal to the number of rows or columns in *RangeReference*.

Example: =**HLOOKUP(1986.5,C5:G8,0)** returns 1986 (contents of D5).

HOUR, MINUTE, SECOND

Syntax: HOUR(*TimeNumber*)

MINUTE(*TimeNumber*)

SECOND(*TimeNumber*)

Usage: Returns the number for the hour, minute, or second, respectively, of the time represented by *TimeNumber*. HOUR returns an integer from 0 through 23. MINUTE and SECOND return integers ranging from 0 through 59. *TimeNumber* can range from 0 through 0.999 to represent the times 12:00 a.m. through 11:59:59 p.m.

Example: =**MINUTE('16:48:30')** returns MINUTE(0.70035), which returns 48.

IF

Syntax: IF(*Condition,ValueIfTrue,ValueIfFalse*)

Usage: Determines whether *Condition* is true or false and then returns either *ValueIfTrue* or *ValueIfFalse*.

Example: If A1 holds the number 20, =**IF(A1>10,B1,C1)** returns the value in B1.

INDEX

Syntax: INDEX(*RangeReference,Column,Row*)

Usage: Returns the value in a cell in *RangeReference* at the intersection of the specified *Column* and *Row*. If either *Column* or *Row* is negative or is greater than or equal to the number of rows or columns in *RangeReference*, Works returns the error value ERR.

INT

Syntax: INT(*x*)

Usage: Returns the integer part of *x*. INT deletes the digits to the right of the decimal point with no rounding. (Use ROUND to round *x* to the nearest integer.)

Example: **=INT(7.9)** returns 7.

IRR

Syntax: IRR(*Guess,RangeReference*)

Usage: Returns the internal rate of return for the cash-flow series specified in *RangeReference*. The internal rate of return is the interest rate that gives the cash flow series a net present value of 0.

This function uses an iterative technique that can have more than one solution. IRR gives the error value ERR if the computations do not converge to within 0.0000001 after 20 iterations. Enter a *Guess* to tell IRR where to begin. Enter a different *Guess* if Works is unable to determine the IRR. Normally a starting value between 0 and 1 yields a meaningful result.

Example: You have an investment represented by these cash flow numbers: (7,000), 2,000, 2,000, 2,000, (3,000), 2,000, and 6,000. It should yield about 10 percent. Use the following formula to determine the internal rate of return:

> **=IRR(10%,A1:G1)**

This formula returns 12.32%.

ISERR

Syntax: ISERR(*x*)

Usage: Returns the logical value 1 (TRUE) if *x* is the error value ERR; otherwise, returns the logical value 0 (FALSE). Use ISERR to test for errors in a spreadsheet and to prevent errors from flowing to other related cells.

Example: If A1 contains the error value ERR, **=IF(ISERR(A1),2,1)** returns 2.

ISNA

Syntax: ISNA(*x*)

Usage: Returns the logical value 1 (TRUE) if *x* is the value N/A. If *x* is not the value N/A, the logical value 0 (FALSE) is returned. Use ISNA to test for N/A values in the spreadsheet. Like ISERR, you can use ISNA to prevent N/A values from flowing to other cells.

Example: If A1 contains the value N/A, **=ISNA(A1)** returns 1.

LN

Syntax: LN(*x*)

Usage: Returns the natural logarithm of *x*, which uses the mathematical constant *e*, 2.71828..., as a base. The value for *x* must be a positive integer.

Example: **=LN(2.7182818)** returns LN(EXP(1)), which returns 1.

LOG

Syntax: LOG(*x*)

Usage: Returns the base 10 logarithm of *x*, which must be a positive integer. The inverse of LOG is exponentiation.

Example: **=LOG(10)** returns 1.

MAX

Syntax: MAX(*RangeReference0,RangeReference1*,...)

Usage: Returns the largest number contained in *RangeReference*. Each *RangeReference* may be numbers, cell references, range references, or formulas. When you use cell references, blank cells are treated as 0. When you use range references, blank cells are ignored. In each type of reference, text is treated as 0.

Example: With values of 97, 95, 83, 70, and 97 in cells B2 through F2, **=MAX(B2:F2)** returns 97.

MIN

Syntax: MIN(*RangeReference0,RangeReference1*,...)

Usage: Returns the smallest number contained in *RangeReference*.

Each *RangeReference* may be numbers, cell references, range references, or formulas. When you use cell references, blank cells are treated as 0. When you use range references, blank cells are ignored. In each type of reference, text is treated as 0.

Example: With values of 97, 95, 83, 70, and 97 in cells B2 through F2, and 1000 in cell G2, **=MIN(B2:F2,G2,70)** returns 70.

MINUTE

Syntax: MINUTE(*TimeNumber*)

Usage: Returns an integer ranging from 0 through 59 for the minute represented by *TimeNumber*. *TimeNumber* ranges from 0 through 0.999 to represent the times 12:00 a.m. through 11:59:59 p.m.

Example: **=MINUTE('16:48:30')** returns MINUTE(0.70035), which returns 48.

MOD

Syntax: MOD(*Numerator,Denominator*)

Usage: Returns the remainder (modulus) of *Numerator* divided by *De-nominator.* The remainder or modulus has the same sign as *Numerator.* MOD returns an ERR value if *Denominator* is equal to 0.

Example: =**MOD(-3,-2)** returns -1.

MONTH

Syntax: MONTH(*DateNumber*)

Usage: Returns a number from 1 to 12 for the month represented by *DateNumber. DateNumber* uses the integers 1 through 65534 to represent the dates January 1, 1900, through June 3, 2079. January 1, 1900, is date number 1, and June 3, 2079, is date number 65534.

Example: =**MONTH(31882)** returns 4. 31882 is the date number for April 15, 1989.

NA

Syntax: NA( )

Usage: Returns the numeric value of N/A. Use NA() to indicate that information is not available.

Example: If A1 holds the number 0, =**IF(A1=0,NA( ),A1)** returns N/A.

NOW

Syntax: NOW( )

Usage: Returns the date and time number for the current date and time. At every recalculation, this value is updated. The integer portion of NOW() is the date number, and the decimal fraction is the time number. The decimal portion is not displayed unless you change the cell format from General to Fixed with two decimal places. Use the Format menu's **T**ime/Date command to display the true date or time.

Example: If the current date and time is 4:48:00 p.m. on April 15, 1989, =**NOW( )** returns 32613.

NPV

Syntax: NPV(*Rate,RangeReference*)

Usage: Returns the net present value of a series of cash-flow payments represented by numbers in *RangeReference* and discounted at a fixed interest rate per period (*Rate*).

If you have a 12 percent annual interest rate but want to discount on a monthly basis, divide the annual interest rate by 12 to find the monthly rate. For a 12 percent annual interest rate, for example, the monthly rate is 1 percent.

RangeReference is the reference for a single cell or part of a single row or column but cannot be a range that holds more than one row or column.

Works assumes that payments occur at the end of periods of equal length. To find the net present value of a cash flow-series in which the first payment occurs at the beginning of the periods, you must add the amount of the first payment to the net present value of the payments that follow. Works uses the following formula to calculate net present value:

$$NPV = N\ Payment[i]$$
$$NPV = \$gs\ \underline{\hspace{2cm}}$$
$$NPV =i=1\ (1+Rate)i$$

Example: You are looking into a rental contract that promises a 10 percent yield with payments at the end of each month for the subsequent five months. Cells B2:F2 contain the expected monthly payments ($500, $1,500, $3,000, $4,000, and $5,000). The value for the investment is entered in B1 as $8,000. Use this formula to calculate how much you should pay for the investment:

=NPV(10%,B2:F2)-B1

This formula returns 1784.8197.

PI

Syntax: PI( )

Usage: Returns the number 3.14159..., which is an approximation of the mathematical constant pi.

Example: **=COS(60*PI()/180)** returns 0.5 (cosine of 60 degrees).

PMT

Syntax: PMT(*Principal,Rate,Term*)

Usage: Returns the periodic payment for a loan or an investment of *Principal* based on a fixed interest *Rate* for each compounding period over a given *Term*. Works assumes that payments occur at the end of equal periods.

Works uses this formula to calculate the periodic payment:

$$\frac{Present\ Value*Rate}{(1-(1+Rate)-Term)}$$

Example: You decide to buy a car, which requires you to get a loan for $12,000 at 9 percent interest per year. Use this formula to determine what your payments would be if you paid the loan with 24 monthly installments:

=PMT(12000,9%/12,24)

This formula returns $548.22.

PV

Syntax: PV(*Payment,Rate,Term*)

Usage: Returns the present value of an ordinary annuity of equal payments (*Payment*), earning a fixed interest rate per period (*Rate*), over a term of several periods (*Term*). Works assumes that the first payment is paid at the end of the first period. The following formula is used for calculating the present value of an ordinary annuity:

$$PV = \frac{Payment*(1-(1+Rate)-Term)}{Rate}$$

Example: You learn that you are to inherit some money from your uncle. You will be paid $1,500 at the end of each year for the next 10 years. You estimate that the annual inflation rate over the next 10 years will be 9 percent. Calculate the value of this inheritance in today's dollars with this formula:

=PV(1500,9%,10)

The formula returns $9,626.49.

RAND

Syntax: RAND( )

Usage: Returns a random number from 0 up to but not including 1. A new random number is generated every time the spreadsheet is recalculated.

Example: =**RAND( )*10+1** returns a random number between 1 and 11, but not including 11.

RATE

Syntax: RATE(*FutureValue,PresentValue,Term*)

Usage: Returns the fixed interest rate per compounding period needed for an investment of *PresentValue* to grow to a *FutureValue* over several compounding periods or terms (*Term*). Use the following formula to calculate the rate:

$$\text{RATE} = \frac{FutureValue\ 1/Term}{PresentValue} - 1$$

Example: You are operating a limited partnership that intends to purchase an apartment building for $750,000. You intend to sell it for $1,500,000 after 6 years. Calculate the annual rate of return for this investment by using this formula:

=**RATE(1500000,750000,6)**

The formula returns 12.25%.

ROUND

Syntax: ROUND(*x,NumberOfPlaces*)

Usage: Rounds *x* to the specified number of places either to the left or right of the decimal point. Insert a positive *NumberOfPlaces*, and the number is rounded that many places to the right of the decimal point. Using 0 for *NumberOfPlaces* forces *x* to be rounded to the nearest integer. A negative *NumberOfPlaces* rounds *x* the specified number of places to the left of the decimal point. *NumberOfPlaces* can range from −14 to 14.

Example: =**ROUND(2.149,1)** returns 2.1.

ROWS

Syntax: ROWS(*RangeReference*)

Usage: Returns the number of rows in *RangeReference*.

Example: If the range B3..D6 is named Table, =**ROWS(Table)** returns 4.

SECOND

Syntax: SECOND(*TimeNumber*)

Usage: Returns an integer ranging from 0 through 59 for the second represented by *TimeNumber*. TimeNumber ranges from 0 through 0.999 to represent the times 12:00 a.m. through 11:59:59 p.m.

Example: =**SECOND('16:48:30')** returns 30.

SIN

Syntax: SIN(*x*)

Usage: Returns the sine of *x*, which is an angle measured in radians.

Example: =**SIN(1.047)** returns 0.866.

SLN

Syntax: SLN(*Cost,Salvage,Life*)

Usage: Finds the amount of depreciation in one period, using the straight-line depreciation method. For *Cost*, insert the amount you paid for the asset. For *Salvage*, insert the amount you expect to obtain when you sell the asset at the end of its life. For *Life*, insert the number of periods you expect to use the asset (usually measured in years). SLN uses this formula to compute depreciation for the specified period:

$$SLN = \frac{Cost\text{-}Salvage}{Life}$$

Example: You buy machinery for $50,000. The machinery should last 10 years, after which you think you can get $8,000 for it. The following formula computes the depreciation expense per year, using the straight-line method:

=SLN(50000,8000,10)

The formula returns $4200.

SQRT

Syntax: SQRT(*x*)

Usage: Returns the square root of *x*. Works returns the error value ERR if *x* is negative.

Example: =SQRT(25) returns 5.

STD

Syntax: STD(*RangeReference0,RangeReference1*,...)

Usage: Returns the population standard deviation of *RangeReference*. The values in *RangeReference* may be numbers, cell references, or formulas. Blank cells are ignored in range references and are treated as 0 in cell references. Text is treated as 0 in any of the references.

The standard deviation of a sample of the population is given by the following formula:

STD(*RangeReferences*)*SQRT(COUNT(*RangeReferences*)/
(COUNT (*RangeReferences*)-1))

Example: =STD(B2:F2) returns 8.43.

SUM

Syntax: SUM(*RangeReference0,RangeReference1*,...)

Usage: Returns the total of all values in *RangeReference*. The values in *RangeReference* may be numbers, cell references, or formulas. Blank cells are ignored in range references and are treated as 0 in cell references.

Example: =SUM(B2:F2) returns 355.

SYD

Syntax: SYD(*Cost,Salvage,Life,Period*)

Usage: Finds the amount of depreciation for a specific period, using the sum-of-the-years-digits method. The amount you paid for the asset is *Cost*. The amount you expect to get when you sell the asset at the end of its life is *Salvage*. The number of periods, usually measured in years, you expect to use the asset is *Life*. The period for which you want to find the depreciation is *Period*.

The formula that follows shows the computation of SYD for a specified period:

$$SYD = \frac{(Cost\text{-}Salvage)*(Life\text{-}Period+1)}{Life*(Life+1)/2}$$

Example: You buy machinery for $50,000. The machinery should last 10 years, after which you will sell it for $8,000. Calculate the depreciation expense for the seventh year, using the sum-of-the-years-digits method, with this formula:

=SYD(50000,8000,10,7)

The formula returns $3,054.55.

TAN

Syntax: TAN(*x*)

Usage: Returns the tangent of *x*, which is an angle measured in radians.

Example: **=TAN(0.785)** returns 1.

TERM

Syntax: TERM(*Payment,Rate,FutureValue*)

Usage: Returns the number of compounding periods necessary for a series of equal payments (*Payment*), earning a fixed interest rate per period (*Rate*), which should grow to a *FutureValue*. Use the following formulas to calculate the future value of an ordinary annuity:

$$TERM = \frac{FutureValue*Rate \; \text{LN}(1+(Payment))}{\text{LN}(1+Rate)]}$$

(when *Rate* is not equal to 0)

$$TERM = \frac{FutureValue}{Payment}$$

(when *Rate* is equal to 0)

Example: Each month you add $200 to a savings account with an 8 3/4 percent interest rate, compounded monthly. Use this formula to calculate how long before you have $5,000:

=TERM(200,8.75%/12,5000)

The formula returns 23.05 months.

TIME

Syntax: TIME(*Hour,Minute,Second*)

Usage: Returns a time number for the time specified by *Hour*, *Minute*, and *Second*. The time number is a fraction ranging from 0.0 through 0.999, which represents time from 0:00:00 or 12:00:00 p.m. through 23:59:59 or 11:59:59 p.m.

Hour is a number ranging from 0 through 23. *Minute* and *Second* are numbers ranging from 0 through 59. If either *Minute* or *Second* is outside the specified range of 0 through 59, TIME adjusts the number to the correct time.

Example: **=TIME(16,48,0)** returns 0.7 (the time number of 4:48:00 p.m.).

TRUE

Syntax: TRUE( )

Usage: Returns the logical value 1 (TRUE). Use TRUE( ) rather than 1 to create more readable logical formulas.

Example: If A1 holds the number 20, **=IF(A1>10,TRUE( ),FALSE( ))** returns =IF(A1>10,1,0), which returns 1.

VAR

Syntax: VAR(*RangeReference0,RangeReference1,...*)

Usage: Calculates the variance in the numbers in *RangeReference*. The values in *RangeReference* may be numbers, range references, cell references, or formulas. Blank cells are ignored in range references and are treated as 0 in cell references. Text is always treated as 0. Use the following formula to calculate the variance of the population:

> VAR(*RangeReferences*)*COUNT(*RangeReferences*)/
> (COUNT(*RangeReferences*)-1)

Example: **=VAR(B2:F2)** returns 71.18. Where cell B2 equals 97, cell C3 equals 83, cell D3 equals 78, cell E3 is blank and cell F3 equals 97.

YEAR

Syntax: YEAR(*DateNumber*)

Usage: Returns the number of the year (from 0 through 179) represented by *DateNumber*. *DateNumber* uses the integers 1 through 65534 to represent the dates January 1, 1900, through June 3, 2079. January 1, 1900, is date number 1, and June 3, 2079, is date number 65534.

Example: **=YEAR('4/15/89')** returns YEAR(31882), which returns 89.

Chapter Summary

In this chapter, you have examined the built-in functions of Works. These functions make constructing complex formulas easy. The key to using functions is to use the correct syntax; without the correct order, Works cannot calculate an answer.

In the next chapter, you examine the Works charting tool. If you have a well-constructed chart, even the most arcane numbers can be deciphered easily.

Creating Charts

You can do a terrific job of manipulating and analyzing numeric information when you use a spreadsheet. A spreadsheet's flexibility enables you to compare hundreds of variables for a particular situation easily. But many people have trouble correlating black-and-white numbers on a piece of paper with their implications for a real-life situation. For this reason, the idea of charting information was developed. With a chart, relationships are grasped more easily because numbers are represented by graphic forms rather than abstract figures.

Works has the capability of creating many kinds of charts to illustrate the information contained in your spreadsheets. You have probably seen many of the types of charts Works can create: bar, stacked bar, 100% bar, line, area line, combination, hi-lo-close, and pie.

In this chapter, you learn how to do the following:

- Create bar, line, and pie charts from the data in your spreadsheets.

- Define a chart and how to specify the data to be used in that chart.

- Enhance charts by adding horizontal and vertical grid lines, chart titles, and legends.

- Print and plot charts.

- Duplicate, modify, or delete charts.

Examining the Basic Chart Types

Before you learn how to create and work with charts, take a look at the many types of charts available with Works. Different types of data require different types of charts. For example, a pie chart is very effective for presenting individual expenses as they relate to total expenses, but are not well suited to showing month-to-month sales trends. Similarly, in order to show a relationship between two variables, such as sales to advertising dollars, an XY chart is ideal, while a bar chart does not fully depict the relationship. In this chapter, a variety of charts has been created to give you ideas on which chart to use to plot your data.

Examining the Bar Chart

A *bar chart* shows differences between categories of data. Such a chart is useful for comparing values at particular points in time. Figure 12.1, for example, shows the seasonal sales variation of two products portrayed in a bar chart.

FIG. 12.1

A sample bar chart

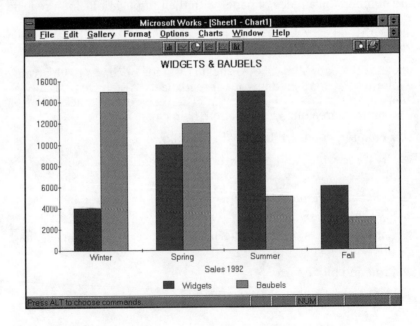

Examining the Stacked Bar Chart

A *stacked bar chart* shows the relative value of a series of numbers as they contribute to a whole. In figure 12.2, the sales of three products are stacked to show their relative contributions to the total sales.

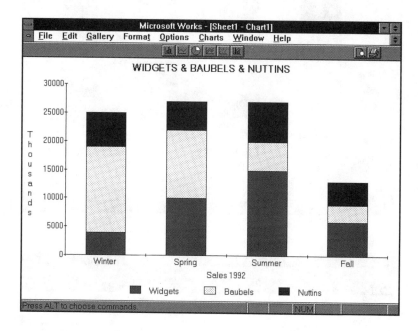

FIG. 12.2

A sample stacked bar chart

Examining the 100% Bar Chart

Displaying data as a portion of a bar that represents 100 percent of the total is another means of portraying separate contributions to a whole. In figure 12.3, the same sales numbers used in figure 12.2 are displayed in a *100% bar chart*.

Examining the Line Chart

The most common chart used in business is the *line chart*. This chart does an excellent job of reflecting trends over time. Figure 12.4 depicts in a line chart a series of sales figures for three products over time.

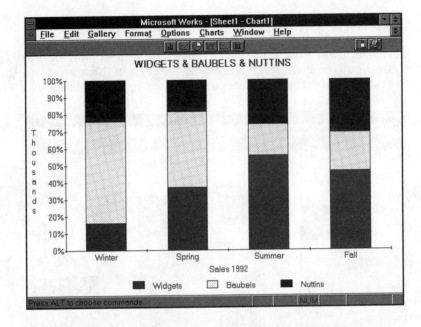

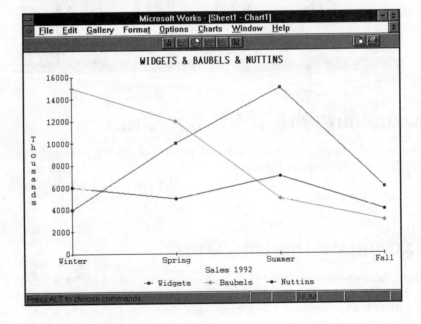

Examining the Area Line Chart

Similar to a stacked bar chart, an *area line chart* stacks the chosen values as a total of the lines plotted. In figure 12.5, the contributions of three products to the total sales are charted in an area line chart. Works calculates the total of each data set at each point in time to determine the point to plot. For example, if the data at a certain point are 50, 100, and 50, Works plots the point at 200. That is, the collective total is the point plotted.

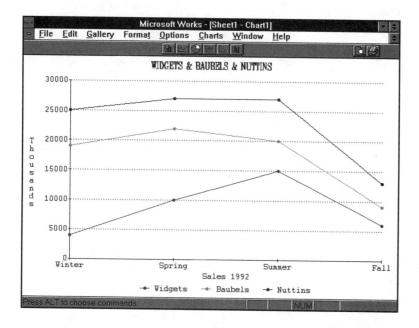

FIG. 12.5

A sample Stacked line chart

Examining the Hi-Lo-Close Chart

The *hi-lo-close chart* is used primarily for tracking the price movements of stocks. The high, low, and closing prices are charted. Figure 12.6 shows a mythical company's stock price changes, in comparison to those of IBM and MicroSoft, displayed in a hi-low-close chart.

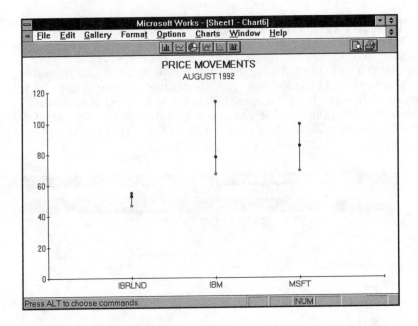

FIG. 12.6

A sample
hi-lo-close
chart

Examining the Pie Chart

A *pie chart* shows the relationship of numeric components to a whole. In figure 12.7, the sales of a product in different geographic areas are charted. If every component is included in a pie chart, the pie itself equals 100 percent of the numbers being charted.

Creating Series Charts

The first step in making a chart is creating the *chart definition*, which tells Works which series of data to use from your spreadsheet. When making a chart, you can specify the chart titles, the scale titles, and the scale itself and can even change the style type. Works assigns in sequence a name to each chart—CHART1, CHART2, and so on—as you create it. (You can change this name if you prefer. See "Naming, Duplicating, and Deleting Charts" in this chapter for more information.)

When you create a chart definition, Works saves it for you. Therefore, you don't have to specify the data for a chart every time you want to create one. Works allows a total of eight chart definitions per spreadsheet, effectively enabling you to build eight distinct charts for each spreadsheet.

The following sections explain the details of creating the various Works charts.

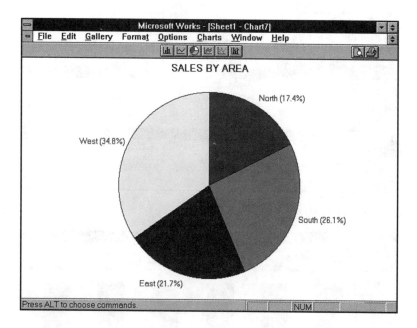

FIG. 12.7

A sample pie chart

Creating a Bar Chart

To create a simple bar chart, the default chart style, display the spreadsheet file that contains the data you want to chart. Suppose, for example, that you want to chart the first six months of data in the sample TENNIS spreadsheet. Follow these steps:

1. Click **File**, and from the menu click **O**pen Existing File, or press Alt,F,O.

2. The File Open dialog box appears. Click on the scroll box until the name TENNIS.WKS appears and is highlighted. Then click OK. Or, type TENNIS.WKS and press Enter.

3. Select the range of cells containing the data you want to chart. In the sample TENNIS spreadsheet, move the cursor to cell B6 and select the range B6..G6, which represents the dues income from January to June.

4. Access the **C**harts menu (see fig. 12.8).

5. Press Alt,N to select Create New Chart. Works displays a chart of the range of cells you selected. This range is called the data *series*. Figure 12.9 shows the bar chart created from the TENNIS spreadsheet.

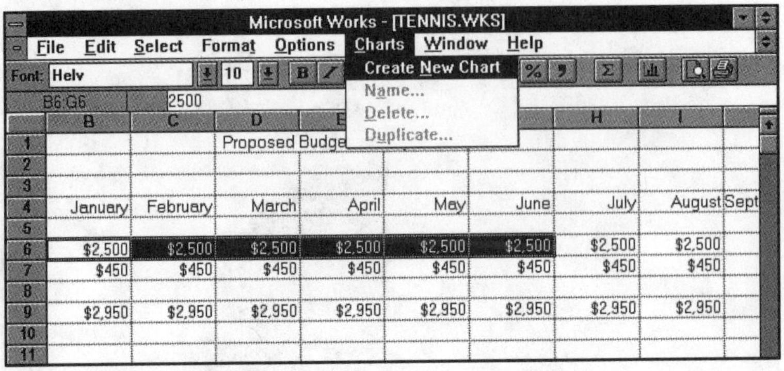

FIG. 12.8

The Charts menu

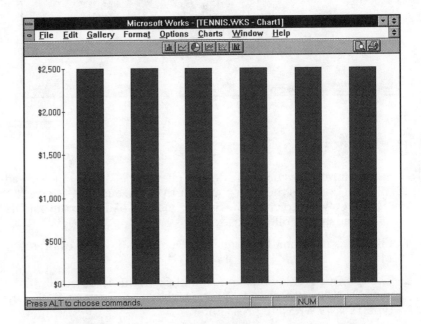

FIG. 12.9

The default bar chart for the TENNIS data

You have created a simple series bar chart. Admittedly, this chart is not very interesting—just a single series of data with no variation in that data. Notice that Works did include numbers on the vertical axis. The program calculates the numbers to be charted and develops the appropriate scale.

To return to the spreadsheet, access the **Window** menu and select the spreadsheet file name (or press Ctrl+F6).

All the series charts have a consistent structure. The horizontal line on the chart is the *x-axis*, and the vertical line is the *y-axis*. When you add data to a chart, Works adds the data as the first series, then the second series, then the third, and so on, with a total of six series allowed. Hence, the x-axis series are charted across from left to right, and the y-axis series, which can be only a single series, is charted from top to bottom on the left side of the chart. (Works does allow for a right-side y-axis when you create a custom chart, which is described later in this chapter.)

To add a second series of values to your chart, follow these steps:

1. With the spreadsheet on-screen, select enough data to represent both a first and a second series. For the example, press Shift+End to select the cells B6..G7, the Dues and Fees row entries.

2. Click the Chart button in the Tool bar.

   The Chart button is third from the right in the Tool bar, between the Sum and Print Preview buttons. Or, press Alt,C to open the **C**harts menu and press N for Create **N**ew Chart.

The new chart includes two bars at each position, with one bar representing Dues and the other representing Fees. Although a bar chart is helpful for many situations, you often may want to change the type to suit your data better.

Changing to a Different Type of Bar Chart

When you have two or more data series in a chart, you may want to change your basic bar chart. Charting the Income section of the TENNIS spreadsheet in the stacked bar format, for example, helps you reflect the total income for every month. A stacked bar chart shows the relative contributions of each value plotted at a given point in time. So, if the purpose of your chart is to determine which value is greatest in relation to others at the same point in time, a stacked bar chart may do that better than a bar chart. To create a different type of bar chart, follow these steps:

1. If you still are looking at the bar chart, click the Bar chart button on the far left of the Tool bar.

2. The Bar chart dialog box appears, as shown in figure 12.10. Notice that the dialog box contains five numbered squares representing the different types of bar charts.

   Bar chart 1 is a bar chart that plots positive and negative values (if any). Each series is plotted individually. Bar 2 is a stacked bar chart, in which the individual data points at a specific time are plotted on top of each other. Bar 3 is a 100% stacked bar chart, in which the total of the values at a specific point is calculated to equal 100, and each individual value is drawn as a percentage of the total bar height. Chart 4 is the same as chart 1 with the addition of horizontal grid lines to enhance readability. Chart 5 includes data labels inside the chart for each bar.

FIG. 12.10

The Bar dialog box

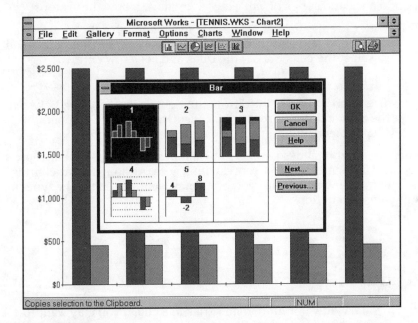

You use the 100% bar chart to look at data from the perspective of a baseline amount. By setting all data to be charted as a percentage of the total data, you can identify more easily the most crucial components. The 100% bar chart is a close relative of the pie chart, because the total pie, by definition, must be 100 percent.

3. Select the type of bar chart you want to create by pressing the appropriate number and then pressing Enter or by clicking the type you want and then clicking OK.

As you can see, you easily can change the type of chart displayed. Simply click the button in the Tool bar that matches the type of chart you want, and select the chart from those offered. Or you can access the **G**allery menu and then select the chart type you want to create. Works uses the same data series as was used in your previous chart.

Figure 12.11, for example, shows the Fees and Dues rows of the TENNIS spreadsheet displayed in a 100% bar chart.

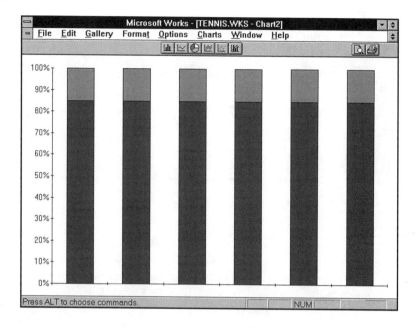

FIG. 12.11

A 100% bar chart

Changing the Data To Be Charted

The spreadsheet and the chart or charts you create from it have an interactive relationship. Changes you make in the spreadsheet are reflected in the chart. So that you can see how this relationship works, modify the data you have selected in the TENNIS spreadsheet for charting. Press Ctrl+F6 to redisplay the spreadsheet. The menu bar offers new menu choices, alerting you that you can modify the spreadsheet entries. Make the following changes in the sample spreadsheet:

1. In cell C6, type **3000**.

2. In cell D6, type **500**.

3. In cell E6, type **4500**.

4. In cell F6, type **4200**.

5. In cell G6, type **1000**.

Figure 12.12 shows the modified spreadsheet.

Now create a bar chart with these new numbers. Click the **Chart** button on the Tool bar, or press Alt,C,N.

FIG. 12.12

The sample
spreadsheet with
new values in the
range C6..G6

	A	B	C	D	E	F	G	H
1				Proposed Budget January 1992				
2								
3								
4		January	February	March	April	May	June	July
5	Income							
6	Dues	$2,500	$3,000	$500	$4,500	$4,200	$1,000	$2,500
7	Fees	$450	$450	$450	$450	$450	$450	$450
8								
9	Total Income	$2,950	$4,450	$950	$4,950	$4,650	$1,450	$2,950
10								

Changing to a Line Chart

A line chart is a better choice when you have many data points to plot.
By using a line chart, you reduce the cluttered look that a bar chart can
render and you make the individual points more recognizable.

To create a line chart, follow these steps:

1. With the default bar chart on-screen, click the Line chart button,
   which is directly to the right of the Pie chart button in the Tool
   bar. The Line chart dialog box appears, with six types from which
   you can choose (see fig. 12.13).

FIG. 12.13

The Line dialog
box

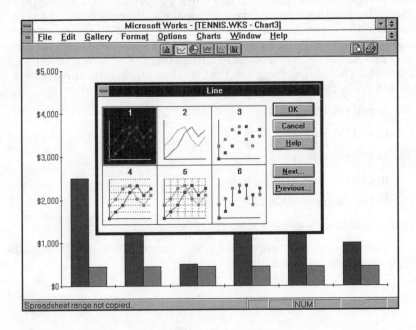

2. To create a basic line chart, press 1 and then Enter or click
   the box numbered 1 and then click OK. Select one of the other
   numbers to create a variation of the line chart.

   Line chart 1 is a standard chart in which each line plots a single
   series and each data point is denoted by a marker. The points are
   connected by straight lines. Chart 2 is the same as chart 1 except
   no data markers are included. Chart 3 is the same as chart 1 in
   that each series of values is represented individually, except that
   only markers appear at data points; no lines are drawn to connect
   them. Chart 4 is the same as chart 1 except that horizontal
   gridlines are drawn. Chart 6 is a unique chart discussed later in
   this chapter.

The chart appears on your screen. Figure 12.14, for example, shows a
simple line chart of the Dues and Fees rows of the TENNIS spreadsheet.
Figure 12.15 shows an area line chart of the same data. This type of
chart reflects the totals of each series as they are added together, in
much the same way as the stacked bar chart does. The first line is
drawn and then the next line is added to the first series, creating the
stacked effect.

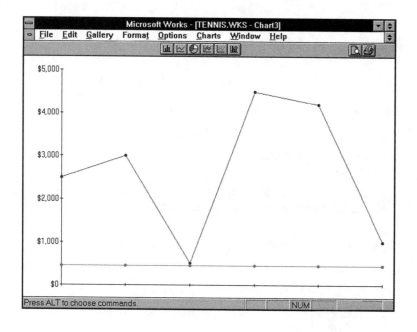

FIG. 12.14

Creating a line
chart

FIG. 12.15

An area line chart

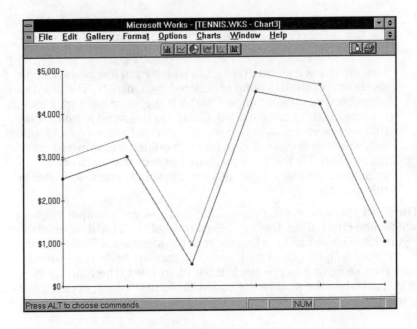

Creating a Pie Chart

A pie chart represents a set of numbers that together create the whole pie. You can, for example, create a pie chart to show the numbers in the Expense section of the TENNIS spreadsheet as pieces of a pie.

To create a pie chart, follow these steps:

1. Press Ctrl+F6 to return to the spreadsheet if you are looking at the previous chart.

2. Select the range of data you want to chart. In the TENNIS spreadsheet, for example, move the cell selector to cell B13 and select the cells in the range B13..B17.

3. Open the Charts menu.

4. Select Create New Chart. Works creates a bar chart by default.

5. Click the Pie chart button in the Tool bar.

6. From the Pie chart dialog box that appears, select item 1 as the type of pie chart.

7. Press Enter or click OK.

   Pie chart 1 is a standard chart with each value of the series represented by a piece of the pie. Chart 2 includes category labels for each of the values represented in the pie. Chart 3 includes labels that express the relation of a particular piece by a percent to the whole series of values selected. Chart 4 explodes the piece of the pie that represents the first value of the series. Chart 6 explodes all the pieces of the pie.

Figure 12.16 shows the TENNIS spreadsheet displayed in a pie chart.

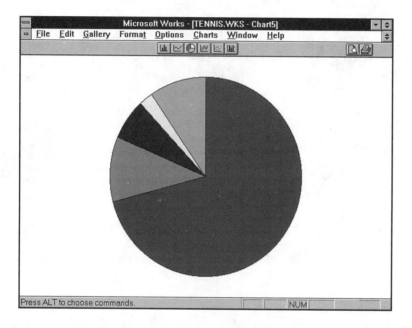

As you can see in figure 12.16, determining which pie slice represents which series of spreadsheet data is impossible. The labels for each slice on a pie chart are thus the most important pieces of information you can add. For information on adding data labels to your chart, see this chapter's section on "Adding Data Labels."

As with any other chart, you can add titles or change the series depicted in a pie chart. Only one series, however, can be displayed at a time in this kind of chart.

Exploding a Slice

After creating a pie chart, you may want to emphasize one of the pieces of the pie. The traditional means to do so is to *explode*, or pull away from the other pieces of the pie, the one piece that represents the data you want to emphasize. Using the pie chart from the preceding illustration, for example, you can explode the Salaries piece. To explode a slice of a pie, follow these steps:

1. When viewing any chart, click the Pie chart button in the Tool bar.

2. Select item 5 from the Pie chart dialog box.

3. Click OK or press Enter. The Salaries piece is exploded, because it is the first value in the series.

Changing Slice Colors and Patterns

Another way to emphasize a piece of the pie is to make it a specific color or pattern. If you have only a monochrome monitor, you can change the pattern of the piece rather than the color. To change the color or pattern of one or more slices of the pie, follow these steps:

1. Open the Format menu.

2. Select **P**atterns & Colors. The dialog box shown in figure 12.17 appears. Notice that the color and pattern for each slice of the pie is listed in the dialog box.

FIG. 12.17

The Patterns & Colors dialog box

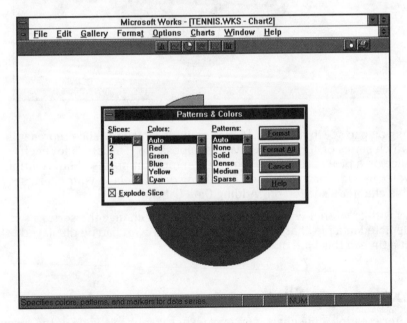

3. For each slice, you can select a different color or pattern. To emphasize the exploded slice in the sample chart, highlight slice 1, which represents the Salaries slice, and select a new color and pattern.

When you select a series of values to be plotted in a pie chart, Works numbers them beginning with the initial value as 1, the next value as 2, and so on. Works also selects the color and pattern of each slice. On a color monitor, each slice is a different color with a solid pattern. In the Patterns and Colors dialog box, the settings for slice 1 indicate that they are both being determined by Works and that the piece is exploded. To change the color and/or pattern of slice, click on the number representing the slice, or press S and use the arrow keys to highlight the slice number. Then, click on Colors and/or Patterns and click on the new color and/or pattern. If you wanted every slice to be the same, select Format **All**.

4. Select the **F**ormat button to reformat the slice.

5. Click the **C**lose button or press Enter.

Figure 12.18 shows an example of an exploded slice that has been formatted in a different pattern.

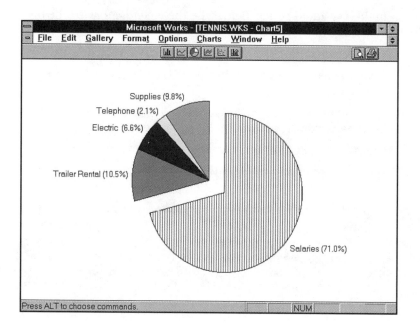

FIG. 12.18

A new pattern for the Salaries slice

Adding a Legend

You use a *legend* in a chart to identify each series of data being charted. The legend appears at the bottom of the x-axis. In the two sample line charts shown previously in this chapter, the two data lines represented the Dues and Fees areas of the TENNIS spreadsheet. You can add these labels to your chart as a legend. To add a legend, do the following:

1. Access the **Edit** menu.

2. Select the **Legend** option. The dialog box shown in figure 12.19 appears.

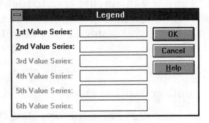

FIG. 12.19

The Legend
dialog box

3. In the **1**st Value Series: field, type the legend entry for the first y-axis series (**Dues**, for example).

4. Click (or press Alt,2) to move to the **2**nd Value Series: field.

5. Type the legend entry for the second y-axis series (**Fees**, for example).

6. Complete the remaining fields of the dialog box, depending on how many data series are included in the chart.

7. Press Enter or click OK.

The legend is added (see fig. 12.20).

T I P   If you think that you might need to change the legends or just want more flexibility, you can type a cell address rather than a text entry in each field of the Legend dialog box. In the preceding example, you can substitute the cell addresses A6 for Dues and A7 for Fees. Then if you change the entries in those cells, the legends on your chart also change.

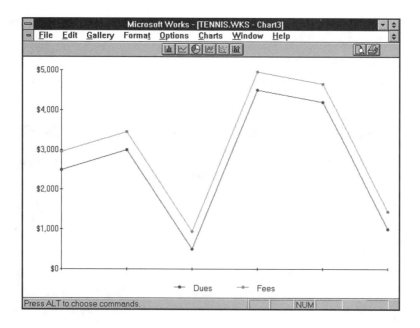

FIG. 12.20

Adding a legend to the area line chart

Adding Titles

You can add a title and a subtitle at the top of a chart. You also can add titles to the x- and y-axes. To add titles to the top of a chart, follow these steps:

1. Open the Edit menu. (You must be looking at the chart to access this menu.)

2. Choose the Titles option. The dialog box shown in figure 12.21 appears.

FIG. 12.21

The Titles dialog box

3. In the Chart Title: field, type the title for your chart. For the TENNIS spreadsheet's chart, for example, you might type **Tennis Club Income**.

4. If you prefer, type a subtitle in the **S**ubtitle: field. For the TENNIS chart, type **1992**.

5. Press Enter or click OK.

The chart appears with the titles displayed at the top of the screen (see fig. 12.22).

FIG. 12.22

Adding titles to the chart

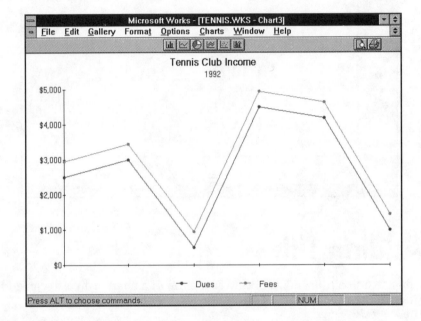

To enhance a chart even more, you can add labels to the x- and y-axes. In the sample chart in figure 12.22, for example, you can add the names of the months across the bottom of the x-axis. To add x-axis labels, follow these steps:

1. Open the **W**indows menu.

2. Select the spreadsheet from which you want to extract the x-axis titles—TENNIS.WKS in the example.

3. Select the range of cells that contains the text you want to use as x-axis labels. In the TENNIS spreadsheet, select the range B4..G4, which contains the names of the months.

4. Access the **E**dit menu.

5. Select the **C**opy option. The cell range is copied to the clipboard.

6. Access the **C**harts menu.

7. Select the chart to which you want to copy the labels—Chart3 in the example.

8. Open the **E**dit menu.

9. Select the **S**eries option. The dialog box shown in figure 12.23 appears.

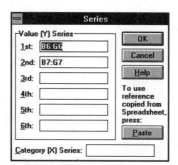

The **C**ategory (X) Series: field at the bottom of the dialog box refers to the horizontal line at the bottom of the chart. Because you have stored the range on the clipboard, the **P**aste button is active.

10. Select the **C**ategory (X) Series option.

11. Select the **P**aste button.

12. Press Enter or click OK.

Figure 12.24 shows the chart for the TENNIS spreadsheet with x-axis labels added.

Adding Data Labels

In some charts, you may find that adding data labels enhances its lucidity. *Data labels* are inserted into the chart at the top of each bar of a bar chart, along the points plotted in a line chart, or beside each slice of a pie chart. Figure 12.25 shows a bar chart with data labels inserted.

FIG. 12.24

Adding the
month names as
the x-axis labels

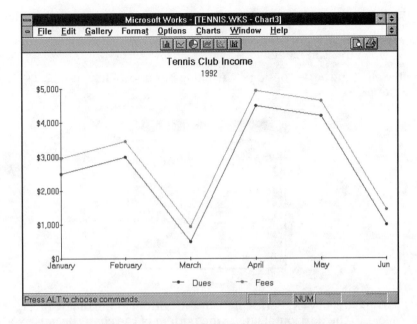

FIG. 12.25

A bar chart with
data labels
inserted

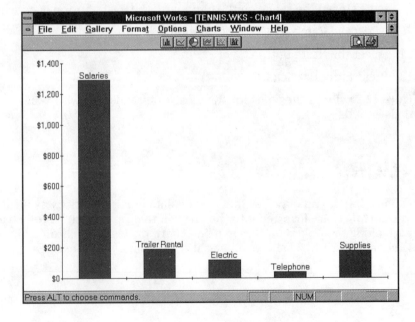

If you want to practice creating data labels, you can create the chart shown in figure 12.25 from the TENNIS spreadsheet. Follow these steps:

1. Press Ctrl+F6 until you return to the spreadsheet.

2. Select the range B13..B17.

3. Open the **C**harts menu.

4. Select Create **N**ew Chart.

To extract data labels from your spreadsheet and add them to a chart, follow these steps:

1. If the spreadsheet is not on-screen, press Ctrl+F6 until the spreadsheet appears.

2. Select the range containing the text you want to use as data labels. For the TENNIS spreadsheet example, select the range A13..A17.

3. Access the **E**dit menu.

4. Choose the **C**opy option to copy the range onto the clipboard.

5. Open the **W**indow menu.

6. Select the chart to which you want to add the data labels—Chart4 if you're following the examples in this chapter.

7. Open the **E**dit menu.

8. Select **D**ata Labels.

9. In the first box, select the **P**aste button.

10. Press Enter or click OK.

    If you want the data labels to be the actual numbers represented by each bar or data point, in the Data Labels dialog box click on Use series data.

To type your data labels in the Data Labels dialog box (rather than extract them from the spreadsheet), follow these steps:

1. Access the **E**dit menu.

2. Select **D**ata Labels. The Data Labels dialog box appears.

3. Type the appropriate cell range in the Cell **R**ange: field at the bottom of the dialog box. For the TENNIS example, type **A13..A17**.

4. Works gives you several different options for applying data labels, the simplest being the **C**ell Contents option (see fig. 12.26). When you select this option, Works displays the contents (such as text labels) as the pie chart's data labels. Works also can calculate the total of the range of values plotted and calculate and display the

percentage each piece represents (the Percentages option) or display the values in the cells in the specified range (the Values option).

Works gives you the option of adding two labels to each piece of pie. If you wish, you can include both the values from the cells and the percentage that value represents in the pie by selecting the 1st label as the Values and the 2nd label as the Percentages.

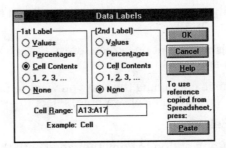

T I P If you have too many data labels on a pie chart, the labels run together on-screen, so you need to experiment with the best way to present your data. Numbering the pieces of the pie may make more sense than adding lengthy text entries.

In figure 12.27, the row labels in the TENNIS spreadsheet (A13..A17) have been designated as the first data labels, and percentages have been added as the second data labels.

Changing Fonts

You can change the font type for the titles or for the X-Y axes labels displayed in your charts. Follow these steps:

1. Select the chart you want to modify.

2. Access the Format menu.

3. Select the Title Font option. The Title Font dialog box appears, as shown in figure 12.28.

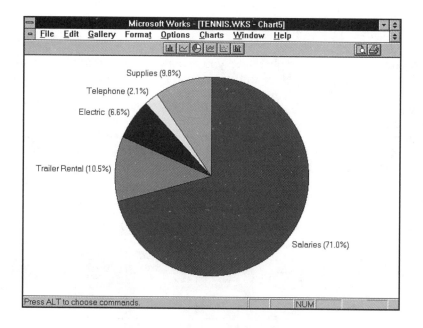

FIG. 12.27

Using double labels in a pie chart

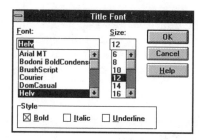

FIG. 12.28

The Title Font dialog box

To select a different font, click Font and click on the name of the font you want to use, viewing the list by clicking the scroll box, and click OK. Or, press the up- or down-arrow keys to highlight the font name and press Enter. You may also adjust the size of the characters. Click Size, or press S. You can select a character size from 6 to 48 point. In addition, you may choose to make Bold, Italic and/or Underline the title characters. Click OK or press Enter to make the change.

To change the font for the X and Y axes labels, select the Other Font option on the Format menu and follow the same method as for the Title Font.

Works provides a dazzling array of fonts and type sizes with which you can experiment. The best way to become familiar with this capability is to try a variety of sizes and fonts to see what you like best.

Using Markers

When you modified the pie chart, you examined the use of colors and patterns for a specific piece of the pie. When you modify a line chart, a different set of options appears in the Patterns & Colors dialog box. Figure 12.29 shows the Patterns & Colors dialog box that appears when you choose Format **P**atterns & Colors with a line chart on-screen. Notice that this dialog box contains a new field named **Markers:**. You use *markers* to plot the exact location of a piece of data. When you are plotting several series of data in the same chart, you need to use different markers to keep the lines distinct. The **Markers:** field lists your options for different marker types.

FIG. 12.29

The Patterns & Colors dialog box with the **M**arkers: field included

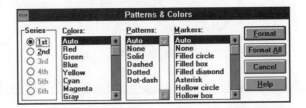

When creating the line chart, Works assigns default marker types to the data points. With the Patterns & Colors dialog box, you can override the marker types assigned by Works. To do so, follow these steps:

1. Access the Format menu.

2. Choose **P**atterns & Colors.

3. In the Series area of the Patterns & Colors dialog box, select the series you want to modify.

4. Press Alt,M to access the **Markers:** field.

5. Highlight the marker type you want to use.

6. Select the **F**ormat button.

7. Press Enter.

The change you have made appears in the chart.

T I P   If you want to have the format change apply to all the data plotted, select the Format **A**ll button rather than the Format button before pressing Enter.

Scaling the Axes

Although Works automatically sets the numbers along the axes to fit your range of data best, you can scale the y-axis and the x-axis yourself. *Scaling* simply means that you determine the frequency of the numbers that are used to enumerate the y-axis.

To scale the y-axis, follow these steps:

1. Access the Format menu.

2. Select the Vertical [y] Axis option. The dialog box shown in figure 12.30 appears.

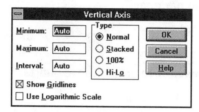

Again, you can learn best about the options by trying many variations. Adding gridlines, for example, enhances the readability of some charts but adds too much clutter to others.

Works does an excellent job scaling the y-axis on its own. If you want to adjust the scaling, you can do so as described in the following:

■ *Minimum* Enter the smallest value you want displayed on the axis. For example, if the numbers you are plotting are all greater than fifty thousand, you may want the smallest number to be 45 thousand.

■ *Maximum* Enter the greatest number you want displayed on the axis. For example, if you are plotting data in which one of the values is much greater than the others, Works may cut off the top of the bar.

■ *Interval* Enter the number increment you want to display on the y-axis. You may need more or less than determined by Works.

■ *Show Gridline* Select this option if you want a horizontal line displayed across the graph at each interval.

■ *Type* The type of mark on the y-axis can be a normal mark or one that corresponds to a stacked bar chart, a 100% chart, or a Hi-Lo-Close chart.

■ *Use Logarithmic Scale* If your data has a huge range, a logarithmic scale converts the increments to a factor of 10 (for example, 100 to 1,000 to 10,000), thereby capturing all the data.

Creating Customized Charts

You may get the idea that you have been creating customized charts throughout this chapter. Actually, however, you just have enhanced the program's standard charts. Four types of charts are not standard:

Charts with a right y-axis

A mixed line and bar chart

A hi-lo-close chart

An XY chart

This section examines how to create these charts.

Adding a Right Y-Axis

A second y-axis enables you to plot disparate data on the same chart. For example, you can combine the cost of new cars with the average income of buyers. The range on the left y-axis might be 5,000 to 25,000, while income may range from 30,000 to 100,000. Normally, the chart could not adequately handle the ranges and still make sense. The second or right y-axis plots the out of range data.

Figure 12.31 shows a typical line chart with two data series. Suppose that you want to add another axis to the right side of the chart. To add a right y-axis, first make sure that you're in a Chart; then follow these steps:

1. Open the Format menu.

2. Select the **T**wo Vertical axes option. The **T**wo Vertical Axes dialog box appears (see fig. 12.32).

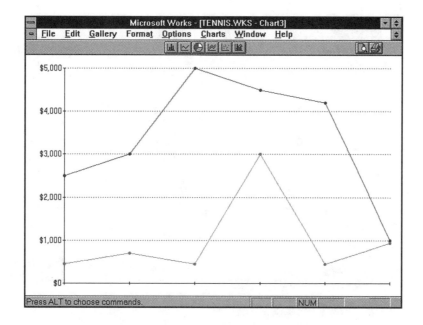

FIG. 12.31

Viewing a typical
line chart

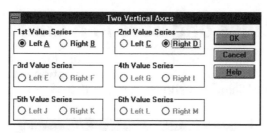

FIG. 12.32

The Two Vertical
Axes dialog box

Notice that in the 1st Value Series box, the first y-axis series
remains assigned to the left y-axis (Left **A** is selected). You can
assign any series to either a left or right axis. In this example,
you want to assign the second y-axis series to the right axis.

For each series in the chart, you can pick to which axis it is assigned. Simply select the series and then the appropriate axis. The
Left choice always refers to the left y-axis and the Right choice
always refers to the right y-axis. Works automatically inserts the
new y-axis and scales it according to the values in the series assigned to it.

This feature may seem complex, but with a little practice, you will feel
comfortable working with the second y-axis. Figure 12.33 shows the
sample chart with the right y-axis added.

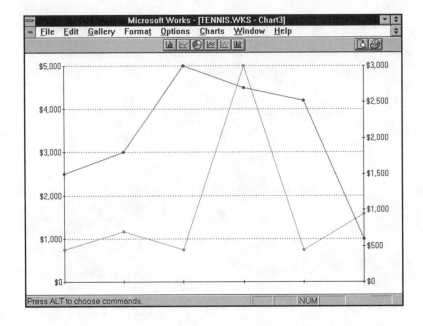

Mixing Lines and Bars in a Chart

Another custom chart you can create is one that incorporates both
lines and bars. Choosing the **M**ixed Line & Bar option from the Forma**t**
menu opens the dialog box shown in figure 12.34.

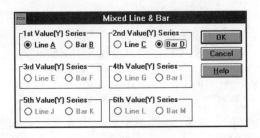

You must decide which series to plot as bars and which to plot as lines.
In figure 12.34, the first series is plotted as a line (Line **A** is selected in
the 1st Value (Y) Series box), and the second series is plotted as a bar
(Bar **D** is selected in the 2nd Value (Y) Series box). For each series in
the chart, you can choose Line or Bar as the display style. The combination of the y-axis on the right and the gridlines creates an interesting
chart.

Making a Hi-Lo-Close Chart

Following trends in stock prices is made easier with the hi-lo-close chart. Three values are plotted for each time period—the high, low, and closing prices of the stock—and they are connected by a vertical line to show the range of movement. Figure 12.35 shows a spreadsheet with the price movements of ZCORP. The time period is one month per plot. Hence, the chart created from that data reflects the highest, lowest, and closing prices for that stock in the entire month (see fig. 12.36). Each month is a single y-axis series with three values. This chart was created by choosing the Line command from the Gallery menu (in chart mode) and selecting option 6, the Hi-Lo-Close option.

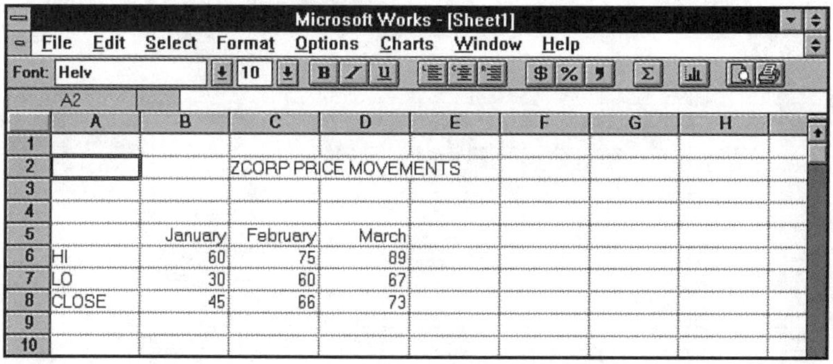

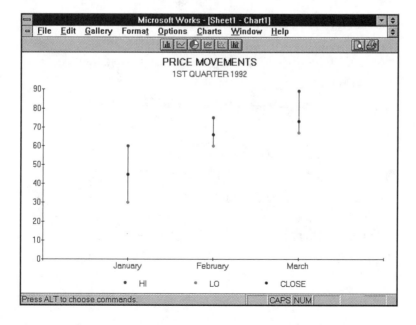

FIG. 12.35

A sample spreadsheet of stock prices

FIG. 12.36

Charting the stock prices in a hi-lo-close chart

Making an XY Chart

XY charts are used most frequently for plotting irregularly occurring data. Figure 12.37, for example, shows a spreadsheet with two columns of numbers—one representing time intervals and the other the number of parts per million of a drug detected in the patient's bloodstream. This type of data—the absorption rate of a drug into a patient's bloodstream—is a good candidate for presentation in an XY chart.

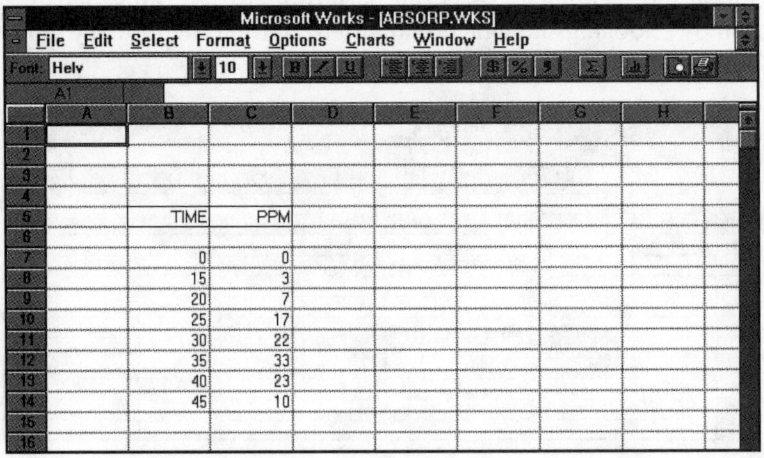

FIG. 12.37

A sample spreadsheet for producing an XY chart

	TIME	PPM
	0	0
	15	3
	20	7
	25	17
	30	22
	35	33
	40	23
	45	10

To create an XY chart, follow these steps:

1. In the spreadsheet, highlight the range that includes the data you want to chart—B7..B14 in the sample spreadsheet.

2. Access the Charts menu.

3. Select Create New Chart. Works creates the default bar chart.

4. Open the Edit menu.

5. Select Series. The Series dialog box appears.

6. In the Category X Series: field, enter *B7..B14*.

7. Select the 1st: field and erase the entry. Replace it with **C7..C14**, which is the measured absorption rate values.

8. Open the Gallery menu, and select XY (Scatter).

9. In the X-Y (Scatter) dialog box, select 1 (see fig 12.38).

Chart 1 is a standard XY chart. Chart 2 includes lines drawn between the data points. Chart 3 includes horizontal gridlines. Chart 4 includes vertical gridlines. Chart 5 includes both horizontal and vertical gridlines. Chart 6 is a markers only chart with a logarithmic y-axis and horizontal gridlines.

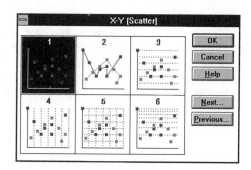

FIG. 12.38

The X-Y (Scatter) dialog box

In an XY chart, the intersection of the x-axis and the y-axis becomes the 0 value for both series.

An XY chart is a good candidate for an additional y-axis, particularly if you have many observations to plot. You also can add a title or the x- and y-axes labels in the same way you do for all other charts.

Naming, Duplicating, and Deleting Charts

The Works default names for charts—Chart1, Chart2, and so on—may not be specific enough for you. You easily can add a more descriptive name to each of your charts.

After you have created a chart to your liking, follow these steps to name it:

1. Access the **Charts** menu.

2. Select **Na**me to open the Name Chart dialog box (see fig. 12.39).

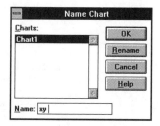

FIG. 12.39

The Name Chart dialog box

3. In the **Charts:** list, highlight the chart you want to name.

4. Press Alt,N to activate the **Name:** box field.

5. Type any name you want, using up to 16 characters.

6. Click Rename, then press Enter or click OK when you are finished naming the chart.

On the **Charts** menu, note that you also have the options to erase (**De**-lete) and copy (**Du**plicate) your charts. Use the **Du**plicate option when you want to experiment with a chart format while retaining the original. When you select **Du**plicate, Works makes a copy of your original chart. The copy becomes the active chart, and you can save it with a unique name and make changes to it.

Viewing a Chart in Black and White on a Color Monitor

If you are using a system with a color monitor, you may want to see how the chart will look in black and white before you print. Previewing the chart in black and white gives you the opportunity to modify the markers or the cross-hatching required for black-and-white printing.

To see a chart displayed in black and white, do the following:

1. Access the **Options** menu.

2. Choose Display as **P**rinted. Works then displays the chart in black and white.

Printing Charts

Works makes the printing process an easy task. But first, you may need to set up the page or the printer. The following sections explain how to prepare for the job and then how to initiate the printing process.

Setting Up the Page, Margins, and Printer

Before you print a chart, you may want to modify the size of the chart in relation to the page or change the size of the paper you are using for printing. For these tasks, you use the Page Setup & Margins dialog box on the File menu (see fig. 12.40).

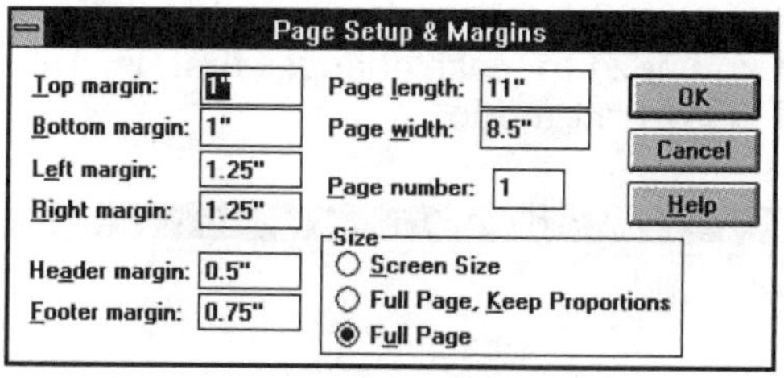

FIG. 12.40

The Page Setup & Margins dialog box

Notice that Works has inserted default settings for the margins, page size, and page number at which you want to start printing. The program assumes that you want to print the chart on standard, 8 1/2-by-11-inch paper in Portrait (vertical) mode, beginning on page 1. To change the orientation of charts from Portrait to Landscape (horizontal) mode, you must access the Printer Setup dialog box (choose File Printer Setup). All the example charts printed in this chapter are in Portrait mode.

The values in the Page Setup and Margins dialog box are calculated in inches. When working with charts, you may wish to be more precise and have the calculations done in centimeters, picas, or points. Changing the measuring units is accomplished via the Options menu and the Works Settings dialog box.

To change a value in the Page Setup and Margins dialog box, click on the box following the setting, and then type in the new value.

Or, with the keyboard, press Alt and then the underlined letter to move the highlight to entry box, then type the new value.

The top, bottom, left, and right margin settings determine the distance from the edge of the paper that Works begins printing. The overall size of the paper is determined by the entries in the page length and page width. If you are adding headers or footers to the chart, and need more space, increase the room for the header or footer, decrease the value in the margin. This sounds wrong, but when you think about it, the larger the margin the less space for the header or footer.

The Size options allow you to manipulate the manner in which the chart is printed. The default setting is Full Page, which means that the chart is printed using the total page. When Works prints the chart, it adjusts the proportions of the chart to fit the page. If you want to print the chart on the full page but keep the same proportions as seen on the screen, select that option. Lastly, you can print the chart so that it is identical to the size displayed on the screen.

Another useful feature is Preview. Before you print your chart, you can use the Print Preview command on the File menu to look at your chart on-screen as it will appear on paper. In view of the time required to print a chart, this feature alone can save you hours if you discover on the preview that you need to make changes first. Figure 12.41 shows a chart previewed in Portrait mode.

FIG. 12.41

Previewing a chart

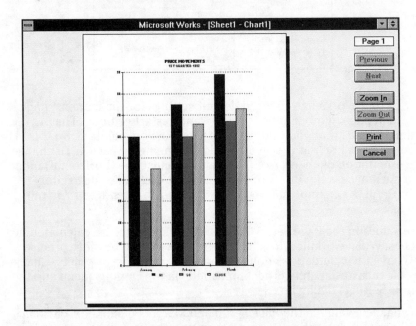

Although by default Works uses the printer driver that you specified when you first started using Windows, you can modify some of the settings. Or, if you have two printers, you can switch from one printer to another. To change these settings, you use the Printer Setup dialog box, which you access by choosing Printer Setup from the File menu. Figure 12.42, for example, shows the Printer Setup dialog box for a system in which an HP LaserJet Series II printer is installed. By clicking the arrow at the end of the field, you can display a drop-down list with the names of other printers. Select a different printer if you prefer and then select the settings that are appropriate for it. Depending on the printer, you can print heavier or lighter graphics, as indicated by the number of dots per inch.

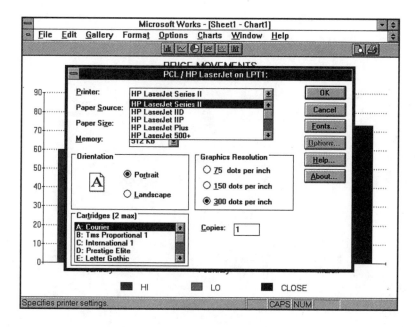

FIG. 12.42

A Printer Setup
dialog box

Initiating the Printing Process

Printing a chart is straightforward if you have installed your printer
correctly. To begin printing a chart, click the Printer button in the
Tool bar or open the File menu and select Print. A dialog box appears,
asking you for input on the number of copies you want to print.
Simply press Enter again to print one copy of the chart. Printing charts
takes a long time, especially if you are using a dot-matrix printer. Use
this opportunity to take a break.

Chapter Summary

Charts illuminate relationships that are difficult to perceive when represented by numbers alone on a spreadsheet. The key to using charts
is to pick the appropriate chart format to illustrate your data. This
chapter has explored the many aspects of creating charts and examined the ease of switching among different chart formats.

In Chapter 13, you examine the Microsoft Works database. A database
enables you to store and recall easily large amounts of information,
such as names, invoices, and part numbers.

Databases

PART

IV

OUTLINE

Creating a Database and Database Report: Quick Start

A database is a collection of related information. For example, a phone book contains the name, address, and phone number of everyone in a geographic area with a phone. With Works, you can create your own phone book of friends or business associates. A further example is an invoice database containing the names and addresses of customers and a list and the cost of items they have ordered plus the shipping destination. With Works, calculating the amount of outstanding invoices or printing a list of overdue accounts is simple. With the information entered into Works it is instantly accessible. Even with a thousand database records, it takes only a matter of seconds to find a particular invoice. In other words, the Works database takes the place of paper methods of recording information. Database information can be sorted, queried, and then output into reports.

This chapter provides a quick overview of the Works database feature. In this chapter, you learn how to do the following:

- ■ Create a database.

- ■ Create, name, enter, and edit fields.

■ Fill fields with data.

■ Change field sizes, alter their styles, and sort the data.

■ Save the new database.

Creating a Database

When you start Works, the Startup dialog box appears on-screen. To create and name a database, follow these steps:

1. Move the mouse pointer to the **Database** button and click to display the database opening screen, as shown in figure 13.1. You are using a new database file in the Form view. The Database Tool bar contains specific buttons as shown in the figure.

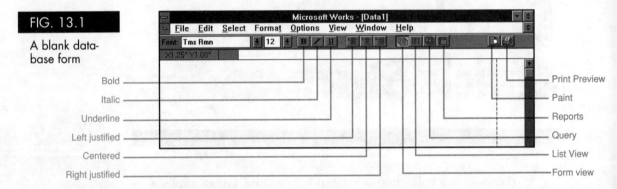

FIG. 13.1

A blank database form

2. Click the insertion point to the desired location, or use the arrow keys to move the insertion point.

3. Type the name of the database across the top of the screen, as shown in figure 13.2.

4. Move the mouse pointer off the label and click.

Naming Database Fields

Information in a database is entered into a field. The field is created by entering a field name followed by a colon.

To name the database fields, follow these steps:

1. Choose the position for the first field and move the insertion point to that location.

2. Type the name of the first field and end it with a colon, as shown in figure 13.2. For the field named *First Name:*, for example, the highlighted entry will look like this:

   First Name:

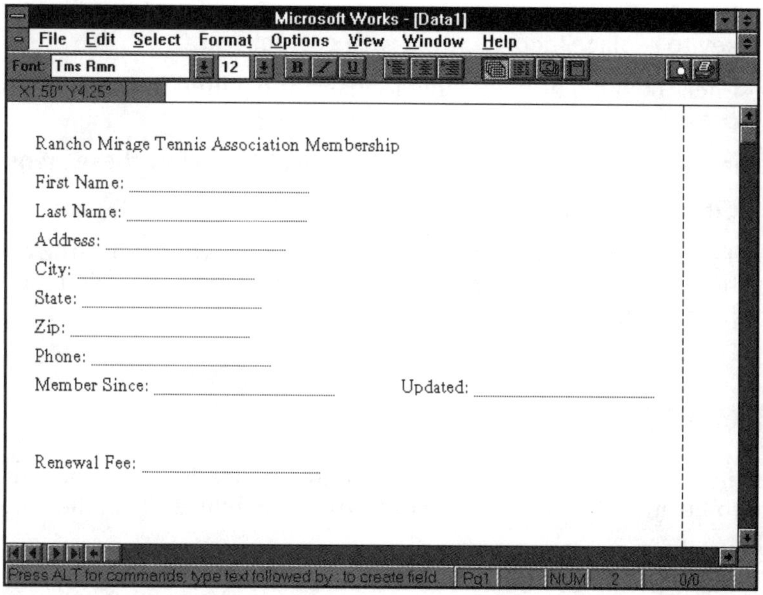

FIG. 13.2

Fields for the database record

3. Move the mouse pointer off the label and click to display the Field Size dialog box. The default width is 20 characters and the default height is 1 line. Accept the default values for the first field by clicking OK, or typing the desired values in the dialog box.

The remaining fields are created by accepting the default values for field Size. After creating a field name, pressing Enter moves the insertion point to the next line down in the form and in alignment with the preceding field name. The Updated: field is created by using the mouse pointer or the arrow keys to move the insertion point after the Member Since: field. A field can be created anywhere in the form.

4. Complete figure 13.2 by entering fields for all the needed information in the database record.

Editing a Field Name

There will always be the need to add or change the information entered into the fields and the best way to do that is by editing the fields. The names of the database fields are easily edited or changed.

To edit a database field name, follow these steps:

1. Click the field name.

2. Press F2, and EDIT appears on the status line, along with the field name.

3. Edit the field name by using the arrow keys, delete key, and insert key to replace incorrect text with correct text.

4. Click the label or field name to insert the edited information, or press Enter.

To change the entire field name (not just edit it), follow these steps.

1. Click the field name.

2. Type the new name and click. The new text will replace the old text. If you decide that you don't want to replace the old text, press Esc.

Entering Data

Each field name is followed by a dotted line indicating the space for the data to be entered. To enter the data shown in figure 13.3, follow these steps:

1. Move the mouse pointer to the data cell for First Name:, and click, or use the arrow keys and press Enter.

2. Type **Bradley**.

3. Click the mouse pointer on the next field to enter the data.

4. Repeat steps one through three for the remaining fields in figure 13.3.

To enter data for the second record, click the first right-facing arrow at the lower left of the form screen. A blank second record appears, indicated by the NUM 2 that appears in the status line below the form screen, or press Tab in the last record. Move the mouse pointer to the data cell for First Name: and begin entering the data for the second record, shown in figure 13.4.

Enter the following information for records 2 and 3:

Tom Collins
13008 Roundup
Rancho Mirage, CA.
92876
(619) 555-1818
5/15/87
1/15/92
140

Moette Champagne
9306 Twin Trails
San Pedro, CA
92222
(619) 555-7895
5/10/86
3/16/92
140

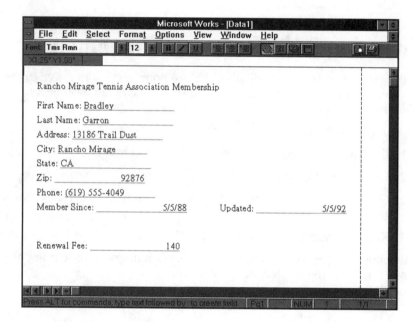

FIG. 13.3

The completed
record

Changing to List View

The database was created in Form view, but is viewed in List view. To change to List view and display figure 13.4, click the List view button on the Tool bar.

In List view, you can view up to eight fields at one time. To view the remaining fields, click the right-arrow key in the scroll bar in the lower-right corner of the form screen until the fields scroll to the left.

FIG. 13.4

A List view of
records

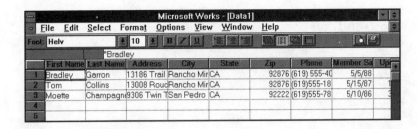

Choosing Field Styles and Alignment

Follow the procedure described in the previous section to move to the
last field, Renewal Fee:, in the database record. The Renewal Fee: field
contains a numeric value.

To change the format of this field, follow these steps:

1. Click Renewal Fee to highlight the field column.

2. Click Format on the Menu bar.

3. Click Currency in the Format menu to display the Currency dialog
   box.

4. Keep the number of decimals at 2. Click OK.

The values that appear in the Renewal Fee column now appear in currency format with two decimal places.

Sorting in List View

A useful feature of a database is the ability to sort records. In this example the records of this sample database are sorted alphabetically by
using the Last Name: field.

To sort alphabetically by using the Last Name: field, follow these steps.

1. Click on the Last Name: field so that the whole column is selected.

2. Click Select from the Menu bar.

3. Click Sort Records to display the Sort Records dialog box, as
   shown in figure 13.5.

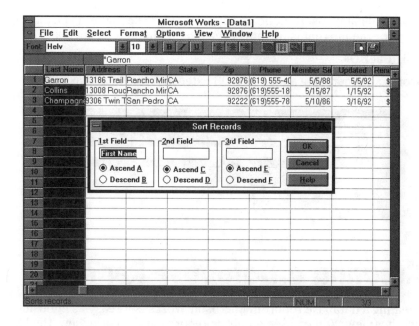

FIG. 13.5

The Sort Records
dialog box

4. First Name appears in the dialog box under the first field to be sorted. Press the backspace key to delete First Name from the box.

5. Type **Last Name**.

6. Sort in ascending order by clicking Ascend or pressing Alt,A.

7. Click OK or press Enter.

Works sorts the records in alphabetical order by the Last Name: field as shown in figure 13.6.

To return to Form view, click the Form button in the Tool bar, or press F9 or open the **View** menu and select **F**orm.

Saving the Database

Although you have created the database form and entered several records, the form and the records must be saved as a specific file.

To save the database you have created, follow these steps:

1. Click **F**ile on the Menu bar.

2. Click Save **A**s to display the Save As dialog box.

3. A blinking insertion point appears under File **N**ame. Type a name for the file that is no longer than eight characters, such as TEST.

4. Click OK.

Works automatically adds the WDB extension to all database files.

FIG. 13.6

Database
records sorted by
Last Name

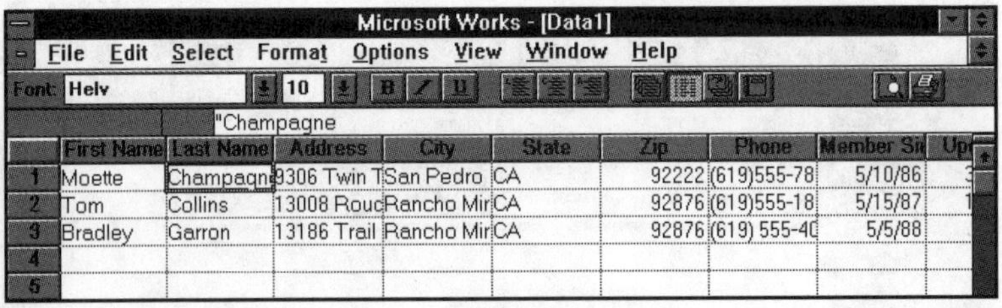

Creating a Database Report

Creating a database report in Microsoft Works is as easy as choosing another view. You can see database records in the Form view, the List view, and, when you are ready to prepare a report, the Report view.

This report example totals the amount in the Renewal Fee: field of all records and provides a count of the number of records included in the total. With a small number of records, this report could easily be done by hand. But when the records grow to several hundred the efficacy of an electronic database is apparent.

From the Form or List view, click the Report button on the Tool bar to display the New Report dialog box. Begin by typing the name of the report in the Report title box. Figure 13.7 shows the New Report dialog box.

Press Alt,T to enter the report name, such as TEST REPORT.

Choosing the Fields To Appear in the Report

On the left side of the Report dialog box is the list of fields for the records created in this database. To choose the fields appearing in the report, follow these steps:

1. Click Last Name and then click the Add>>> button. The Last Name: field is inserted in the Fields portion of the Report box, or press Alt,S to select last name, then press Alt,A to add.

2. Repeat this procedure to include Phone number and Renewal Fee in the Report box.

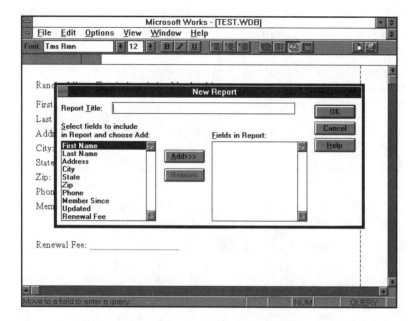

FIG. 13.7

The New Report dialog box

Defining the Report

The specific output of the report is established by choosing the data, how the data is to be presented, and by defining the printer setup. To define the report output, follow these steps:

1. Click OK or press Enter to display the Report Statistics dialog box.

2. With Renewal Fee highlighted, click **S**um, to give you a sum of the renewal fees. Or press Alt,F, highlight Renewal Fee, and press Enter.

3. With Last Name highlighted, click on **C**ount or press Alt,C to get a total of the records in the report.

4. Press Alt,U or choose **U**nder each column by clicking that option in the lower right of the dialog box. The Sum and the Count will display below each column.

5. Click OK or press Enter and you are notified that the report definition is created.

6. Click OK to display the Report design screen.

7. Works displays a message alerting you that the Report Definition has been created. Click OK, or press Enter.

8. Click the Print Preview button to see the report. Or press Alt,F,V.

The mouse pointer is shaped like a magnifying glass. Click once or twice on the text you want magnified until you can read the text easily.

Three records are included in the report with a total of $420.00 expected in renewal fees.

Sorting Reports

Reports can also be done from the Select option on the Menu bar, by following these steps:

1. Click Cancel or press Esc to exit from the report created in the previous section, and display the Report Definition screen.

2. Click Select on the Menu bar.

3. Choose Sort Records to display the Sort Records dialog box. In this dialog box, you can sort by three fields, and you may also break sorted groups either by group or by first letter.

4. For each field by which you want to sort, supply the following information:

   Type the name of the field.

   Indicate whether you want the sort in descending or ascending order.

   Choose to break by group or by first letter.

To make your sort selections, you can select the options you want by either pointing and clicking or pressing Alt and the corresponding letter. For example, to sort the 1st Field you have selected in ascending order, press Alt,A. Works also allows you to break the sort by inserting a summary row each time the information in that field changes. For example, if the field contained ZIP codes, when a new ZIP code is encountered Works breaks the sort and totals the number of records with the previous ZIP. This technique is available only when you create a report.

The option, 1st Letter, works in combination with the Break option in the following manner: if the entries in the field are letters (such as names) then Works breaks the sort when the first letter in the field changes. For example, if there are 50 records with Smith in the Last

Name: field and the next record is Thomas, Works inserts a summary line in the report, noting that 50 records were counted with the Last Name of Smith.

5. After defining the sort, Click OK or press Enter.

Because you began the sort process in the report definition screen, you must click either the Form button or the List button to see the records. The records in the database are listed according to your sort choices.

Preparing a Query

A query helps you locate a specific record or records in the database. For example, suppose that you want to locate all records in a specific ZIP code. You enter the ZIP code you want to match in the database form and select Report and Works searches the database for a match or matches as follows:

1. Start in the Report definition screen, by clicking the Report Definition button, or by opening the **View** menu and selecting 1 Report1, from the list of options. The prior report definition, created earlier in this chapter, appears on-screen.

2. Click the Query button. Works presents you with a blank database form.

3. One of the entries in the database has a ZIP code of 92222. Press the Tab key to move the highlight to the ZIP code field or click on the field.

4. Type: **92222** and press Enter or click on the check mark to the left of the edit bar at the top of the screen.

5. Click on List or open the **View** menu and select **List**. Works displays the records that match in List format as seen in figure 13.8.

You can save the query in a report format with the following steps:

1. With your mouse pointer in this list of records, create a new report by clicking **V**iew on the menu bar, and Create New Report, to display the New Report dialog box.

2. Type the name for this query in the Report Title box to create a new report with a new title, such as ZIP 92222.

3. Click OK.

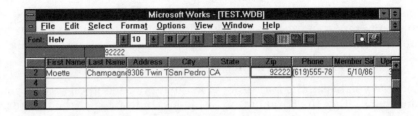

FIG. 13.8

One record
matching the
92222 ZIP code

Printing the Report

With the mouse pointer in the Report Definition screen, click the Print button on the Tool bar, to display the Print dialog box. Specify the options you want, including multiple copies, and click OK to print the report.

 A Print Settings dialog box may appear that reminds you to set up the printer and printing options. When this task is complete, click Continue.

Saving Reports

Save your report by clicking File on the Menu bar, and Save. Works will save your report as a component of the database in which you are working. This includes any variations on reports that you have made.

Chapter Summary

In this chapter, you learned about the basic steps of creating a database, creating database field names and fields, editing database field names, entering information into a record, sorting records, and creating reports.

In the next chapter, you take a more detailed look at building and modifying database forms.

Creating and Using Databases

Your life is full of data and information—from the people listed in your address book to your list of suppliers. A database helps you store and organize this information. In Chapter 7, you used the Works-Wizards to create a simple database of names and addresses that you then inserted into a form letter. In that example, you accepted the Works design and so did not customize the database. In this chapter, you learn more about databases—what they are, what they can do, and how they are designed and customized.

The Microsoft Works database helps you organize information, analyze this information in a variety of ways, and print the results in a report or in a word processed document. Because this is done electronically, these activities are done quickly and easily on your computer, in your network, or in a remote location. The integration features of Microsoft Works ensures maximum utilization of your database, by making it easy to interface with other applications.

In this chapter, you learn how to do the following:

- Create a database.
- Enter field names and data into a record.
- Change and edit cell contents, and enter dates and move fields and records.
- Search a database for specific records.
- Select records, and sort records.

- Copy, delete, and clear data.
- Add functions to database tasks.
- Protect the confidentiality of a database.
- Hide field names, fields, and records.

Creating a Database

At the Works welcome screen, shown in figure 14.1, click the Start **Works** Now button to display the Startup dialog box. You may choose whether to open a new word processing file, a new spreadsheet file, a new database file, a new WorksWizards file, or an existing file, as shown in figure 14.2. Click the mouse pointer on the Database button.

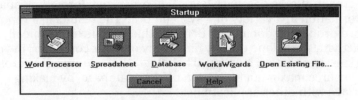

The database screen displays a database window named DATA1. The work space is clear and ready for you to create a database. Before you begin creating a database, take a moment to learn the various database components:

Database Record. This holds all the information about one person, one company, or one event on your list, and consists of database fields. All the records in one database file will hold the same information about each person, company, or event.

Database Field. In a database of companies, each piece of information about the company is a field. The name, address, and phone number of the company, the type of company, and the main contact person are all fields in the record for that specific company.

Label. A title or note is considered to be a label, which means that you will not be adding field information to it. The name at the top of the database is an example of a label.

Cell. When you list or report information that is in a database, the information is presented in rows and columns. A cell is the point where a row and column intersect.

Planning Your Database

Before beginning to construct your database, plan what you want your database to do, how to construct the database, and how to use the database. Decide what information is going to be crucial, what information you would like to add, and what order or format to enter the information you want. For example, a database for personal names and addresses will be different than one for suppliers.

You can create a format that is easy to read and easy to use for everyone having access to the database by adhering to the following procedures:

■ Abbreviations used for entering information should be easily understood by everyone using the database.

■ For information entered the same way every time, type an example in the field name, such as Date (MM/DD/YY). Date format is especially important because information is often retrieved by date.

■ Enter the information in a logical order. When you rearrange the conventional sequence of name, company name, address, city, state, and ZIP code, data entered by other database users is likely to be inconsistent.

■ Field names should be meaningful, unique, and understandable to others. Use a secret code only when you are the sole person with access to the database.

Mailing labels may use first names, last names, professional titles, or all three. Add sufficient space for long addresses, plus a field for the company name. Academic or government institutions may require all the following information:

- Name (Joe Brown, Ph.D., D.D.S.)
- Title (Director)
- Department (Public Health Dentistry)
- School (School of Public Health)
- Institution (University of Minnesota)
- Branch of Institution (Duluth)

With some entries, such as expert consultants, you may want to include professional credentials—M.D., M.S.W., M.B.A., or Ph.D. —as a separate field.

You may want to add a number for each record. Purchase orders and invoices often have numbers assigned to them. Add one field to each record that holds a field number.

Entering Field Names

The month is April 1990, and the Rancho Mirage Tennis Association wants to remind members that they'll have to renew their membership in May. In this section, you create a membership database for the Association that contains the members' name, address, phone number, date of membership, date of most recent membership payment, and the annual dues payment.

For this example, the information in the database is limited to the fields just named, although much more information could be added for each member. Other fields could list a member's playing level, tournament standings, doubles partner, locker number, and the last time the member had his or her racquet restrung.

NOTE Remember to maximize the Application window and the Document Window with the Control buttons.

To create your database, follow these steps:

1. Move the mouse to the upper left corner of the database work space screen, and click. Type **Rancho Mirage Tennis Association**. The text is highlighted in the database work space and also appears in the Formula bar, below the Tool bar, as shown in figure 14.3.

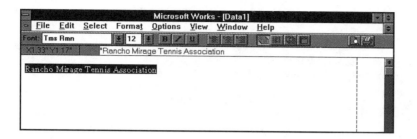

FIG. 14.3

Text on work space screen and in Formula bar

2. Move the mouse down two lines and click to create a new insertion point. Type **First Name:**. The colon tells Works that a field is being entered into the database.

3. Click to display the Field Size dialog box, as shown in figure 14.4. The default value for field length is 20 and for field height is one. When information exceeds the default values, change the value by typing in a higher number. For this example, choose the default values by clicking OK.

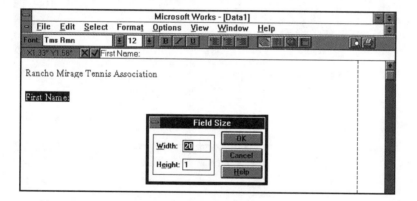

FIG. 14.4

Field size dialog box

4. Repeat steps two and three, entering the following fields with the field lengths shown in parentheses:

- Last Name: (30)
- Address: (30)
- City: (20)
- State: (5)
- Zip: (7)
- Phone: (20)

■ Member Since: (20)

■ Updated: (20)

■ Renewal Fee: (10)

> **NOTE** Separate the first name and last name fields. This step makes it easier to search your database for a last name.

The work space screen should appear as shown in figure 14.5.

FIG. 14.5

Completed
database form

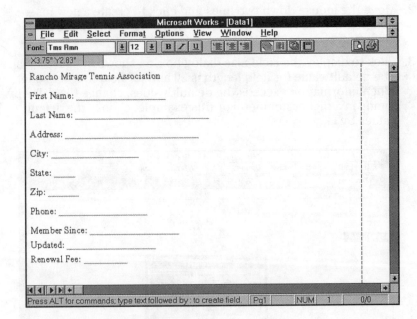

Entering Data into a Record

With the database format completed, you are ready to enter data. Follow these steps:

1. Click to highlight the data cell to the right of *First Name*:, as shown in figure 14.6. The highlighting covers the specified field length of 20 spaces. Type **Bradley**.

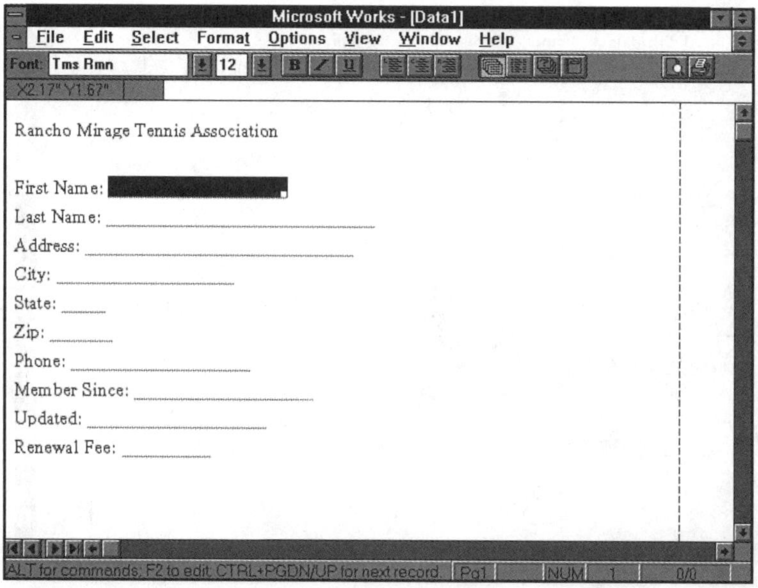

FIG. 14.6

Highlighted field
data cell

2. Repeat step one by clicking or pressing Tab to move to the next field, and enter the following data:

- Garron

- 13186 Trail Dust

- Rancho Mirage

- CA

- 92876

- (619) 555-4049

- 5/5/88

- 5/5/88

- 180

You have just completed one database record containing all information—in fields—about one member, Bradley Garron. This completed record should appear as shown in figure 14.7.

3. Before proceeding to the next record, locate the four arrows at the bottom left of the screen. Two point to the left and two point to the right. The inside arrows move you from record to record, and the outside arrows move you to the first record in the database and to the last. Click on the right-facing inside arrow to move to the next record as shown in figure 14.8. The same fields appear but are blank.

FIG. 14.7

Completed data record

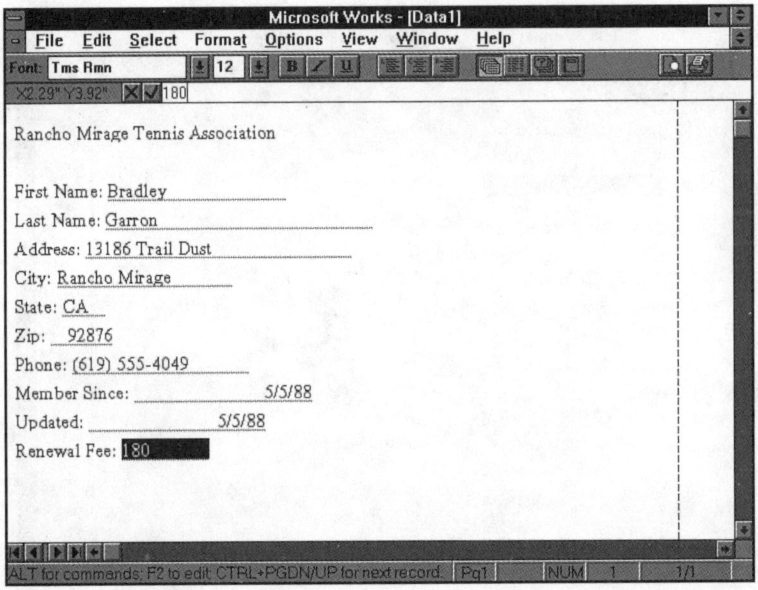

FIG. 14.8

Blank second record

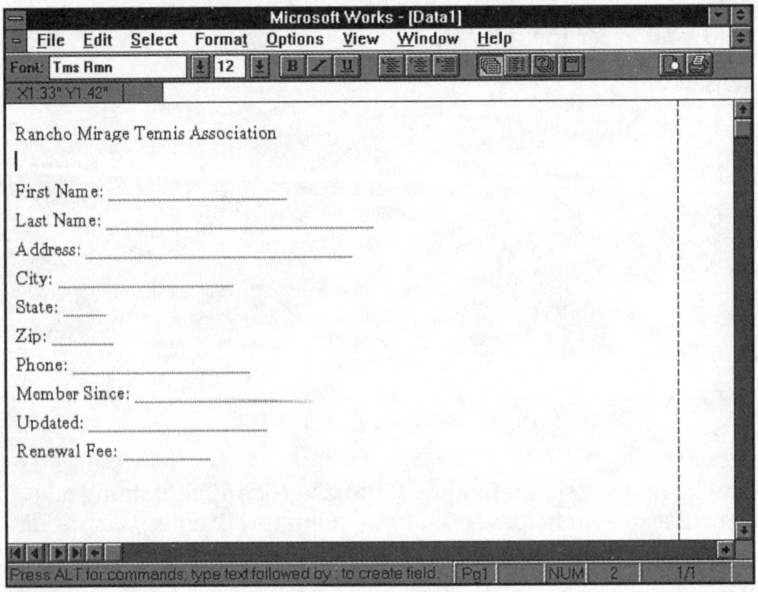

The Record number indicator appearing at the lower right side of the screen displays NUM 2, to show you are now in the second record of this database.

4. Follow the procedure for the first record to complete the second
   and third records with the following information:

Record 2:	Record 3:
■ Moette	Tom
■ Champagne	Collins
■ 9306 Twin Trail	13008 Round Up Ave.
■ San Pedro	Rancho Mirage
■ CA	CA
■ 92929	92928
■ (714) 555-3838	(619) 555-4989
■ 5/10/86	5/15/87
■ 5/2/88	5/25/88
■ 140	140

Examining the Form View Database Screen

With Record 3 on-screen, as shown in figure 14.9, study the database
screen. The database screen displays a great deal of information to
help you keep track of where you are and what you are doing.

Title bar. The name of the file in which you are working appears at
the top of the screen. When you're in the database, Data1 is displayed on this line.

Works Menu bar. The second line from the top of the screen is the
Works Menu bar. Access these menu selections by clicking the
menu name.

Tool bar. The third line from the top, the Tool bar, holds the buttons that control file activity. In this case, the form button is highlighted on-screen to show you are in Form view. Other options are
List view, Query view, and Report view. To move to another view,
click the appropriate button.

FIG 14.9

Completed third
record

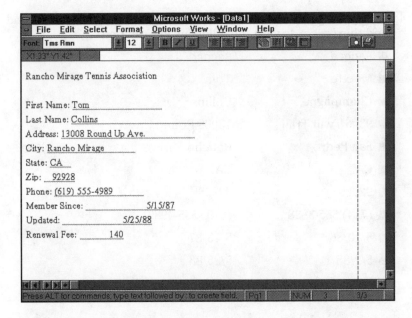

Formula bar. The fourth line from the top is the Formula bar, which displays the contents of the active cell. Click the data cell to the right of *First Name:*, and *"Tom* appears on the Formula bar. The quotation mark that appears before Tom indicates this element to be data entered into a field, or data entered into a label such as the name of the database. Click the cell *Rancho Mirage Tennis Association*, and *"Rancho Mirage Tennis Association* appears on the Formula bar.

Whenever you enter field names, text, numbers, or field formulas, they are displayed in the Formula bar and in the active cell. Clicking the mouse inserts the entries into the active cell. Works provides the opportunity to change the entries before placing them in the database. You can, of course, edit them after entries are made in the active cell by pressing F2 to edit.

Specific information about your location in the record is displayed at the left end of the Formula bar. Like a spreadsheet, the database is divided into cells, and the X and Y notations indicate your present cell position. As you move across the screen, following the x-axis by clicking the mouse pointer across the page to the right, the numbers sequence from X1.25 to X7.17.

As you move down the screen, following the y-axis, the sequence moves from Y1.00 to Y4.58. Using these position indicators, you can find specific locations in a small or large database.

Work space. The work space takes up the majority of the Works database screen, showing the name of the database and listing the fields and their contents.

Scroll bar. Mouse activity occurs on the shaded line directly below the work space, called the scroll bar. The four arrows (called scroll arrows) at the lower left corners of the scroll bar are the navigation buttons. Two point to the left and two point to the right. The inside arrows move you from record to record, and the outside arrows move you to the first record in the database and to the last. Click each of these buttons to move through the database records.

Use the scroll arrows to scroll left or right and up or down in the work space. Click on the scroll arrows to move in small increments. Click and drag the boxes (called thumbs) in the scroll bars to scroll over larger spaces.

Status bar. Below the scroll bar is the status bar. At the far right of the status bar you see 3/3. All three records can be seen. After a Query with a larger database, a number such as 28/40 may appear, telling you that 28 of the 40 possible records in that database can be seen in response to the Query.

Pg 1 appears near the center of the status line, denoting that this is a one-page record. As databases develop, records often have more than one page. You can look in the Status bar to find which page of the record holds the mouse pointer.

The Record indicator NUM 3 on the status bar indicates you are viewing record number three of the records in this database. Click the right-facing navigation button, and record number four appears.

In the short space that holds the record number, to the right of the word NUM in the status bar, you will see the name of command modes you are presently using. Press F2 to go into the Edit mode and Edit displays on the status line, replacing the record number.

Message bar. The Message bar is located at the left end of the status bar, and offers a one-line help message for any task you perform. In figure 14.9, the Message bar reads ALT for commands; F2 to edit.... Press Alt and the Message bar displays the message Press letter on menu title, or use arrow keys and press Enter. Click the Select menu and the Message bar reads Selects specified record or field. You are constantly receiving a cue with each mouse click.

Now that you are aware of the information available on-screen, practice editing a field.

Changing the Size of a Field

Click the underlined section next to the Last Name field. Click Format on the Menu bar, and then click Field Size to display the Field Size dialog box. Type **20**, instead of the 30 chosen earlier, for the size of this field. Leave the height at one line. Click OK.

Editing Data in a Field

Data entered incorrectly into a data cell is corrected by using the edit key (F2), or by typing in new data. When the data contained in a cell is small, typing in the new information may be easier. For example, change the date in the Member Since data field by highlighting that field and typing 5/22/87. Click, or press Enter, to insert the data into the field.

Use the edit key (F2) when you have a long entry in the field or when you are editing something that is difficult to spell. Click the field you want to correct, press F2 and EDIT appears on the status line. By using the arrow keys, move the cursor to the incorrect text in the formula bar and edit as you would in the word processor. Press Enter to apply the correction or Esc to ignore it.

For example, click on the address field where it says 13008 Round Up Ave. Press F2. Press the left arrow key until it is to the right of the number 8. Press the backspace key one time, then type **9**. Click the mouse button to insert the corrected address number, or press Enter to apply the correction. Press Esc to ignore the correction.

Selecting Fields and Records in Form View

When you prepare to edit, move, or copy records or fields, you must first select them. In Form view, a field is selected by just clicking the field name or data field, but you are able to select only one record or field at a time. In Form view, Go to the section on List view if you want to learn how to select more than one record or field.

Select a record by clicking the mouse pointer in a record in Form view. Do not click on a field. To move, copy, or delete that record, click **Edit** on the Menu bar to display the **Edit** menu. For a record, the editing choices are to cut the record, copy the record, paste, delete the record, insert a record, insert a page break, or add headers and footers.

Select a field or data cell by pointing to the cell and clicking. The selected cell is highlighted.

Moving a Field

In the Form view, fields are moved easily to make reading and finding data more convenient. For example, in figure 14.9 the dates would be more easily spotted were they on one line. To position them on one line, the Updated field needs to be moved to the right of the Member Since field. Follow these steps:

1. Point to the Updated: field and click to highlight the field being moved, as shown in figure 14.10. The mouse pointer is a hand for moving the field.

2. Click, hold down the mouse button, and drag the field to the new location.

3. Release the mouse button when the field is positioned correctly, as shown in figure 14.11.

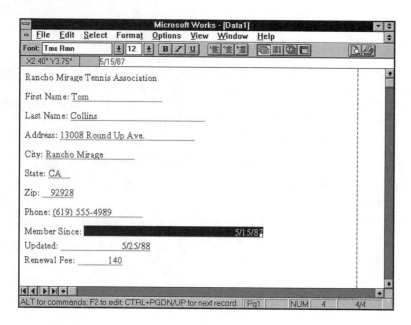

FIG. 14.10

Highlighted field to be moved

FIG. 14.11

Field moved to
new location

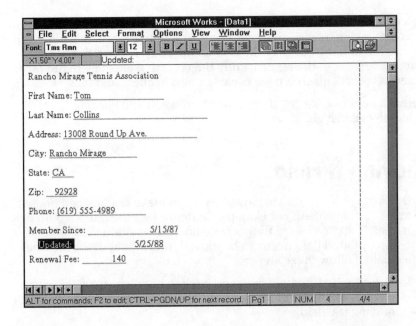

Click the left-facing record button to see the two remaining records in
this database, and you will notice that the change you made in one
record appears in every record. This convenient feature means that
you don't have to repeat the move procedure in every record.

Moving a Record

Records can be moved from any position in the record list and inserted
anywhere else in the list. Subsequent records are renumbered automatically when records are moved. To change the order of the records
in your database, follow these steps:

1. Click the mouse pointer in the record you want to move.

2. Click **Edit** on the Menu bar, and then Cut Record.

3. Move the mouse pointer to a blank record using the record
   buttons.

4. Click **Edit** and then click **P**aste Record. The data from the record
   that was cut inserts in the blank record.

Copying Labels

You cannot copy field data or field names from one record to another by using Works. Actually, there is no need to do so because once you establish a database form, every field name appears in every record.

You may choose to copy a label from one database to another. Follow these steps:

1. Click to highlight the label you want to copy.

2. Click **E**dit on the Menu bar, and then click Duplicate Label to display the highlighted label with the menu pointer appearing as a small hand.

3. Move the highlighted label to the new location and click.

Copying and Replacing

Use the **C**opy Record command to copy an entire record to a new location and replace an existing record. Follow these steps:

1. With your menu pointer in the record you want to copy, click the **E**dit menu, then click Copy Record.

2. Use the navigation buttons to move to the record to be replaced.

3. Click the **E**dit menu, then click **P**aste Record to copy the record and replace the previous record.

When you do not want to replace an old record, move to a blank record and click **E**dit, then **P**aste Record. The record is copied, but no other record is replaced.

Deleting and Clearing Data

Deleting and clearing data are two distinct tasks. Deleting data removes records or fields you no longer need, including their formatting. Clearing data removes the contents of a cell but leaves the formatting commands so that new information placed in the cell has the same format as the replaced information. Clear a cell when you want to erase the data you have and replace it.

To delete data, follow these steps:

1. In the Rancho Mirage Tennis Association database, click the Renewal Fee: field.

2. Click **E**dit on the Menu bar to display the Edit menu shown in figure 14.12.

NOTE The Edit menu will display different menu options, depending on what you have highlighted. In this case, **D**elete Field is listed; however, the menu would list Delete Label when a label was selected.

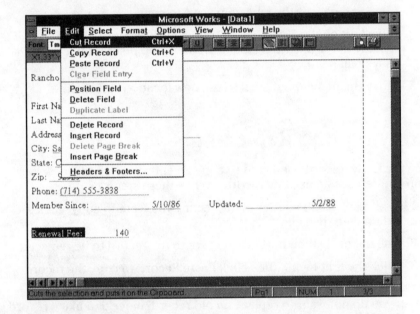

3. Click **D**elete Field to display a warning box asking whether to delete the data in this field.

4. Click OK to delete the field. Click **C**ancel to save the field. You also can click Help when you need the Help system at this time.

To clear data, follow these steps:

1. Click to highlight the label or data you want to remove.

2. Click **E**dit on the Menu bar, and click Clear Field Entry in the **E**dit menu.

By choosing this option, you can reenter data into these cells with the same formatting previously employed.

Examining the List Screen and Functions

Until now, you have been working with the Form database screen and the Form view functions. In Form view, you see one record at a time while viewing the fields in that record. When you want to see more than one record at a time to compare field data, use the List database screen.

For the examples that follow, a database has been created with 25 entries. The 25 entries are names and addresses, all outside the United States, used for an advertising mailing. In this database, you are going to track the response, noting which persons purchased products as a result of the mailer and the length of time for the order to arrive (purchase date). By tracking this information, you can determine cost-effectiveness of advertising outside the United States. You can create this database by copying the screen or by using your own database.

With this database, you can keep track of much more information. For example, you might want to record the date the order was received, the date the order was shipped, the transit time, whether the order was returned, or the recipient's fax number.

Before proceeding further, save the existing file as a backup copy to prevent inadvertently losing your work. Click File on the Menu bar, then Save As. Type **TENN**, then click OK. The file is saved as TENN.WDB.

In the Form view screen, click the List button on the Tool bar to display the List view screen, as shown in figure 14.13. The List view displays the database in spreadsheet fashion. The List view button is highlighted while you are in the List view mode.

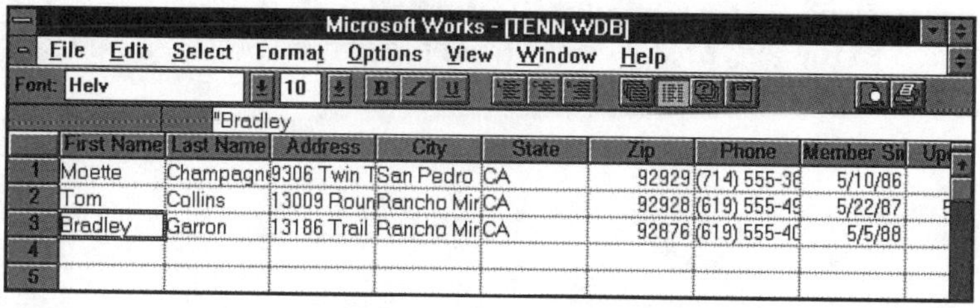

FIG. 14.13

List View of Database

On this List view screen, the Menu bar, Tool bar, and Formula bar are located in the same positions as in the Form view. The Formula bar displays the entire entry of a highlighted cell in the list. For example, click the cell 13009 Round Up Ave. in the address column. The entire entry appears on the Formula bar, as shown in figure 14.14.

FIG. 14.14

Address on the
Formula bar

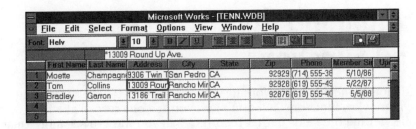

Move the mouse pointer to the right, and you see the remaining fields.
Use the scroll bar to move to Updated. After Updated, find Renewal Fee,
as shown in figure 14.15.

FIG.14.15

Updated and
Renewal fee

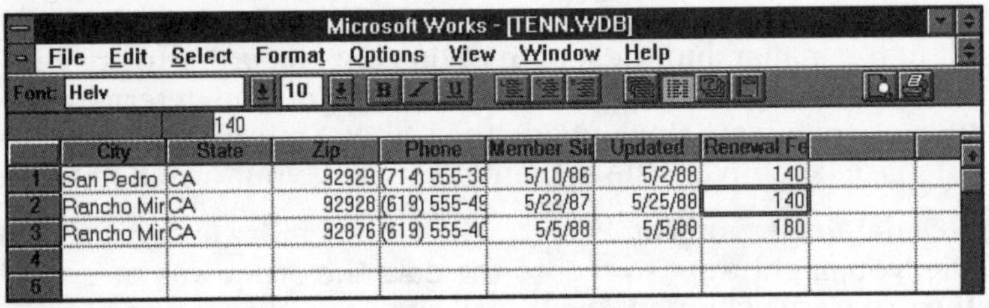

A column of numbers appears on the left side of the work space, indicating the number of the database record. The numbers 1 to 20 appear
on one screen.

The remaining List view screen appears much as the Form view screen.
For the examples that follow, more records have been added to this
database. You may copy these entries from the screen or use your own
database.

In the work space, the fields are listed from left to right in the same
order they were entered in Form view. The numeric field, *Zip*, has two
alignments. Because the Canadian postal codes start with letters, they
are aligned to the left; postal codes from the United States, made up of
numbers, are aligned to the right.

Selecting Data in the List View

In the Form view, you can select only one field data cell or record at a
time. In the List view, you can select and hide several records, select
and move fields, and select and copy any portion of the data.

To select and highlight one cell, move the pointer to the cell and click.

To select three records out of a 25-record database, follow these steps:

1. Move the mouse pointer to the column of record numbers beside the leftmost field of the records you want to select.

2. Click and drag the mouse pointer to highlight the three records.

3. When all fields in these records are highlighted, release the mouse button. Three records are highlighted, except the initial field, as shown in figure 14.16.

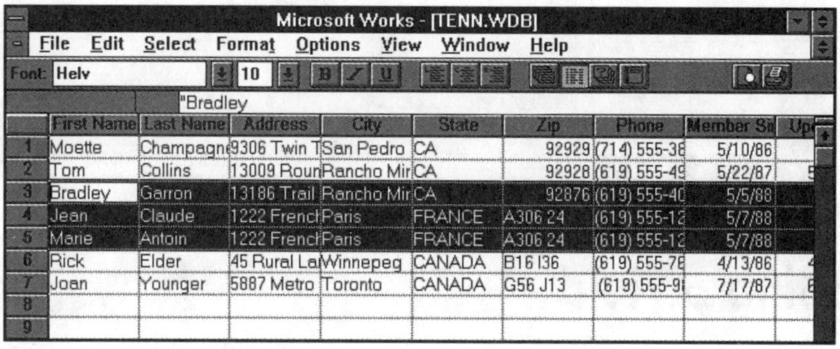

FIG. 14.16

Highlighted records

4. Now you are ready to move, copy, and delete records as described in following sections.

Undo the records selection and turn off the records highlighting by clicking a cell that is not included in the three records selected.

Select a field by clicking the field name at the top of the column to highlight the vertical column of cells.

Clicking and dragging to format, move, hide, copy, or delete the entire database can be inconvenient. Instead, click **S**elect on the Menu bar, and then the **A**ll option to highlight the entire database. To undo this selection, click any single field in the List view to turn off the highlighting.

In larger databases, use the **G**o To... command to quickly select a specific record or field. Follow these steps:

1. Click **S**elect on the Menu bar, and then the **G**o To... command to display the Go To dialog box.

2. All the fields in your database are listed in the Go To dialog box. Move the highlighting to the desired field and click. Alternatively, type the field name or data cell entry in the Go To box. In this example, Updated was selected as shown in figure 14.17.

3. Click OK. Your mouse pointer is positioned in the Updated field.

FIG.14.17

The Go To dialog box

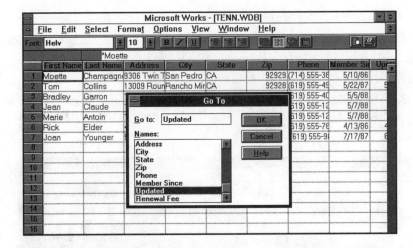

Editing a Field

The process for editing a field in the List view is basically the same as for the Form view. Start by clicking to highlight the field. To edit, follow one of these procedures:

- Replace the old text by typing new text.

- Press F2 to edit, and a cursor moves to the entry on the Formula bar. Delete and reenter text as needed.

Changing the Size of a Field

When you want to see the entire width of a column, for better viewing while in the List view, follow these steps:

1. Move the mouse pointer to the column you want to expand, and click the field name for that column. In this example, use the Address column.

2. Click Format on the Menu bar, then click Field **W**idth to display the Field Width dialog box. The current width is 10. Type **30**, as shown in figure 14.18.

3. Click OK, and the width of the Address column expands to 30 characters.

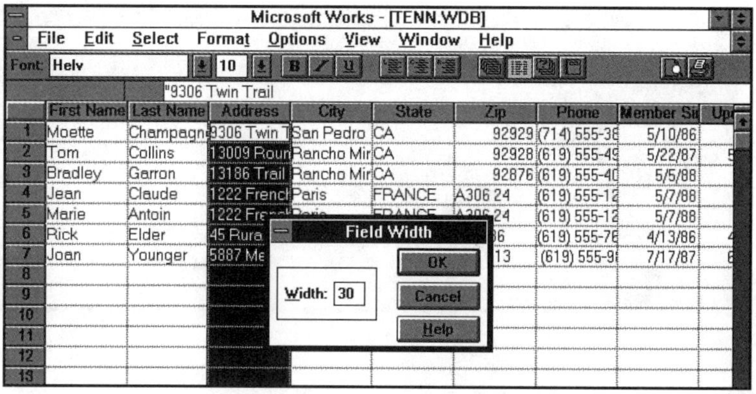

FIG. 14.18

Field Width
dialog box

As you move down the page, you can see the entire address for every record in this database. Notice that the database looks neater with some space between the columns. To make the List view even easier to read, continue increasing the size of other columns so that no overlap occurs. You can also change the width of columns by putting the mouse pointer on the division between field names (the pointer will look like a left-right arrow with a vertical line through it) and clicking and dragging to the new width.

Moving a Field

Eventually, this database will be sorted alphabetically, according to last name. To make the List view easier to read, move the Last Name field to the left margin. Follow these steps:

1. Click *Last Name* in the Last Name field column so that the entire column is highlighted.

2. Click **Edit**, then click Cut.

3. Use the scroll bars to move the mouse pointer to the First Name field.

4. Click **Edit**, then click **Paste** to insert the Last Name field to the left of the First Name field, as shown in figure 14.19.

5. Use the steps outlined in the last section to widen the Last Name field to 13 spaces.

FIG. 14.19

Last Name field
moved to the left
margin

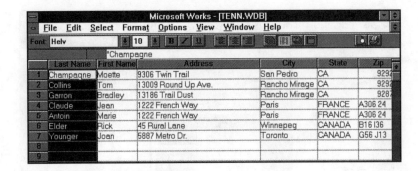

Editing the Field Name

Occasionally, you may want to change a field name in the List view. To change the name of the field Zip to *Zip Code*, follow these steps:

1. Move the mouse pointer to any cell in the column Zip.

2. Click **Edit** and then click Field Name to display the Field Name dialog box.

3. Type **Zip Code**, the new field name for this column. The Field Name dialog box with the new name is shown in figure 14.20.

FIG. 14.20

The Field Name
dialog box

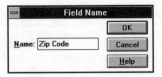

> **NOTE** There is a 15-character limit on field names. Also, when you type the new field name, do not include the colon as you did in the Form view. Works already knows this is a field name.

4. Click OK to display the List view database screen, as shown in figure 14.21. The new field name, Zip Code, appears at the top of the column.

Moving a Record

In List view, the records appear horizontally across the screen. To move the first record to the end of the list, follow these steps:

	Microsoft Works - [TENN.WDB]						
	Last Name	First Name	Address	City	State	Zip Code	Pho
1	Champagne	Moette	9306 Twin Trail	San Pedro	CA	92929	(714) 55
2	Collins	Tom	13009 Round Up Ave.	Rancho Mirage	CA	92928	(619) 55
3	Garron	Bradley	13186 Trail Dust	Rancho Mirage	CA	92876	(619) 55
4	Claude	Jean	1222 French Way	Paris	FRANCE	A306 24	(619) 55
5	Antoin	Marie	1222 French Way	Paris	FRANCE	A306 24	(619) 55
6	Elder	Rick	45 Rural Lane	Winnepeg	CANADA	B16 I36	(619) 55
7	Younger	Joan	5887 Metro Dr.	Toronto	CANADA	G56 J13	(619) 5
8							
9							

(Font: Helv, 10; cell contents: 92928)

FIG.14.21

Database screen with new field name, Zip Code

1. It's faster to click the row number. It automatically highlights the whole row. This allows you to eliminate blank records (if you want to completely remove the data or want to move it to the end of the database).

2. Click and drag the mouse pointer across the record until all fields in the record are highlighted.

3. Click **Edit**, and then click **Cut**.

4. Move the mouse pointer to the new location, and click. In this case, choose line 8.

5. Click **Edit**, then click **Paste**. The first record is placed on line 8.

 **CAUTION** To protect your data, save your file before moving records and fields. For instance, moving and pasting a record at record number 10 would replace record 10, and record 10 would no longer exist. To move a record or field to a new location among other records or fields, create blank space in which to insert the data before you start the move process. This procedure prevents replacing data. When you replace something accidentally, return to the saved database file.

When you replace data on a saved database, retrieve the saved file with the following steps:

1. Click **File** on the Menu bar, then click the **Close** option.

2. Works displays a dialog box asking if you want to save the changes to the file in which you are working. Click No.

3. Click **File**, and then click **Open** Existing File to display the list of files.

4. Click the same file in which you were working. Click OK and the file opens, appearing as previously saved. Works does not save the changes. You retrieve your original data and do not lose anything that may have been replaced.

Copying Data

Apply the same caution when copying data as when moving data. Save the file before you start copying procedures and leave blank space in which to copy data. When replacing, you do not need to leave blank space.

When in List view, you can copy multiple records, fields, or cells. Follow these steps:

1. Select the records, or fields, you want to copy. In this example, copy the Renewal Fee field. With the mouse pointer in the upper left corner of the data you want to copy, click and drag to highlight the data to be copied.

2. Click **E**dit and then click **C**opy.

3. Move the mouse pointer to the new location, at the right of the last field column with data in it, and click.

4. Click **E**dit and then click **P**aste. The Renewal Fee column remains in the original location and is copied to the new location.

This same data can be copied several times in different files or different parts of a file, while selecting the data only once, by repeating these copy commands.

Deleting and Clearing Data

Select data to be cleared when you want to keep formatting but want to remove the cell contents. Delete data when you want to erase the data and the formatting from the cell. You can clear or delete data by performing the following procedures:

Clear data: Click **E**dit and then Clear Field Entry.

Delete data: Click **E**dit and then **D**elete Record/Field.

In the List view, you can delete multiple records, fields, or cells at the same time, saving several steps when compared with the procedure for deleting multiple records (one at a time) used in the Form view.

You are now familiar with the List view and the List view functions. In the next section, you learn how to use the Works search function. To use the search function, stay in the List view.

Searching a Database

In List view, you can search the entire database, search selected fields, or search selected records. In the Form view, you can search the entire database only.

Data you need can be found quickly and easily with a database search. Using the search function, you can designate groups of records to print, to include in a report, or to add to a word-processed document.

The search feature can be used to study potential customers' native country. For instance, to search the database for records where the country field matches Canada, follow these steps.

1. Click **Select** on the Menu bar, and then click **Find** to display the Find dialog box.

2. Type the data for which you are searching. In this case, type **Canada**.

3. Click the **All** records radio button, as shown in figure 14.22.

NOTE The Next record radio button enables you to find only the next occurrence of the data you entered. When you find one record, press F7 to continue the search. No records are hidden when you choose the Next record option.

4. Click OK to display the records that match the search criteria, with all other records hidden from view, as shown in figure 14.23. Two records appear.

FIG. 14.22

The Find dialog box

FIG. 14.23

List View of
Records From
Canada

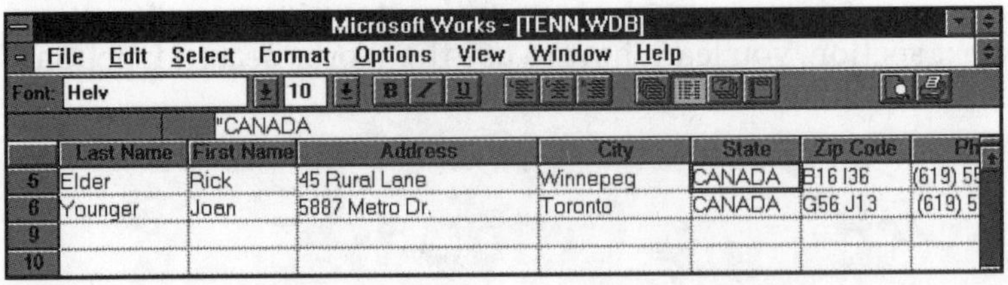

FIG. 14.24

The Select menu

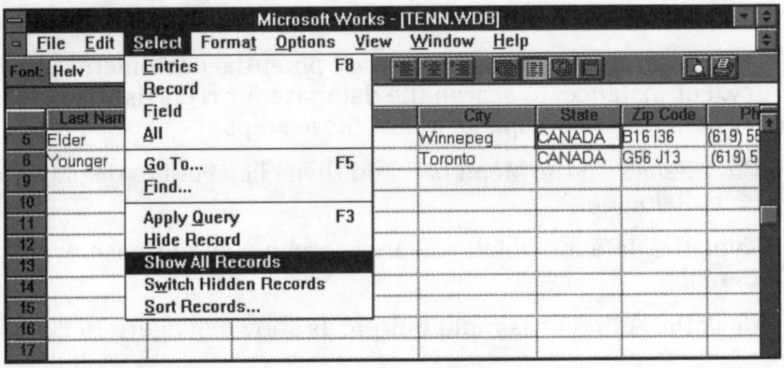

To return to the List view with all records displayed, click Select and then click the Show All Records option, as shown in figure 14.24. The entire database is again on-screen.

You can search for any character or string of characters in a database. When you cannot remember the exact spelling or sequence of a string of characters, use the Works wild cards. A question mark (?) represents any single character, and an asterisk (*) represents any string of characters. Works finds all uppercase and lowercase references to the words for which you are searching.

For example, when you search for *Christens?n*, Works will find Christensen and Christenson. If you search for *a*y*, Works will find anatomy, allegory, and androgyny, as well as any other words that begin with A and end with Y.

When you need to search for ranges of data, you need a query. A query is useful when you want to find Zip Codes higher than 90000, for example, or last names that begin with the letters L through S. The Query view and information on executing queries is presented in Chapter 15.

Sorting Records

Placing the database records in a specific order can save time. For instance, putting records in the Zip Code in order ensures printing the labels in proper order for a bulk mailing. Records can be arranged in ascending order by invoice number. Or you can list the Last Name field in the database according to alphabetical order.

Works enables you to specify up to three sort fields at one time. Put the most important field first, with the remaining two fields in descending order. An ascending sort is done from the beginning to the end, as in A to Z or 0 to 100. Descending order is the opposite, as in Z to A or 100 to 0.

As an example, do a sort of this database with the most important criterion being the state, and with a secondary concern being the Last Name. Both sort criteria will be done in ascending order. Follow these steps:

1. Click **Select** and then click **S**ort Records command to display the Sort Records dialog box.

2. In the **1st Field** box, you see the name of the field in which the mouse pointer was located when the menu selection was made. Type **State** in this box. Click the Ascend **A** radio button.

3. In the **2nd Field** box, type **Last Name** and again click ascending order, as shown in figure 14.25.

4. Click OK.

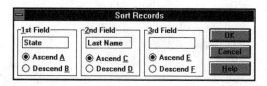

FIG. 14.25

Sort Records dialog box

The records in the database are listed in ascending alphabetical order by country. Within each country, the people are listed alphabetically by last name.

You can sort by more than three sort fields. For instance, to sort by using four criteria, do one sort with the least important fields listed. Then do a second sort with the more important fields entered into the Sort Records dialog box.

Using Formulas in a Database

Formulas are used in database cells as they are in spreadsheet cells—to create a proposed response in a field where one condition is likely to be true or to use the values from fields in algebraic calculations. To use formulas, follow these rules:

■ Formulas must be preceded by an equals sign (=), as the resulting value from the formula will equal the value that appears in the cell.

■ Only one formula is allowed per database field. A formula entered into a field in one record is automatically entered in every other record in that database.

■ When calculating a value based on values in other fields, use the name of the other fields in the formula. For example, in an invoice record, you may have a Purchase Amount field, an Amount Received field, and a Balance Due field. In the Balance Due field, use the following formula:

=Purchase Amount–Amount Received

You can take this example a step farther and create an incrementing value. For example, you want a balance due for each invoice, but you also want the total amount due for this time period. Use a Total Balance Due field and add the Total Balance Due field from the previous record to the Balance Due field in the current record. The Total Balance Due formula would be as follows:

=Balance Due+Total Balance Due

Works will then add the Total Balance Due from the field in the previous record to the Balance Due from this record, giving you a running total.

■ A formula also can be used with text. For example, 95 percent of the Rancho Mirage Tennis Association members live in Rancho Mirage. Instead of entering Rancho Mirage in the City field of 500 records, just type the following in the City field:

="Rancho Mirage

The equals sign (=) tells Works this is a formula to be inserted into every record. The quotation mark (") tells Works this is text. For the few members who live in another city, enter their city name as you normally would, and the typed text will replace the universal text you typed in the formula.

■ Database formulas can contain operators such as +, –, *, /, constant values, field names, and functions. The Works operators are listed in table 14.1.

Table 14.1 Works Operators

Operator	Meaning
^	Exponential
–	Negative or subtraction
+	Positive or addition
*	Multiplication
/	Division
=	Equal to
<>	Not equal to
<	Less than
>	Greater than
<=	Less than or equal to
>=	Greater than or equal to
~	Not
|	Or
&	And

■ The same functions that work in the spreadsheet also work in the database. These functions and their descriptions are found in Chapter 7. Insert these built-in mathematical equations in formulas to reduce the time required to enter complex formulas.

As an example of using a formula in the database at hand, you are going to obtain a running total of the Renewal Fee. Follow these steps:

■ Add a new field in the Form view. Return to the Form view by clicking the Form view button in the Tool bar.

■ Move to the bottom of the first record. Type **Total:** and click. Type **40** for the field size.

■ With the cursor in the highlighted data cell, type the following formula

=Renewal Fee+Total

■ Click, and a value appears in the data cell. The formula you entered appears on the Formula bar. This formula gives you a running total by adding the Purchase Amount of the current record to the Total for the previous record. As you move through the records, the Total becomes larger. Figure 14.26 shows the Total value for record six. Notice the formula on the Formula bar.

Formula calculates running total

Rancho Mirage Tennis Association

First Name: Marie
Last Name: Antoin
Address: 1222 French Way
City: Paris
State: FRANCE
Zip Code: A306 24
Phone: (619) 555-1234
Member Since: 5/7/88   Updated: 5/7/88

Renewal Fee: 120

Total: 940

In a database, you might have fields for Purchase Amount, Amount Received, and Balance Due; data are entered for the Purchase Amount and Amount Received. Let Works do the work of calculating the Balance Due. Follow these steps:

■ Click the field data cell for Balance Due.

■ Type the formula **=Purchase Amount–Amount Received**, and click to display the value in the data cell and the formula on the Formula bar.

As you scroll through the records, you will see that Works has done the calculations for you.

Formatting Data

Numbers in the database can result from formulas or from data entered directly into a field. The way these numbers are displayed is controlled through the Format menu shown in figure 14.27. The top portion of the menu lists the numerical display options from General to Time/Date.

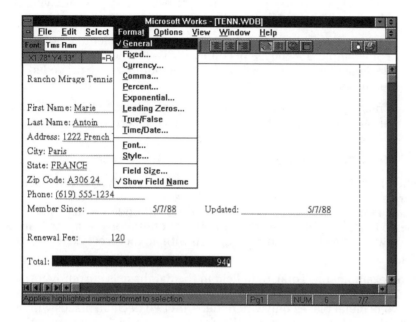

FIG. 14.27

The Format menu

Numbers are formatted differently when they are dates, when they appear in a balance sheet, or when they are being rounded. A description of the various number formats is found in the following list:

General. The General format is the default number format, used when you do not specify a format. Integers are stated precisely, for example 548.989. Numbers exceeding the cell field length are written in exponential notation, such as 5.48E+06. Negative numbers are preceded by a minus sign.

Fixed. This format specifies the number of decimal places to be displayed. Specify three decimal places, and .05898 will appear as .059. Negative numbers are preceded by a minus sign.

Currency. This format displays a currency sign, commas every three spaces, and a decimal point to two locations. When you enter data with a currency symbol, Works recognizes the symbol and formats the number as currency. Negative numbers are placed in parentheses. The number of integers behind the decimal can be changed.

Comma. This format inserts commas at every three places, and negative numbers are placed in parentheses.

Percent. This format displays numbers as percentages with the specified decimal places. For example, .67 becomes 67% with zero decimal places specified. Negative numbers are preceded by a minus sign. As with the Currency format, type a percent symbol after a number and Works recognizes the Percent format.

Exponential. This format displays numbers in scientific notation. For example, 158600000 becomes 1.59E+08 when two decimal places are specified. Negative numbers are preceded by a minus sign.

True/False. This format displays logical values. Cells with a value of zero display FALSE, and cells with a nonzero value display TRUE.

Time/Date. This format is explained in the next section.

When formatting a number that begins with a zero, type a quotation mark and then type the number. This makes the number text rather than a numeral. For instance, you enter the ZIP Code for San Juan, Puerto Rico, by typing **"00913**. Without the quotation mark, the leading zeros would be eliminated, leaving you with an incorrect ZIP Code of 913.

As an example, the Total: data field in the database is currently formatted in general format. The Total is a calculated value, and is displayed to two decimal places only when there are two decimal places with a numerical value. For example, the Total in figure 14.28 appears with no decimal values.

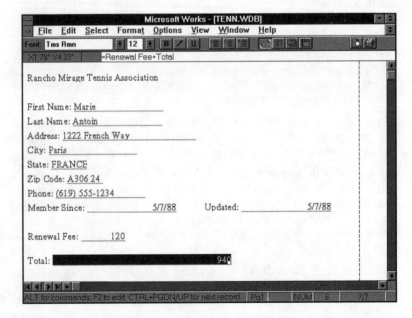

FIG. 14.28

Total in General format

Change the Total: field to currency format. Follow these steps:

1. Click Format, and then click Currency to display the Currency dialog box.

2. Specify the number of decimals at two by clicking OK with the default value of 2 on-screen.

The value of the Total: field is reformatted with a dollar sign and two decimal places as shown in figure 14.29.

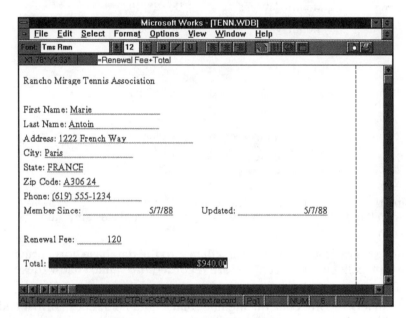

FIG. 14.29

Field data field in currency format

NOTE When you format a data cell in one record, the data cells for that field are changed in all other records.

Using the Time and Date

As in a spreadsheet, date and time can be used as data in cells as well as in formulas. Table 14.2 shows the date formats that Works recognizes.

Table 14.2 Date and Time Formats Recognized in Works

Format	Contents	Type
Short	Month, day, year	12/28/55
	Month, year	12/55
	Month, day	12/28
Long	Month, day, year	Dec 28, 1955
	Month, year	Dec, 1955
	Month, day	Dec 28
	Month only	Dec
12-hour	Hour, minute, second	7:36:00 PM
	Hour, minute	7:36 PM
24-hour	Hour, minute, second	21:18:00
	Hour, minute	21:18

Type the date or time, using the formats shown in table 14.2, in any field cell in the database, and Works formats the dates and times as shown.

When several people are entering data into the database, formatting the date cell ensures all entries are recorded the same. Follow these steps:

1. In any record, click the Member Since data field. Click Format and then click Time/Date to display the Time/Date dialog box.

2. Choose the format for the date. In this example, choose Month, day, year as the format for entering dates. You can also choose the Long or Short option. With the Long option, December 1, 1989 displays. The Short option displays 12/1/89. Click the Short option.

3. Click OK, and the field data cell is formatted. A month, day, and year typed in any format appears in a standard format every time. For example, type **Dec 1, 89** and 12/1/89 displays in the data cell.

You can also enter the current date and time in a database cell:

■ To insert the current date into a data field, highlight the field in the Form or List views, and press Ctrl+;.

■ To insert the current time into a data field, highlight the field in the Form or List views and press Ctrl+Shift+;.

Using Different Character Styles and Alignment

Works provides many choices in character styles and alignments. Choose boldface, underline, or italic character styles. Data can be left-aligned, right-aligned, centered, or justified. Works also has a *slide-to-left* feature to prevent printing blank spaces. These options are available from the Style dialog box, accessed by clicking Format and then clicking the **S**tyle option. Figure 14.30 shows the Style dialog box.

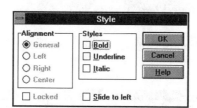

FIG. 14.30

The Style dialog box

Default settings for character styles are left-aligned in Form view. In List view, text is left-aligned and numbers are right-aligned. A specified alignment appears in both the List and Form views.

Character styles can be used to accent specific fields. For example, accent Renewal Fee to readily show who owes you money with the following steps:

1. Click the Renewal Fee: field and click Forma**t**.

2. Click **S**tyle to display the Style dialog box.

3. Click Bold and an X appears next to Bold, indicating that the option is turned on.

4. Click OK.

Renewal Fee now appears in boldface on-screen. As you scroll in Form view, the Renewal Fee field is easily spotted on the page.

Figure 14.31 shows postal codes that begin with letters to be left-aligned, and postal codes that are numbers to be right-aligned. To make the entire column left-aligned, follow these steps:

1. Click the List view button on the Tool bar.

2. Click the Zip Code field label at the top of the Zip Code column. Click Forma**t**, then click the **S**tyle option to display the Style dialog box.

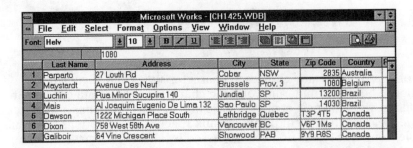

FIG. 14.31

Zip Code
Alignment

3. Click **L** for left-aligned text. Click OK, or press Alt,L and press Enter.

The postal codes in the Zip Code column are now all left-aligned as shown in figure 14.32.

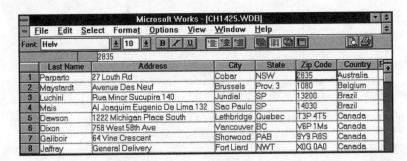

FIG. 14.32

Left-aligned
postal codes

When printing forms, use the *Slide to left* feature. This feature enables the text to slide to the left so that less blank space is printed. Follow these steps:

1. Select the text you want to slide to the left.

2. Click Forma**t** and then click **S**tyle to display the Style dialog box.

3. Click the Slide to left option.

When printing this form, no leading spaces will be printed before the selected field or label.

NOTE The Slide to left option is available only in Form view.

Using Different Fonts

Changing fonts is another effective way to customize your database forms. To change a font, from the Form view, click the down arrow to the right of the Font box on the Tool bar. A list of available fonts is displayed, as shown in figure 14.33. Your ability to change fonts will depend on the capabilities of your printer.

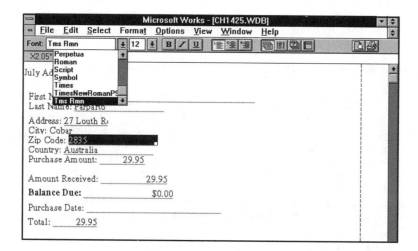

FIG. 14.33

List of available fonts

Click to choose any of the fonts listed, and the entire form will change to the specified font. Figure 14.34 shows the form in a Script font.

Point size of the type can also be selected. Click the point size down-arrow on the Tool bar, and the options are: 6, 8, 10, ..., 48.

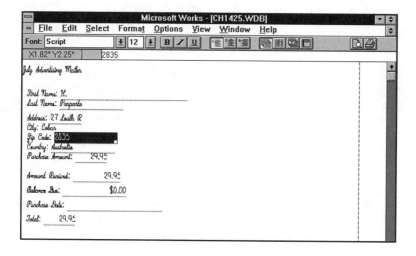

FIG. 14.34

Form view in script font

Protecting a Database

You have completed development of your database. The field names and data cells are correct. The characters are formatted and aligned, and the printed version of the Form view fits the paper form you have to print. It's perfect!

Now is the time to protect your work. You can protect your database two ways:

■ *Protect Form* — You can protect the form design while still being able to enter and edit data. Protect the form design, and other employees can enter and edit data but cannot change the field names, labels, format, or size.

Works will lock the fields and cells in a database when you protect it. This is especially useful when other people will be entering information. Locked fields and cells cannot be formatted or changed when the database is protected until you unlock the field or cell.

Protect the database form design by clicking Options on the Menu bar, and then clicking the Protect Form option, accessed from the Form View only. When the Protect Form option is on, the indicator symbol (check mark) appears on the menu as shown in figure 14.35.

With the Protect Form Option activated, return to the Form View screen and click Format, and then click the Style option. Notice that you cannot access the Style dialog box, and nothing can be changed in the Form. The Form will remain protected until you turn off the option via the Options menu.

■ *Protect Data* — With the data entered in the Protect Form mode, you can still continue to enter and edit data. When you are ready to lock the entire database, and not just the form, click Options and then Protect Data, and the indicator appears next to this option.

With the Protect Data option activated, locked fields and data cells cannot be edited or entered. For instance, a student can access his or her grade report but cannot change the final grade. An employee can look at his or her work schedule but cannot add a few extra hours of overtime.

Unlock the database by clicking Options and then clicking Protect Data and/or Protect Form. When you click these options, the indicator (check mark) is removed to tell you they are turned off.

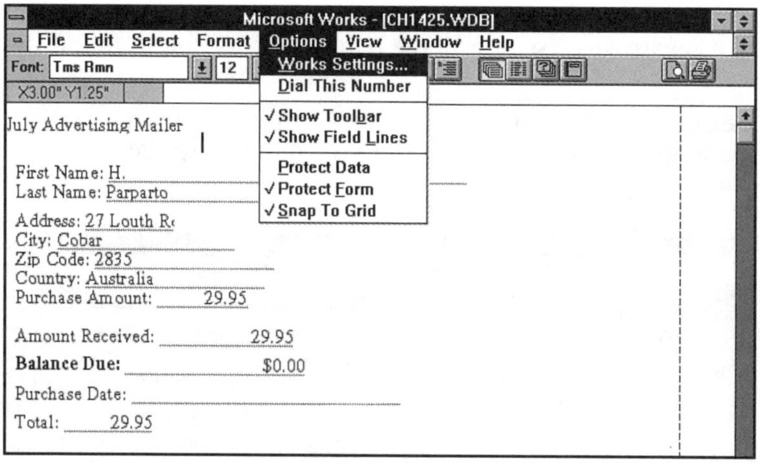

FIG. 14.35

The Protect
Form indicator
turned on

Hiding a Field Name, Field, or Record

While protecting a database keeps others from changing, rearranging, or editing data, hiding fields or records keeps database information completely confidential. To control which records are included in a report or which fields should be seen by you alone, use the Hide Record command.

When you searched the database to find all the addresses from Canada, for example, you were hiding those records that were not from Canada and displaying the ones that were. In addition, the Hide Record command enables you to choose which records you want hidden, regardless of searches.

A hidden record is not listed in List view and does not appear in Form view. A hidden record cannot be included in a report or printed with other records. The status line shows the number of displayed records compared to the total number of records. When 22/25 appears on the status line, for example, 22 of the total 25 records are displayed; three records remain hidden.

To hide a record while in Form view, follow these steps:

1. Move the mouse pointer to the record you want to hide.

2. Click Select and then click the Hide Record option. The record disappears from the screen. On the status line, you see that one less record is displayed. In the database on-screen, 24 of 25 records are available.

In List view, you can select several records and hide them all with one series of keystrokes. To hide all the records from Canada, follow these steps:

1. Select the two records from Canada using the click and drag method. Figure 14.36 shows the screen before the records are hidden.

Selected records to hide

	Last Name	Address	City	State	Zip Code	Country	F
4	Mais	Al Joaquim Eugenio De Lima 132	Sao Paulo	SP	14030	Brazil	
5	Dawson	1222 Michigan Place South	Lethbridge	Quebec	T3P 4T5	Canada	
6	Dixon	758 West 58th Ave	Vancouver	BC	V6P 1Ms	Canada	
7	Galiboir	64 Vine Crescent	Shorwood	PAB	9Y9 R8S	Canada	
8	Jaffray	General Delivery	Fort Liard	NWT	X0G 0A0	Canada	
9	Leja	105 45th Avenue	Lanchine	PQ	H8T 2RS	Canada	
10	McCallum	Herring Cove Post Office	Herring Cov	NS	78787	Canada	
11	Petty	91 Cosgrove Crest, #203	Red Deer	AB	T4P 2Z6	Canada	
12	Bansdorf	78 Bauer St.	Frankfurt	BV	8777	Germany	
13	Friberger	65 Munchen Square	Munchen	BV	8778	Germany	
14	Neussendorf	Box 729	Humacoa		958 666	Germany	
15	Romigen	AM Krebsbruckles	Crailsheim		7180	Germany	
16	Washek	91 Coomb Flat	Hong Kong		8885	Hong Kong	
17	Dolan	Pearse Road	Dublin		87401	Ireland	
18	Luigi	Casella Postale 7045	Roma		162	Italy	

2. Click **Select**, and then click **Hide Record**. The List view screen now displays five of seven records.

When you are ready to display all records including the hidden records, click **S**elect, then click Show All Records. Five of seven records are displayed.

When you hide a field, you get a slightly different result than when you hide a record. Hide a field in the List view, and the field is still displayed in the Form view. You may want to hide a field while in the List view to make other fields more visible.

For example, suppose you are working in a database and are only interested in the last name of the person on the mailing list and his or her postal code. By hiding the Address field, the last name and the postal code are nearer each other on the screen. Follow these steps:

1. Move your mouse pointer to the Address field column.

2. Click Format, then click Field **W**idth to display the Field Width dialog box, as shown in figure 14.37.

3. Type **0**, and click OK. The Address field is no longer displayed. The address information is still there, in memory, although the address field is not visible on-screen.

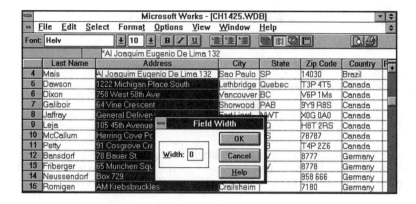

FIG. 14.37

Field Width
dialog box with
zero width

Use the **G**o To. . . command to return the hidden field to the display by
following these steps:

1. Click **S**elect and then click **G**o To, to display the Go To dialog box.

2. Click Address, as shown in figure 14.38.

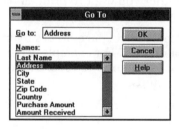

FIG. 14.38

Address high-
lighted in Go To
dialog box

3. Click OK to choose the hidden field, even though the hidden field
   is not displayed.

4. Click Forma**t**, then click Field **W**idth. In the Field Width dialog box,
   type any value greater than 0. In this example, type **30**, the previous field width.

5. Click OK, and the Address field displays in the original location.

Printing a Database

You are now ready to print your database, and you want to print from
the Form view one record per page. While in the Form view, Click the
Print button on the Tool bar to display the Print dialog box as shown in
figure 14.39.

FIG. 14.39

The Print dialog
box

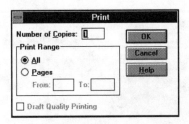

Choose the number of copies and whether to print all records or the
selected record. When you have made all the necessary decisions, Click
OK to print the Form view of the database.

> **NOTE** The dialog box options that are dimmed are not available in
> the view from which you are printing. Monochrome moni-
> tors have options without reverse-video letters.

Print from the List view by Clicking the Print button on the Tool bar to
display the Print dialog box. In the List view, you can choose the number of copies and whether you want to print all pages or just some selected pages. Click OK and the list of records will print.

In the List view, you can control page breaks by inserting a page-break
marker into the list of records. For example, when you want 20 records
per page, move the mouse pointer to record number 21 in the List view,
click, and follow these steps:

1. Click **Edit**, then click Insert Page **B**reak to display the Insert Page
   Break dialog box.

2. You can choose **R**ecord or **F**ield. Choose Record and Click OK to
   insert the page-break symbol at record 20. The page break is
   shown as a dotted line across the List view.

To remove the page break, click record 21 and then click Edit and click
Delete Page Break.

Chapter Summary

In this chapter, you learned to create a Works database, a most useful
tool. You began by planning the database — the information you
wanted to include and how to format the information. You entered
fields and data, and you learned how to use the Form view and List
view modes of the database.

You selected, moved, copied, and deleted text from the Form view and the List view. You learned to search and sort data. You learned to use formulas, and about formatting cells, character styles, and text alignment. Finally, you learned to protect your form design and your data, and how to hide fields and records.

In Chapter 15, you learn to create reports from your data. After you learn how to query the database for the data you want, you learn to duplicate, delete, sort, view, and customize reports. After creating the report, you learn to format the report with headers, footers, fonts, and titles. Finally, you learn the printing options available for reports.

Creating and Using Database Reports

B uilding and maintaining extensive databases is useless unless you know how to extract specific information from the databases when you need it and in formats that make the most effective use of the information.

In this chapter, you learn how to do the following:

- Create and print database reports.
- Prepare queries.
- Duplicate, delete, sort, view, and customize reports.
- Format reports with headers, footers, fonts, and titles.
- Print reports.

Creating a Database Report

In this section, you create a report and learn the components of the report display. Several more names have been added to the TENN database for the following examples. To create the report, follow these steps:

1. From either the Form view or the List view, click the report button on the Tool bar to display the New Report dialog box shown in figure 15.1.

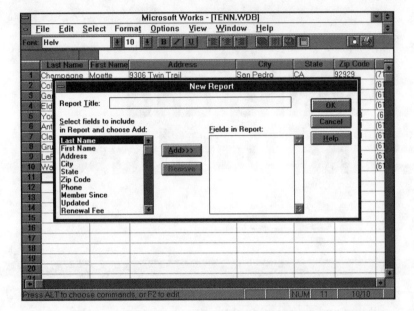

2. A blinking cursor appears in the Report Title: box. Type the name of the report **Members by Country**.

3. On the lower left side of the New Report dialog box, you are asked to choose the fields you want included in the report. Choose some or all of the fields listed by clicking the field name, then clicking the Add>>> box in the center. The fields chosen are listed in the **F**ields in Report: box located in the lower right of the dialog box. Add the Last Name field, the State field, and the Renewal Fee field, as shown in figure 15.2.

4. Remove fields from a report by clicking the field name in the lower right box, then clicking Remove.

5. When you have completed choosing the fields for your report, click OK to display the Report Statistics dialog box. The fields you have chosen are listed in the left box. Choose the statistics you want in the report by clicking the field, then clicking the statistics you want for that field by following these procedures:

    Click State, then click Count to include the number of records in the report.

Click Renewal Fee and then click Sum to include the sum of the amount received in the report.

6. Position the statistics under each column by clicking the Under each Column option in the box at the right.

7. Click OK to display the Report Definition screen as shown in figure 15.3, which shows the report title, column labels, and summary formulas. Across the top of the Report Definition screen are the field name headings. Down the left side of the screen are the following row names:

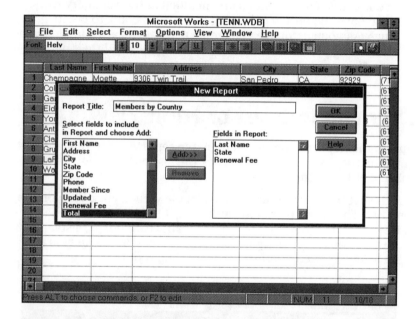

FIG. 15.2

Three fields added to the report

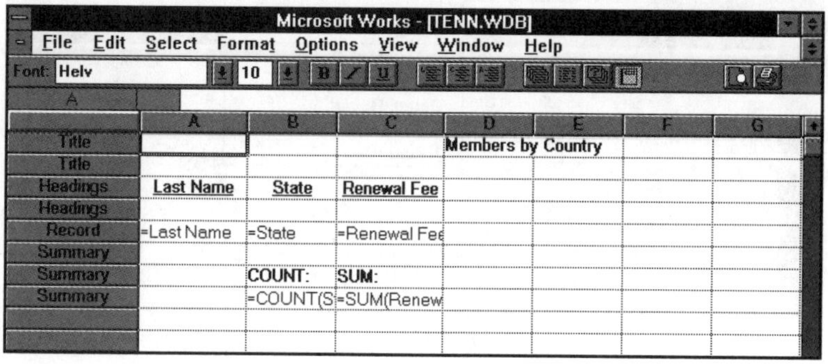

FIG. 15.3

The Report Definition screen

Title. Two Title rows display at the top of the report. The text entered for the report title appears here.

Headings. The text in these rows is printed at the top of every page. Usually they hold the field name. However, you can add to or change the text in the Headings rows.

Record. The Record row holds the record data for each database. One entry for each record is listed.

Summary. The Summary rows appear at the end of a report.

Your statistical selections are included in the Summary rows. You also have the option of leaving these rows blank to create groupings. As you customize your report, new rows are added beyond these basic row definitions. These new rows and their definitions are discussed when they occur.

Returning to a List or Form View

While in the Report Definition screen, the report button remains highlighted on the Tool bar. You can click the List or Form view buttons to return to either of these views.

Click the list button to return to the List view, then click View on the Menu bar. The check mark indicator is next to List, showing that you're in List view. The report you just defined above, Report 1, also appears on the menu as shown in figure 15.4. From this View menu, you can create a new report, or return to the existing report.

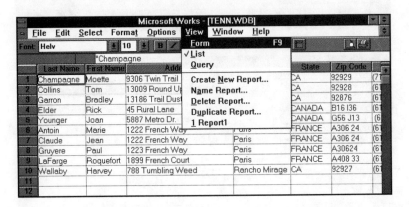

Click the report button on the Tool bar to view the report you just created.

Sorting a Report

In Chapter 14, this database was sorted alphabetically by country. Sorting can be accomplished in the Report view as well. Sorting in the Report View can be more specific, enabling you to create breaks and summaries where needed.

When sorting records in the Report view, the Sort dialog box appears slightly different than in List view. In addition to listing the fields by which you can sort, the dialog box offers the option of creating breaks after each group created by the sort.

From the Report Definition screen, click **S**elect on the Menu bar, and then click **S**ort Records to display the Sort Records dialog box shown in figure 15.5.

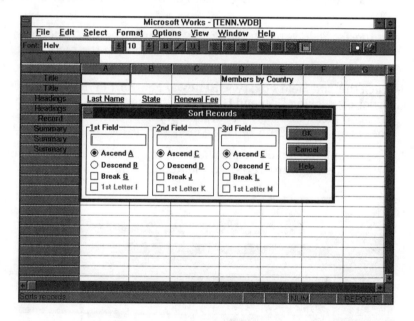

FIG. 15.5

Sort Records
dialog box

You can sort up to three fields at a time by naming the fields to be sorted in the field name boxes, with the first field name for the most important criteria. Below the field name boxes, choose to sort in ascending or descending order or to break the sorted data into groups. With Break turned on (indicated by an X next to the option), Works creates a grouping by inserting a blank summary row in the report when the contents of the field change.

Choose the 1st Letter option, and Works creates a grouping in the report when the first letter of the sort changes.

The break by letter, the default break, is used most often. The length of the database suggests the type of break to use. With only 10 records, a break after every change in 1st letter would create a break after almost every record. However, a database of 1,000 entries may have 60 records with a last name that starts with S.

When making sorting and grouping decisions for a report, consider the original goals when you created the database. In this example, the purpose in this report is to list members by their country.

Sort this report and set up breaks by following these steps:

1. With the mouse pointer in the Report Definition screen, click **Se**lect and then click **S**ort Records to display the Sort Records dialog box.

2. At the **1**st Field prompt, type **State**. Sort in ascending order, and turn on Break by clicking Break **G**. Works breaks the record list after each country.

3. Click the **2**nd Field box, type **Renewal Fee**. Sort in descending order by clicking Descend **D**. Do not choose the break option for this 2nd Field; choosing the break option for this field would break the records after each separate monetary value.

4. The completed dialog box is shown in figure 15.6. Click OK to confirm the settings and return to the Report Definition screen.

FIG. 15.6

Completed Sort Records dialog box

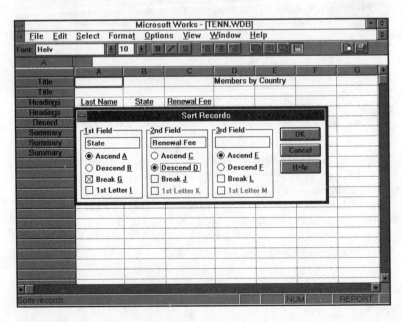

Below the record entries, the row `Summ State` is inserted. For the State field the equation `=Count(State)` appears in the Summ Country row. When viewing or printing this report, the total number of records per group appears in this cell. As you move the mouse pointer to the right, the equation `=SUM(Renewal Fee)` appears in the Renewal Fee field, and on the Formula bar as shown in figure 15.7. At the end of the list of purchases, you get a total of the Renewal Fee per State.

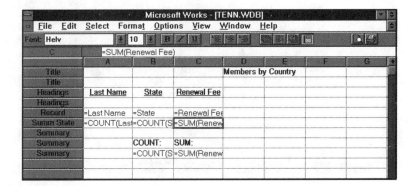

FIG.15.7

SUM formulas

To save the file, click **F**ile, and then click **S**ave. The report just created is saved with the file.

Now view the results of your sort. Click the preview button on the Tool bar to display the report, as shown in figure 15.8. If, instead, a Question box displays, click Continue, or complete the Page and Printer Setup to display the report.

In figure 15.8, the countries appear in alphabetical order. To the right of the countries, the renewal fees are listed in descending order by country. For instance, the renewal fees for Canada are $180 and $180. The records are grouped by country and the total renewal fees for each country appear at the end of the group. Use the scroll bars to view the remaining countries and purchase amounts.

Using Functions in a Database Report

Functions can make complex mathematical equations as easy as typing a single line in a cell. In the example just completed, the functions *=SUM(Renewal Fee)* and *=COUNT(State)* were added to the database report for Works to provide additional information from the existing data.

FIG. 15.8

Report preview
on-screen

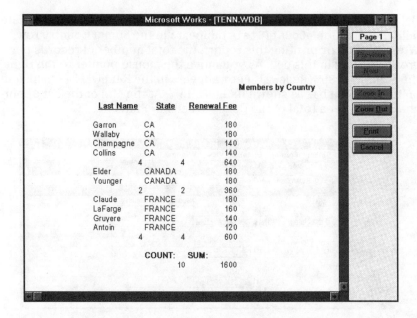

Now you would like to know the average renewal fee. To add this function to the report, follow these steps:

1. Click cancel to exit the preview screen.

2. Click the mouse pointer under the Renewal Fee field in one of the summary rows.

3. Type **=AVG(Renewal Fee)**, and click to insert the function in the cell.

Works adds all the purchase amounts and divides by the total number of records to calculate the average renewal fee. For more information about functions, see Chapter 11.

Using Formulas in a Database Report

Formulas in a database report can be treated almost the same as formulas in a spreadsheet. Enter the formula of your choice in one of the Summary rows. Always start the formula with an equal sign (=). Use operators such as an asterisk (*) for multiplication, a slash (/) for division, a plus sign (+) for addition, and a minus sign (-) for subtraction.

Developing a Query for a Database Report

Use a database query to look for records in your database that meet two or more criteria. To find records meeting just one criterion, a search is easier. When you want records that have France in the State field, for example, use a search. However, when you want records that have France in the State field, and a renewal fee equaling $140, use a query. The result of your query can be a report.

When you apply a query, you establish criteria for each field in the database. Works searches the hidden and displayed records to find records that match the criteria. All data in the fields in the records can be used in queries.

With the mouse pointer in the List view, Click the query button in the Tool bar to display what looks like a Form view of a record but with no data in the fields. You are ready to type the criteria for your query in the blank spaces.

Using Query Formulas

Set up a query formula to find an exact match to two or more criteria. Very complex queries may be executed by using the following general equation for queries:

=(*formula stating search conditions*)/combining operator(*formula stating search conditions*)

Comparison operators, shown in table 15.1, are used in a *formula to state search conditions* for ranges of data. The table provides examples of the operator, the field queried, the formula, and the records found by the query.

Table 15.1 Comparison Operators

Operator	Field	Formula Used	Finds These Records
Equal to (=)	State:	="Canada"	State is Canada
Not equal to (<>)	State:	<>"Canada"	State is not Canada

continues

Table 15.1 Continued

Operator	Field	Formula Used	Finds These Records
Less than (<)	Renewal Fee:	<140	Balance due is less than $140
Greater than (>)	Renewal Fee:	>140	Balance due is more than $140
Greater than or equal to (>=)	Renewal Fee:	>=140	Renewal Fee is equal to $140 or more
Less than or equal to (<=)	Renewal Fee:	<=140	Renewal Fee is equal to $140 or less

Logical operators, shown in table 15.2, find records that meet more than one set of conditions. For example, when you write the formula Renewal Fee: >50 AND <1000, the logical operator AND queries for amounts above $50 and below $1,000.

Table 15.2 Logical Operators

Logical Operator	Symbol
AND	&
OR	|
NOT	~

Entering a Query

To find the records with orders from France and renewal fees greater than $140, follow these steps:

1. You should already be in the Query view. If not, move to the List view and click the query button on the Tool bar to display the Query view shown in figure 15.9.

2. Click to highlight the State: field data cell. Type **France** and click.

3. Move the mouse pointer to the Renewal Fee: field, and click to highlight the data cell. Type **>140** as shown in figure 15.9, and click.

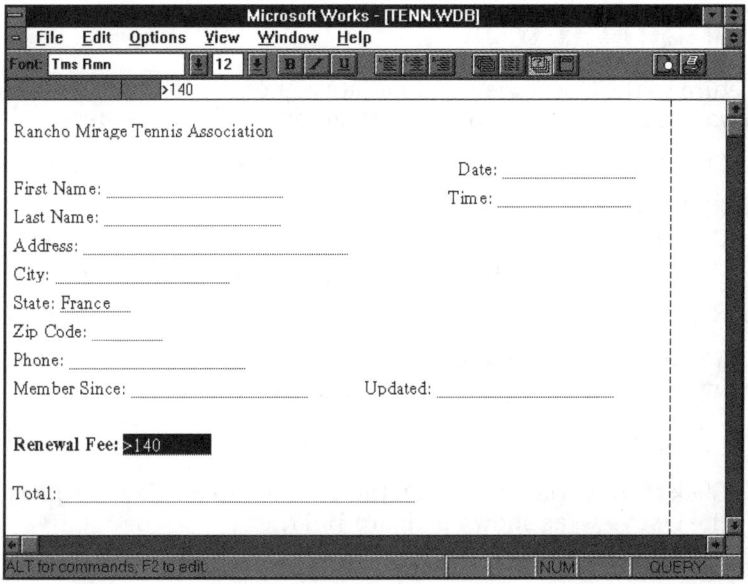

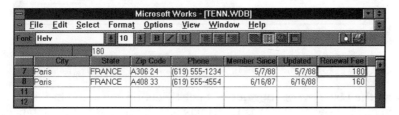

FIG. 15.9

Query screen
with entries

4. Execute the query by clicking the list button on the Tool bar to
   display the records matching your query in the List view.

The results of this query are shown in figure 15.10. Two records show
members from France with renewal fees over $140.

FIG. 15.10

Query results

	City	State	Zip Code	Phone	Member Since	Updated	Renewal Fee
			180				
7	Paris	FRANCE	A306 24	(619) 555-1234	5/7/88	5/7/88	180
8	Paris	FRANCE	A408 33	(619) 555-4554	6/16/87	6/16/88	160
11							
12							

T I P

Use wild cards in a query. For example, type **C*** in the Last Name
data cell when searching for all last names that start with C as one of
the operators. The asterisk (*) stands for any string of characters. In
this example, Works finds Christens, Cook, Curren, and Climer with
the C* entry.

Changing a Query

To return to the Query view and initiate a query for records showing a renewal fee greater than 0 and less than 140, follow these steps:

1. Click the query button on the Tool bar to display the Query view.

2. Clear the State field data cell. Click to highlight the State data cell. Click **E**dit and then click C**l**ear Field Entry to erase the query criteria, and retain the cell's formatting and style conditions.

3. Repeat step 2 to clear the Renewal Fee field.

4. Move the mouse pointer to the Balance Due data cell, and click to highlight the cell. Type the formula **>0&<140** asking Works to locate all records showing a renewal fee greater than 0 and less than 140. Click to enter the formula into the data cell.

5. Click the List view button on the Tool bar to display the query in the List view, as shown in figure 15.11.

In this example, one record appears with a renewal fee exceeding 0 but less than $140.

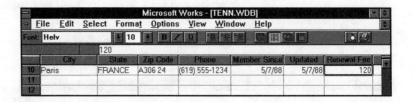

Returning to Your Complete Database

From the List view of your query, click **S**elect on the Menu bar, and then click Show All Records to display all the records in this database.

NOTE   When you use the Show All Records option, the active query is not deleted. Click the query button on the Tool bar to display the most recent query form. After executing a query, you may add, change, or delete records, and then apply the active query again.

Viewing Records Not Matching the Query

Your query has produced a list of selected records. To view the records not matching your query, click Select, and then click Switch Hidden Records to display all records not matching the query. By using this menu path, you can go back and forth between the query results and the records that do not match the query.

Deleting a Query

When your query is completed, you do not need to clear or erase each cell individually. To delete the query, follow these steps:

1. Move to the Query view by clicking the query button on the Tool bar.

2. Click Edit and then click Delete Query to erase all data cells displayed in the Query view.

3. Add new data or return to the List view. Return to the List view to display the complete database.

Copying Data in a Database Report

Copy rows or columns in a database report by selecting the rows or columns to be copied and then moving them to the desired location. To copy, you must be in the Report Definition screen of the Report view. As an example, to copy the Last Name fields to the end of the report, follow these steps:

1. Click and drag to select the Last Name field in the Report Definition screen. Click Edit and then click Copy.

2. Move the mouse pointer to the right of the Renewal Fee field and click.

3. Click Edit, and then click Paste to copy the Last Name field to the new location.

4. Preview the report to see the Last Name field on the right and left side of the report.

Deleting Reports

There are several reasons to delete a report.

■ You have several similar reports, but need only one to work with or print.

■ You have created eight reports and need one more. You must delete an old database report before you can create a new one, because the limit is eight.

■ You no longer need the report.

To delete a report, follow these steps.

1. Move to the Report Definition screen of the Report view.

2. Click View, and then click **D**elete Report to display the Delete Report dialog box with the list of reports you have created, as shown in figure 15.12. Click Cancel to change your mind and exit the Delete Report dialog box.

3. Click to highlight the report, then click to delete.

4. Repeat these steps to delete other reports.

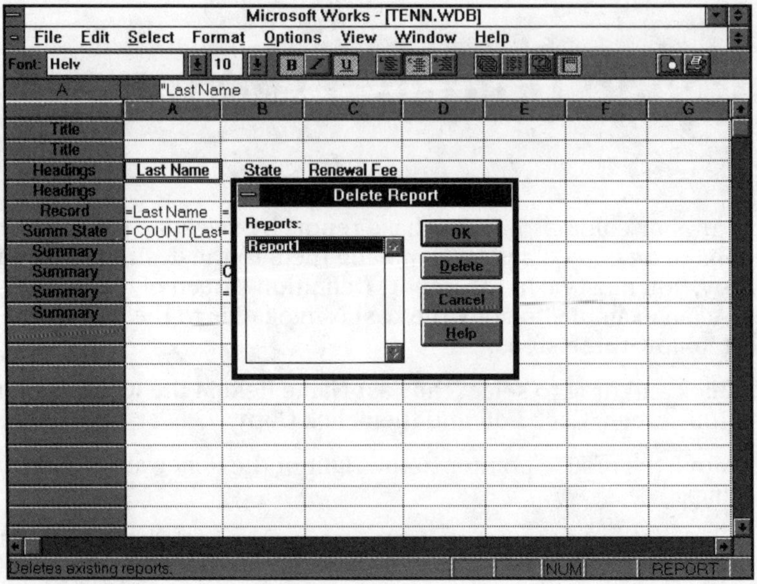

FIG. 15.12

Delete Report
dialog box

Renaming a Database Report

To rename a database report, follow these steps:

1. Move to the Report Definition screen in the Report view.

2. Click **View**, and then click **N**ame Report to display the Name Report dialog box with the list of reports you have created.

3. In this example change the name of Report1 to Members by State, which is more descriptive. Click Report1, and type **Members by State** in the Name: box as shown in figure 15.13.

4. Click **R**ename to replace Report1 with Members by State.

5. Repeat these steps to rename other reports. When finished renaming reports, click OK to leave the Name Report dialog box.

Duplicating Database Reports

You have prepared a report for the board of directors. Now you want to create a similar report, from the same database, for your management staff and another report for your own records. Create these variations on a report by duplicating the report and then making changes to the duplicated report without changing the original report.

 Remember, the limit is eight reports per database. When you already have eight, you must delete a report before you can duplicate a report.

To duplicate a report, follow these steps:

1. Move to the Report Definition screen in the Report view.

2. Click **View**, and then click D**u**plicate Report to display the Duplicate Report dialog box with the list of reports you have created, as shown in figure 15.14.

FIG. 15.14

The Duplicate Report dialog box

3. Click to highlight the report to be duplicated, and then click the Duplicate box. Use the Name Report command to rename the duplicate report. You can view and customize the duplicated report to reflect specific information.

4. Repeat these steps to duplicate other reports. Click OK when finished.

Customizing a Report

When customizing a report, you work with the rows of the Report Definition screen, just as you did when creating a database report at the beginning of this chapter. In the Report Definition screen, the rows are named down the left side of the screen, while the columns appear across the top of the screen and usually contain field names and records.

The rows in a database report are listed in a predetermined order and are described in the following list.

Title. Two Title rows display at the top of the report. The text entered for the report title appears here.

Headings. The text in these rows is printed at the top of every page. Usually they hold the field name. However, you can add to or change the text in the Headings rows.

Record. The Record row holds the record data for each database. One entry for each record is listed.

Summary. The Summary rows appear at the end of a report.

Earlier in this chapter, you sorted the database by grouping the data by state and then listing the renewal fee in descending order. When you sorted this database on-screen, or any other database of your choice, other rows may have been added.

Many of the actions involved in customizing a database report also affect the established rows. You can choose to delete rows, add or insert rows, or modify rows. In addition, you can modify the contents of the rows by changing the formatting of cells, or including character styles and number formats. The steps for customizing reports are the same as for customizing the database.

 The actions taken to customize a report must occur in the Report Definition screen. You cannot access the menus while viewing the report unless you are in the Report Definition screen.

Deleting a Row or Column

To practice deleting a column, move to the report named Members by State and follow these steps:

1. Move to the Report Definition screen.

2. Click to choose the column Field Name, and then click **Edit** to highlight the **Edit** menu as shown in figure 15.15.

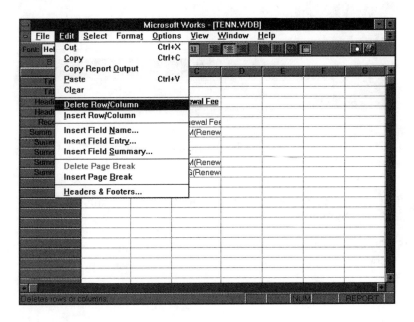

FIG. 15.15

Edit menu

3. Click the **D**elete Row/Column option to display the Delete dialog box.

4. Click **C**olumn, and then click OK, to delete the column from the Report Definition screen.

Follow the same procedure to delete a row.

Inserting a Row or Column

To insert two rows to include more calculations at the end of the Members by State report, follow these steps.

1. Move to the Report Definition screen.

2. Click to highlight the shaded cell below the Summary row.

3. Click and drag to highlight two full rows as shown in figure 15.16.

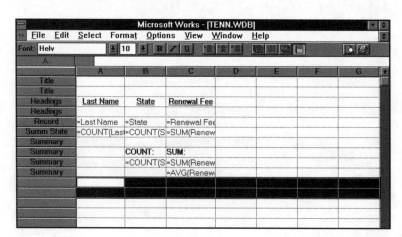

4. Click **E**dit and then click **I**nsert Row/Column to display the Insert row dialog box.

NOTE   Works knows you want to insert rows because you have highlighted rows.

5. Choose the type of row you wish to insert. Click Summary as shown in figure 15.17.

NOTE Works also assumes, because you have selected rows at the bottom of the report, that you want to insert in Summary rows.

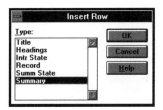

FIG. 15.17

Insert Row
dialog box

6. Click OK to insert two additional rows in the Report Definition screen.

Follow the same procedure to insert columns.

Entering Information in a Database Report Cell

From the Report Definition screen, you can add data, labels, formulas, or functions to cells. At the top of the screen are two Title rows, which appear on the first page of the printed report.

To add a date to the first title row, move the mouse pointer to the leftmost column in the first Title row, type **11/18/89**, and click.

NOTE When editing a cell, press F2 to edit data on the formula bar.

Click the report title that says Members by State. Notice that the text entered was preceded by a quotation mark ("), indicating the date text is a label.

Now add a formula in the additional Summary rows you entered at the bottom of the Report Definition screen. Move the mouse pointer to the bottom Summary row, and click the Renewal Fee column to highlight the cell shown in figure 15.18. You previously have added the SUM function and the AVG function to this column.

FIG. 15.18

Highlighted cell
in Renewal Fee
column

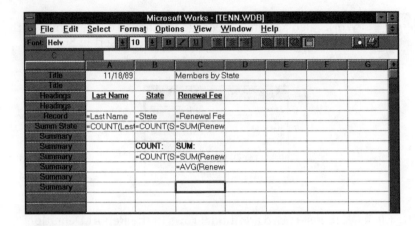

To add the standard deviation, a statistical calculation described more
fully in Chapter 11, follow these steps:

1. Click the **E**dit and then click Insert Field **S**ummary to display the
   Insert Field Summary dialog box shown in figure 15.19.

2. The fields in this database are listed at the left side of this dialog
   box. On the right side of the box are statistical calculations available for a report. Click Renewal Fee.

3. Click STD, and then click OK.

FIG.15.19

The Insert Field
Summary
dialog box

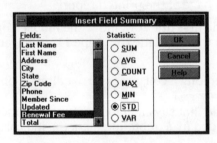

Table 15.2 lists and describes the statistical calculations available in
the Insert Field Summary dialog box.

Table 15.2 Statistical Functions in the Insert Field Summary Dialog Box	
Function	**Description**
SUM	Total of the group
AVG	Average of the group
COUNT	Number of items in the group
MAX	Largest number in the group
MIN	Smallest number in the group
STD	Standard deviation of the group
VAR	Variance of the group

Inserting Field Names and Field Contents

To insert field names or contents in any cell, follow these steps:

1. Move the mouse pointer to the selected cell, and click to highlight the cell.

2. Click **E**dit to display two options: Insert Field **N**ame and Insert Field Entry.

3. Click Insert Field **N**ame to display the fields of this database in the Insert Field Name dialog box. Use this list to insert any field name as a label at the mouse pointer location.

4. Click cancel to exit the Insert Field Name dialog box.

5. Click **E**dit and then click Insert Field Entry to display the Insert Field Entry dialog box shown in figure 15.20. Use this list to change cell entries in a Record row. Choose any option on this list and Works inserts =fieldname in the cell. The actual contents of the cell appear when you view the report.

FIG. 15.20

The Insert Field Entry dialog box

Changing Character Style

The title of this database appears in the third column of the first Title row. Set off the title of the report by making it both bold and underlined. Follow these steps:

1. Click and drag to highlight the title, Members by State.

2. Click Format and then click Style to display the Style dialog box.

3. The style options are Bold, Underline, and Italic. Click Bold and Underlined.

4. Click OK to format the report title as shown in figure 15.21.

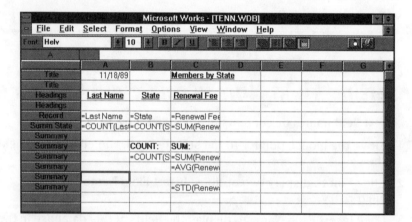

Use the same procedure to format cells in a report with any of the available cell alignment and character styles. For more details on how to change styles and formats, see Chapter 14.

Formatting a Report

Before printing a report, add some final touches to give your document a more finished, professional look.

Changing Fonts

Alter the fonts in your report based on the fonts available with your equipment. To see the available fonts, click the Font box on the Tool bar. The font selection menu for one hardware setup is shown in figure 15.22. Your screen may be different, depending on the printer selected in the setup program.

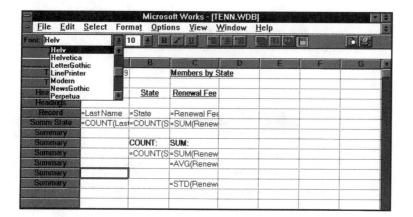

FIG. 15.22

Font selection list

Next to the Font box on the Tool bar is the point size box. Click the down arrow next to the box to display a list of available sizes for the font highlighted in the font selection menu. The sizes are listed in points. One point is approximately 1/72 inch.

To change the font, follow these steps:

1. Click the down arrow to remove the list from the screen display.

2. Use the scroll bars to move up and down the list of fonts.

3. Click to choose the desired font.

4. Click the font selection button to exit from the font selection menu and display the chosen font. You may choose one font for the List view, one for the Form view, and a separate one for the Report view.

Adding Headers and Footers

In the word processing chapters, two types of headers and footers were discussed—paragraph headers and footers, and standard headers and footers. The paragraph headers and footers were used in word processing documents. Standard headers and footers are used in spreadsheet and database documents.

To add headers and footers, follow these steps:

1. Click **Edit** and then click **Headers & Footers** to display the Headers & Footers dialog box. Notice how the paragraph header and footer option is dimmed, indicating this option cannot be used in a database report.

2. Click either the Header or Footer box, then type the text you want to appear on the top of every page for a Header or the bottom of every page for a Footer. For this example, type **Board of Directors** in the **F**ooter: box as shown in figure 15.23.

3. Click OK.

FIG. 15.23

Headers & Footers dialog box

The footer you added to the document does not appear on the Report Definition screen. View the footer by clicking the preview button on the Tool bar. Figure 15.24 shows how the footer looks at the end of the first page of the report.

FIG. 15.24

Report preview with footer

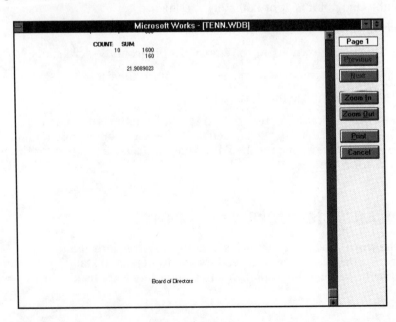

Printing Database Reports

When printing a report, you can choose to print the entire document or specified rows from the document. Choose the report you want to print by placing the mouse pointer on that report in the Report Definition screen, and then clicking the print button on the Tool bar to display the Print dialog box shown in figure 15.25.

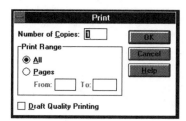

FIG. 15.25

The Print dialog box

In the Print dialog box, specify the number of copies you want, and then whether you want to print some or all of the pages. Finally, you may choose **D**raft Quality Printing for first drafts. When you have completed your selections, click OK.

Chapter Summary

In this chapter, you learned many aspects of Works database reports. Many of the tasks you previously learned for database creation also apply to database reports, such as sorting, grouping, and using functions and formulas.

You learned how to create and use queries, copy parts of a report, duplicate a report, delete a report, and rename a report. In addition, you learned how to insert rows and columns, add statistical summaries, and customize reports. Finally, you learned about formatting and printing reports.

In the next chapter, you take a look at tying all the programs together into an integrated package.

Integrating Applications

PART

V

OUTLINE

Tying It All Together

The three primary computer applications are word processors, spreadsheets, and databases. At the beginning of the personal computer revolution, these applications had to be purchased separately. Unfortunately, separate software programs could not easily share common information. With separate software, for example, to create a form letter meant that you had to be skilled in database creation and elementary programming in order for two disparate programs to work together.

With Works for Windows, however, these same three programs are seamlessly integrated so that you can switch among the three applications effortlessly. The Windows environment further extends this feature by allowing you to "cut and paste" any or all portions of screen information, regardless of its type, from one application to another. Thus, if the information you need to complete a letter containing a competitive bid is in a spreadsheet file, it can be cut and pasted into the letter with little work. Or, if you want to send the name and address of one friend to another friend, you do not have to retype the information. Instead, you simply cut the information from the database and paste it into a letter.

Before continuing with this chapter, you may want to review the basics of file management and the concept of windows. These functions allow information to be transferred from file to file or from component to component.

In this chapter, you learn how to do the following:

- Integrate text, database information, and spreadsheet data.

- Create integrated financial reports by using copying skills you learn in this chapter.

- Use templates.

To get started integrating your Works components, you need to open three files. You may select files you have created for your own use or select sample files used in this book. The three files used in this chapter's examples are RMTA.WDB, RENEW.WPS, and TENNIS.WKS.

Using Microsoft Works Windows

Windows enables you to work in a number of files without having to close one file before you can open another. Works can display up to eight windows at one time, each holding a different file. The active window contains the cursor. Move the cursor to another window and click the mouse or press F6 and the file in that window becomes the active file. The active window appears in a different color (if you are using a color monitor) and has a double-lined border at the top and mouse scroll bars. All information displayed on the figure bars (Title, Menu, and so forth) pertain to the active window.

You can make any window smaller or larger, and you can arrange and rearrange a window by placing it in different locations on-screen. Windows also can be cascaded or tiled. You can perform these features by using the keyboard or mouse.

Click **W**indow or press Alt,W to activate the Window menu, which contains a list of files (see fig. 16.1). Press the number to the left of the file you want. The cursor appears in the window of the file you selected.

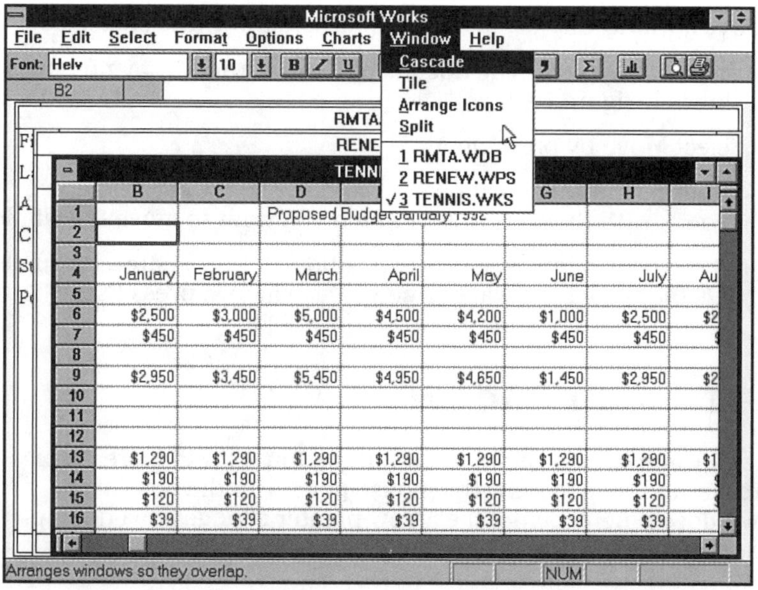

FIG. 16.1

The Window
menu

Switching between Windows

You can use the procedure described in the preceding section to make
a different window active. Again, just access the **W**indow menu and
choose the number of the window in which you want to work.

You also can use the hot keys to move between windows. For example,
press Ctrl+F6 to move to the next window; press Shift+Ctrl+F6 to move
to the previous window.

The mouse provides the fastest way to switch between windows. If you
opened the files as directed in the preceding section, and did not maximize the file window, the active file appears at the top of the windows.
Use the mouse to move the arrow to the window you want to activate
and click the mouse button.

Moving a Window

You can use either the mouse or the keyboard to move a window by
using the **W**indow menu and the cursor-movement keys. To move a
window with the mouse, perform the following procedure:

■ Click on the Title bar on the top of the window and drag the window to the position you want.

To move a window by using the keyboard, follow these steps:

1. Press Alt+hyphen. The document Control window menu opens, as shown in figure 16.2.

2. Select **M**ove by pressing Alt,M.

3. A four-headed arrow appears. Press the arrow key that corresponds with the direction in which you want to move the window.

4. When the window is properly positioned, press Enter. If you decide that you don't want to move the window, press Esc.

Resizing a Window

Resize a window by selecting the window you want to increase or decrease, and then moving the mouse pointer to the border of the window. When you do, the arrow pointer changes to a double-headed arrow. To resize a window by using the mouse, take these steps:

1. Move the mouse pointer to the border of the window you want to increase or decrease.

2. Press and hold the left mouse button.

3. Drag the border to the position you want.

4. Release the mouse button.

To resize a window by using the keyboard, follow these steps:

1. Press Alt+hyphen. The document Control window menu opens, as shown in figure 16.2.

2. Select **S**ize by pressing Alt,S.

3. A four-headed arrow appears. Press the arrow key that corresponds to the border you want to move. For example, if you want to move the bottom border of the window down, press the down arrow. If you move the border too far, press the arrow opposite to the move you have made.

4. When you are satisfied with the new window position, press Enter. If you decide not to move the border, press Esc.

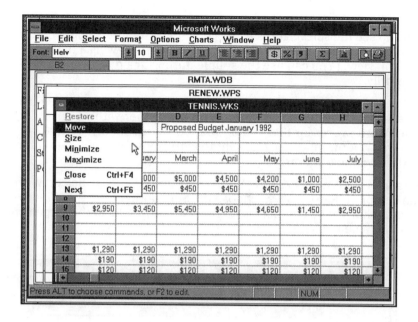

FIG. 16.2

The document
control window
menu

Maximizing a Window

Assume that you had several windows showing on-screen, each containing an open file, and you want to work with one file for a while without the others appearing on-screen. You can do so by maximizing the window in which the file appears. To maximize a window by using the mouse, follow this procedure:

■ Either click on the up arrow in the upper-right corner of the document window, or click on the document control button and select Maximize.

To maximize a window by using the keyboard, take these steps:

1. Press Alt+hyphen and the document Control window menu appears.

2. Press Alt,X.

Splitting a Window

A Microsoft Works window can be split into panels, with each panel displaying a different part of the same file. This feature is of great benefit when working with a large file because you can see two parts of the file at the same time. When using a spreadsheet, for example, you may want to see the sales figures while you look at total revenue. You cannot use the split feature, however, when you are viewing a database file in Form view. (You can use the split feature with a database file in List view only.)

With the exception of word processor files, panels can be located side by side with a vertical split or one above the other with a horizontal split. Word processor files can be split only horizontally. To make active the window in which you want to work, move the mouse pointer into the window and press F6.

To split a window, access the **W**indow menu and choose **S**elect. With the cursor on RENEW.WPS, choose the **S**plit option from the **W**indow menu. A horizontal split line is inserted in the middle of the screen, and includes a new ruler line. (see fig. 16.3).

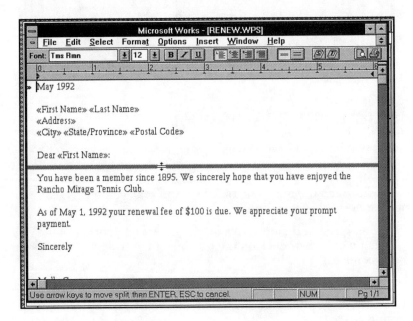

Press the up- or down-arrow key to move the split line, and press Enter when the horizontal line is in the desired location. In RENEW.WPS, you can see the horizontal split in the file. In the top panel, you can see the date and heading of the letter; in the bottom, you can see the closing of the letter (see fig. 16.4).

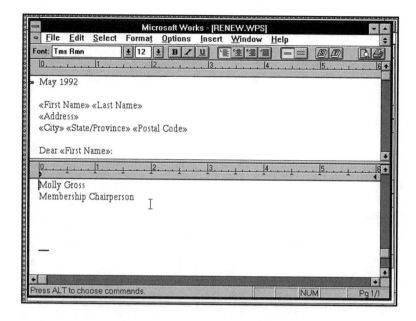

FIG. 16.4

Date, heading,
and closing
visible in the
panels

You can remove the split by pressing Alt,W,T. Then, move the horizontal line back to the ruler line position at the top of the screen, and press Enter. You also can remove the split by moving the mouse pointer onto the top of the second ruler line. The pointer changes shape to a double-headed arrow, with one arrow pointing up and another pointing down. Click the mouse button and drag the line to the top or bottom of the screen. You now should have only one panel on-screen.

When working with a spreadsheet file, click **W**indow and choose **S**plit, or press Alt,W,S. You will see a vertical and horizontal split line. Move the left- and right-arrow keys to move the vertical line. Move the up- and down-arrow keys to move the horizontal line. Press Enter when the lines are in the desired positions. As you may have already figured out, you can simultaneously view up to four panels at one time when working with spreadsheet files, with each panel displaying a different part of the file.

Figure 16.5 shows four sections of the file TENNIS.WKS. You can move the cursor between panels by positioning the mouse pointer in the panel and clicking or by pressing F6 or Shift+Ctrl+F6 (to move back to the previous panel).

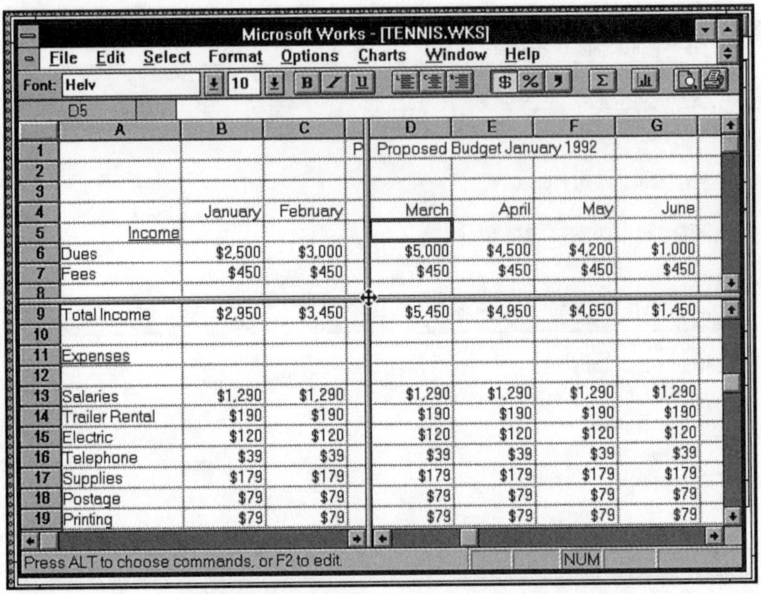

FIG. 16.5

Four sections of
the file
TENNIS.WKS

Splitting the Spreadsheet with the Mouse

You can also use the mouse to split windows into panels. For a horizontal split, point to and click the short double lines at the top-right of the window, just above the scroll bar arrow. For a vertical split, point to and click the double lines to the left of the scroll arrow at the bottom-left of the window. In the database screen, these double lines are in the same position as in the spreadsheet. In the word processing screen, the double lines are at the top of the vertical scroll bar.

With the pointer on the double lines, press the mouse button and hold it down while you drag the double lines to the horizontal or vertical position.

To remove a split line from the screen, use the mouse to point at the line and then press and hold down the mouse button while you drag the line off the screen. Then release the mouse button.

Use the mouse to move between panels by moving the pointer to the panel you want to work in and then clicking the mouse button.

Arranging Windows On-Screen

If you have a window maximized, and you want to see all the windows you're using at the same time, use the **Window** menu. To view all the open files through the windows, click **Window** or press Alt,W and then select Tile. All the open files will appear (see fig. 16.6).

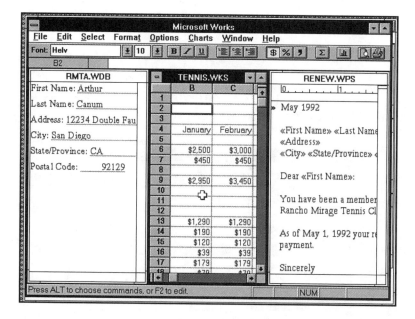

FIG. 16.6

Your working
windows in Tile
format

You can use the **S**ize and **M**ove options to arrange the windows in a variety of ways. You can arrange the screen to display all three windows or to display only two. Use the skills you have just learned, and the mouse or the keyboard. Figure 16.7 shows a possible new arrangement.

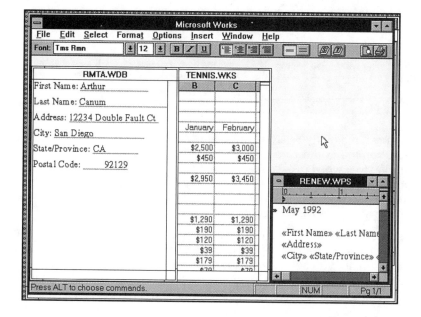

FIG. 16.7

A different
arrangement of
windows in Tile
format

Cascading the Open Windows

Another item on the Window menu is Cascade. This option arranges the open windows one on top of the other with just the file name visible at the top of the window. You can use the mouse pointer to click the name of the file you want to make active. Figure 16.8 shows the windows after the Cascade option has been selected.

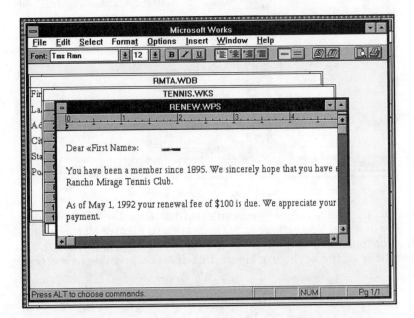

Cutting and Copying between Windows

You may have many reasons to copy text or data from one file to another. You may want to copy a group of figures from a spreadsheet, for example, to a word processing file. You can place the numbers in a report, letter, or memo. Or you may want to include a list or record from a database in a report, letter, or memo. Or you may want to copy or move numbers from the spreadsheet to data cells in the database.

The procedure for moving is almost identical to that used to copy information. The only difference between the two procedures is that, from the Edit menu, you select the Cut option to move and the Copy option to copy. When you want to leave the original in its present location and create a duplicate elsewhere, choose the Copy option. When you want to remove the original from its present location and insert it elsewhere, select the Cut option.

Because the procedures for copying and moving are almost identical, only the copying procedure is examined here. Begin by indicating the text you want to copy. You can indicate the text in the following ways:

- Press and hold down the Shift key and move the cursor-movement keys until the text you want to copy is highlighted.

- Press F8 multiple times.

- Click the mouse at the beginning of the text you want to highlight and drag until the text you want to copy is highlighted.

- Remember the hot keys for moving and copying. Press Ctrl+X for the Cut option and Ctrl+C for the Copy option.

- Cutting and copying text from one Works program to another will be much quicker and less cumbersome if the origination file and the destination file are both open and displayed in windows before you start any of the following tasks. The origination file is the one from which you are copying text or data. The destination file is the one to which you plan to paste text or data.

Copying from the Spreadsheet to the Word Processor

To copy material from the spreadsheet to the word processor, follow these steps:

1. Select the information in the spreadsheet that you want to copy.

2. Press Ctrl+C. Works copies the selection to the Clipboard.

3. Press Ctrl+F6 to move to the window in which you want to paste the selected text.

4. Move the cursor to the location where you want to paste the selected text.

5. Press Ctrl+V.

Figure 16.9 shows an example in which the total income line from TENNIS.WKS is copied to RENEW.WPS.

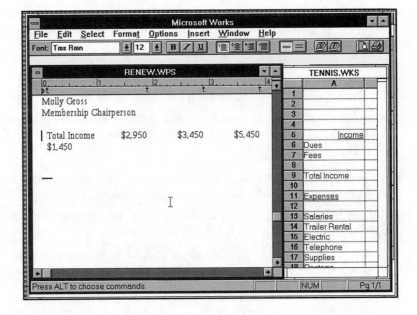

Copying from the Database to the Word Processor

To copy material from the database to the word processor, follow these steps:

1. In Form view, select the record. In List view, select the record, records, field, or fields. In Report view, select a portion of a report.

2. Press Ctr+C. Works copies the selection to the Clipboard.

3. Press Ctrl+F6 to move to the window in which you want to insert the selected text, or open the **W**indow menu and select the name of the file.

4. Move the cursor to the location where you want to insert the selected text.

5. Press Ctrl+V

Figure 16.10 shows a record from the database copied to RENEW.WPS.

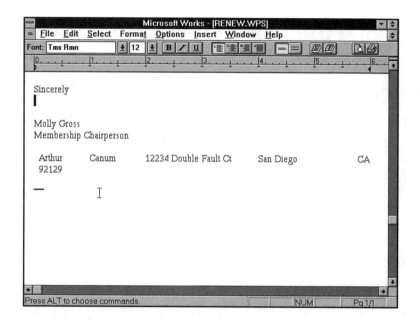

FIG. 16.10

Sample database
record copied to
the word
processor

Copying from the Word Processor to the Spreadsheet

To copy material from the word processor to the spreadsheet, follow these steps:

1. Select any text, memos, or notes from the word processing component of Works.

2. Press Ctrl+C. Works copies the selection to the Clipboard.

3. Press Ctrl+F6 to move to the spreadsheet window in which you want to insert the selected text.

4. Move the cursor to the location where you want to insert the selected text.

5. Press Ctrl+V.

The word processing text is inserted into the spreadsheet.

Copying from the Database to the Spreadsheet

To copy material from the database to the spreadsheet, follow these steps:

1. In Form view, select a record. In List view, select the desired records or fields. From a database, select portions of a report.

2. Press Ctrl+C. The selection is copied to the Clipboard.

3. Press Ctrl+F6 to move to the spreadsheet window in which you want to insert the selected text.

4. Move the cursor to the location where you want to insert the selected text.

5. Press Ctrl+V.

Copying from the Word Processor to the Database

To copy material from the word processor to the database, follow these steps:

1. Select a name, data element, or block of text from the word processing file.

2. Press Ctrl+C. Works copies the selection to the Clipboard.

3. Press Ctrl+F6 to move to the database window in which you want to insert the selected data.

4. Move the cursor to the location where you want to insert the selected text.

5. Press Ctrl+V.

In figure 16.11, a name from the word processing file is inserted in the database file under the First Name: field. When copying the name and address of a new correspondent from the word processing file to the database file, insert the data or text one field at a time.

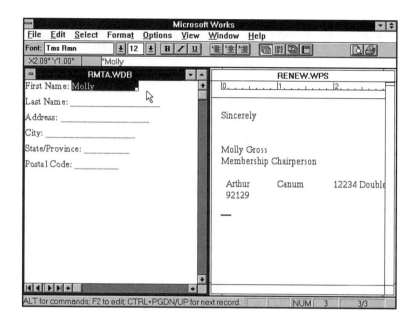

FIG. 16.11

A name from the
word processing
file inserted into
the database file
First Name: field

Copying from the Spreadsheet to the Database

To copy material from the spreadsheet to the database, follow these steps:

1. Select a row or column of data to be inserted in the database file. The results of the calculations will be copied. The formulas will not be copied.

2. Press Ctrl+C. Works copies the selection to the Clipboard.

3. Press Ctrl+F6 to move to the database window in which you want to insert the selected text.

4. Move the cursor to the location where you want to insert the selected data.

5. Press Ctrl+V.

Other Features of Works

Besides the many features you've read about and worked with earlier in this chapter, Works provides additional features that can help you gain additional proficiency with the Works programs.

Using the Works Settings Dialog Box

The Works Settings are the automatic or default settings used every time you use one of Works' programs: the word processor, the spreadsheet, or the database. An example of a Works setting is the opening screen that appears when you start Works. The default, or automatic setting, is the Startup dialog box that appears and welcomes you to Works. Although it is considerate of Microsoft to welcome you to its program every time you start, it is not necessary or particularly useful. Thus, in the Works Settings dialog box, you have the option of directing Works to not show the Startup dialog box, and instead take you directly to the screen where you select a particular enhancement to use or to open an existing file. A further enhancement of the start-up process enables you to direct Works to save the workspace as you left it, which means that when you restart the program you begin exactly where you left off when you stopped.

Examine the Works Settings dialog box by clicking **O**ptions and choosing **W**orks Settings option, or by pressing Alt,O,W. The Works Settings dialog box appears (see fig. 16.12).

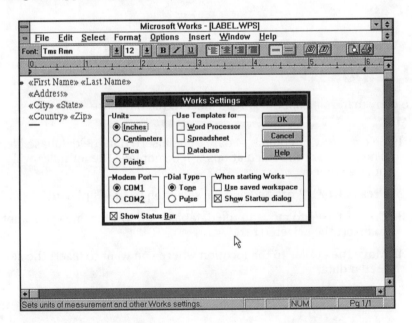

FIG. 16.12

The Works Settings dialog box

The following list provides a description of each option in the Works Settings dialog box:

Option	Description
Units	Inches is the default for most numbers that have units. Works assumes you mean one-half inch when you type .5 in the Tab dialog box. If you type numbers with other dimensions, Works converts them to inches. If you type 2 cm, for example, Works converts the measurement to .787 inches. If you want to work with a unit other than inches, select the unit you prefer from the Units section of the Works Settings dialog box. The unit you select becomes the default. If you select Points and then type 2, Works assumes that you mean 2 points.
Modem Port	This item identifies the port to which your modem is connected. A port is the term used to describe the connection of your computer hardware to external devices. For example, to use a modem it must be installed in one of the communication ports of your computer. Usually, the mouse is connected to COM1 and the modem is connected to COM2. Communication Ports (COM) are serial ports as opposed to your printer port, which is a parallel port.
Dial Type	With this option, you can select the dial type—Pulse or Tone—used by your phone.
Use Templates for	When you select the Create New File... option from the File menu, you can tell Works to open a template file rather than a standard Works file. The next section provides more information on setting up template files.
When starting Works	If you have used several files in the course of your working session, you can set the Use saved workspace option to reopen those same files, in the same position, the next time you start Works. This item coordinates with the Save Workspace option on the File menu. With the Show Startup dialog option, you can choose not to have the Startup dialog box displayed when you start Works. Otherwise, the Startup dialog box will be displayed when you start Works.
Show Status Bar	The Status bar is displayed across the bottom of the screen. The menu command descriptions and other information as to the status of Works are displayed in the status bar. As you become more proficient in the use of Works, you may wish to turn this off, creating more screen space.

Creating Templates

Suppose that you are running a business with two divisions, and you are setting up a budget for each division. Instead of having each division develop its own budget format, you can create a budget template so both departments will use the same format. Only the numbers will change between the departments.

In the same way, you can use a template in a word processing file to establish a format for certain documents. All reports to shareholders, for example, may include a header, footer, font, and format. Instead of creating these special settings each time you send a report, you can use a template that contains these settings. A template file can be created for any Works component to help you improve consistency.

Set up a template file by clicking File or pressing Alt,F to activate the File menu, and selecting or pressing N to Create a New File. Select the type of file you want to create from one of the three components. Then, set up the template file format exactly as you want it for each use. In a spreadsheet, you may want to list income and expenses that will be consistent throughout your organization. In a database, you can create an invoice format to be used in each division.

After the file is created, access the File menu and select A for the Save As option. While in the Save As dialog box, press Alt,T, or click the Save File as Type dialog box. The list of available formats will appear. When you are saving a word processing document as a template, the template format is identified as WP Template. When Works saves the file as the template the extension added is PS.

When you are ready to enter text in the template, make sure that the Works Settings dialog box is turned on for templates. If you have templates developed for both a spreadsheet and a word processing file, these two options in the Works Settings dialog box should be marked with an X. (To access the Works Settings dialog box, press Alt,O,W for the Works Settings option.)

Return to the File menu by pressing Alt,F. Press N to Create a New File. Select the component of Works in which you want to create a new file. If you have templates for the spreadsheet and word processor, select either one of these components. When you create a new file, Works will open a file with the template you have created.

Enter the data or document you want, and it will be entered according to your established template.

If you find that you want to change a template file, open the existing template file by pressing Alt,F,O. From the List Files of Type box, select All Files (*.*). The template files are named as follows:

TEMPLATE.PS	Word processor
TEMPLATE.KS	Spreadsheet
TEMPLATE.DB	Database

Select the template you want to change and press Enter. Make the necessary changes and save the file again with the same file name.

Later, you may find that your needs for a template have changed. In that case, you can create a new template by following the procedures for creating a template outlined in the preceding section. By using this method, you may add entirely new formats, titles, headers, and footers.

Opening Files

At the bottom of the File menu, Works lists the most recently used files, making it easy for you to reopen those files without having to specifically remember the name. Simply open the file menu and select the file you want to open.

Dialing a Number

With Works you can highlight a phone number and have Works dial it for you. You can highlight a phone number by using F8 or the cursor keys; then open the Options menu and select Dial this Number. If you have installed your modem, you hear the modem dialing via the computer speaker. As the number is being dialed, pick up the phone and proceed with your call.

Chapter Summary

In this chapter, you took advantage of Works' integrated environment. You learned how to size, move, and arrange windows. With your window skills sharpened, you learned the tips and tricks for copying between windows. You also explored the techniques of merging a word processing and database file to create mailing labels.

In the next chapter, you learn how to use the Windows Accessories with macros.

Using Windows Accessories and Macros

The original version of Microsoft Works was not compatible with Windows because it was written for DOS-based systems. Thus, initial Windows programs were not available to many users because the computer hardware needed to deliver performance in a graphic environment was not widely available.

However, with the new, more powerful systems based on the 80286 and 80386 processors, Windows and all its diverse accessories is becoming the environment of choice for many computer users. This chapter describes the Windows accessories you can use to enhance and extend the performance of Works. In this chapter, you learn how to do the following:

- Open the Accessories window.
- Use the Terminal.
- Receive a file.
- Use the Notepad.
- Use the Calendar.
- Use the Cardfile.
- Use the Recorder.

Learning about Windows Accessories

In the DOS version of Works, Microsoft included several accessory tools that most users found helpful. These tools included a macro recorder, an alarm clock system, a pop-up calculator, and a module devoted to communicating with other computers via phone lines.

When Windows 3.0 was brought to market, Microsoft included a series of accessories, including those mentioned in the preceding paragraph, that will work with any program running in Windows. Thus, Microsoft Works for Windows no longer includes the macro recorder, alarm clock, calculator or terminal (communication) program. Instead, you can access these programs in Windows and add them to the desktop.

The following list describes the Windows accessories and how they can be used with Works. You may want to have some of the accessories running in the background while you are working in Works. Others, such as the Terminal, you probably will access only when finished with a Works session.

Accessory	Function
Terminal	Sends and receives computer files directly into Works. You need a modem connected to a phone line to use the Terminal program.
Paintbrush	Similar to Works Draw, Paintbrush includes several additional features that enable you to create more elaborate pieces of art. The art then can be imported into a Works file.
Notepad	If you need to make a quick note while operating in Works, you can open a Windows notepad, type the note, and retrieve the note later. When you retrieve the note, you can print it or cut and paste it into a Works word processing document.
Write	The Write program is a miniature word processor that includes features such as Search and Replace, font settings, and paragraph and document formatting.
PIF Editor	Non-Windows applications also can be used in the Windows environment. The PIF editor creates a "program information file," which Windows needs to correctly use a non-Windows program.

Accessory	Function
Calendar	The Calendar program is used to schedule events and set alarms for events. You can create Multiple alarms and calendars.
Calculator	In Chapter 2, you learned about the Windows calculator and added it to the Task List to use it in a spreadsheet.
Clock	The Windows clock is not a tool, but can be included on the desktop to track time.
Cardfile	The Cardfile is an electronic version of an address card file. You can record the names, addresses, and phone numbers of friends, business associates, club members, and other acquaintants. Because you are working in Windows, you can cut and paste the card file information in a word processing document.

Opening the Accessories Window

To begin using Windows accessories, you must first open the Accessories window. You can open the Accessories window before starting your Works session, or you can open it from Works.

To open the Accessories window before starting your Works session, follow these steps:

1. From the Program Manager, click the **W**indow menu.

2. Click the Accessories item. The Accessories Window opens (see fig. 17.1). You also can just double-click the icon for the Accessories window.

FIG. 17.1

The Accessories window

In figure 17.1, the Accessories window is open and has been maximized.

NOTE   Your Accessories window will not include an icon for Collage, the screen capturing program used for this book.

To access the Accessories window from Works, take the following steps:

1. Click the application Control window button or press Alt+ space bar.

2. Select Minimize. The Works window shrinks.

3. Click the Window menu.

4. Select the Accessories item.

Using the Terminal

The Terminal program enables your computer to communicate with other computers by telephone. With Terminal, you can send or receive text files or binary files. In most cases, you will be sending or receiving text files. When you save a word processing file in Works that you want to send to another computer, use the Save As option on the File menu, and save the file as Text under the Save File as Type option. You can save a database or spreadsheet file as Text and Commas, or Text and Tabs. Either can be sent via the terminal.

After you have the Accessories window on-screen, double-click the Terminal icon. The first step you take is to enter the settings needed to connect to the other computer. Each computer you call may require a different settings file because of the differences in terminal protocols. Thus, you must know the protocols of the computer you plan to call (called the *host computer*). For example, you must know the baud rate, data bits, parity, and number of stop bits expected by the host computer. (The manual that comes with your modem will explain all these terms.)

The baud rate, data bits, stop bits, parity, and phone number are the protocols for connecting with another computer. Rather than entering the protocols every time you want to connect to a different computer, you can create a settings file that contains all the information necessary to communicate with the other computer. Settings files have a TRM extension.

1. Click the Settings menu.

2. Click the Phone Number item. The Phone Number dialog box appears (see fig. 17.2).

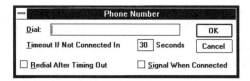

FIG. 17.2

The Phone
Number dialog
box

3. Enter the phone number of the computer you are going to call.

4. Click OK.

   The default settings in the Phone Number dialog box probably will
   not need changing. If you are certain they do, however, change
   them now.

5. The next step is to select the Communications item from the
   Settings menu. When you do so, the Communications dialog box
   appears (see fig. 17.3).

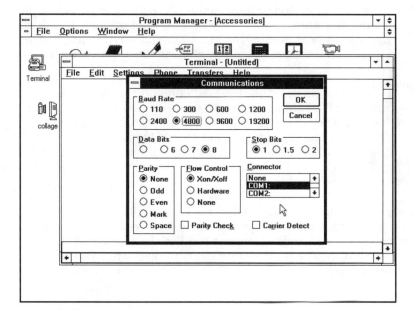

FIG. 17.3

The Communica-
tions dialog box

6. Enter the settings that reflect the host computer's protocols by
   moving the mouse pointer to the item and clicking. In figure 17.3,
   the baud rate is set at 4800.

   You may have to refer to your modem manual or your Windows
   documentation to verify that the settings are correct.

436

7. When finished setting the correct protocols for the host computer, click OK.

8. The final Settings dialog box to access is the Modem Commands item. In this dialog box, you select the type of modem you have or a choice that is compatible with those listed. The most common modem is Hayes or Hayes compatible.

9. When finished selecting the type of modem, click OK.

10. Save the **S**ettings file by clicking **F**ile and the Save **A**s option; enter a name for the file.

11. Click the **P**hone menu and select Dial. Windows sends the phone number to your modem, and the exchange of protocols occurs.

12. Click the **T**ransfers menu, and select the Send Text File option. Windows opens the Send Text File dialog box. Enter the directory and the name of the file you want to send.

13. Click the OK button to begin sending the file. The file scrolls in the Terminal window as it is being sent. At the bottom of the Terminal window you can control the flow of the file—either pausing or stopping the transmission—by clicking the appropriate button.

> **NOTE** If you do not know the host computer protocols, try sending the file in binary form. To do so, access the **S**ettings menu and select the Binary Transfers item. Choose either XModem or Kermit; either should work. Dial the number and after connecting, select Send Binary File from the **T**ransfers menu. Binary files do not have to be in text format to be transferred.

One of the salient features of Windows is its ability to execute several programs simultaneously. If you are sending or receiving a large file, you can minimize Terminal and use the Task List (press Alt+Esc) to switch to Works. The transfer process continues while you proceed with other work.

Receiving a File

After you dial into the host computer as described in the preceding section, access the **T**ransfers menu and choose the Receive Text File option. The Receive Text File dialog box appears. Enter a directory and the name of the file; then click OK. The file begins down-loading to your computer system. You may even append (add to) an existing file by entering the name of an existing file and clicking the Append File option.

Using Paintbrush

The Paintbrush program enhances and adds more flexibility to creating art objects than does the Works Draw program. You can create an object with Paintbrush that can be inserted into Works, as described in Chapter 6. Simply save the file to the MSWORKS directory, and then use the Insert menu in the word processor to bring it into a document.

Using Notepad

If you're like many people, you'll have occasion to jot down a phone number or a reminder to yourself when using your computer. Windows enables you to create many notepad files. For example, you can create a notepad that pertains to your Works spreadsheets and nothing else. Then, when you are working in a spreadsheet, you can have the corresponding notepad open on the desktop. Notepad is one of the accessories you will find useful when operating with Works.

To open a notepad, follow these steps:

1. In the Accessories window, double-click the Notepad icon.

2. Type a short note, such as, **My spreadsheet notes**.

3. Open the File menu, and select Save. The File Save As dialog box opens.

4. Enter the file name. You can include the directory where Works is located, that is, MSWORKS, or you can select the appropriate directory from the Directories box. In this example, the file is named SPREAD.

5. Click OK.

6. Click the Notepad Window control button and select the Minimize item.

At this point, if Works is already running in a window, use the Task List to switch to Works. If Works is not running, use the normal steps to start Works.

1. Press Ctrl and Esc together, or double-click a blank area in the Windows desktop (the area beneath Program Manager). The Task List dialog box appears, listing the currently open windows. In Figure 17.4 the Task List appears with the SPREAD.TXT Notepad highlighted.

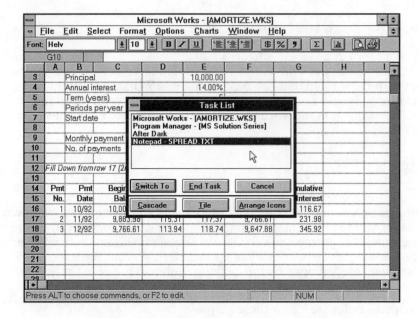

2. Double-click the Notepad SPREAD.TXT item and the window
   appears over the spreadsheet (see fig. 17.5).

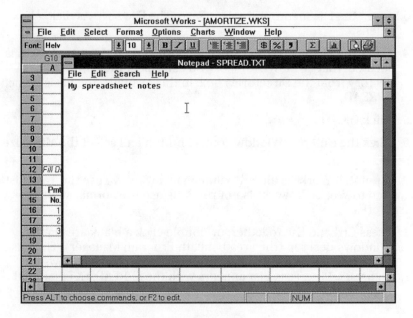

Now you can enter notes pertaining to the spreadsheet or any other matter. The main point to remember here is that Notepad is only a keystroke or two away.

Using Write

The Windows Write program is not as full-featured as Works' word processor and is not meant to replace it. This accessory is for Windows users who do not have a word processor installed as part of their Windows configuration.

Using the Calendar

If your business day includes scheduling meetings and specific times for phone calls, you may want to create a calendar file for use on the desktop. You can then set alarms to remind you of meetings or to check your schedule. To use the calendar, take the following steps:

1. From the Program Manager Accessories window, double-click the Calendar icon. The calendar appears as shown in figure 17.6.

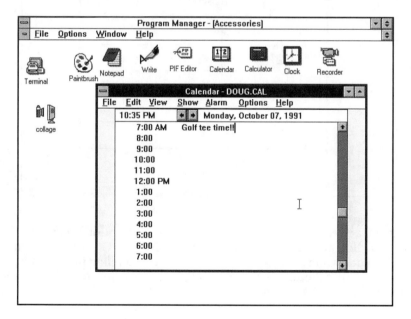

FIG. 17.6

The Calendar

2. Open the **F**ile menu and select the **S**ave item. The File Save As dialog box appears. Enter a name for the calendar file.

3. Click OK.

To see a previous date, click the left-pointing arrow at the top of the window next to the time. To see a future date, click the right-pointing arrow. Once you retrieve the date you want, move the mouse pointer to the time slot in which you want to make an entry. Type the text of the appointment.

If you want to set an alarm, access the **A**larm menu and choose the Set item.

The Calendar can be viewed in either day mode, as in figure 17.6, or in month mode. To see a full-month calendar, as shown in figure 17.7, press F9 or choose Month from the View menu.

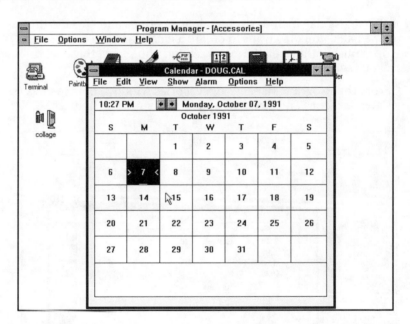

After you activate the Calendar, use the Minimize option then open Works. Follow the steps as described in the Notepad section to open the Calendar while using Works. Now when your golfing buddy calls, you can easily schedule the event, including an alarm, so that you cannot possibly miss your tee time.

Using the Calculator

In Chapter 2, you opened the Windows Calculator and pasted a calculation into a spreadsheet. The Calculator comes in two forms: Standard, as explained in Chapter 2; and Scientific. Figure 17.8 shows the Scientific form.

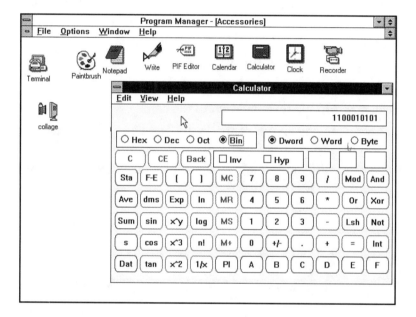

FIG. 17.8

The Calculator in Scientific form

To change the form of the Calculator, choose either Standard or Scientific from the View menu. After deciding which calculator you want to use, click the Window Control button, and select the Minimize item, or click the Minimize button, or press Alt,N. Adding the Calculator to the desktop makes those quick golf handicapping calculations a snap. To access the Calculator, refer to the steps described earlier in this chapter.

After calculating a result, press Ctrl and Ins to save the value on the clipboard. Minimize the Calculator and press Shift and Ins to paste the value into a document, spreadsheet cell or database field.

Using the Clock

The Windows Clock is not an accessory essential to Works. It can be added to the desktop to check the time, either in digital or analog form.

Using the Cardfile

The Cardfile accessory is designed to be used as an electronic address file, storing the names, addresses, and phone numbers of friends, associates, club members, and other acquaintances. The Index line at the top of the card is used by Windows to search for specific cards. For example, if you want to enter the names of your friends, follow these steps:

1. Click the **Edit** menu and select the Index item.

2. Type a name into the Index Line box.

3. Click OK.

You can now add the text you want to the card.

4. Press F7 to add another card. In the Add box, type the name you want to appear on the index line.

5. Save the card file by opening the **File** menu and selecting **S**ave. Figure 17.9 is an example of a series of cards.

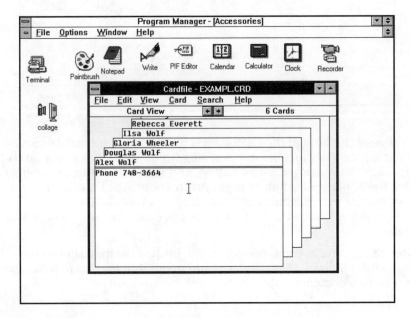

FIG. 17.9

The Cardfile

With the names and phone numbers of your business associates or friends entered in the card file, you can use the Task List to switch to the card file and find that needed phone number in an instant. Use the **Card** menu and the Autodial item to dial the phone.

Using the Recorder

Now that you have a better idea of all the fun accessories included in Windows, you may want to have them available every time you use Works. Does that mean, though, that you must open every accessory, select your specific file, and then minimize it each time you start Works? Not at all. With the Recorder accessory, you can design a *macro* that does all these laborious steps for you. You simply execute the macro, and the windows accessories are at your command.

A macro is a series of recorded keystrokes that you use over and over. In Chapter 10, you used the SUM icon on the Tool bar to quickly create the summing formula for a column of numbers. The SUM icon is a macro. Because the summing formula is used so frequently in spread-sheets, Microsoft decided to attach the SUM macro to an icon.

To learn how macros work, follow these steps to create a simple macro that adds the signature line to a document:

1. From the Program Manager Accessories window, double-click the **R**ecorder icon, or press Alt,R.

2. Start Works as you normally would.

3. Open a new word processing document.

4. Switch to the Program Manager Accessories window by clicking the Window Control button and selecting the Switch To option, or press Ctrl+Esc. The Task List dialog box opens.

5. Double-click the **R**ecorder item. At this point, it is untitled.

6. Open the **M**acro menu and select the Record item. The Record Macro dialog box appears as shown in figure 17.10.

7. Enter a name for the macro. In this example the name is SIGNATURE.

There are many other macro options, as described in the following sections. (Steps 8-16 follow the next several sections on macro options.)

Using Playback

Playback means that you are pressing the key combination to rerun the macro. After you have recorded a macro, the following options can be set that effect the playing back of the macro:

FIG. 17.10

The Record
Macro dialog
box

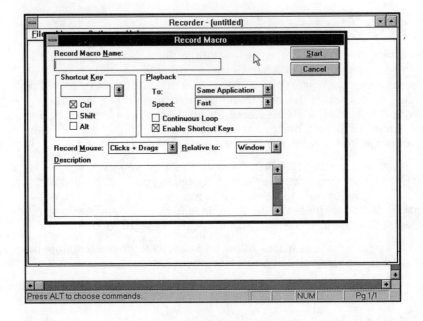

Option	Function
To:	You can specify that the macro play back in any application or only the application in which it was recorded.
Speed:	You can specify that the macro playback occur at the same speed as it was recorded or very quickly. Most of the time, you will want the macro to play back at the fast speed. If the macro seems to misstep when played, you can slow it down by changing the speed to Recorded Speed.
Continuous Loop	Because a macro is a small computer program it can run continuously if you so specify.
Enable Shortcut Keys	Set this option to *on* so you can use a key combination to execute the macro, instead of opening the macro file and selecting it from your list of macros.

Using Record Mouse

Because program actions in Works (and Windows) can be activated either by using the mouse or keystrokes, you can have the macro ignore the mouse movements, record every move, or record only the clicks and drags that occur. Use keystrokes to record all your macro steps if possible. Otherwise the application and document windows have to be in the same relative position when you run the macro as when it was created. Windows does attempt to mitigate this problem with the next option, *Relative to*. The *Description* entry is to identify the macro's purpose. For our example, set this option to Ignore Mouse.

> *Relative to:* Because the desktop can be moved and resized, you must instruct Windows whether the macro should respect the screen boundaries as it plays, or the window boundaries. Leave this setting as Window.

> *Description:* Always enter a text description of what the macro is designed to do.

8. For the description, enter "This macro creates a letter signature line."

The final playback step is to assign the macro recording to shortcut keys. The first choice is to use the Ctrl, Shift, or Alt key.

9. Click the Ctrl key. An X will appear in the small box.

10. Click the down-arrow key in the Shortcut **Key** box. A list of keys that can be used with the Ctrl, Shift, or Alt keys appears (see fig. 17.11).

11. For this example, select the F1 key.

12. Select Start. Windows takes you to the application you were using when you opened the Recorder, which in this example is a word processing file in Works.

    Now the macro can be recorded and later executed by pressing Ctrl+F1.

13. Type **Sincerely yours,** press Enter twice, and type **William James**.

14. End the recording by pressing Ctrl+Break.

Windows displays the Recorder dialog window.

15. Click the Save Macro item.

16. Click OK.

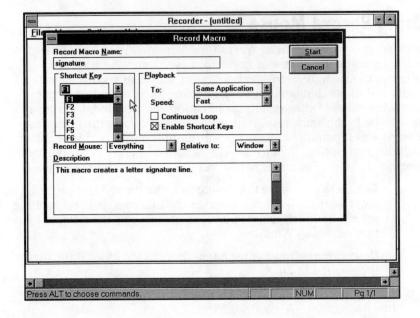

Testing the Macro

The macro is saved. To test it, press Enter a couple of times, then press
Ctrl+F1.

Saving the Macro File

Although you have recorded the macro, assigned it to a keystroke combination, and given it a description, that doesn't mean it is saved for-
ever. To do that, you must save it as a file. Then the macro file exists
and is available every time you run Windows. To save the macro, take
these steps:

1. Click the Window Control button and select the Switch To option.

2. From the Task List, press Ctrl+Esc.

3. The Recorder window reappears. Open the **F**ile menu and the
   Save option. Enter the name of the file and click OK.

Creating the Startup Macro

Now that you have the conceptual basis for a macro, you can create
one that opens the various tools and files you will use.

When you start Windows, most likely at the C:\> prompt, type **WIN**. Windows starts and you decide which application you want to open first. However, instead of simply typing WIN, you can type the following and then press Enter:

WIN DOUG.CAL

Windows starts and the calendar file named DOUG appears first. Now take the idea a step further. Suppose that your macros are stored in a file named DOUG.REC (REC is the extension for all macro files in this program) and at the C:\> prompt you type the following and then press Enter:

WIN DOUG.REC

After Windows appears, the first application to appear is the macro file named DOUG.REC. At this point, you could select the macro that opens all of the other accessories you want to have available before starting your Works session.

Chapter Summary

In this chapter, you learned how to open the Accessories window and how to receive a file. You also learned about the Terminal, the Notepad, the Calendar, the Cardfile, and the Recorder.

This chapter completes the main part of the book. The appendix provides information about electronic, service, and newsletter source files.

Using Microsoft Works with Other Programs

In this appendix, you learn how to use Works with other programs and how to save files that you want to transmit electronically. You also examine a list of enhancement resources, including templates and electronic databases.

Sharing Works Information

Because of the great number of software programs on the market today, Microsoft Works has been designed to share the information in Works files with other popular programs. In addition, the information in other programs can be imported into Works.

Using Lotus 1-2-3 Spreadsheets

The best-selling spreadsheet (as of this writing) is Lotus 1-2-3. Works can interact directly with 1-2-3 files created by Releases 1A and 2.0, without having to convert. Lotus Development has recently released a version of 1-2-3 for Windows. According to the 1-2-3 documentation, Works cannot open a file created with the Windows version.

Works' spreadsheets also will perform without any converting of 1-2-3 file formats, because the 1-2-3 Release 1A file format is also used by Works. This feature enables the key parts of the spreadsheet—formulas, formats, values, and range names—to be recognized.

Avoiding Data Loss

Because Microsoft Works and 1-2-3 spreadsheet features are not identical, you might lose information if you perform one or both of the following procedures:

- Create and save a file in Microsoft Works.

- Open the same file in Lotus 1-2-3, and then save it in Lotus 1-2-3.

The information that can be lost are Works- or Lotus-specific attributes. These attributes represent capabilities unique to Works or 1-2-3. The reverse of the preceding sequence also can result in lost information (Lotus-created files opened in Works and then saved).

Lotus 1-2-3 Release 2.0 uses a string-combination operator (the & sign), which Works does not support. In addition, the following Release 2.0 functions are not recognized by Works:

- All string functions.

- All database statistical functions.

- The date and time functions: $CADATEVALUE and $CATIMEVALUE.

- The logical functions: $CAISNUMBER and $CAISSTRING.

- The special functions: CACA, $CACELL, and $CACELLPOINTER.

 Using a 1-2-3 file with these functions results in the values being retained, but not the formulas.

Opening a 1-2-3 File

To open a 1-2-3 file in Works, use the same procedure you use to open a Works file. Click File, then Open, or press Alt,O. Select the file name and press Enter.

1-2-3 does not use the same file extension as Works. If the 1-2-3 file name does not appear, click on the Type field, or press Alt,T, and select the All Files (*.*) option. Works then displays the file names of every file in the C:\MSWORKS directory. If the file is on a different disk drive, click on Drives or press Alt,V to select the correct drive. You may also select a different directory, by clicking Directories or pressing Alt,D. Click on the directory containing the 1-2-3 file.

Working with Other Databases or Spreadsheets

A popular database program is dBASE. To transfer files from Works to dBASE, open the Save As dialog box and from the Save File as Type box choose the version of dBASE you want. Click OK and the file is saved to the disk with the appropriate extension.

For spreadsheets that are not compatible with 1-2-3, you must convert the Works files to ASCII (text) files that can be loaded by other programs.

Converting a spreadsheet file to an ASCII file makes fundamental changes in the structure of the file. Formulas are not going to be retained—only the values that the formulas produced. For example, if a cell contains the formula C1+C2, which results in the value 10, only the value 10 will be converted in the ASCII file.

ASCII files use commas as delimiters, which are symbols that mark the end of one section of a command and the beginning of another section.

When Works converts the spreadsheet file to text, the end of a row or the end of a record is separated by a carriage return and a line feed.

Saving a File in ASCII

To save a file as an ASCII text file, follow these steps:

1. Click File and choose the Save As option, or press Alt,F,A.

2. The Save As dialog box appears. Type a unique name for the file.

3. Click the Save File as Type box. Choose the Text & Commas option.

4. Click OK.

The original file you have been working with remains on-screen, and the new ASCII file is saved on the disk.

Opening Files from Other Programs

For Works to open a file from another spreadsheet or database, the file first must be saved as an ASCII text file. Lotus 1-2-3 files and dBASE files, however, can be opened by using the List Files of Type box in the Open file dialog box.

Individual pieces of information in text files are delimited (separated) either by commas (for spreadsheet files) or tab marks (for database files). A spreadsheet row is separated by a carriage return. An entire database record also is separated by a carriage return.

After a file from another program has been saved as an ASCII text file, the file can be used in Works. To use the file in Works, click File and then Open, or press Alt,F,O. Type the name of the file to open, and Works will recognize that the file is not in the Works format. A dialog box asks you to select the tool (the Works word processor, database, or spreadsheet, for example) into which the file should be opened.

Using Other Word Processing Files

Virtually all word processing programs can save files as ASCII, which means that the files are saved as text only. When a file is saved in this manner, no formatting is retained. To use files from other word processors, ask the person giving you the file to save it as ASCII, or in one of the formats Works recognizes.

You may find that trying to put in ASCII format all the files you need to access is impossible or impractical. However, Works provides you with a limited ability to convert several file formats to Works format. In doing so, many original formatting commands are retained. Works recognizes the following word processing formats:

Microsoft Interchange Rich Text Format (RTF)

WordPerfect 5.0, 5.1

Microsoft Word for Windows

Windows Write

 You can convert a Works word-processed file to any of these file types.

To convert a Works word-processed file to another format, click File and choose the Save As Option, or press Alt,F,A. Type the file name of the file you want to convert and then click open the Save file as Type box. Press Enter and the file is converted and saved under the new name with the appropriate extension.

Using Electronic, Template, and Newsletter Services

Because you are working in the Windows environment, you have access to the Terminal program that is part of Windows. If you have a modem (either stand-alone or installed in your computer) you can communicate with other computers and transmit and receive information or files. To access the Terminal program in the Accessories window, you must leave Works either by minimizing the Application window or exiting from Works. Open the Accessories window from the Program Manager.

An example of one of the many electronic services is CompuServe. It literally has everything from up-to-the-minute news, stock quotes, games, product forums, an electronic encyclopedia and so on. You can do product research, academic research, and search for lost friends by using the CompuServe phone number bank. To become a subscriber, contact the company at the following address or telephone number:

CompuServe
5000 Arlington Centre Blvd.
Columbus, OH 43220
800-848-8990

Templates

If you write to the following company, you will receive a free catalog of products:

Heizer Software
P.O. Box 232019
Pleasant Hill, CA 94523

Newsletter

To receive a newsletter that focuses on using the attributes of Microsoft Works, contact the following company:

The Cobb Group
The Workshop
9420 Bunsen Parkway #300
Louisville, KY 40220
800-223-8720

Symbols

C

S

X-Y-Z

Teach Yourself
With QuickStarts From Que!

The ideal tutorials for beginners, Que's QuickStart books use graphic illustrations and step-by-step instructions to get you up and running fast. Packed with examples, QuickStarts are the perfect beginner's guides to your favorite software applications.

1-2-3 for DOS Release 2.3 QuickStart
Release 2.3

$19.95 USA
0-88022-716-8, 500 pp., 7 3/8 x 9 1/4

1-2-3 for Windows QuickStart
1-2-3 for Windows

$19.95 USA
0-88022-723-0, 500 pp., 7 3/8 x 9 1/4

1-2-3 Release 3.1 + QuickStart, 2nd Edition
Releases 3 & 3.1

$19.95 USA
0-88022-613-7, 569 pp., 7 3/8 x 9 1/4

dBASE IV 1.1 QuickStart,
Through Version 1.1

$19.95 USA
0-88022-614-5, 400 pp., 7 3/8 x 9 1/4

Excel 3 for Windows QuickStart
Version 3 fo rWindows

$19.95 USA
0-88022-762-1, 500 pp., 7 3/8 x 9 1/4

MS-DOS QuickStart, 2nd Edition
Version 3.X & 4.X

$19.95 USA
0-88022-611-0, 420 pp., 7 3/8 x 9 1/4

Q&A 4 QuickStart
Versions 3 & 4

$19.95 USA
0-88022-653-6, 400 pp., 7 3/8 x 9 1/4

Quattro Pro 3 QuickStart
Through Version 3.0

$19.95 USA
0-88022-693-5, 450 pp., 7 3/8 x 9 1/4

WordPerfect 5.1 QuickStart
WordPerfect 5.1

$19.95 USA
0-88022-558-0, 427 pp., 7 3/8 x 9 1/4

Windows 3 QuickStart
Ron Person & Karen Rose

This graphics-based text teaches Windows beginners how to use the feature-packed Windows environment. Emphasizes such software applications as Excel, Word, and PageMaker and shows how to master Windows' mouse, menus, and screen elements.

Version 3

$19.95 USA
0-88022-610-2, 440 pp., 7 3/8 x 9 1/4

MS-DOS 5 QuickStart
Que Development Group

This is the easy-to-use graphic approach to learning MS-DOS 5. The combination of step-by-step instruction, examples, and graphics make this book ideal for all DOS beginners.

DOS 5

$19.95 USA
0-88022-681-1, 420 pp., 7 3/8 x 9 1/4

To Order, Call:
(800) 428-5331 OR (317) 573-2500

Find It Fast With Que's Quick References!

Que's Quick References are the compact, easy-to-use guides to essential application information. Written for all users, Quick References include vital command information under easy-to-find alphabetical listings. Quick References are a must for anyone who needs command information fast!

To Order, Call:
(800) 428-5331 OR (317) 573-2500

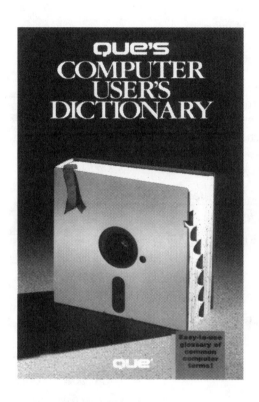

Enhance Your Personal Computer System
With Hardware And Networking Titles From Que!

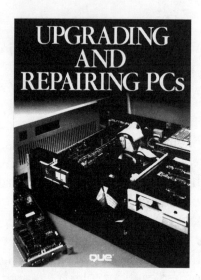

Upgrading and Repairing PCs
Scott Mueller

This book is the ultimate resource for personal computer upgrade, maintenance, and troubleshooting information! It provides solutions to common PC problems and purchasing descisions and includes a glossary of terms, ASCII code charts, and expert recommendations.

IBM Computers & Compatibles
$29.95 USA

0-88022-395-2, 724 pp., 7 3/8 x 9 1/4

Hard Disk Quick Reference
Que Development Group

Through DOS 4.01
$8.95 USA
0-88022-443-6, 160 pp., 4 3/4 x 8

Introduction To Personal Computers, 2nd Edition
Katherine Murray

IBM, Macintosh, & Apple
$19.95 USA
0-88022-758-3, 400 pp., 7 3/8 Xx9 1/4

Networking Personal Computers, 3rd Edition
Michael Durr & Mark Gibbs

IBM & Macintosh
$24.95 USA
0-88022-417-7, 400 pp., 7 3/8 x 9 1/4

Que's Computer Buyer's Guide, 1992 Edition
Que Development Group

IBM & Macintosh
$14.95 USA
0-88022-759-1, 250 pp., 8 x 10

Que's Guide to Data Recovery
Scott Mueller

IBM & Compatibles
$29.95 USA
0-88022-541-6, 500 pp., 7 3/8 x 9 1/4

Que's PS/1 Book
Katherine Murray

Covers Microsoft Works & Prodigy
$22.95 USA
0-88022-690-0, 450 pp., 7 3/8 x 9 1/4

Using Novell NetWare
Bill Lawrence

Version 3.1
$29.95 USA
0-88022-466-5, 728 pp., 7 3/8 x 9 1/4

Using Your Hard Disk
Robert Ainsbury

DOS 3.X & DOS 4
$29.95 USA
0-88022-583-1, 656 pp., 7 3/8 x 9 1/4

To Order, Call:
(800) 428-5331 OR (317) 573-2500